MANAGEMENT, WORK AND ORGANISATIONS

Series editors: **Gibson Burrell**, Warwick Business School
Mick Marchington, Manchester School of Management, UMIST
Paul Thompson, Department of Business Studies, University of Edinburgh

This series of new textbooks covers the areas of human resource management, employee relations, organisational behaviour and related business and management fields. Each text has been specially commissioned to be written by leading experts in a clear and accessible way. An important feature of the series is the international orientation. The titles will contain serious and challenging material, be analytical rather than prescriptive and be particularly suitable for use by students with no prior specialist knowledge.

The series will be relevant for a number of business and management courses, including MBA and post-experience courses, specialist masters and postgraduate diplomas, professional courses, and final-year undergraduate and related courses. The books will become essential reading at business and management schools worldwide.

Published:

Paul Blyton and Peter Turnbull   **The Dynamics of Employee Relations**
J. Martin Corbett   **Critical Cases in Organisational Behaviour**
Sue Ledwith and Fiona Colgan (eds)   **Women in Organisations**
Karen Legge   **Human Resource Management**
Harry Scarbrough (ed.)   **The Management of Expertise**

Forthcoming:

Helen Newell and John Purcell   **Business Strategy and the Management of Human Resources**
Helen Rainbird   **Training in the Workplace**
Harvie Ramsey   **Involvement at Work**
Michael Rowlinson   **Organisations and Institutions**
Adrian Wilkinson, Mick Marchington, Tom Redman and Ed Snape   **Total Quality Management**

Series Standing Order

If you would like to receive future titles in this series as they are published, you can make use of our standing order facility. To place a standing order please contact your bookseller or, in case of difficulty, write to us at the address below with your name and address and the name of the series. Please state with which title you wish to begin your standing order. (If you live outside the UK we may not have the rights for your area, in which case we will forward your order to the publisher concerned.)

Standing Order Service, Macmillan Distribution Ltd,
Houndmills, Basingstoke, Hampshire, RG21 6XS, England

WOMEN IN ORGANISATIONS

Challenging Gender Politics

Edited by

Sue Ledwith

and

Fiona Colgan

MACMILLAN
Business

First published 1996 by
MACMILLAN PRESS LTD
Houndmills, Basingstoke, Hampshire RG21 6XS
and London
Companies and representatives
throughout the world

ISBN 0–333–60504–7 hardcover
ISBN 0–333–60505–5 paperback

A catalogue record for this book is available
from the British Library.

10   9   8   7   6   5   4   3   2   1
05   04   03   02   01   00   99   98   97   96

Copy-edited and typeset by Povey–Edmondson
Okehampton and Rochdale, England

Printed in Great Britain by
Antony Rowe Ltd
Chippenham, Wiltshire

To John, Maureen, Fergus, Margaret,
Syd, Pauline, Pete, Harry and Kate

Contents

List of figures

List of tables

Notes on the contributors

Anne Brockbank is a Lecturer in Continuing Education at City University, London. She took degrees in mathematics (Manchester, 1976) and social science (Manchester, 1985), followed by counselling training. She contributed to the development of the retail degree at Manchester Metropolitan University, and carried out the retail skills research project there. Her current research and consultancy interests include management development; interpersonal skills; women in management; and the learning process. She is author of *Life Choices* (1985) and has recently contributed articles to *Women in Management Review* and the *International Journal of Retail and Distribution Management*.

Fiona Colgan is Director of the Centre for Equality Research in Business (CERB) at the University of North London. She graduated from the University of Sheffield in 1979 (geography and politics) and from McGill University, Montreal, Canada in 1986. While in Canada, she worked as a researcher on projects concerning gender and labour force restructuring and women's alternative social service organisations. In 1988 she joined the Business School of the University of North London where she is currently a Senior Lecturer in Industrial Relations and Organisation Studies. Her current research includes an Economic and Social Research Council (ESRC) funded project on trade union democracy and the strategies of women trade unionists (with Sue Ledwith), equal opportunities in employment and services delivery within the transport sector, and issues of social equity and diversity within organisations.

Larraine Gooch is a Senior Lecturer in Management for Oxford Brookes University and manager of the University Diploma in Personnel Management course. She graduated in 1969 from Sheffield University and gained her MA in HRM from Thames Valley University in 1993. She became a Fellow of the Institute of Personnel and Development in 1995. She has experience in personnel management in both the public and the private sector, having spent a number of years as a personnel manager in J. Lyons (now Allied Lyons) and BBC Television.

Geraldine Healy is a Principal Lecturer in Industrial Relations in the Business School of the University of Hertfordshire. She has researched and published on gender and labour market issues. She is currently undertaking a large-scale study of teachers' employment and change in collaboration with the National Union of Teachers (with David Kraithman). The subjects of recent publications have been: the employment of women with young children, business and discrimination, professionalism and trade unionism, and teachers' employment and change.

Susan Johnstone is a Principal Lecturer in Law at the University of North London Business School and a member of the School's Centre for Equality Research in Business (CERB). She worked as a researcher and writer on employment law for the Industrial Relations Law Bulletin and now lectures in employment law. She is interested in international comparative research into equal opportunities legislation and recently spent time in Canada researching Ontario's equal opportunities legislation. Currently she is researching equality legislation in the member states of the European Union, and its impact on women in the labour market.

David Kraithman is a Principal Lecturer in Economics in the Business School of the University of Hertfordshire. He has researched and published on labour market issues on women and young people. He is currently undertaking a large-scale study of teachers' employment and change in in collaboration with the National Union of Teachers (with Geraldine Healy). The subjects of recent publications include local labour market issues, the employment of women with young children, and teachers' employment and change.

Caroline Langridge is an experienced general manager with a longstanding interest in women's issues. Her early career was in local government where she held a variety of posts moving to an executive officer post in the then Department of Trade and Industry in 1968. She became the secretary of Wandsworth Community Health Council when it was established in 1975 and while there was instrumental in establishing a number of innovative community care projects and the Blackshaw Nursery Centre, the first shiftworkers' day nursery in the UK. In 1986 she gained her MA in Public Policy Studies from the University of Bristol. In July 1986 she became the Unit General Manager, Community Services, West Lambeth Health Authority, before moving on to secondment to the Department of Health in August 1989 to join the NHS Trust Unit. Caroline was appointed as head of the NHS Women's Unit in October 1991. She is a Fellow of the Royal Society of Arts, a member of Forum UK and the Parrot Club.

Sue Ledwith is a sociology graduate of London University and is now a Principal Lecturer in the School of Business, Oxford Brookes University, where she is also a member of the University's Equal Opportunities Action Group. Much of her working life has been spent juggling family and jobs, and she has been active in a number of dual and triple roles, such as chairing her former polytechnic's workplace nursery management committee, being a school parent-governer and more recently as a committee member of her local branch of the Institute of Personnel and Development. For ten years she was also editor of the women's pages of *SOGAT Journal* (the journal of the print and paper trade union SOGAT '82). Currently she and Fiona Colgan jointly hold an ESRC award for the research they are carrying out with the trade unions UNISON and the Graphical, Paper and Media Union (GPMU) about women's trade union activism.

Amanda Martin Palmer teaches sociology and social policy as a Senior Lecturer at Oxford Brookes University and as a Staff Tutor at Kellogg College, Oxford. She read human sciences at St Catherine's College, Oxford, and maintains links with the Human Sciences programme at Oxford. She completed a PhD in the sociology of education at Warwick University during the 1980s after an initial career in the Civil Service and local government. Amanda acts as an equal opportunities and training consultant to a variety of government departments and has conducted in-house research on personnel issues for HM Customs and Excise. She also has longstanding links with the School of Business at Oxford Brookes University and in this capacity she has undertaken self-development work with senior women executives in the NHS and worked with teachers in the development and implementation of school equal opportunity policies.

Steve Shaw is a Senior Lecturer in Transport and Tourism at the Business School, University of North London. Following a previous career in planning and business development, he has worked in higher education since 1986, teaching mainly on management courses for people working in the travel industry. He is the author of *Transport: Strategy and Policy* (1993). Research interests include social equity issues in service delivery, and he has written a number of articles on the response of public transport undertakings to the travel needs of women, people with disabilities, and ethnic minorities. He is a member of the Transport Research and Consultancy Unit (TRaC) and the Centre for Equality Research in Business (CERB).

Frances Tomlinson is a Principal Lecturer in Organisational Behaviour and a member of the Centre for Equality Research in Business at the University of North London. She graduated from Bristol University in 1970 with a degree in psychology and philosophy. After working for several years in the National Health Service, she joined the Polytechnic (now University) of North London.

Her current research interests include gender and HRM philosophy and practices, and cross cultural management.

Joanne Traves is a Lecturer in Retail Management at the University of Surrey. After gaining her degree in psychology (Aberdeen, 1985), and experience in retail management, she contributed to the development of the retail degree at Oxford Brookes University. On completion of her MBA in 1994 she began work on her current reearch interests which include women in management, careers in retail management, and organisational culture.

Sylvia Wyatt studied human sciences at Oxford before joining the NHS in 1978 as a national management trainee. She worked in the NHS over a period of 11 years in a variety of roles including strategic planning, operational management and asset management, combining a family and a career. She joined the Price Waterhouse Healthcare Consultancy in 1989 to help implement the internal market; in 1991 she spent a year at Stanford Business School, USA. On her return to the UK, Sylvia spent more than two years with IHSM Consultants as the Principal Researcher on the Creative Career Paths (CCP) Project. She then moved to the London Health Economics Consortium, part of the London School of Hygiene and Tropical Medicine in December 1994, where she is undertaking health policy and health services research. She is also a non-executive director of East Surrey Health Authority. She considers one of her major achievements to have been working part-time for eight years while at the same time making career progress.

Preface and acknowledgements

The decision to put this book together came out of many conversations with research collaborators and colleagues working in the areas of equal opportunities, gender and management and organisations. Together we have speculated about the similarities and differences among women and men, and above all whether or not women's activism makes a difference to gendered organisational life. Our conclusion was that: yes, women do make a difference. How much difference, however, is the question to which the answer will always be elusive.

On the one hand women are more and more becoming mainstream participants in the world of work, with their successes in reaching senior positions in traditional male strongholds being heralded as major break-throughs – which they are. Alongside these achievements, however, are frequent reports of personal disappointment and harassment suffered by women in many work organisations. In addition, every day we are faced with the hard facts of women's continued material disadvantage at work.

As researchers our main task is to try to discover and then understand the processes and discourses and contradictions of women's everyday experiences in their work organisations. We have been able to draw on others' research and literature about women from a wide range of disciplines, across a spectrum including management and organisational behaviour, labour market studies, sociology, psychology, industrial relations, human resource management, feminism and gender studies.

Our overriding and central interest, however, is 'what are women themselves doing about organisational gender politics?' Too many texts, we think, discuss what organisations are doing to and for women, but take little account of women as real people. Well, women are real: they have views and abilities, and what they think and what they do, and how they go about it are key to an understanding of the struggles and strategies for equality, parity and organisational transformation.

So women and change are the key themes of the book. The first chapter identifies strategies and skills which women as active change agents may use.

xvii

In particular it proposes different approaches taken by different types of women. The context in which these are set is one of patriarchy and the gender politics of organisations. Organisational equal opportunities responses are also identified and assessed. The discussion draws on a wide body of theory and research, and builds on this to introduce a model of women's consciousness and activism. This forms the framework for the eight research-based case study chapters which follow. These cover book publishing, retailing, personnel management, the Customs and Excise service, school teaching, the health service, the public transport sector and trade unions.

In feminised industries such as retail and healthcare, change in women's aspirations and management styles are examined; opportunities offered through political and structural change are assessed in studies of women's projects in book publishing, teaching, trade unions and in the public transport sector, especially in Canada; the role played by women in the personnel function is investigated in relation to its potential for a re-visioning of women's careers in personnel, and women's developing consciousness and strategic courses of action in the overwhelmingly male culture of the Customs and Excise Service are identified. The final chapter draws some tentative conclusions from the case studies: that women who can accurately read their gendered organisational structures and politics are likely to be a significant force for change, especially when working together with others. The chapter then concludes with a discussion about women's role, strategies and potential for change in decision-making fora in Europe. During our research and writing, most of the organisations studied were experiencing change and transition, and so were many of the women. In such dynamic situations, it is impossible to see how women will eventually fare, so some of our comments are necessarily tentative and speculative. Nevertheless, we hope that the debates and discussions we have found useful and stimulating will also be of interest and use to our readers.

As editors we would like to thank the many individual women and men who have participated in the research so sharing with us some of their life experiences and providing us with rich insights into their organisations. We would also like to thank all the contributors for making the process of developing the book so enjoyable, and for their tolerance with our questions and requests. In particular go thanks to Pauline Baseley, Geraldine Healy, Frances Tomlinson and Peter Case for their helpful comments on some of the theoretical issues, and to the series editors and our publishers Stephen Rutt, Tracy France, Beverley Tarquini and Keith Povey for their patience and support.

CHAPTER 1

Women as organisational change agents

Fiona Colgan and Sue Ledwith

Introduction

This is a book about women, their work organisations, and change. It focuses on the strategies which women develop in order to survive, develop and progress in gendered organisational life, and by which women may become organisational change agents. The increasing movement of women into the labour market is in itself a significant source of change. Just by 'being there' women inevitably bring new and different perspectives on employment issues and so become catalysts for change within their organisations. In this book our main exploration is of women's own agency: ways in which women themselves assess their position and role in their work organisations, how they cope with gender politics and work out and negotiate ways and means of progressing their own, and perhaps a wider, more 'women-friendly' organisational agenda. Our enquiry is set within the context of recent significant restructuring of work and work organisations; the product of wider social, political and economic changes. Thus change, and the opportunities and challenges it offers to women and men, supplies the main underpinning theme throughout the studies in this book. However, the book's major concern is with the impact of women as active 'change agents' within organisations.[1]

These themes are examined through a series of eight empirical case studies of women in a range of organisations, industries and professions – book publishing, the retail sector, personnel management, the customs and excise service, trade unions, the teaching profession, the health service and public transport sector.

In this first chapter we start by surveying the influence of current major political, social and economic changes for women in the labour market, work organisations and management. We then move on to consider women's responses and to develop a theoretical and conceptual framework of women's consciousness of gender politics and their own organisational roles, which in turn informs the case study chapters. In the final chapter, drawing on the case study research, we consider the range of women's activism and equality strategies and identify some possible directions for the future.

Women and change

Women are increasingly moving into the labour market, into employment and work organisations. By the mid-1990s, women comprised 47 per cent of the UK workforce, with nearly three-quarters of adult women in or available for paid work (Sly, 1993). Both through their presence in the workplace and in a growing number of occupations, women pose a challenge to the traditional gendered division of labour prevalent in most societies and organisations (Redclift and Sinclair, 1991). Women challenging the status quo provide a potential force for change within organisations as they question the existing split between public and private spheres within society and seek to widen traditional definitions of 'employment issues' and 'organisational priorities'.

Women bring to the workplace their own particular mix of skills, learned through a lifetime of socialisation and honed at home in the managing and organising of domestic and family life (Johnson Smith and Leduc, 1992). So-called 'female' attributes, such as interpersonal skills, consensus, teamworking, negotiation and being able to handle several projects at a time, were beginning to be acknowledged within organisations in the late-1980s as comprising the missing components of a newly discovered 'soft' leadership style. It was predicted that these 'female' ways of organising and managing would be more appropriate to organisations by the millennium (Rosener, 1990; Institute of Management, 1994). In addition to having these 'natural' skills women have also become increasingly well qualified. Thus they have been catching up with and in some cases outstripping their male peers in gaining formal qualifications (Grant, 1994; EOR, 1992a, Simpson, 1995).

In the late 1980s, it appeared that women were ready and well-placed to fill the gap left by the demographic time bomb. However, the 25 per cent fall in the number of school leavers entering the labour market in the 1990s (NEDO, 1988) was more than compensated for by recessionary forces (Dickens, 1989). For women in employment, and for the new supply of women flooding onto the market in the early 1990s, the going rate of pay remained low, work was predominantly part-time (less true among ethnic minority women, two-thirds of whom work full-time (Sly, 1994), casual, flexible and – with the deconstruction of the employment contract – job security became ever more tenuous. The effect of gender segregated labour markets was that over 80 per cent of women worked in the service sector, compared with 56 per cent of men (Sly, 1993). Vertical gender segregation also continued to significantly disadvantage women (Equal Opportunities Commission, 1993). Research has shown that at the beginning of their careers, women with qualifications may start off level with men, but they quickly fall behind. For example a longitudinal study of graduates found that after only three years following graduation, 40 per cent of the men were in higher grade management or the professions. Only 17 per cent of the women were in equivalent positions. Over a third of the men were high earners, but only 19 per cent of the women were (MccGwire, 1992; Institute of Management, 1994).

Twenty-five years after the first equality legislation in Britain, only a handful of women have reached the top in their organisations and professions. More often women were bunched together just under the glass ceiling, with only the few breaking through this 'intractable barrier' (Hansard, 1990). The Hansard Society's (1990) report on women at the top identified the absence of women in positions of influence and power in management, in education, the professions, trade unions and public and political life. It confirmed that wherever they work, women typically continued to hold secondary, not primary positions. Numerous other reports showed this as a consistent pattern at all levels of work, from the top jobs down (Hansard, 1990; Equal Opportunities Commission Annual Reports; Serdjenian, 1995). Among the CBI's top 200 companies, for example, women were only 6.7 per cent of top management, and 81 per cent had no women directors at all on their main boards (Hansard, 1990). As the Hansard Society points out 'the higher the rank, prestige or influence, the smaller the proportion of women'.

However, a review of women's position within organisations over the last 25 years is not all bad news. By sheer force of numbers women have been continuing to move forwards into the workforce and upwards within organisations, with this movement itself bringing changes. There is now public acceptance of women's right to paid work as well as this right being enshrined in equality legislation. Equal opportunities measures once labelled 'loony' are commonly espoused, although only a small proportion of employers actually practise them. In 1988 a British Institute of Management (BIM) survey of 350 member organisations showed that although about half had a commitment to equal opportunities, less than a third were taking active steps to ensure they were put into practice (MccGwire, 1992). Recent studies do, however, indicate a number of benefits to employers who pursue positive action programmes in favour of women's and ethnic minority employment (Welsh, Knox and Brett, 1994; Serdjenian, 1995).

By 1994 Opportunity 2000, the voluntary campaign set up in 1991 'to increase and improve women's participation in the workforce' (Opportunity 2000, 1994) claimed 278 member employers representing 25 per cent of the UK workforce. Although a range of equality initiatives were in place in the majority, take up among employees of flexible measures such as job sharing and homeworking was at a very low level of around 10 per cent. In addition, less than half the member organisations had checked that their staff received equal pay for work of equal value.

Yet increasingly, these 25 years have found a generation of women who at both a practical and a personal level are frustrated at the intransigence of their labour market position and the snail's pace of change within organisations. The BIM described the tempo as 'glacial', and the Hansard Society in its report called for speed in covering the 'last long mile' of the journey towards women's equality (quoted in MccGwire, 1992). The Southern and Eastern Region Trade Union Congress Women's Rights Committee, reflecting on women's progress within trade unions, called their recent report 'Struggling for Equality' and wondered if they should add a little anger and irritation to the title, given the slow pace of change being experienced by women in trade unions and in the workplace (Southern and Eastern Region TUC, 1994).

British women are not alone in their frustration at the slow movement towards equality. Their experiences are shared and articulated by women across Europe (Hellman, 1987; Pillinger, 1992), in Australia (Grieve and Burns, 1990) and Canada and the United States (Backhouse and Flaherty, 1992; National Action Committee on the Status of Women, 1993): Eastern Europe (Rai, Pilkington and Phizacklea, 1992) and the developing countries (Ostergaard, 1992). The position of women and existing inequalities in terms of access to employment, economic and physical resources and senior positions within organisations is the subject of concern in both national and international fora of debate including the United Nations' Fourth World Conference on Women at Beijing in 1995. Indeed, some authors identify the establishment and spread of women's movements around the world accompanied by the exchange and diffusion of ideas and publications as evidence of the formation of a key and influential social movement (Barry, Honour, MacGregor and Palnitkar, 1994).

The last 25 years have been important years of cumulative experience and learning for women working within organisations: learning, both through working within 'non-women-friendly' environments and identifying and experiencing various forms of direct and indirect discrimination within organisations; learning by researching, analysing and publishing evidence of this discrimination, and by endeavouring to understand better and combat its root causes within organisations and society. It is our proposition in this book that women's increasing awareness of gender politics, combined with a willingness to actively challenge, change or work towards the transformation of organisations is a key ingredient in the liberation of women (and of men). We do not however envisage some grand feminist revolution – however welcome that might be. Our project in this book is to identify a range of strategies which women as change agents may take incrementally, purposefully or intuitively, in pursuit of their own woman-friendly or feminist projects in their work organisations, occupations and professions.

These embrace both women's individual agendas of hierarchical progression and status, plus more wide-ranging collective agendas for women, such as those aspired to through trade unionism and women's organisations. Such strategies involve a number of interrelated endeavours. Prerequisites include women's knowledge and understanding of gender relations generally, the gender structure, culture and politics of their particular work or occupational setting, and their own role and relationship within this. The level and depth of understanding and awareness will vary among different types and groups of women and will be significant in the choice of strategies and their effects. We aim to show that, among such women, understanding may unfold on a trajectory of developing feminist consciousness, moving from an acceptance of women's traditional role and position in society to a range of more questioning, critical and potentially feminist positions.[2]

Strategic action may or may not follow from the development of women's consciousness of gender inequalities, but, where it does, political skills are demanded if women as challengers to the status quo, indeed as change agents, are to have an effect. Many existing texts on women's position within organisations and the labour market describe the gender inequalities which exist and analyse the barriers women face (Crompton and Sanderson, 1990; Rees, 1992b; Walby, 1990; Witz, 1992). This book will seek to show how women actively challenge the status quo within their organisations on an individual and/or collective basis. In each of the eight chapters, contributing researchers explore the awareness and strategies of women in their endeavours to manage their gender roles and to work for change in their various organisations and industries.

This chapter now proceeds to provide a theoretical and conceptual framework for the sectoral studies. Firstly, it outlines and draws on the concept of patriarchy in order to situate the subsequent discussion of gender inequality and the contradictions women face between work and organisational life and their domestic and familial roles. Secondly, it reviews prevailing organisational responses to discrimination within organisations and their underlying rationale. Finally, the theme of women as change agents within organisations is explored through the development of a typology of women's political consciousness plus a discussion of the political skills required to bring about change within gendered organisational environments.

Explanations of gender inequality

A number of social science and management texts now recognise that there are structures and processes within society that systematically lead to the oppression of women (Fine, 1992; Rees, 1992b; Walby, 1990). This discrimination is reflected in gendered job segregation in the labour market and the enormous imbalance between the representation of women as workers in organisations and their occupation of positions of power in organisations (Colgan and Tomlinson, 1991; Lovenduski and Randall, 1993; MacEwen Scott, 1994).

Walby (1988) has criticised the social sciences for only slowly incorporating gender at both theoretical and empirical levels. She points to three major approaches in the literature so far with a potential fourth in progress. The first is the almost total neglect of gender, the result being that, in much social science, industrial relations and management studies research, workers and managers are assumed to be male, with any acknowledgement of women being reduced to a footnote. The second is the stage of critique when the flaws and fallacies in previous research have been exposed by feminist research. The third is the adding on of the study of women as a special case, as compensation for their previous neglect. Finally the fourth is the integration of gender relations into the analysis of work and organisations (Walby, 1988).

Studies on the significance of gender and the gender division of labour at work and in the home have much to contribute to an understanding of why such gender inequalities occur and how they are maintained and reproduced. Since the 1970s a growing number of authors have argued that an analysis of gender and gender relations is crucial to an understanding of organisations and their management (Dickens, 1989; Marshall, 1984; K. Purcell, 1990; Acker, 1990; Witz and Savage, 1992; Mills and Tancred, 1992).

This section will draw on some of the more recent research which has sought to recognise the significance of gender and the gender division of labour at work and in the home in order to explain the position of women (and men) in employment and within organisations. In doing so we acknowledge the contribution to knowledge made by differing perspectives within feminist research and discourse (summarised by Beechey, 1987; Rees, 1992b, and Walby, 1990). We will follow the example of Cockburn (1991) in this book by taking the view that a study of the position of women in organisations and their equality strategies calls for an approach that does not reject 'as heretical any of the three significant tendencies within feminism (often called liberal feminism,[3] socialist feminism[4] and radical feminism[5] but draws on insights from all' (Cockburn, 1991); that there are many feminisms – 'liberal, radical, cultural, socialist, post-modern, eco-feminism' (Townley (1994), as well as those of black women, lesbian women, disabled women and, although there are differences, there are sufficiently common themes from which to extract a shared view of the world which may inform a set of practices (Townley, 1994).

On patriarchy

Patriarchy is one of the major concepts used to explain the position of women in society and the analysis of gender inequalities. As Beechey (1987) points out, the concept of patriarchy is not new, it was used by early feminists such as Virginia Woolf, the Fabian Women's Group and Vera Brittain as well as by the sociologist Max Weber (1947) to refer to a system of government in which men ruled societies through their position as heads of households. The meaning of the term has evolved since Weber, as the concept has more recently been elaborated by writers such as Hartmann (1979), Walby (1986, 1990) and Cockburn (1983, 1985, 1991).

The concept of patriarchy which has been developed within feminist writings is not a simple or single concept but has a whole variety of meanings (Beechey, 1987). For example, radical feminists have used patriarchy to refer to male domination and to the power relationships by which men dominate women (Millett, 1969; Firestone, 1970) whereas socialist feminist writers have attempted to analyse the relationship between the subordination of women and the organisation of prevailing modes of production (Hartmann, 1979; Beechey, 1987). It is not our purpose here to elaborate the differences in usage in the literature, but to introduce the concept as a useful tool in the development of an analysis of gender inequality within organisations.

Walby (1990) has sought to provide one of the most comprehensive overviews of the variety of ways of explaining women's subordination in contemporary society and she and a number of other researchers have argued that the concept of 'patriarchy' is indispensable to any analysis of gender inequality (Cockburn, 1991; Witz, 1992). Walby's most recent definition of patriarchy is as 'a system of social structures and practices in which men dominate, oppress and exploit women' (1990). Walby identifies six different patriarchal structures: the patriarchal mode of production (domestic labour); wage labour; the role of the state; male violence; patriarchal relations in sexuality; and the formation of cultural institutions. She suggests that an individual's experience of patriarchy will depend on the interrelationship between these six structures (1990).

The concept of patriarchy has been used in a number of ways to try to explain gender inequalities within employment and organisations. Analyses have included segmented labour market theory (Dex, 1987) and the use of women as a flexible reserve army of labour (Beechey, 1977; Breugal, 1979; Rubery and Tarling, 1988). However, the five major bodies of work which will be discussed here include: women's familial role, dual systems theory, labour process theory, the analysis of the process of gendering and patterns of occupational segregation, and finally a gender paradigm for organisational analysis and research.

Familial role

Prior to joining the workforce, the material factors of women's work lives are influenced and structured by attitudes and behaviour informed by normative societal values about women's familial role and responsibilities as wives and carers, and especially as mothers. Anthias and Yuval-Davis (1983) point to the importance of taking both gender and ethnic divisions into account when examining male and female roles in the household. It has been argued extensively that women's subordination within the sphere of the family and their subordination in the sphere of paid employment are dynamically inter-related and reinforce one another (Witz, 1992). Thus it becomes clear how both perceived and actual familial demands on women also dominate their rela-tionship with paid work.

The impact is illustrated by the extensive evidence of how women's parti-cipation in the labour market is shaped by both having children and by the numbers and ages of their children throughout their working lives (Hewitt, 1993). In Britain, by the end of the 1980s, 45 per cent of women who had worked through their pregnancy were back at work within nine months. (In 1979 the figure was only 24 per cent.) However, those women who took longer breaks found that they returned to work in positions inferior to those they had left to go on maternity leave (Kandola and Fullerton, 1994a). Only a handful of employers provided formal career breaks, supported by training for women to keep up to date in readiness for their return to work.

The actual length of women's own career breaks has reduced over the last decade due to a combination of economic necessity, the provision of state maternity rights and benefits, and among 'best' employers (MccGwire, 1992; Kandola and Fullerton, 1994a) childcare provision and flexible working fol-lowing the return to work. Meanwhile, however there has been little or no re-education of men and women, and especially employers, towards challenging the expectation that it will be mothers who will give up paid work, take career breaks, care for their children in sickness and in health, as well as holding down a job, quite possibly as a single parent, and later on find themselves caring for their ageing parents (Central Statistical Office, 1995). Rubery and Fagan (1994) provide a useful discussion of the role of motherhood and childcare, social and economic policies such as the taxation system, in addition to social attitudes, in explaining the variations in women's activity rates across Europe. Cynthia Cockburn (1991) points out that cultural and political context seems to make little difference to the likelihood of men becoming more domesticated. In countries as different as Sweden, Norway, the former Soviet Union and China and America, despite extensive parental and other child-care-related leave benefits applying equally to both sexes, women continue to be the main domestic workers.

In Britain, after their maternity leave, the majority of women return to work part-time, taking short-term, casual jobs to fit around their young children. As their children get older, they return to work for longer hours (Equal Oppor-tunities Commission, 1995).

Meanwhile, however, it is assumed that a woman's domestic role involves her taking on the bulk of unpaid work in the home: succouring the primary (and presumably male) worker and rearing and socialising ('investing in') the next generation of workers (Delphy, 1984). In order to pay for all this, the male 'primary' wage earner claims as his right, a 'family wage' in acknowledgement of his breadwinning role. A common reading of this by employers is that when women arrive onto the labour market, they are working as 'secondary' wage earners and so are less committed to a career than men are (Beechey, 1987; Hartmann, 1979). This patriarchal view, combined with the resulting perception of the erratic nature of women's participation and commitment to work, serves to both lower their value on the labour market and to deny women a female identity independent of family.

So it becomes evident that when women reach the workplace, or return to it with additional family responsibilities, they find that they are required to fit into a system which has already been structured by those who got there first – men – around a full-time, lifetime career of commitment and progression; a system predicated on expectations by and about men's work; a system of patriarchy.

Dual systems theory

Dual systems theory argues that there are two separate systems operating in society, an economic system and a sex-gender system. Within the dual systems framework, capitalism is perceived as growing on top of an existing patriarchal system. The main focus of attention is the articulation between these two systems (Rees, 1992b).

Hartmann (1979), for example, views the two as having the same interests in that both systems benefit from women's unpaid domestic labour within the family. She views the capitalist mode of production as defining positions within society, whereas patriarchy determines who will fill them. Within dual systems theory capitalism structures a hierarchy of jobs which are then filled to the disadvantage of women. As summarised by Hartmann,

> Capitalist development creates the places for a hierarchy of workers, but traditional marxist categories cannot tell us who will fill which places. Gender and racial hierarchies determine who fills the empty places. Patriarchy is not simply hierarchical organisation, but hierarchy in which particular people fill particular places (Hartmann, 1981, quoted in Fine, 1992).

Walby (1988), however, suggests that at times the interests of patriarchy and capitalism may be in conflict. Thus conflicts may arise between the interests of capital in utilising cheap labour and those of patriarchy in restricting women to domestic labour or very limited forms of paid work. She points to two distinct patriarchal strategies to account for the resulting gender inequality: one is the exclusion altogether of women from the structures that men dominate, the other is women's segregation from men within these structures to hold them in positions of subordination, that is, segregation where exclusion fails (1990).

Studies which provide evidence of these patriarchal processes at work within organisations (including trade unions and the professions) include those conducted by Cockburn (1983, 1991), Crompton and Sanderson (1990), and Witz (1992). However, the dual systems approach has been criticised for being race-blind. Anthias and Yuval-Davies (1992) argue that it prioritises the relations between men and women within the patriarchal system and the relations between social classes in the capitalist system, so neglecting both the social relations of race and ethnicity and the existence of 'racialised genders' which can lead to a gender *and* race heirarchy of subordination. As Cockburn (1991) suggests, the buyer of labour is never indifferent to sex, ethnicity or skin colour.

Dual systems theory has been criticised by Marxists and feminists such as Barrett (1980), Rowbotham (1981) and Fine (1992). Fine (1992), for example, has expressed reservations about an analysis whereby patriarchy is primarily blamed for job exclusion and lower pay for women against the 'dull but liberalising forces of capitalism'. Nevertheless, the advantage of the dual systems theory approach is that it addresses the existence of patriarchy and its articulation with the prevailing economic system in a historically contingent way. Thus the forms that patriarchy takes in the family, the labour market and so on can be seen as changing and dynamic over both space and time (Rees, 1992).

Labour process theory

In the labour process literature, women's lives are considered to be defined as much by employment as by family and reproduction (Braverman, 1974; Cockburn, 1986; Knights and Willmott, 1986). Key components of this view are well summarised by Fine (1992) as follows. Firstly, work and the workplace is a terrain of conflict between capital and labour. Secondly, capitalism has a tendency to deskill and degrade jobs as accumulation substitutes machinery for labour. Thirdly, as the definition of skill is socially constructed – neither independent of, nor determined by, the requirements of the job itself – there is conflict and negotiation over what shall be defined as higher or lower grade jobs. Finally, each of these processes is gendered, resulting in an ongoing sexual division of labour and skills (Phillips and Taylor, 1980; Cockburn, 1985).

Specifically associated with the theory of the labour process is the idea that the restructuring of skills as a consequence of automation, mechanisation and so on can degrade and cheapen jobs, as shown for example by Smith and Morton (1990) in the newspaper industry. In line with patriarchy theory such jobs may be abandoned by men and left to women. Conversely, where jobs and skills are threatened in conjunction with mechanisation, men may agree to accept the changes only subject to the continuing exclusion of women (and ethnic minority workers). In the first case there is segregation, in the second exclusion (Fine, 1992). Men move out of jobs (and up) as they are occupied by women, due to greater male bargaining power, with men systematically devaluing women's work by constructing it as non-technical and inessential (Cockburn, 1988).

This approach has been useful in linking labour process change with the gendering of jobs. It recognises that both the regional and international gender division of labour is opened up through the stimulus of economic restructuring and labour process change (Massey, 1984; Bagguley *et al.*, 1990). It also recognises that employers, under renewed pressure from competition and in a powerful position relative to their workers during a recession, may seek to develop a 'flexible firm' (Atkinson, 1985). One important aspect of this for the study of organisational gender relations is the process whereby male workers are likely to form the majority of the 'core' workforce (enjoying more stable employment, training and development and better terms and conditions of employment) whereas women are more likely to be found in the 'peripheral' or casualised workforce (Walby, 1990; Storey, 1995a).

Gendering and occupational segregation

The gender segmentation of labour markets is now generally recognised as an important area of social science research (Beechey, 1987). This segregation has been shown to be strongly related to inequalities in pay, career prospects and employment protection. In fact, some working in the field argue that it has proved to be one of the most profound dimensions of labour market inequality and the most enduring (MacEwen Scott, 1994). Existing research has shown that despite legal, economic and social changes, occupational segregation by sex has shown little decrease in Britain (Hakim, 1987; MacEwen Scott, 1994). It has also acknowledged that the labour market is not a gender (or race) neutral context to which women and men come, rather it is 'permeated by an implicit gender ideology activiated through the practices of management, unions, male workers and women themselves' (Sinclair, 1991).

Gender segregation in employment is the product of complex interrelationships between employers, employees and households (MacEwen Scott, 1994). Employment indices suggest that there has been little change over the years despite substantial change in the structure of employment. Men are still twice as likely as women to work in highly segregated jobs and only half as likely to work in unsegregated jobs. Amongst both men and women, segregation remains much higher in manual than non-manual work. About a fifth of women work in 'exclusively female' jobs with a tendency for male exclusivity to be associated with highly skilled manual work, and female exclusivity with low-skilled manual and non-manual work (Colling and Dickens, 1989; Ledwith, 1991). According to MacEwen Scott (1994), major inroads into 'men's' territory have been limited, and confined to the professions, within which gendered segmentation remains strong. This corroborates studies of the increasing entry of women into the professions as a result of greater access to appropriate credentials, at the same time as the relegation of women to lower-status, lower-paid areas of work (Crompton and Sanderson, 1990; Jenkins and Walker, 1993; Roberts and Coutts, 1992).

Increasingly, studies have shown how gender[6] is constructed and reconstructed during the course of all spheres of daily life (Westwood, 1984; Sharpe, 1984; Yeandle, 1984; Coward, 1992) and through history; and that this needs to be adequately reflected and reproduced analytically (Connell, 1987). Cockburn (1985) in particular has argued that work itself is a gendering process whereby the social process of gender construction and formulations of gender difference which are learned by men and women from an early age continue into their working lives. Thus all behaviours become gendered and all interpretations of behaviour too. It is important to recognise as a key element in this process the persistence and dominance of forms of men's presence within organisations and the significance of this for power relations and the gendering of occupations within organisations (Cockburn, 1983; Hearn *et al.*, 1989; Collinson, Knights and Collinson, 1990).

As researchers and writers such as Acker (1990) and Rees (1992b) have pointed out, there is now recognised to be a relationship between both the gender and the sexuality of those who do a particular job, the value put upon the skills involved and the level of pay with which those skills are rewarded. The social construction of skill also depends on how those skills were obtained, for example, those acquired via education, training or experience are valued more than innate characteristics or skills learned on the job. The most consistantly undervalued jobs are those characterised as 'women's jobs', particularly where, 'A gendered job was one which capitalised on the qualities and capabilities a woman gained by virtue of having lived her life as a woman' (Davies and Rosser, 1986a). Thus the ranking of women's jobs are often justified on the basis of women's identification with childbearing and domestic life, while at the same time the gendered definition of some jobs 'includes sexualization of the woman worker as a part of the job' (MacKinnon, 1979, quoted in Acker, 1990).

Vogler (1994) has sought to understand the effect of sexist attitudes on the persistence of gender segregation. She defined sexism as a belief in the legitimacy of gender inequality. In trying to identify why an informant's job was gendered, she reported a low emphasis on skill, domestic constraints or employers' hiring policies. Much more stress was placed by individuals on social factors relating to gender roles (MacEwen Scott, 1994). Vogler (1994) noted that sexism was higher among men than women although less so among the 'higher and better educated social classes' who exhibited less sexism and also worked in less segregated environments. She concluded that even if sexist attitudes do not 'cause segregation, they play an important part in justifying gender inequality in the labour-market and in interpreting it as "natural"'.

The development of this literature on gendering and occupational segregation has played an important part in pin-pointing the centrality of gender relations in the analysis of work, power and organisations.

Gender and organisations – a theoretical framework and a research paradigm

Analysis of the gendering of organisations is comparatively recent (Ferguson, 1984; Acker, 1990; Mills and Tancred, 1992; [Tancred-]Sheriff and Campbell, 1992); Billing, 1994). A major reason for this, according to Acker (1990) is that in spite of feminist recognition that hierarchical organisations are an important location of male dominance, most feminists writing about organisations have assumed that organisational structure was gender neutral.

Acker comments that some of the best feminist attempts to theorize about gender and organisations have been trapped within the constraints of definitions of the theoretical domain that cast organisations as gender neutral and asexual. Such neutrality is given expression in what she terms 'organisational logic', or the underlying assumptions and practices that construct most contemporary work organisations.

As part of her explanation of the persistence of this neutrality, Acker (1990) uses the example of how sexuality is dealt with and controlled within organisations through organisational power relations. The separation of work and sexuality and the 'suppression of sexuality is one of the first tasks the bureaucracy sets itself' (Burrell, 1984, quoted in Acker, 1990). This is in order to try to control the interferences and disruptions to the 'ideal functioning of organisations' caused by sexuality, procreation and emotions (Acker, 1990). The resulting 'silence on sexuality' (Acker, 1990) also includes control of homosexuality through insistence on hetereosexism or celibacy, oppressing lesbians and gay men, many of whom feel forced to conceal their sexuality at work (Palmer, 1993). The assertion of male (and heterosexist) power and control through forms of sexuality (Ramazangolu, 1989) and sexual (and racial) harassment within organisations is increasingly being explored (Amos and Parmar, 1984; Phizacklea, 1983; Hearn and Parkin, 1987; 1989; Hall, 1989; Cockburn, 1991; Brant and Too, 1994). Thus Hall (1989) uses the concept of 'double jeopardy' to characterise the subordination and oppression experienced by lesbians at work as a result of their gender and their sexuality, whereas the concept of a 'double burden' has been utilised by Amos and Parmar (1984) in order to recognise the specific and cumulative forms of oppression experienced by ethnic minority women at work.

Acker's (1990, 1992) argument for a systematic theory of gender and organisations recognises the significance of work organisations as arenas in which widely disseminated cultural images of gender and individual identity are invented and reproduced. She is mainly concerned with the integral part which gender analysis plays in the analysis of the social processes of gendering of organisations and without which, she asserts, these cannot be properly understood.

Four interacting sets of processes are identified which, although analytically distinct, are in practice parts of the 'same reality' (Acker, 1990, 1992). These are: the construction of gender divisions among men and women, with men almost always in the highest positions of organisational power; the construction of symbols and images that explain, express, reinforce or sometimes oppose those divisions, such as language, dress and media image; interactions among and between women and men; and the gendered components of individual identity and presentation of self, described as 'the internal mental work of individuals' as they consciously construct their own conceptualisation of the organisation's gendered structures, including persona and the demands for gender-appropriate behaviour and attitudes. Similar models for theorising gender at these different levels – structural, symbolic and individual – have been developed by Harding (1986), and Scott (1986), and Beechey (1988) has affirmed the utility of analysis which keeps these different levels in play at the same time.

As well as Acker's call for a systematic theory of gender and organisations, and Mills and Tancred's (1992) for the whole of organisational analysis to be rethought on the basis that a fundamental gendered substructure characterises the workplace, Witz and Savage (1992) have outlined a 'gender paradigm' for use in the study of organisations. They argue that until the 1980s there was little dialogue between organisational studies and feminist research and debate, but that new currents in social theory have now placed the issue of the relationship between gender and bureaucracy firmly on the agenda. Drawing on a burgeoning dialogue between organisational studies and feminist research, plus insights from the work of Clegg (1989) and Giddens (1984), they assert that a key element of the new paradigm is the need to move away from 'general notions of bureaucratic organization in order to recognise historically and spatially specific ways of organising, which can be shown to rest on gendered foundations' (1992).

Central to their proposed paradigm is the relationship between gender and power within organisational settings. They argue that this involves moving away from formalist analyses of bureaucracies towards a recognition of both how they are shaped by specific struggles and how they in turn lead to specific types of gender configurations (Witz and Savage, 1992). As an example of historical specificity, Witz and Savage suggest that the modern organisation came into being depending on cheap female labour, thus helping to define women as subordinate workers to men within emergent white collar labour markets (1992). This is a view substantiated by the work of Zimmick (1992) on the Post Office and of Crompton and Le Feuvre (1992) on the finance sector in Britain and France.

The paradigm is developed through a conceptualisation of how bureaucracies are gendered, drawing especially on the work of Kanter (1977), Ferguson (1984) and Pringle (1989) in order to carry out a 'feminist interrogation of bureaucracy' (Witz and Savage, 1992).

The recognition of a gender paradigm for the study of organisations raises important issues for women and men seeking to change the patriarchal nature of organisations (Witz and Savage, 1992). Whereas Kanter (1977) expressed the expectation that the integration of women into bureaucratic power structures will alter these structures in a significant way, Witz and Savage (1992) counter that view, drawing on the work of Ferguson (1984) who suggests that it is more likely that women will become co-opted. Ferguson suggests that individual women may have to learn to act like men in order to function effectively at senior levels (1984). Whereas this leads her to advocate a separatist strategy for women *vis-à-vis* male bureaucratic structures, Watson's article (1992) on the Australian Femocrat strategy provides an example of women working as feminists fairly successfully (although not without some personal conflicts and dilemmas) within male dominated bureaucratic structures. The potential costs and stresses borne by senior women working within 'male' organisations are increasingly being explored in the management and organisation studies literature (Marshall, 1984; Alimo-Metcalfe, 1993; Powell, 1993; Tanton, 1994).

The proposals offered by contributors to the organisational debate, such as Acker, Mills and Tancred *et al.*, and Witz and Savage, that organisations are seen to be inevitably shaped by a wide variety of social forces, gender notably amongst them, is a significant shift for organisation theory. Morgan and Knights (1991) and Kerfoot and Knights (1993) illustrate this by looking at how important issues of corporate strategy revolve around the gendered nature of particular jobs. Thus, this approach recognises the key role gender divisions may play in affecting the process of organisational and sectoral restructuring (Beechey, 1987).

Patriarchy as a conceptual tool

There still remains some unease about the use of the concept of patriarchy as a conceptual tool of analysis (Bradley, 1989; Fine, 1992). Crompton and Sanderson (1990) see the concept as an imperfect but useful descriptive tool whereas Walby (1990) and Witz (1992) seek to salvage it and recast it to further the understanding of male dominance and the complexity of gender relations and inequity within organisations and society.

Key criticism of the concept of patriarchy has revolved around its limited use on the grounds that it provides a biologically determinist and ahistoric analysis of gender inequalities (Barrett, 1980; Rowbotham, 1981; Fine, 1992).

Other criticism has been levelled at its insensitivity to the experiences of women of different cultures, classes and ethnicities (Barrett, 1980; Rowbotham, 1981; hooks, 1984; Anthias and Yuval Davis, 1993).

In responding to these criticisms Walby (1990) and Witz (1992) take the view that the concept of patriarchy can have explanatory potential if used in a historically sensitive way. For Walby, the concept of patriarchy is essential to capture the depth, pervasiveness and interconnectedness of different forms of gender inequality over time, class and ethnic group. However, she also acknowledges 'the danger in theorizing gender inequality at an abstract level and acknowledges the need for any discussion to deal with historical, cultural and spatial variations' (1990).

It is now acknowledged in the literature on patriarchy and its forms that there are different patterns of both patriarchy and capitalism. Further, there are complex historically specific ways in which the structures and practices which make up those systems intersect (Walby, 1990; Witz, 1992). In general, we agree with the view of Fine (1992) and Anthias and Yuval Davis (1993) who, despite reservations, allow that patriarchy has been a useful tool in describing and investigating female oppression and as such provides an important method of enquiry or investigation. In our view also, it is important to be sensitive to the experiences of women of different cultures, classes, races, sexualities and ethnicities, and women with disabilities.

Chapters within the book illustrate the insights provided by the bodies of work summarised in this section. Patriarchy therefore provides the overall framework for much of the subsequent discussion on women in organisations. In the book we recognise that as cultures and societies variously differentiate between the relative status of men and women and prescribe rules governing the relations between the sexes, similarly within different occupations and organisations a range of traditions, values and expectations exist which mediate the way in which women and men (and ethnic minorities) are deployed within them (Colgan and Tomlinson, 1991; Redclift and Sinclair, 1991).

Organisational approaches to inequality

In North America, Europe and Australia women's and other equity-seeking groups have campaigned for legislation outlawing discrimination on the grounds of sex, race, sexuality and disability in the workplace and in the provision of goods and services (Adam, 1987; Anthias and Yuval-Davis, 1992; Backhouse and Flaherty, 1992; D. Cooper, 1994; Coote and Campbell, 1987; Thornton and Lunt, 1995). They have also campaigned, with varying degrees of success, for shifts in organisational policies and practices using both human rights and 'business case' arguments to address organisational inequality.

According to the latter, it has been argued that organisations need to make the best use of their human resources and compete successfully in the provision of goods and services by recognising the challenges and opportunities provided by an increasingly diverse population (Hicks-Clarke and Iles, 1994; McNaught, 1993; R. R. Thomas, 1991).

A range of practical legal, institutional and organisational equal opportunities actions have been taken in response to these demands, and the now well-publicised empirical and incontravertible evidence of gender inequality in the labour market and at work. In the UK these equality and equal opportunity measures have been catalogued and evaluated in an increasing number of publications (Hansard, 1990; MccGwire, 1990; H. Collins, 1992; Davidson and Cooper, 1993; King, 1993). Nevertheless, the overriding conclusions which are commonly articulated are that 'women's advance into what have been traditionally men's jobs, particularly into the higher-status professions in business and management, has been very slow' (Davidson and Cooper, 1992) and 'however they play it, women in the UK are still losing out' (King, 1993).

We move now to consider the practical equality initiatives taken in work organisations, and the problems arising from the pragmatic manner in which these have been developed within a mainstream managerial paradigm, with little or no acknowledgement to explanations of patriarchy and the gender processes discussed in the previous section. In light of this, we would question, in this section, the existence of a political will to introduce, resource, implement and sustain equal opportunity initiatives effectively in patriarchal organisations.

The management literature, in acknowledging the lack of progress and continuing imbalance, has sought to evade the centrality of gender and race relations in the analysis of work, power and organisations. Rather it has recast the debate concerning equal opportunities away from a moral and human rights framework which acknowledged systemic discrimination against specific groups, to a focus on the individual, the 'business case', and issues of corporate strategy. This can be seen for example in much of the recent human resource management (HRM) literature, which appears to be gender-blind in its consideration of human resource issues as it strives to align HRM more closely with corporate strategy (Guest, 1987; Colgan and Tomlinson, 1995; Legge, 1995; Storey, 1995a; Purcell and Ahlstrand, 1994).

This HRM approach is exemplified in a study carried out by the Ashridge Management College Research Group (Hammond and Holton, 1991). This provided the business-case argument for the Opportunity 2000 Campaign whose aim is to increase the quantity and quality of women in the workforce by the year 2000. Hammond and Holton (1991) applied four criteria for the successful management of change to organisations' equal opportunities programmes. These were: demonstrating commitment from the top all the way up and down the organisation; changing behaviour; communicating and building ownership of equal opportunities, and making the investment in time and resources. In their view, it was the absence of these which accounted for the failure of equal opportunties initiatives, and only when equality issues were integrated with business objectives was the position of women likely to change. This is a similar argument to that made for recasting personnel management into a business framework and calling it Human Resource Management. Personnel management had been seen to have failed largely because of its lack of integration into business strategy (Guest, 1987; Storey, 1995a; Purcell and Ahlstrand, 1994), and like equal opportunities, which is often located within personnel departments, had not contributed sufficiently to the bottom line.

A second approach has emerged from the strategic HRM school – 'the management of diversity'. This claims to 'move on' from equal opportunities towards 'valuing diversity' into more sophisticated programmes where difference is celebrated and maximised in everyone's interests (Ross and Schneider, 1992; Kandola and Fullerton, 1994a). Kandola and Fullerton (1994b), outlining the approach, suggest that 'diversity takes individuals as the primary focus of concern, not groups'. They also argue that such an approach 'will mean that certain group-based equal opportunity actions need to be seriously questioned, in particular positive action and targets'. We take the view that it is too soon to claim that diversity management in the UK is a more effective or innovative approach. Much of the research on managing diversity programmes has been conducted in North America where they are being implemented within quite a different context. For example, there appears to be a stronger vision of equal opportunities and civil rights plus a more radical legislative framework to address discrimination in the United States and Canada than currently exists in the UK (Hicks-Clarke and Iles, 1994).[7]

In our view, on their own, business problem solving approaches ignore the power relations of gender and race in their analysis of organisational discrimination and equal opportunities; they operate within a liberal approach to equal opportunities. Thus we consider a more useful and thoroughgoing insight into organisational equality initiatives is offered by Jewson and Mason (1986) and Cockburn (1991) who explicitly deal with these power relations. First, we will consider Jewson and Mason's (1986) exposition of two opposing yet complementary positions – the liberal and radical approaches to equal opportunities.

The liberal approach to equal opportunities

The liberal approach lays emphasis on the development of 'fair' and visible procedures in order both to be acceptable and to deliver equality, with the requirement that the *process* of that delivery must also be seen to be fair. Liberal systems are about removing handicaps for disadvantaged groups in order to enable everyone to participate equally on a level organisational playing field. In the case of women, it is possible to identify two main types of removal: first, the elimination of discriminatory organisational and labour market practices and material detriments, and second, the easing of women's burden of family responsibilities.

Measures aimed at the elimination of discriminating structures and practices include ensuring the provision of equal terms and conditions of employment and material benefits. It may also involve action to prevent organisational members' overtly sexist, homophobic, racist or disablist behaviour, including the introduction of non-discriminatory procedures and systems, supported by training, across the range of personnel and employment activities such as recruitment and promotion, and interpersonal behaviour in the workplace. The second category of measures aims to help lighten women's domestic load via maternity rights, childcare support, flexible working, career break schemes and training to make up the deficit between the sexes. Neither type of measures challenges the existing gender roles of women and men: rather, they reinforce the general expectation that women are those responsible for their children's care.

In liberal terminology these measures are designated 'positive action', the aim of which is to redress past discriminatory practices and promote free and equal competition among individuals (Jewson and Mason, 1986). Both the definition of 'positive action' and some of the rights are legitimised in the anti-discrimination laws in many industrialised countries, and are among the most common equal opportunity systems now in use in work organisations. (H. Collins, 1992; MccGwire, 1992). The liberal approach to establishing equal opportunities has been formally operating in Britain now for around 25 years. But despite increasingly creative approaches, it is still seen to have failed women, as the discussion of women's continuing subordinate position at work earlier in this chapter has shown.

Instead, it is characterised as doing little more than inviting women and ethnic minority applicants to succeed within organisations on 'white, male terms' (Webb and Liff, 1988), being an individualistic, meritocratic approach which is power (gender and race) blind (Collinson, Knights and Collinson, 1990). In addition it provides a plausible justification for unequal outcomes, is based within the control of a managerial (and usually patriarchal) framework, and fails to challenge or attempt to change the existing organisational power structures.

As indicated above, by the early 1990s the rationale for liberal approaches was increasingly being framed within a strategic human resource management approach, with the emphasis on the 'business case' for equal opportunities, thus shifting concepts of fairness into the dominant ideology of the market, individualism and business efficiency.

The radical approach to equal opportunities

A radical approach is more than making existing procedures and systems fair, or 'tinkering at the margins': it is about challenging existing structures, attitudes and cultures in pursuit of change. It seeks to intervene directly in organisational practices in order to achieve a fair distribution of rewards among groups as measured by some ethical and moral criterion. As such it focuses on fairness in *outcomes*, calling for positive discrimination and consciousness raising in order to 'release a struggle for power and influence' (Jewson and Mason, 1986).

Radical equal opportunity initiatives which involve 'positive discrimination' ('affirmative action' in the USA) include measures which involve establishing that women are different from men, making women visible, setting men-only structures. This is seen by liberals and traditionalists (both male and female) as not only illegal in the UK (except in trade unions), but undesirable (Institute of Management, 1994).

Radical approaches have been introduced more commonly where work organisations also have explicitly political or ethical/altruistic values. For example in the UK elected local politicians, in alliance with equality-seeking activists (predominantly within Labour local authorities), who could see that liberal measures were insufficient, developed a range of innovative 'separatist' structures for groups experiencing disadvantage (e.g. women, ethnic minorities, lesbian and gay and disabled) overseen and resourced by lay political committees (Halford, 1992; Buswell and Jenkins, 1994). In the US, Canada, Australia and parts of Europe the state in its role as employer has taken both legislative and structural measures to expedite the more speedy progression towards equity for women, people of colour and other disadvantaged groups. It is clear that, in both British and North American examples, the radical approach in large measure builds on policies and practices developed at the liberal level of equal opportunities.

Nevertheless, although the theoretical and political positions of the two viewpoints may be clearly differentiated, and in some cases are fundamentally in conflict, within organisational politics, they are often confused and conflated through a 'systematic pattern of muddle and deception' (Jewson and Mason, 1986). In particular, argue Jewson and Mason, the preferred procedures of the liberal approach are widely assumed to result in the outcomes preferred by the radical school.

The long agenda: transformational change

This approach has been set out by Cynthia Cockburn (1989) to cope with the tensions and contradictions inherent in what she characterisises as the 'liberal/radical dichotomy'. She feels that a recognition of both a short and long agenda in the development of equal opportunities offers a broader approach within which to understand differing equal opportunities initiatives.

Given the complex nature of power and the various kinds of challenge which equal opportunities activism can present to the forms in which power is reproduced, she proposes that we should be wary of identifying radical approaches as inevitably the most progressive. She suggests that if the major contradiction of the liberal approach is that 'it cannot achieve what it proclaims', then the major contradiction of the radical is that 'it seeks to give some disadvantaged groups a boost up the ladder, while leaving the structure of that ladder and the disadvantages it entails just as before' (Cockburn, 1989).

Following Cockburn's argument, the radical approach towards organisational equal opportunities is thus likely to be viewed with suspicion by the majority of members who may seek to resist it. This is particularly the case where it is seen to be the vehicle for the pursuit of vested minority interests by one group (women for example) in order to gain power at the expense of existing power holders rather than to offer a transformational route to power sharing (Colgan and Ledwith, 1994).

Examples of the backlash to equal opportunity initiatives are many and widespread (Cockburn, 1991; Dunant, 1994; Faludi, 1992). To try to avoid such situations, Cockburn advocates the need to see the development of equal opportunities in terms of a short or long agenda. At its shortest, it involves measures to minimise bias in recruitment and selection procedures, and as such focuses on the formal and bureaucratic. At its longest, it is at its most progressive, establishing a project of transformation for an organisation, and can be expected to involve changes to structures, attitudes and cultures.

She proposes that there is likely to be greater support for the long equal opportunities agenda which coherently argues the need to make changes to the organisation on the grounds that 'the on-going chances of all groups are to be equalised and sustained, democratised and opened' (Cockburn, 1989). This is the challenge which confronts those seeking to shift patriarchal, racist disablist and homophobic organisational structures, attitudes and cultures, so encouraging organisations to function more effectively by recognising and valuing the diversity of individuals and their experiences.

Women's perspectives on organisational gender politics

In the rest of this chapter, therefore, we discuss ways in which women themselves may and do meet the challenge of organisational gendering, both for themselves as individuals and through collective equality strategies which aim to bring about transformational change within organisations. We do so by identifying key processes and stages in the development of women's own consciousness of gender relations, their understanding of organisational gender politics, and strategies which they may adopt in order to survive, progress or work for change in their organisations. This discussion then provides the framework for the empirical case study chapters which follow.

Understanding organisational gender politics

Moving now to women's consciousness and activism within their work organisations,[8] we would expect these to differ according to a woman's wider background and experience and the fit with the specific circumstances of the gendered structure and culture at her workplace and her perception of these. The case study chapters illustrate these differences and show how women's strategies do take account of organisational specificity.

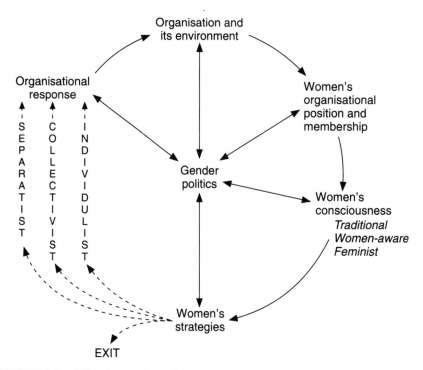

FIGURE 1.1   **The dynamics of women's consciousness and activism in organisations**

Figure 1.1 illustrates a cycle of gendered organisational change. It summarises some key features in the dynamic relations between organisational gender politics, women's consciousness and activism and women's potential role as change agents.

Organisational analysis needs to recognise that a fundamental gendered substructure characterises the workplace (Mills and Tancred, 1992; Witz and Savage, 1992), so creating and reproducing horizontal and vertical segregation by gender within organisations. This results in a complex process well described by Podmore and Spencer (1986) whereby women (and men) may 'prefer' and/or be 'pressurised" into working within specific occupations/departments within a given organisation. In seeking employment, women (and men) thus need to balance their own interests and career aspirations with their perception of the opportunities, threats and barriers that arise in gendered work organisations.

This process is illustrated for example in the chapter on personnel management by Larraine Gooch and Sue Ledwith whereby women wishing to work in management may on the one hand value and be attracted to working 'with people' as a personnel manager; however they may also find themselves doing so within an organisation which provides limited opportunities to women within line management roles. As a result, women may find themselves 'pressured' into and trapped within the junior echelons of a personnel department with limited opportunities for career progression in management within the organisation. Similarly, women may choose to enter teaching as a 'feminised' profession within which they may hope to develop a career while balancing personal and family aspirations only to find themselves experiencing horizontal and vertical gender segregation within a profession which prioritises the requirements and norms of the 'male full-time career' as shown in the chapter on teaching by Geraldine Healy and David Kraithman.

The strategies women develop to survive and progress in gendered organisational life will depend in the first instance on their consciousness and awareness of gender politics within the organisation. The degree to which women accept, conform to or challenge gendered patterns of occupational segregation and gender politics within their organisation will depend on a balance between their consciousness of discrimination and career barriers; their reading of organisational politics and their willingness to adopt individualist, collectivist and/or separatist strategies.

For example, in order to survive and progress, women working in a very masculine environment such as HM Customs and Excise are shown by Amanda Palmer to adopt solely individualist strategies of career progression, even though the organisation provides a host of formal equal opportunity measures, and is puzzled at their apparent lack of effect. Women such as teachers, however, as shown by Geraldine Healy and David Kraithman, may adopt collectivist strategies through the established professional organisations and trade unions in order to challenge the wider patriarchal structures, while also pursuing individual approaches to their own career management. Yet other women may decide to follow a separatist (women-only) feminist strategy, working collectively solely with other women, as illustrated by some of the women depicted in the chapters on women in the book publishing industry by Fiona Colgan and Frances Tomlinson, and in trade unions as shown by Fiona Colgan and Sue Ledwith. In practice, women will use some or all of these strategies during the course of their working lives. It is also the case that a woman may decide that the most appropriate strategy open to her is to leave an organisation which she perceives as hostile and unlikely to improve, as can be seen in the chapters on book publishing, HM Customs and Excise, the transport sector and the National Health Service.

Thus women's understanding of and engagement with equality and gender issues will differ in their level and development both within and between organisations. Similarly, and informed by this understanding, women's objectives will vary from individual career progression through to wider collective projects of organisational change.[9] Where women's actions are sufficient to provoke an organisational response (positive or negative) this will trigger further adjustments by women and men, thus contributing to a cycle of gendered organisational change.

A trajectory of women's consciousness and activism

Because of the complexities involved and the multiple directions and dimensions of women's consciousness and activism, we present this as a trajectory. At one end lies a traditional consciousness, and the trajectory extends in a number of directions to encompass a range of overlapping feminist consciousnesses.

Traditional women

At the traditional end of the trajectory we place women with a lack of awareness of gender politics. Being a traditional woman implies broad acceptance of women's gendered place in society, the family, the labour market and work organisations. It does not necessarily mean agreement with the terms and conditions which women actually experience, although it could denote a high level of tolerance and conformity with the dominant (male) culture.

A traditional view would be likely to confine women's courses of action to those generally expected within patriarchal structures and cultures, as such women would be unlikely to conceive of challenging these. Our women's traditionalism is similar to Kakabadse's (1986) 'Traditional' political style. The characteristics of Kakabadse's traditionalists were that they wished to fit in with the rest of the organisation, accepting the way things were done, even if this was detrimental to their own interests. Such strategies for individual progress are likely to be pursued by those who believe that the difference in status and power between men and women in organisations is legitimate, that procedures are fair and that they as women need to demonstrate their own ability within the prevailing climate and not look for 'special treatment' as women. Indeed, traditional women may well be anxious to be accepted within their organisations as 'one of the lads', as found for example by Tomlinson, Daniel and Ledwith (1992) in their study of women business students on work placements.

In her study of women managers, Judi Marshall (1984) constructed a sequence of increasing gender awareness, identifying groups of women managers at three broad stages in the move towards development of a 'clear sense of themselves as women'. Her first group may be seen as 'traditional'. Although not unaware, nevertheless in their professional lives they denied their womanhood while simultaneously identifying the disadvantages of being female and explaining how they avoided or coped with discrimination. Marshall suggested that these women used a tactic of muting their own awareness of being women and different from men by preferring not to see themselves as *women* first at work, but as professionals. They did not welcome visibility and avoided being 'one of the girls'. These women also hinted that if they did become more aware of being a woman they would encounter more difficulties. This may frequently be the case for women working in predominantly male environments, as reflected in Amanda Palmer's chapter on women in HM Customs and Excise who invoked individual strategies of seeking to demonstrate their worth as 'effective colleagues rather than as women' to male co-workers. Traditional women in trade unions may act collectively (on the basis of trade union cultural norms) *against* women's equality projects. In the trade union chapter Fiona Colgan and Sue Ledwith show how such women sought to emphasise the benefits of trade union unity and solidarity by speaking out and voting against what they described as 'divisive' special measures for women.

Women 'in transition' along the trajectory

Moving along the trajectory to women with an awakening consciousness, we can place Marshall's second group of women managers. They were in 'painful turmoil' (Marshall, 1984), talking at length about the problems of being a woman. This state of 'acute consciousness' had been brought about by changes in their relationships to work. One woman recounted how hitherto she had 'been blind to what has been truly happening'. In carrying out her research, Marshall describes her own transition from reform to radical feminism: 'as my reading and thinking touched my personal sphere in this powerful way, I experienced a new sense of myself – as a woman, and with new freedom. I began the delicate, engrossing process of developing my own feminism.' She described the women in her study as developing a new sensitivity to apparent prejudice and discrimination, going on to record that they had not yet found a new way of behaving. The women often felt they were behaving inappropriately: how to be and to behave, especially in close relations, had become problematic. Neither had they evolved a new set of values or perspectives which acknowledged their awareness of gender. This pattern also emerges from the study in Larraine Gooch and Sue Ledwith's chapter, of young women personnel professionals trying to chart a career in a profession which they recognised had a number of gendered occupational barriers, but for which they had no coping strategies.

We characterise such women as being 'in transition'. In the chapter about women trade union activists, a group of such women were questioning the reality to them as women of the traditional trade union concepts such as 'unity' in the light of their experiences of opposition from their own trade union brothers . In their search for an understanding of what was going on in their union, these women gained a better understanding of how their male colleagues held onto power. Subsequently they sought out men and women who were sympathetic to women's issues, and worked together with them to use the existing rules to get 'women's issues' onto the trade union agenda.

Women in transition along the trajectory like this may be unsure about their identity and role, and at this stage are often anxious to distance themselves from being labelled as feminists. Research among women in a range of women's groupings and their activism, found this to be the case especially among younger women, who had a much less developed sense of self-confidence about being women, and were reluctant to be identified as feminists (Kelly and Breinlinger, 1994). This position is evident among women in all the case study chapters. In the 1990s, being labelled 'feminist' was increasingly being seen by some women as problematic. This was found to be the case particularly among young women even when they shared the aims and values of the women's movement (Siann and Wilkinson, 1995). Marshall (1994) points out that in most studies many women comment on the negative stereotypes of feminism in employment and the pressure on women not to identify with its issues. Such attitudes are not altogether surprising, existing as they do within a robust patriarchal hegemony, a system whose values of gender relations are, as Cockburn (1991) suggests, possibly the strongest, and invisible, force against women. As feminist ideas seep 'almost subliminally into mainstream thinking' (Siann and Wilkinson, 1995), this hegemony may be mobilised as oppositional response or backlash.

Feminism and feminists: differences in aims, strategy and action

Moving to sites of feminist consciousness on the trajectory, and in identifying feminist ideas and feminists, we draw on the debate over formulations which distinguish different feminisms. Firstly, a broad, universal feminism is seen as embracing practical action, consciousness, and theory: a 'vision of *all* women challenging sexualised, gendered, racialised and economic control over our lives through ideology and politics' (Bhavnani, 1993). Such unity of purpose encompasses the 'political theory and practice that struggles to free *all* women: women of colour, working class women, poor women, disabled women, lesbians, old women – as well as white economically privileged heterosexual women' (B. Smith, 1982, quoted in Bhavnani, 1993).

Delmar (1986), while acknowledging the title of feminist as any group that has tried to change the position of women, or ideas about women (Banks, 1981, cited in Mitchell and Oakley, 1986), identifies the problem of distinguishing between many feminisms, including conscious and unconscious feminism. Building on the history of feminism, she cites at one level the view of Ray Strachey (1928) that while a sense of awareness of grievance might be sufficient to bring someone into the ambit of women's politics, it does not make that person a feminist.

A feminist, according to this perspective, is someone whose central concern and preoccupation lies with the position of women and their struggle for emancipation; someone who puts women's rights in the centre of her work, and for whom feminism is also a conscious political choice (Strachey, 1928). Thus, together consciousness and activism allow a relatively objective differentiation between feminists and non-feminists. In this type of feminism, feminists are distinguished as the leaders, organisers, publicists, lobbyists of the women's movement. 'The social movement provides the context for feminism; feminists are its animating spirits' (Delmar, 1986). However, Delmar also asks: How would one place individuals and women's groups who reject the label of 'feminist'?

This is particularly pertinent in organisational gender politics, where a distinction between feminists and non-feminists is not straightforward and may call for situationally specific, politically expedient and non-overt strategies. In Marshall's (1984) study, women managers whose work experiences had contributed to a new more feminist consciousness had become advocates of women's rights. Although they found this tough, it was also 'challenging and exciting' (Marshall, 1984). However, some of the women also found that being an 'animating spirit' turned out to be at their own expense and subsequently they tried to 'unthink this response' in order to take care of themselves first (Marshall, 1984). Nevertheless, Marshall's view is that the development of awareness is progressive: 'as there is no going back from the conclusions that they have reached, they must go forward'. Women like this can be seen to be developing a clearer sense of themselves as women and their affinity to women as a group. Thus on our trajectory we have found it useful to differentiate between what we have described as a 'women-aware'[10] and a fuller 'feminist' position.

First we need to define the 'women-aware' position. We noted that although women may recognise and be impatient with the barriers they experience as women within work organisations, they may for a number of ideological and pragmatic reasons opt to embrace an individualist and short agenda approach to women's progression at work. As Delmar (1986) suggests, 'you don't have to be a feminist to support women's rights to equal treatment'. This can be seen particularly to be so among some of the women discussed in the retail and personnel chapters, who were prepared to identify themselves in some cases as 'holding feminist beliefs' within a managerial ethos of individual ambition and career.

A 'women-aware' approach therefore would not preclude women from taking collective or separatist action, both in pursuit of personal career goals and the furthering of women's position in management more generally. For example, such a separatist, albeit temporary, strategy among women managers was revealed in a 1993 BBC programme, 'Business Matters', by a group of women health care administrators in the United States. They had developed a collective strategy to ensure that at least one of them became a chief executive officer (CEO) within a certain timescale. Their approach turned out to be so successful that within two years a number of the women had in fact become CEOs.

A 'women-aware' perspective can be further differentiated from a fuller feminist one in terms of the aims, strategies and actions prioritised to challenge gender inequalities within organisations and sectors. Tomlinson (1987), for example, in her study of women's organisations (which she identified as part of the broader women's movement) differentiated between organisations which she classified as 'conservative' in that they wished to act moderately, present a 'safe image' by avoiding the label 'feminist' and involve men (e.g. the City Women's Network, Women in Banking and Women in Management) and those that had a more feminist campaigning philosophy (e.g. Women in Publishing, Women in Media and Women in Libraries). Thus the more 'conservative' or 'women-aware' organisations, recognising the barriers faced by women, set out to create self-help networks rather along the lines of the 'old boys network'. These organisations (and the women within them) sought to pursue liberal equal oportunities policies and promote a positive and 'sensible' image of women, particularly to management, and were keen to have men as members and patrons of their groups. The feminist groups in the study adopted a more separatist strategy consciously choosing to operate as women-only self-help networks, they sought to improve women's position by creating a women's network, but also sought to operate as pressure groups, challenging gendered organisational structures and cultures and campaigning around women's employment issues (Tomlinson, 1987).

Moving to the feminist areas of our trajectory, we find women whose values, knowledge and gender awareness explicitly inform feminist strategies of challenge and change, putting women's rights 'in the centre of' their work (Strachey, 1928). The objectives of feminists are likely to be about both removing obstructions to women's attempts to participate, progress and remodel the world of work, and the transforming of patriarchal structures and cultures. In the case study chapters such women are most evident in the book publishing industry, the teaching profession, trade unionism and among political activists in the Canadian public transport chapter. For feminists, both the process and the results are about developing feminist consciousness and activism, combined with a willingness to be identified as feminists and with the women's movement. Aims, strategy and actions are likely to be informed by all strands of feminism, and individualist, collective and separatist forms of action utilised in pursuit of the more radical, long agenda approach to equality. In addition, an altruistic sense of reciprocity and sisterhood is a key value among women with a feminist perspective.

Inevitably, despite the recognition of and desire to challenge gender inequalities within organisations, there will be differences between the women-aware group and feminists on equal opportunities priorities and how to move the equal opportunities agenda forward. Nevertheless, where the interests of both groups overlap, alliances can be made and at times a long agenda, aiming for transformative culture change, can accommodate the goals and methods of both the women-aware group and feminists. Evidence of women-aware and feminist alliances can be found in the the NHS Women's Unit in Sylvia Wyatt's chapter on the health service, and in the Toronto Transit Commissions's Equal Opportunities Unit in the chapter on the transport sector. There Fiona Colgan, Susan Johnstone and Steve Shaw describe the elaborate and sustained collaborative campaigning by a range of equity-seeking pressure groups in order to get political and thus legislative change. The chapter also illustrates how women managers and workers have built on these initiatives in order to argue effectively for equal opportunities at the Toronto Transit Commission.

Women as organisational change agents

Clearly then, there are differences in the aims, strategies and sorts of action women might wish to take, and also what is possible in particular circumstances. The type and direction of a woman's activism will be related to her particular consciousness and her perception of the gender politics within her organisation. Nevertheless, it can be seen that women with a developed sense of gender awareness, and those with a feminist consciousness, are in a variety of ways a potential force for change. In this next section we review the political strategies which women may use as they seek to initiate change in gendered work organisations.

In identifying such women as change agents, we can draw on Kirton's (1991) model of adaptors and innovators to discuss the actions they may take.

Kirton (1991) described a change agent as a 'competent individual who has enough skill to be successful in a particular environment'. Adaptors are seen to typically produce ideas stretching and extending agreed definitions of the problem and likely solutions. Their effort in change is in improving and doing better within the existing set of rules and structures. Innovators, however, are more likely to pursue change by reconstructing the problem, separating it from the existing accepted thought and customary viewpoint and showing disregard for the rules. Innovators are less concerned with improving existing structures and more with doing things differently, and so their solutions are less likely to be acceptable.

Kirton (1991) also speculated that people who were most willing to cross boundaries were likely to be innovators. The more boundaries there are and the more rigidly they are held, the more innovative an individual has to be to cross them. Thus research on women managers indicates that they are more likely to be innovative than their male counterparts (Kirton, 1991; White, Cox and Cooper, 1992). Successful women were found to be less concerned to conform to the rules, supporting the contention that women must defy what is considered to be normative female behaviour if they are to work successfully in male-dominated situations (White, Cox and Cooper, 1992).

In addition, Kirton (1991) found that innovators were more likely to be present as change agents when organisations were fluid and themselves going through change – as are almost all the organisations in the case studies in this book. We would expect that women innovators will most likely be drawn from the feminist and woman-aware groups on our trajectory. Given the challenges and opportunities facing individuals in the 1990s as a result of the sectoral restructuring and organisational changes discussed earlier in the chapter, optimists might expect women innovators to be in a particularly good position to take advantage of these opportunities to work for transformation and change. Geraldine Healy and David Kraithman, for example, report some evidence of this in their chapter considering the implications of change in the education sector for women teachers. Fiona Colgan, Susan Johnstone and Steve Shaw illustrate the key role of a woman innovator seizing the opportunity to push the case for equal opportunities as part of a major change programme at the Toronto Transit Commission.

Political skills

To be an effective change agent, however, it is necessary to be familiar with the organisation's gender and power relations. Power is elusive and complex and located in a variety of sites in organisations. Traditional analysis has seen organisational power as ubiquitous, essentially male, and controlling the currency by which male domination is maintained (Hearn and Parkin,

1992): 'preference for men = preference for power' (Kanter, quoted in Hearn and Parkin). For women working within such a patriarchal paradigm, gaining admission to the 'male' power structures is likely to be difficult and hazardous. Nevertheless, among individual women managers intent on developing their careers within traditional (male) routes, there is often a strong concern to access organisational power and the political processes, but a lack of knowledge and skills of how to do so (D. Sheppard, 1994). Yet women are also seen, and see themselves, as reluctant, and ambivalent about engaging in organisational politics. D. Sheppard (1994) found women managers being less inclined to be calculating and politically aware, and frequently eschewed playing political games. What follows here is a discussion of political skills which women who wish to operate within the patriarchal power paradigm may consider using.

Political skill has been described as 'the elusive and increasingly demanded ingredient of success and survival in organisational life' (Baddeley and James, 1987). Here we draw on the work of Arroba and James (1987), who identify two interacting dimensions of political skill. The first is 'reading' which involves an awareness or understanding of an organisation, for example the ability to read its organisational and gender politics. The second is 'carrying': 'an awareness of one's disposition to behave in certain ways, in other words what one "carries" or brings from a person's internal world into a working situation' (Baddeley and James, 1987). The level and type of political skill is derived from the dynamic of the interaction between reading and carrying.

Reading

At one end of the reading dimension is acute political awareness. This refers to the ability to read an organisation, both formal and informal, the decision processes, the overt and covert agendas, the location and bases of power inside and outside the organisation, one's own power bases and abilities to exercise influence, the organisational culture and its style, its political purpose and direction. At the other end of the reading spectrum is an unwillingness or inability to recognise these things (Baddeley and James, 1987).

We have already seen, from the trajectory of women's consciousness and activism, that there are differences in women's awareness and perception of gender politics. For women, accurate reading of informal structures of male power and domination is often problematic. Organisational hierarchies are constructed around the dominant symbolism and 'images of masculinity such that a successful organisation is lean, mean, aggressive and competitive with a tough, forceful leader' (Wajcman, 1994). Job segregation may also function to prevent women from observing at close quarters behaviours suitable for gaining positions of power. For as already established in our earlier discussion, the gendered nature of organisational life, serves to both exclude women from the male inner circles of power and influence, and to obscure from them and other 'outsiders' the complex detail of how these work. Thus, for many women, organisational politics may be foreign territory.

It is not surprising to find therefore – as is shown in the chapter on book publishing – that one critical evaluation by men of women's behaviour in organisations is that 'they' (women) do not understand the complexities of informal organisational activities and politics. In patriarchal organisations, dominated by white men, informal rules and the masculine discourse of management establish the requirements of conformity to the dominant culture – Acker's (1990) 'organizational logic'. Measures such as sexism, racism and sexual and racial harassment may be taken by the dominant group to control, repel and exclude outsiders. Amanda Palmer identifies how in HM Customs and Excise, sexual harassment is privatised and individualised and so hampers women's attempts to challenge or stop such behaviour. In these ways, even if accurately read, organisational and gender politics remain intimidating and inhibiting for 'outsiders' (Davidson and Cooper, 1992)

Kanter (1977) is particularly concerned with this aspect of organisations: what she calls 'relative number' and its impact on women (and other outsiders) and the way in which they read and respond to organisational gender politics. She identified organisations as 'tilted' (with a male: female ratio of say 65:35) and 'skewed' (with a ratio of around 85:15). In these situations, because women are so few, they are highly visible, may become tokens and are subject to continuous organisational scrutiny. As Cockburn (1991) suggests, 'for women who want to be taken seriously for their skills and career potential, it is a continual problem to know when to hide their difference from men and when to assert it'. Thus women (and other 'outsiders' such as ethnic minority groups, people with disabilities, lesbians and gay men) are excluded from insider élites and networks unless perhaps they are introduced by a mentor or sponsor. Although the benefits of mentoring for women can be great (White, Cox and Cooper, 1992; Kanter, 1977), the problems of cross-sex mentoring have also been recognised as being especially difficult for women, who may be perceived as having procured promotion through sexual favours to senior management (Clutterbuck and Devine, 1987).

Exclusive external male-specific networks such as freemasonary, private clubs and so on, add to women's difficulties. Yet a 1994 Institute of Management report concluded that women would not achieve real success until they had the 'key to the men's club' (Coe, 1992).

The male homosociability embodied in men's clubbing represents one of the main ways in which management becomes a closed and gendered circle (Witz and Savage, 1992; Simpson, 1995). The manner in which this may develop and its effects in controlling and excluding women are well illustrated in the Customs and Excise chapter. The problems of being in a minority, attempting to play a game in which men have made the rules has meant that women become 'travellers in a male world' (Marshall, 1984) mapped by men (Gulati and Ledwith, 1987), and face different 'interactional contexts' from their male counterparts (Kanter, 1977). Women managers who are in an isolated minority may not know how to proceed or what to say in various circumstances and, unlike male management 'learners', do not have a reference group whose direct advice or example is available. This leaves women, in trying to develop their own strategies, being keen to discover how their male counterparts manage and think and behave (D. Sheppard, 1992). In their chapter on retailing management, Anne Brockbank and Joanne Traves explore how women managers report comfort while working among other women at middle management level. However, in attempting to comply with what they perceive is required of a senior management role within their organisation (predicated on a male management model, and dominated by men) they expressed disquiet and discomfort.

Management education and training programmes are another source of information for women about how managers are expected to manage and to behave. However these, like the mainstream management and organisational literature, remain mainly gender-blind. In fact their content and prescriptions for 'good' leadership and management are still largely based on tacitly masculine models, and are often resistant to or are ignorant of a more female orientation or the use of the few available gender and equality aware texts. Alternative approaches offered through women's training courses and programmes and gender and equality aware texts, while increasingly available, have yet to make it into the mainstream.

These are just some examples of the difficulties women may have in reading patriarchal structures and cultures which may be segregated, skewed, alien and impenetrable at work, outside work and across the boundaries between them, and which are significant when women come to take action. This is also the case of course for ethnic minority women – and men – in most corporations (Kanter, 1977).

Carrying

The second dimension of political skill as identified by Baddeley and James (1987) is 'carrying'. At one end of the carrying dimension is integrity, and at the other a disposition to play ego-defensive games (Baddeley and James, 1991). 'Carrying' refers to a person's internal life. This relates firstly to a predisposition to behave in certain ways, and secondly to the level of awareness of what one is carrying into a given situation (Arroba and James, 1987).

For example, in their study of women's career development, White, Cox and Cooper (1992) identified significant early family and school influences among successful high-flying management and professional women – Innovators – who had crossed the boundaries of traditional expectations of women's role at home and at work. These women had also achieved accuracy in both 'reading' organisational and career politics and in maintaining their female integrity when 'carrying' into their chosen paths. Top women in the health service chapter can be seen to share many of the family background influences with 'innovators', especially having mothers whom they regarded as powerful.

However, women also have to take into account and manage 'sex role spillover' – the carrying over of expectations based on gender (such as motherhood and childcare, or sexual roles) that are inappropriate for work and not inherent in the job itself, yet shape women's (and men's) role and expectations within it (Gutek and Cohen, 1992). For example, women in the retailing and personnel chapters clearly articulated how the expected conflict between their career and a future family shaped their aspirations and limited their horizons. Sex role spillover will affect women regardless of their sexuality or whether or not they have children, and stereotypical attitudes towards women predicated on women's general lack of commitment to work because of their families is a powerful process structuring gender heirarchies, and is illustrated in all the empirical chapters. Similarly, women from ethnic minority groups are likely to have to manage sex *and* race role spillover.

As already identified, key elements in 'carrying' are a woman's awareness of her own identity (e.g. class, race, sexuality, etc.), her organisational image and credibility, and her subsequent presentation of self. To be seen as a woman, or not, is often the question. As Morgan (1986) points out, 'most people in an organization soon learn the rules of dress and other unwritten requirements for successful progress to higher ranks'.

So far, in this chapter, we have seen that women with a low awareness of gender politics tend to seek to be absorbed into the dominant male culture, and to avoid being labelled as feminist. They also try not be singled out 'as women', whereas for those with a greater awareness of organisational gender politics there is a fine balance between being true to oneself as a woman and knowing how to be 'successful' when reading and carrying within gendered organisational environments. These dilemmas are found in many occupations and professions. For example, among women engineers presentation of self as an engineer took precedence over being seen as a woman in a climate where, 'For an engineer, both image and identity are male and white.' (Carter and Kirkup, 1990). For female engineers this led to a range of dilemmas, over dress and personal presentation, particularly for black women (Carter and Kirkup, 1990). Credibility and acceptance (by men) may be seen by women managers as being achieved through 'blending in'. This also helps to reduce the sense of isolation which women experience in male-dominated environments such as management (D. Sheppard, 1992).

Thus managing the presentation of self, dress and demeanour in patriarchal organisations is a major concern for women. On the one hand, Kanter (1977) confirms the utility for women of visibility based on their gender: in order for their activities to enhance their power, women have to attract the notice of significant others. But she cautions that visibility must be used judiciously; problems may arise for women who are perceived to 'flaunt themselves'.

Two further conditions for being a successful change agent can be added to *carrying*. In his discussion of innovative and adaptive managers referred to above, Kirton (1991) stipulates that as well as job know-how, change agents must be able to gain the respect of their colleagues and superiors (this gains them commensurate status), and also to have a 'general capacity' for leadership. It is now well established that leadership is usually defined as a construct premised on male characteristics, and that women have alternative approaches to offer. The differences exemplified by Rosener (1990) as Transactional (male) and Transformational (female) imply that women will require a high level of skill in successfully managing such role complexity. Anne Brockbank and Joanne Traves discuss in their chapter the case for an androgynous management style in retailing through adopting styles accommodating both male and female characteristics, and going on, like Ferguson (1984, cited in Witz and Savage, 1992) to favour such forms.

Another interesting illustration of the fine tuning involved comes from our research with women trade unionists. One experienced woman trade union activist said that when presenting information or proposals to the male-dominated executive of her union, she used what she described as a 'swashbuckling' style developed over the years of working in a masculine culture and which gains her important credibility. When with her women members she adopted a softer, more sympathetic, participative, womanly manner.

It can be seen therefore that, in 'carrying', individualist innovative career women may eschew feminist labels in favour of the pivotal values of the organisation, but at the same time attempt to adapt these for their own use. As White, Cox and Cooper (1992) suggest, these women will reject 'relevant' organisational rules, and rather than conforming to the male model of success will integrate their femininity into a sense of their own womanly identity.

Here we are in agreement with the proposition from Breinlinger and Kelly (1994), that the strength of identification with women as a group is not related to choice of strategy in a straightforward manner, and that, while consciousness may be a prerequisite to action, a particular type of action is not an inevitable outcome of consciousness. In work organisations women's activity is mediated by the prism of gendered organisational culture.

Nevertheless, where women do identify themselves as feminist, they also identify strongly with women collectively (Kelly and Breinlinger, 1995). Clearly women can gain strength and power from feminist unity to use in their collectivist strategies. Where such identity is congruent with, for example, an oppositional class position, as in socialist or trade union politics, there is also likely to be strong collective activity, since it is the cultural norm (Phillips, 1987). Tensions may arise, however, where women feel it is important to organise separately as women, as well as 'caucussing' within a broader class or cultural/ethnic grouping, since this may be perceived as threatening or dangerous to the unity of the particular grouping (A. Walker, 1983; Briskin, 1993). It may, however, also be important for feminists to organise across identity political groupings: with black women, working-class women, lesbians or women with disabilities, as well as within the broader women's movement.

Thus, women on the collective, socialist and some radical feminist sections of the trajectory may be more ready to challenge forms of organising which are exclusive and are gender, race-blind, homophobic and disablist, or to incorporate change into their longer strategic agenda. While some feminists choose to work collectively within the existing, patriarchal paradigms (e.g. of trade unions, political parties), others will be more ready to work across and outside these. Radical feminists may elect to work entirely outside existing patriarchal structures in woman-only organisations and collectives.

Women's political styles

These examples of the complexities of gendered role negotiation illustrate how reading and carrying interact with one another in many different ways. Building on a model developed by Arroba and James (1987) we propose that these interactions may result in four styles of women's behaviour for managing political situations within gendered work environments. These are identified by Arroba and James (1987) as 'wise', 'clever', 'innocent' and 'inept' styles of behaviour.[11]

Wise behaviour

Wise behaviour entails accurate organisational reading, and acting with integrity. Arroba and James (1987) suggest it requires intuition. This stems from sensitivity to others, awareness of personal feelings and values, and an intimate knowledge of the context. The majority of White, Cox and Cooper's (1992) high-flying women seemed to be wise. Three-quarters of them emphasised that politics required sensitivity to the organisational climate and its male-dominated systems of influence. As one woman said 'there are norms for behaviour. You can get away with challenging these up to a point, but you need to be sensitive to the line that you can't cross'. They also stressed the dangers of becoming too entrenched in political games. Kanter (1977) proposed a similar course of action for women in skewed organisational settings. However, such skills do not come cheap. 'Such dexterity requires both job-related competence and political sensitivity that could take years to acquire' (Kanter, 1977).

Types of wise behaviour available to individuals will vary a great deal between organisations. For example, within retail and personnel management, wise behaviour is most likely to include individual action aimed at personal career progression. In the chapter on HM Customs and Excise the women are seen as choosing to demonstrate their worth as effective colleagues rather than as women, and in doing so sought to 'educate' their male colleagues – a strategy which the author Amanda Palmer identifies as being a wise one in view of the prevailing culture in the Service.

Accurate reading of predominantly male career routes in order to time their career moves to maximum advantage is proposed by White, Cox and Cooper (1992) as wise behaviour by high-flying women. The factors influencing the careers of these successful women were found to be 'surprisingly similar to those reported for successful men' (White, Cox and Cooper, 1992). For example, they took care not to fall into the 'trap' women often find themselves in of becoming 'functional specialists' and getting stuck in functional dead ends, rather than recognising that high flying requires mastery of the range of management functions.

Similar strategies of career management through the building of credible portfolios through making the 'right' career moves can be seen among senior women managers in the health service chapter. These women also illustrate how accurate reading of the power and gender politics helps to negotiate their way around a sector undergoing wholesale restructuring, and of accessing resources such as those on offer from the NHS Women's Unit and its support systems and networks.

The use of networks and alliances, with and between other women and men, is a key strategy commonly used by organisational politicians. Male alliances of the 'old school tie' kind are well catalogued and widely known (see above). However, women's networking as a means of career progression is relatively new and little researched (Tomlinson, 1987). Women's networking skills and experience are not disputed. Women typically organise a whole range of voluntary support systems around their families – school runs, after school and holiday playschemes, childcare, and so on. Perhaps because these sorts of networks are inherently democratic rather than heirarchical, relying on mutuality and cooperation, women are often reluctant to use networking more generally for their own personal gain. In addition, as politics and networking are bound up with power, and power is still predominantly held by men, women may still need to learn how to break into the male-dominated networking system (Davidson and Cooper, 1992). The chapters on women in publishing, women in trade unions and the transport industry do provide evidence of women networking and making informal alliances. Yet, as outlined in the trade union chapter, some women may feel uncomfortable caucussing and 'doing deals' to advance their own agenda. Others, however, have explicitly sought to use and develop their interpersonal skills in order to build supportive networks and political alliances within their trade unions.

Clever behaviour

Clever politicians typically are seen to behave opportunistically to further their own individual interests. 'A shrewd understanding of how the organisation works is used to personal advantage' (Arroba and James, 1987). They advise that acting cleverly and playing psychological games can get things done, but such short-term gains may backfire, as Kanter (1977) describes how 'A few women flaunted themselves in the public arena in which they operated and made a point out of demonstrating their 'difference' . . . parading their high-level connections or by passing the normal authority structure. Kanter (1977) goes on to point out that such boldness was usually accompanied by top management sponsorship, but this was a risky strategy because of shifting power alliances at the top. She adds that these women 'felt less consciously aware than the other women of the attendant dangers, pressures, psychic costs, and disadvantages'.

Inevitably, these women adopted individualist strategies which could leave them fairly exposed in a competitive organisational environment. It would appear that such women were not always able to accurately read the organisation's gender and sexual politics, especially where power was fluid. In this way they could be in danger of a worse fate, of behaving ineptly.

Inept behaviour

Inept behaviour is considered by Baddeley and James (1987) to be an outcome of prioritising personal needs, combined with dysfunctional reading. They categorise it as involving psychological game playing and political unawareness. Both inept and clever behaviour can involve getting oneself out of difficult situations at the expense of others. They may also land the person 'in a mess' themselves (Arroba and James, 1987). Such behaviour is more likely to be undertaken individually and can result in women being stereotyped and dismissed in one of the 'deviant roles' frequently attributed to women by men in organisational politics (e.g. 'Queen Bee', 'Token woman', 'Seductress' or 'Man-hater': Kanter, 1977; Morgan, 1988).

Being perceived by organisational power holders as being aligned with a sectional or vested interest can also lead to charges of ineptness and to marginalisation within organisational politics. To overcome such problems, campaigning for 'women's issues' requires a delicate balance within gendered organisations if they are to gain the support of key and powerful organisational members. One potential strategy which frequently provokes controversy is separatist or 'women-only' organising. For active women, the exclusion of men from women's groups is seen as critical to the development of women's own solidarity, analysis and skills (Kelly and Breinlinger, 1994). On the other hand, excluding men was frequently mentioned by non-active women in the Kelly and Breinlinger study (1994) as being problematic, and by women-aware groups in Tomlinson's research (1987). For some of Kelly and Breinlinger's (1994) women, keeping men out was 'wrong and counter-productive' and a 'politically hopeless activity'. This tension between aims, objectives and strategy among women is also identified in the chapter on book publishing, concerning the work of the fairly high profile campaigning group 'Women in Publishing'. The fact that some women (and men) consider separate organising (by women) as an inept style of organisational behaviour – whereas for feminists it might be considered as being true to self and to feminism, and therefore 'wise' – indicates the depth and strength of patriarchal structures and attitudes, and gender relations in society.

Innocent behaviour

A fourth type, innocent behaviour, is typified by a blindness to power, including patriarchal power structures. It emphasises formal managerial and professional rationality above all else, denying or not seeing the informal organisation and leading to innaccurate reading and inappropriate behaviour.[12]

As Hayes (1984) has observed, 'individuals who do not acknowledge the informal system will become politically incompetent' (cited in White, Cox and Cooper, 1992). Such behaviour may be either inept or innocent. The difference lies in innocents' unawareness of organisational and gender politics, whereas inept organisational players choose to deny them.

Trying to become 'socially invisible' could be construed as both inept and innocent behaviour. Frequently in studies of women and organisations women are found trying to minimize their sexual attributes in order to blend unnoticeably into the predominant male culture, perhaps by adopting 'mannish dress' (Kanter, 1977). Such women aim to avoid conflict, risks, or controversial situations, and are happy to step into assistant or technical staff jobs such as personnel administration (Kanter, 1977). Women making this choice blended into the background. This 'fear of visibility' is similar to Marshall's (1984) group of women who muted their awareness of femininity and subordinated it to their managerial role. Like Carter and Kirkup's (1990) women engineers, they were intent on gaining approval for their ability on the prevailing terms – men's.

Innocents have integrity but expect all organisational members, including themselves, to abide by the formal rules. When these are breached, innocents see this as 'unlawful' action which they could not condone or participate in themselves. Such behaviour is exemplified by both the traditional women and the women in transition on our trajectory. For example, innocents may respect formal equal opportunities policies and procedures but may be puzzled at their failure to deliver the real thing. For such women a critical event may trigger an awakening awareness of organisational gender politics, leading to a loss of innocence and movement along the transitional road towards more strategic action.

Women exiting 'male' organisations: across the boundaries

The focus of this chapter has been primarily on women's action within conventional and patriarchal bureaucratic work organisations. However, women searching for better, more women-friendly opportunities may choose to leave these in order to establish their own autonomy.

Several studies have shown that after prolonged periods of struggling within organisations some women decide to 'take control of their lives' (Marshall, 1994, 1995) by exiting the organisation (Goffee and Scase, 1985; B. Lawrence, 1987; Cockburn, 1988). These women see business ownership, or working freelance or single-handedly as a professional, as a strategy to overcome labour market related gender subordination and sexism. This is also the case for ethnic minority women who may wish to overcome racist and sexist barriers to their career progression (Bhachu, 1988; Kalsi, 1995).

Women leavers would probably have been able to read accurately their organisations and their own role within them, but may have themselves lacked the patience, the political skills or the will to carry forward their own ambitions within patriarchal organisational structures and cultures, or found the weight of patriarchy too profound. Moving out to be herself may also be intensely liberating for a woman.

Carter and Cannon (1994) have identified one type of entrepreneurial women – re-entrants – coming from high-flying management and career backgrounds, who had been frustrated by gender-related career blocks. These women were highly aware of gender-related barriers in the labour market, and were also reported to be the most radical in their feminist beliefs. Furthermore, women entrepreneurs running their own organisations have developed strategies in order to operate effectively in the predominantly male business world (Allen and Truman, 1993; Carter and Cannon, 1994).

In some cases, women's consciousness and activism may lead them to leave conventional organisations in order to establish more 'women-friendly' structures. These often set out consciously to identify and meet the needs of women consumers through the provision of goods or services. Such examples can be seen in women's cooperatives (Cholmely, 1991; Norton, 1993), women-only trade unions (Davis, 1993; Milkman, 1985) and women's support services such as rape crisis centres and refuges (Colgan, 1986). Some of these may set out to be separately organised alternatives run along feminist and separatist lines. As explained by Briskin (1993), separate organisation often includes an explicit refusal to work with men. It usually focuses on the building of alternative structures as a solution rather than attempting the transformation of patriarchal structures. The only examples of such feminist organisations in this book are to be found in the chapter on women in book publishing. Clearly, although they are outside of the remit of this book, such women-centred organisational forms are essential areas of further study (Brown, 1991; Griffin, 1995).

Summary

In this chapter we have set out a framework for examining the range and variety of women's strategies for individual progression and for collective approaches in the pursuit of change in their mainstream work organisations. This includes a trajectory of women's consciousness and activism and a model for evaluating the political skills and behaviour of women working as change agents. We recognise that the reality experienced by women every day in work organisations, the structures, processes and relationships, are complex and 'riddled with ambiguity' (K. Purcell, 1990), and this is illustrated in the case study chapters. The women themselves in these comprise a rainbow across race, class and ideology, occupation and ambition, age and experience, and, as indicated here already, clearly draw on a range of contrasting themes and realities in making sense of their lives and choosing their strategies.

Against this exists the weight of patriarchy and the associated dynamics of organisational gendering within which women negotiate their working lives and their careers. Certainly the breakdown of traditional career paths and organisational heirarchies, and the increasing fluidity of organisational structures and cultures has opened up opportunities for those – women and men – who are well informed, well placed and well organised. The test for women is to what extent they have been able to develop strategies, individual, collective and separatist, to take advantage of such opportunities. This is the main question addressed in the empirical chapters which follow, and which is revisited in the final chapter.

Notes

1. The term 'change agent' is commonly used to refer to people who play a significant part in bringing about change in an organisation (Williams, Dobson and Waters, 1989).
2. In common with other feminists, we recognise the need to take account of the increasing variety of feminisms (Townley, 1994; Wolf, 1994), and that ethnic, racial and sexual diversity among women is stressed more than ever before in feminist theory (Mitchell and Oakley, 1986). Thus different feminisms inform the multiplicity of aims, strategies and types of action that women might wish to take and which will themselves vary according to women's consciousness and relations with the gender politics within their organisations.
3. Liberal feminism focuses on individual rights and choices which are denied women, and ways in which the law, education, and – as we have already seen – equal opportunities measures can put right these injustices. One 'unhelpful' stereotype of liberal feminists is to see them as 'naïvely reformist' (Stacey, 1993). Although they may hold feminist beliefs, liberal feminists are often equivocal about being labelled a 'feminist', and may be unlikely to challenge the gender power structures and attitudes in their organisations.
4. Socialist feminists, sometimes linked to and sometimes separated from Marxist feminisists, see women's oppression tied to forms of capitalist exploitation of labour. In this model women's paid and unpaid work is analysed in relation to its function within the capitalist economy: hence the concept of the 'family wage' discussed earlier. The liberation of women, and socialism, are joint goals. (Stacey, 1993). Socialist feminist activism is by definition collective action, although, as we shall see, collective feminist action may be perceived as conflicting with socialism since by identifying as a separate group women are perceived to be undermining the socialist values of unity and solidarity.
5. Radical feminism tends to focus on men's control of women's sexuality and reproduction, seeing men as a group as responsible for women's oppression. (Stacey, 1993). The values and thus the activities of radical feminists are geared towards collective, non-hierarchical mutuality and sisterhood.
6. A useful definition of gender is Scott's (1986, cited in Acker, 1990): 'The core of the definition rests on an integral connection between two propositions; gender is a constituitive element of social relationships based on perceived differences between the sexes, and gender is a primary way of signifying relationships of power.'
7. Although by the mid-1990s severe backlash was building up in the USA against affirmative action, as evidenced by the Supreme Court's 'sharp narrowing' of the scope of legitimate affirmative action in 1995 (Freedland, 1995).
8. It must be recognised that a degree of self-selection occurs as different women may be attracted (or discouraged) from applying to specific occupations and/or organisations, given their perceived personal and career needs and their

perceptions of gender politics and the terms and conditions on offer within a specific organisation.

9. Using Purcell and Ahlstrand's (1994) discussion on collectivism as a starting point, we use the term to cover a wider range of interrelated collectivisms: collectivism may be solidaristic in the sense of organised labour; it may by altruistic and mutual in the spirit of the women's movement; it maybe individually instrumental or selfish, with careerists using collective means to further their own progress. None of these are entirely mutually exclusive.

10. We have used the term 'women-aware' to describe a specific group of women who may hold some feminist beliefs but do not wish to be identified as feminists. We do not wish this term to be confused with Alice Walker's use of the word 'Womanist' to describe a black feminist or feminist of colour (1983).

11. The terms 'wise', 'clever', 'inept' and 'innocent' are used by Baddeley and James (1987) in the model of political skills they developed and have used in management training of local government officers. This model was also used by Arroba and James (1987) to identify women's political skills in order to encourage women to overcome a perceived reluctance to engage in organisational politics – a 'key area for women managers'. We see the possibility of using the model in two main ways: identifying the perceptions of women by other organisation members, especially those in key positions of power, and women's own perceptions of themselves.

12. Baddeley and James (1991) have further distinguished a group they characterise as powerfully innocent. These are typically managers, who through their nurture, their sense of belonging to a particular social category or class, or membership of particular institutions such as church, regiment or profession, display an apparently natural confidence – a 'secure centricity that comes from being white, male, upper or middle class, heterosexual and English'. Their innocence stems from the secure and cocooned sense of self-identity, and their power from their class position. By definition this category excludes women and people of colour. Powerful innocence clearly demonstrates the robustness of the partnership between patriarchy and capitalism and represents an expression of the concept of dual-systems.

CHAPTER 2

Women in book publishing – a 'feminised' sector?

Fiona Colgan and Frances Tomlinson

Introduction

The book publishing industry is frequently cited as exceptional in that it 'seems to have let women through at the very top – at the business end – in a way that . . . no other industry in the country can equal' (*The Guardian*, 1988). However, although women comprise the majority of publishing employees and are the major purchasers of both new and secondhand books[1] (Book Marketing, 1995), they continue to be under-represented in senior positions within publishing. Gendered patterns of vertical and horizontal segregation persist within the book publishing industry as in other 'feminised' sectors (Acker, 1989; Tomlinson and Colgan, 1989; Crompton and Sanderson, 1992). Indirect exclusionary practices can be identified within publishing as within other white-collar and professional sectors (Crompton and Le Feuvre, 1992; Walsh and Cassell, 1995; Witz, 1992). Thus our research has shown that women are more likely to be steered into 'jobs' with limited prospects than the 'careers' which can lead to positions of power within publishing companies (Colgan and Tomlinson, 1991).

As such, the book publishing industry provides a useful case study of the structural and attitudinal barriers that may block women's progression in organisations: firstly, because it is hard to justify the inequalities which exist in the industry on the grounds that women are inherently less suited to work in publishing than men, given the nature of much of the work (literary, creative, administrative etc.) and the high qualifications of many of the women entering the industry.[2] Secondly, because book publishing provides an example of a sector which is undergoing substantial sectoral change with major ramifications for corporate structure and culture, together with a need to evolve a less profligate approach to the management of its (predominantly female) human resources.

Restructuring within the sector has required publishing companies to take a more sophisticated and commercial approach to the production, marketing and selling of books. It has also had major repercussions for the organisation and structure of publishing companies and for their human resource requirements (Clark, 1988; Faith, 1991). In the late 1980s some publishing companies had begun to formalise human resource policies and practices. They began to acknowledge the extremely low representation of ethnic minority groups within the publishing workforce. They had also begun to address the 'wastage' of female employees by developing equal opportunities policies and practices as a result of the demands of female employees, trade union collective bargaining and management concerns about projected demographic changes in the labour market (Colgan and Tomlinson, 1989). These shifts seemed to herald a more 'woman-friendly' approach to human resource management within book publishing. However, the recession faced by the industry in the 1990s has led to further employment change and a hard-nosed reassessment of corporate human resource strategies and priorities.

In this chapter we examine the influence of gender relations on the progress and prospects of women working within the book publishing industry. In so doing, we intend to focus on the changing patterns of male and female employment within the sector since 1987. The chapter will offer a preliminary assessment of both the impact of corporate restructuring and changing human resource policies and priorities on male and female employment prospects within book publishing between 1987 and 1994.

An overview of the book publishing industry

The UK book publishing industry forms one element of the mass media industry. As such, it has undergone a period of substantial restructuring, reflecting the strategic responses of publishers to technological developments within publishing, the restructuring of related media sectors, public cutbacks in educational and library expenditure and recurring periods of recession. The broad picture is one of concentration, internationalisation, an increase in new book titles with shorter print runs and a shrinking workforce (Stanworth and Stanworth, 1994).

Comparatively low entry costs and the freedom to publish had encouraged the development of many small, independently owned publishing companies. Following a wave of mergers and acquisitions in the 1980s, over half of the home market has become dominated by a few large international groups which have increasingly swallowed up the diminishing number of medium-sized companies (Clark, 1988). The structure of the industry has become increasingly polarised between a few large international groups and a number of smaller, more specialised operations and a mass of tiny publishers.

Conglomeration within the sector occurred as hardback and paperback houses came together, as weak and undercapitalised publishers were bought out by bigger firms and as publishing houses sought transatlantic and European links (Hely Hutchinson, 1991). The impact on employment in the 1980s was limited as sales during the 1980s rose steadily and there was little pressure for change. However, as a number of commentators have suggested, the 1990s recession and the poor prospects for both trade and academic book sales in the 1990s (Faith, 1991) meant that the industry was forced to address some of the following issues: inappropriate structures, high overheads, excessive expenditures on authors' advances and corporate acquisitions, overproduction, inadequate market responsiveness, poor management and high borrowings (Hely Hutchinson, 1991).

As companies restructured, reduced overheads and improved corporate management, major changes have been made in the staffing levels of publishing houses. Redundancies in 1990 and 1991 caused the *Bookseller* to recall the year as the 'bloodiest that anyone in the business can remember in terms of job loss' (1991b). Employment in publishing reduced from 24,850 in 1990 to 22,190 in 1991 and to 21,670 in 1992 (*Bookseller*, 1993). Overall employment, according to figures produced for the Publishers' Association, has fallen by 12 per cent since 1990 (Bouwman, 1994) as British publishers have, in the words of one publishing MD, 'focused on our core business and have cut operating costs to the muscle if not to the bone' (Glover, 1991).

British publishers can no longer afford to be the 'languid dilettantes with gentlemanly manners and old-fashioned inefficient methods' of popular image (*Bookseller*, 1993). A more professional management style has been adopted, accompanied by a shift away from 'literary' to 'financial' business goals. A commercial ethos has replaced the liberal and rather paternalist ethos which had characterised many publishing houses prior to the mid-1980s. In large (often foreign-owned) publishing houses, bureaucratic decision-making has altered the work environment of in-house publishing staff with financial and marketing concerns often taking precedence over creative and literary priorities (Stanworth and Stanworth, 1994). As a result tensions exist within many large publishing houses over the degree to which corporate publishing strategy is to be 'editorially' or 'sales and marketing' led.

The need for sectoral restructuring has also been a key feature influencing the human resource priorities and strategies of both large and small publishing companies. Companies have sought to make changes within the labour process, cut labour costs and increase productivity and flexibility, given fragile markets, by adopting a strategy composed of one or more of the following elements:

- formalisation of human resource policies and practices;
- introduction and improvement of training for in-house staff;
- rationalisation of in-house staffing levels;
- increase in the use of freelances;
- increase in the use of new technology;
- marginalisation/derecognition of trade unions.

As trade unions have been marginalised or derecognised, organised opposition to the changes imposed by management has been limited. In addition, the gains made through collective bargaining in negotiating progressive terms and conditions (especially parental leave, childcare and new technology agreements) have been halted and are being undermined in a number of book publishing companies (Labour Research Department, 1992; NUJ, 1993).

It is hard to fit the textbook description of 'strategic human resource management' (Beer and Spector, 1985; Fombrun, Tichy and Devanna, 1984; Guest, 1987; Storey, 1989; Legge, 1995) with most of the managerial policies and practices that we have encountered in publishing. Indeed the majority of publishing companies did not have a personnel function or human resources function until the mid-1980s, thus we would agree with Whipp (1992) that until fairly recently there was little evidence of what could be termed 'strategic HRM' within the book publishing sector. However, between 1988 and 1993 we did find evidence of a shift from a paternalistic, reactive approach to HRM to a more structured, strategic approach in some of the larger publishing companies, particularly those which formed part of a larger media group (Colgan and Tomlinson, 1994).

We wish to examine the impact of these changes on male and female employment patterns given the existing gendered division of labour within publishing. In addition, we wish to focus on the dynamics of gender relations and job segregation during a period of intense sectoral change in order to offer a preliminary assessment of both the impact of corporate restructuring and changing human resource policies and priorities on men and women within the book publishing industry between 1987 and 1994.

Employment patterns of male and female employees

The following employment data draws on two surveys of publishing houses conducted in 1988 and 1993. In each case, a postal survey of 100 publishing companies, including all the major houses, was undertaken.[3] The surveys provided statistical information on the employment, salaries and age profile of men and women working within publishing houses. The survey data was supplemented by in-depth interviews with senior managers within the industry, eight in-depth company studies and two postal surveys (1988 and 1993) of freelance workers to explore the advantages and disadvantages of this form of work.

Evidence of vertical job segregation

Between 1988 and 1993 the composition of the in-house publishing workforce by gender has changed as can be seen from Table 2.1. In 1988 the workforce was 60 per cent female: by 1993 the percentage had dropped to 53 per cent. This suggests that women working within publishing have been disproportionately affected by the restructuring of employment within the industry.

Evidence from both surveys suggests that despite the industry's image of 'letting women through at the very top' and the large number of women graduates employed within it, women are under-represented in the top tiers of publishing. However, the representation of women in senior positions relative to their representation as employees has improved across the industry between 1988 and 1993.

Although we found evidence of the improved representation of women at company board level, this is less apparent at group board level, which remains an overwhelmingly male preserve. Given the concentration and internationalisation that has taken place within publishing, this is significant for, as one woman company director said concerning women and power, 'I don't think that we've got there. The further up the ladder you get, the further away you realise the real power is.'

Interestingly, the general trends in women's position within publishing are not consistently reflected in the employment data available from our case

TABLE 2.1   **Comparison of male and female publishing employees, managers and directors, 1988 and 1993**

Percentage	Women		Men	
	1988	*1993*	*1988*	*1993*
Employees	60	53	40	47
Managers	40	50	60	50
Company Directors	22	30	78	70

Source: Surveys, 1988, 1993, and WiP (1993).

study companies. Table 2.2 presents data on the percentage change in women's employment within six of the case study companies between 1988 and 1993. All six companies have a formal equal opportunities policy and are considered to exemplify 'good practice' in human resource management within the publishing sector (the companies are codenamed to preserve confidentiality).

With the exception of Academic, all these companies have rationalised in-house staffing levels between 1988 and 1993. The figures from these companies indicate that, despite the overall job loss, women continue to make up a growing proportion of publishing employees within these companies. It is interesting to note, however, that the company where women were less likely to succeed to management and board positions ('Academic') was the only company expanding in employment terms during the study period. This raises questions concerning corporate structure, culture and human resource strategy and the dynamics of gender relations, in understanding the relative position of women and men working within publishing organisations.

These questions are further encouraged by the differences in salaries earned by men and women working within publishing. In 1988 we found that 18 per cent of men working within the industry were in the high-earning £19,000-plus category whereas this was only true for 3 per cent of the women working within the industry. Thus men working within the industry were six times more likely to be high earners (Colgan and Tomlinson, 1989).

TABLE 2.2   **Percentage change of female employees, managers and directors in selected case study of publishing companies between 1988 and 1993**

	Total emp. %	Women emp. %	Total mgt %	Women mgt %	Women dir. %
1. 'General' (large)	−20	+4	−25	+17	+18
2. 'Academic' (large)	+14	+2	+52	−7	+2
3. 'Highbrow' (medium)	−23	+6	n/a	n/a	+25
4. 'Media' (medium)	−16	+5	n/a	n/a	−13
5. 'Texts' (small)	−14	+44	n/a	n/a	n/a
6. 'Feminist' (small)	−14	−14	n/a	n/a	0

Note: n/a – data not available.
Source: Surveys, 1988 and 1993.

Industry-wide data on salaries was harder to obtain from our 1993 survey; however data from our case study companies is shown in Table 2.3. Although there has been some marginal improvement in women's representation in the high-earning group,[4] particularly in 'General', men are still far more likely to be the high earners within the six publishing companies ('Feminist' employs women only). 'Feminist' and 'Highbrow' both illustrate the trend towards delayering of management structures in publishing in order to achieve a leaner corporate structure.

TABLE 2.3   Comparative data on women in higher earning groups in two publishing companies

	% of all employees in high-earning group	% of men in high-earning group	% of women in high-earning group
'General'			
1987–8	6	11	2
1992–3	10	15	7
% change	+4	+4	+5
'Academic'			
1987–8	6	15	1
1992–3	9	21	3
% change	+3	+6	+2
'Highbrow'			
1987–8	8	15	3
1992–3	5	9	2
% change	−3	−6	−1
'Media'			
1987–8	6	10	2
1992–3	16	32	8
% change	+10	+22	+6
'Texts'			
1987–8	n/a	n/a	n/a
1992–3	13	23	11
'Feminist'			
1987–8	23	n/r	23
1992–3	16	n/r	16
% change	−7	n/r	−7

Note: n/a – data not available; n/r – not relevant.
Source: Surveys, 1988 and 1993.

A discussion of gendering processes, corporate culture and the impact of human resource policies on patterns of vertical and horizontal occupational segregation will be developed in this chapter. We will focus particularly on changes within the publishing company identified as 'General', given that it provides evidence of an improvement in the position of women within the company.

Evidence of horizontal job segregation

In order to explore some of the structural barriers which may operate to limit women's career progression within publishing, it is necessary to examine the horizontal patterns of job segregation in the industry. A useful initial division is between publishing-specific and non-publishing-specific functions.

Publishing-specific functions

These provide the routes to the professional publishing careers which exist within the editorial, publicity, sales and marketing, rights and production functions. These are the functions to which arts graduates aspire – the attraction being the ability to decide which books are published, their content, image, design and marketing.

Non-publishing-specific functions

These include finance, accounts, computing services, a variety of non-specific clerical occupations and warehouse and distribution. Large numbers of women are employed in clerical or warehouse positions, processing orders and accounts and performing other general administrative tasks. Opportunities for progression into professional publishing careers from these roles are extremely limited within large publishing companies, although professional qualifications (e.g. accounting, computing) may allow movement up non-publishing-specific career routes.

Many large publishing companies have located their accounts, customer services, distribution and warehouse functions in a secondary location outside central London to cut costs (this is true for example of our case study company 'General'). Thus large publishing companies (unlike small companies) allow little sideways movement from non-publishing-specific clerical and administrative work into publishing-specific clerical work. Whereas small companies can offer a useful apprenticeship to aspiring publishing professionals by encouraging a 'jack/y of all trades' approach to gathering publishing experience, large publishing companies tend to create and reinforce two distinct occupational cultures.

Publishing employment 1988

The majority of publishing employees worked in sales and marketing (17 per cent), editorial (17 per cent), warehouse/distribution (20 per cent) and 'other' areas according to the 1988 survey data.[5] No other function other than accounts (11 per cent) employed more than six per cent of the remaining publishing employees.

As Figure 2.1 illustrates, women were more evenly spread across the functional areas of publishing than men because they performed many of the secretarial and administrative duties necessary to each department. Women worked mainly in the areas of sales and marketing (13 per cent), editorial (21 per cent), accounts (13 per cent), warehouse/distribution (14 per cent) and

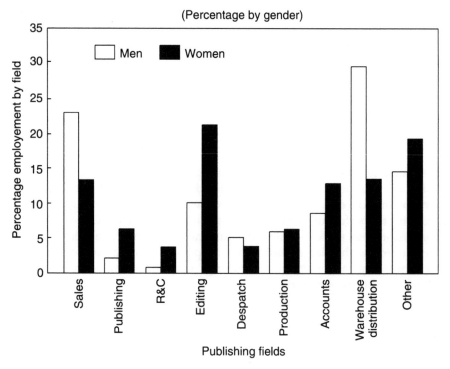

FIGURE 2.1   Employment: men and women in publishing

Source: F. Tomlinson and F. Colgan (1989) *Women in Publishing: Twice as Many, Half as Powerful?*

'other' areas (19 per cent). Men worked mainly in the areas of sales and marketing (23 per cent), editorial (10 per cent), warehouse/distribution (30 per cent) and 'other' areas (15 per cent).

Gendered patterns of occupational segregation were found to exist between and within functions in publishing. In sales and marketing, for example, men made up most sales representative and managerial employees, while women were more likely to be in sales services and junior, clerical positions. In editorial, men were most likely to be in commissioning editor or assistant editor positions: women also held these positions but were more likely to predominate in both secretarial and copy-editing positions. Rights and publicity were two functions predominantly composed of women employees. In the non-publishing-specific areas of publishing, it was common to find predominantly male management structures superimposed on to a primarily female workforce working in administrative and warehouse positions with limited opportunity for progression (Colgan and Tomlinson, 1991).

Publishing employment shifts 1988–1993

Shifts in employment patterns have occurred as large-scale reductions in employment have accompanied the concentration and centralisation of publishing companies into large groups. Changes have also occurred on an on-going basis within both large and small companies as a result of the rationalisation of in-house staffing levels, increased use of freelances and an expansion in the use of new technology.

Concentration and centralisation within the sector has brought widespread job-loss. This large-scale change affects all sections of the workforce where a company has been sold, merged with another or dismembered by its parent company. Thus, for example, when Headline bought Hodder & Stoughton in 1993, 120 of the 640 UK Hodder & Stoughton staff were made redundant. Senior managers and staff in publishing-specific areas did lose their jobs but the majority of redundancies occurred in areas of perceived duplication following the merger. Economies of scale meant this was mainly possible in the (predominantly female) secretarial, administrative, clerical and accountancy support areas (*Bookseller*, 1993). Another example is provided by the Pearson Group's decision to reorganise its holdings, within the publishing sector in 1994. As a result, Longman (an independent publisher for 250 years) was merged with other Pearson holdings bringing the immediate loss of 100 jobs (including those of its board and female chief executive), with many more scheduled to follow (*Bookseller*, 1994).

Accompanying this large-scale job-loss are on-going changes in employment linked to the rationalisation of in-house staff, and increases in the use of freelances and new technology.[6] The sections of the workforce most affected by these changes are the predominantly female areas of copy-editing, indexing, design and picture research where in-house jobs have been replaced by using freelances. Also badly hit are female areas such as secretarial, customer services, accountancy and sales support following the expansion of new technology and staff rationalisation.

Both male and female employment levels have been affected by new technology and rationalisation in production and the warehouse/distribution area. Finally, the predominantly male sales representative workforce and management of many publishing houses has been reduced as publishing houses restructure their sales forces in line with new distribution arrangements and the merger of hardback and paperback sales (*Bookseller*, 1991a).

Our case study company 'General' is predominantly in trade publishing[7] and is part of a larger international media group. It has not changed ownership during our study period although it has taken over a number of smaller publishing companies which it has integrated into its own operation. It has reduced the number of new titles published and cut its backlist to improve efficiency and reduce overheads.

Gendering processes in publishing

In this section we explore processes leading to the differentiation between male and female employment patterns. Use will be made of data from interviews with individual publishing employees carried out between 1987–89 and 1993–94.

Entry points

Many graduates are attracted to the idea of working in publishing: 'General' receives about 2,000 speculative letters a year from 'highly qualified graduates' (mostly women) who are primarily interested in working as an editor though 'most of them don't know what the jobs are'. Interviews with male and female publishing staff indicated that despite marginally superior qualifications women had entered publishing in more junior roles than men. One-third of the women in our original interview sample had started their publishing career as a secretary; none of the men had entered this way.

Secretarial work is generally perceived as women's work, and the majority of applicants for secretarial jobs in publishing are women. In one company we were told 'we will generally not take on men secretaries, they are seen as too ambitious . . . yet some men are prepared to go out and get secretarially qualified and work hard'. The minority status of male secretaries means that their progress within companies is often subjected to particular scrutiny. Thus we were told about a certain resentment amongst female secretaries towards 'the one male . . . who joined as a secretary and six months later he's an assistant editor'.

How men do enter the industry is less clear; entry via sales was perceived as one route. Male entrants in our interview sample had entered via a wider range of functions than women and were more likely to have been taken on as trainees. However the structure of companies is such that many more women than men enter the industry. This is reflected in the age profile: whereas men are more evenly spread across the age ranges, women are concentrated in the 21–30 age band. A senior manager in a large publishing company defended always choosing males for its graduate trainee scheme by saying 'it was fair because men couldn't come into the company as secretaries'.

It seems that the secretarial route is still the most common route via which women enter publishing. According to one personnel manager: 'Unfortunately what you still need in publishing is secretarial skills'. However the limited prospects of many secretarial jobs and their tendency to be gender stereotyped led one successful woman publishing director to assert: 'I always advise people: don't get a secretarial role, go into sales, go into rights. . .'

'General' – entry points

In 'General' there had been an attempt by the new female personnel director to formalise and monitor the recruitment and selection process. This was most easily done for junior publishing and non-publishing-specific occupations. For example, the recruiting of new entrants from the numerous speculative applications had been systematised and formalised. According to the personnel director: 'It still works for graduates to come into publishing through either a secretarial or a rights assistant or a publicity assistant route and then find their way into their heart's desire . . . which is usually commissioning'. They had created a register of graduates who had attended recruitment fairs organised by them. Applicants from this register were invited for permanent and temporary secretarial posts within the company: 'there is always a need for temporary secretaries . . . we virtually never bring people in from agencies . . . they are usually direct temporaries from our register. . .'.

However when seeking to fill more prestigious, publishing-specific positions informal recruitment methods were still used at 'General': for example in editorial: 'you do that [identifying candidates] by asking around . . . you phone up and say I haven't seen you for a long time, it would be nice to have a drink. . .' [male publishing director]. Thus, despite the development of formal policies, at this level line managers continued to use informal practices to seek out the publishing professionals with 'flair' and a good reputation by using the 'grapevine'.

Career paths

Career paths are often visualised as steps up a ladder – from the bottom to the top of an organisation. However, an individual may enter an organisation on a ladder which has few rungs and then stops, a career seeker must move across to progress further. Management trainees enter an organisation assuming there is a ladder potentially prepared for them. In small companies ladders to the top are relatively short. Positions on company boards represent the tops of a series of ladders. Ambitious individuals who want to become board directors will need at some point to move to a ladder which goes 'all the way' if not already placed on one.

However positions at the top are few compared to those at the bottom, so that there will be competition at different stages for who can move to the next rung up. Individuals on short ladders may have to accept that this is as far as they will go, some people will leave the organisation in order to get on a ladder elsewhere, some will decide to stay at the point they are, whilst others may experience disappointment and frustration as their attempts to progress are thwarted and they see others move past them on the way up. Our research indicated that more women than men considered themselves to have reached a 'dead-end' in their career.

Within large companies, the ladders which lead to board level positions are editorial, sales and marketing, production, distribution, finance and perhaps computing and personnel. The shift from 'literary' to 'financial' business goals has meant that although the editorial function remains the most prestigious, the sales and marketing and financial functions have grown increasingly powerful (Jones, 1994). Within smaller companies, the board would be comprised of a managing director, publishing director(s), financial director, sales and marketing director and perhaps a production director.

Taking a job as a secretary in most cases means stepping onto a ladder with only one rung. In publishing, however, secretarial employment is seen as a significant entry point, particularly for women. In order to progress, a secretary must make a transition into a role which is a rung on a ladder which leads somewhere.

Editorial career ladder

The most desirable ladder in publishing is generally perceived as that leading to the position of commissioning editor from where it is possible to move through roles such as senior editor, publishing director to managing director and ultimately chief executive. It is sometimes possible to access this ladder from a secretarial position. A male publishing director described the process within his company:

> Each of the publishing directors has an assistant . . . otherwise being a secretary is a completely dead-end job . . . there's a job [editorial assistant] that if you advertised it you'd get a thousand applicants; it's a great transition job, if you do it well you can make the breakthrough to being an editor . . . .

Appointments to these positions were made internally, usually from the secretarial pool: '[it would be] very unfair to recruit from outside, particularly as there's a great pool of talent here, it does mean that the assistant editors are always likely to be women.'

A female director in another company described her experiences with two secretaries:

> we've got an assistant editor who's been given that opportunity to make that leap . . . [but] she's not actually doing the job we need her to do . . . not sure that she can make that leap . . . we've got another one who's terribly bright, got to find another job for her, otherwise we're going to lose her.

Whereas an editorial assistant working for a commissioning editor may be relatively well placed, a graduate in a desk-editing department has fewer opportunities. The commissioning and desk-editing functions appear increasingly separated, particularly in large companies. More women are concentrated in desk editing where the career ladder is relatively short, usually leading to the position of managing editor. A man in this position felt that: 'at managing editor level you either do the same job until you retire or you do the same job in another company'.

The separation of the two editorial functions presumably explains why 'very few desk editors seem to make it through to commissioning editor, not necessarily the case in the old days', and 'once you've been a copy editor for a few years people are very reluctant to look at you as a commissioning editor'. These jobs were differentiated in terms of skills: desk editing was seen to involve: 'detail and organisation, making sure everything is correct, meticulously checked'. It was sometimes contrasted with the 'judgement', 'creativity and flair' associated with commissioning. However, commissioning involved financial as well as creative judgement. A desk editor contrasted the roles as: 'the commissioning editor looks at the book more from the point of view of finance . . . he looks at the book as a financial unit, we look at the book more as an aesthetic, qualitative thing really'.

These various perceptions reflect ideas that are often gender stereotyped: women may be preferred as copy-editors for their 'attention to detail' and as managing editors because: 'they know that women can keep a lot more balls in the air and hold things together. . .'. Men are thought to be more suitable as commissioning editors: given its status as 'a powerhouse job for the industry'.

The copy-editing or desk-editing function provides a good example of a predominantly female career ladder cut off or truncated during the 1980s as many publishers sought to make cuts in overhead costs. Copy-editing and proof-reading were identified as appropriate parts of the editorial role to sub-contract to freelances. Thus a number of publishing houses closed their in-house copy-editing departments (Bennet, 1992). The resulting pool of redundant publishing staff either left the industry or had little option but to work as freelances. Thus many female employees were jettisoned into a precarious and low-paid section of the labour market. Publishers retained a managing editor in-house to oversee the freelances and gained from a reduction in overhead costs. However, concerns now exist about the skill/training needs of the freelances, publishers' undercutting of NUJ minimum hourly rates and the standard of editing in British publishing (Jones, 1994).

Sales career ladder

An alternative to the editorial 'ladder' often mentioned to us was the 'sales route'. Both editorial and sales are seen as significant because 'that's where power and decision-making lies'. Men still make up the majority of most sales forces, partly because of the perception that sales representatives need to be 'pushy' and 'on the road'. A male editor suggested: 'sales I think will never be dominated by women because it is almost impossible with young children. . .'. However a sales manager in the same company disagreed: 'I'm not sure if it's more difficult than any other job . . . you could argue that it was slightly easier . . . you can to an extent manage your time more than you could in an office situation . . . '. His explanation of the under-representation of women in his own sales force of which only one was female was that 'fewer women apply' for sales jobs and that few women had the right sort of experience.

Sales, then, represents an area in which men still predominate, as sales reps and sales managers. As far as we could ascertain sales managers are all ex-reps; none has been promoted from amongst sales administration staff, the majority of whom are women. Companies which were 'sales-led' were described to us as very 'male-orientated'; one women who had worked as a sales representative said she had experienced a 'tough time' in a company she described as 'male-orientated' and 'hardnosed, sales-led, nasty and ruthless'. As indicated, however, corporate sales forces have been one of the casualties of the economies of scale sought by corporate restructuring and the changing sales and marketing of books (Nelson, 1991; Waterstone, 1991).

Other publishing-specific career ladders

Two publishing-specific areas outside editorial which are seen to offer opportunities for women to enter and progress are publishing and rights. Women make up the majority of employees in both (81 per cent and 87 per cent respectively). Discussion of this tended to focus on 'glamorous' associations: 'It helps to be personable and pretty, there is a horrible tendency to be called publicity girls', and: 'Some rights directors use their sexuality with editors . . . [There are] some quite attractive women doing that job'. Perceptions that doing a job effectively is linked to factors such as attractiveness and youth, being thought of, as one male publicity director described it, as 'literary air hostesses' are clearly limiting for women who want to progress further: 'If you're good at publicity it doesn't mean you can't do anything else' and as one woman rights director who felt she had reached a career ceiling said, 'Women rights directors are not the ones who become the international marketing directors . . . it is not seen that rights equals sales'.

Directors of publicity and rights are now less frequently found on company boards, particularly of large companies where their functions may be subsumed by directors of sales and marketing, and publishing directors. In order to transfer onto these 'ladders' the skills of employees working in these areas, skills for example of negotiation and of financial and marketing acumen, need recognition. According to one female publicity director, publicity was becoming a 'more exact science of targeting and promoting a particular book'. She welcomed more men in publicity, reflecting an often-held view that the presence of a significant number of men helps an organisational function to be taken more seriously.

Gendered managerial responsibilities

Upwards progression involves individuals taking on roles where managerial competence is more significant than technical or creative ability, and further progression will depend on the perception that they will function successfully at successively senior levels. Comparison of the responsibilities of our original interview sample (see Table 2.4) indicated that because of occupational segregation most women managers supervised other women in a 'female' environment, and that whilst many male managers had only women subordinates they also had more opportunities to manage women and men. In order to move on from such segregated roles women have to convince senior managers they can manage in environments employing men and women and that they have the necessary 'staying power' to be worth appointing.

Traditional patterns of male management superimposed upon a predominantly female workforce are often found in 'non-publishing-specific' areas

TABLE 2.4   **Comparison of supervisory responsibilities of women and men in publishing**

	With no supervisory responsibility (%)	With only female subordinates (%)	With male and female subordinates (%)	Total
Women	46	45	9	100
Men	28	28	43	99 *

*Figures may not add up to 100 because of rounding

Source: Interviews in eight publishing companies, 1987–9 (60 women and 40 men).

such as finance and customer service. Thus the first woman to be appointed as an accountant in a large company described how her male management colleagues would:

> drink in the bar at lunchtimes . . . I go sometimes but I don't like drinking at lunchtimes . . . when I first came people [men] didn't know how to take me . . . it took a bit of adjusting, they'd keep apologising for swearing . . . for me it was part of the learning process.

As a result, she mainly associated with the more junior, female staff in her department.

'General' – career paths

The company reduced the number of its employees by 20 per cent between 1988 and 1993. However, the percentage of women employees increased from 61 per cent in 1988 to 65 per cent in 1993. Similarly, the percentage of women in management increased from 41 per cent to 48 per cent and women's representation on the company board from 18 per cent to 33 per cent. 'General' retains a copy-editing department in-house but uses freelances in editorial, production and design. Following the introduction of new technology it has reduced staff in its predominantly female customer services area and has reduced both male and female staff in the warehouse. It has sought to rationalise staff throughout the operation, a particular casualty being the predominantly male sales force. There have been a few small growth areas related to media links and merchandising.

Training and career development

Organisations introduce activities such as training, performance appraisal and succession planning to improve the current performance of individuals, but also to identify potential and assist career development. In 1988 research indicated that such activities were largely undeveloped in publishing companies, reflecting an industry containing many small companies, where much recruitment at senior and middle levels took place through informal head-hunting and poaching from other companies rather than internal promotion, and where some key skills were described to us as 'intuitive' and 'untrainable' (Book House Training Centre, 1988; Colgan and Tomlinson, 1989). Vande-velde and Forsaith (1991) expressed their shock at finding that 49 per cent of the publishing companies participating in their survey offered no formal training to their staff.

It is agreed that publishing companies are now much more committed to formalised training and development. This is particularly true for their core in-house staff (managers, commissioning editors) where training is focused on management, financial, marketing and commercial skills (*Bookseller*, 1993). To assist in identifying training needs, formal performance appraisal schemes have been introduced in many large houses in the 1990s. However whilst a number of large companies have developed in-house training, increased the number of staff on Book House Training courses and adopted National Vocational Qualifications (with reservations) resources are a key constraint, particularly for small companies (PQB, 1993). A key group who do not benefit from in-company publishing training initiatives is the pool of freelances who often find the cost of training prohibitive (Bennet, 1992).

'General' training and career development

The personnel director of 'General' had been charged with training as a key priority on her appointment. She had appointed a training manager, and training initiatives included induction training (since 1991), a performance appraisal system (since 1992), a management development programme (attended by 8 women and 4 men in 1993) and NVQs. Details of courses available were circulated around the company in an annual training brochure. Financial constraints had led to a reduction in the training budget, but in her view the company 'still managed to run a pretty full programme'.

Interviews within the company confirmed the impression that the company now encouraged training within an organised system. However, some felt training was more geared towards managers, supervisors and commissioning editors, and that access to training depended on individual line managers' willingness to share information. An appraisal scheme had been introduced;

its primary focus was on training needs. It was greeted with a certain amount of suspicion: one worry cited concerned the capability of managers to appraise effectively, another that unrealistic expectations could be raised as appraisees identified training and development needs that were subsequently unmet. But it was generally thought to be a good thing in principle.

Formal systems of training and appraisal are often seen as favourable in an equal opportunities context, through creating conditions whereby women (and members of other target groups) can develop their skills and progress on merit. The absence of such systems may favour those whose 'face fits' and serve to reproduce an élite from a particular gender, class or cultural background. Women managers in 'General' were benefiting from training opportunities; however, the company still contained areas with predominantly male management structures, including the warehouse where all the management team and 10 out of 12 supervisors were men. Here the company was assisting two 'promising young people' in obtaining additional qualifications: both were men.

Men, women and mothers; childcare provision

In an industry employing large numbers of women, most of whom are young, questions arise of how, when these women have children they will manage the 'dual role' of primary care giver and employee. This creates a situation whereby women become differentiated into 'women' and 'mothers' whereas men remain regarded as a homogenous group.

Our interviews revealed concern amongst some managers that women might be less likely to fit into career positions and perform to company standards. One male director said: 'If a woman had small children, I think it would concern me . . . The demands we're making in many areas wouldn't be compatible with bringing up small children'. Another senior male manager expressed the view:

> Women around the age of thirty, without children, are likely to be viewed with caution when they're being considered for a job that requires a fairly long and committed time scale. There is the niggling thought that they might have kids. . . It's potentially a source of discrimination.

Thus both mothers and women who might become mothers may be viewed with some reservations by male managers. Young women fear that this management perception could affect their career prospects. We found that over half the women in our original sample had been asked questions at interview concerning their domestic arrangements or plans for children. There can often only be one answer to such questions: 'If they're planning to promote you they'll ask if you're planning to have children . . . I know it's happened to some people – they've automatically said no!'

The taking of maternity leave can be unpopular: 'They (senior management) don't like people taking six months off'. In a period of rapid restructuring it may also entail a certain risk: we were told that in the sales and marketing department of one company: 'people returning from maternity leave found their jobs had disappeared'. A woman sales rep on maternity leave was excluded from training in portable computers because her managers did not believe she would come back; the training had to be separately provided for her on her return. We found that many mothers we interviewed at senior and middle management levels had felt obliged to shorten their period away to minimise the inconvenience to their departments.

Our interviews with senior women and men managers showed that in common with other industries the women were less likely to have children than their male counterparts who almost without exception had children and a wife to look after 'all their domestic concerns'. However, some women have combined having children with the attainment of top-level publishing positions. Their achievements were often regarded as extraordinary if not superhuman by male colleagues: 'I imagine it's ghastly . . . [they] have to be terribly efficient and organised, it amazes me that they are able to put the time into the job that they do'.

Equal opportunities policies are introduced into organisations to counteract the discriminatory attitudes described above and to support working parents through measures such as maternity and paternity leave, childcare payments, workplace crèches, flexible working patterns and career break schemes. During the 1980s trade unions (NUJ, MSF, SOGAT) had effectively bargained to improve these provisions in companies where they were recognised. At the time of our original survey (1987–8) the issue of equal opportunities (EO) was receiving increased attention generally, associated primarily with concern about demographic trends (it was predicted that there would be one-third fewer school leavers in the 1990s) and accompanying skills shortages. We found a number of senior managers in publishing concerned about their continued ability to attract and retain high quality personnel. Unfortunately, in the current recessionary climate, publishing managers have suggested that equal opportunities is no longer a priority.

Our second survey (1992–3) indicated that whilst certain publishers have introduced more formal human resource management systems, including performance appraisal, training and job evaluation schemes, within the last five years there is less evidence of recent EO initiatives. Only one company had introduced a written EOP in the last three years, and all six companies offering maternity leave above the statutory minimum had done so for more than five years.

Women in Publishing (WiP) conducted a survey of maternity and childcare provision in publishing companies in the latter part of 1992.[8] Of the 56 companies who responded, 35 had a written/formal policy on maternity benefits. However only 13 provided financial support with childcare and 4 nursery provision. Seven offered job sharing and 3 a career-break scheme.

'General:' childcare provision

'General' is regarded as one of the industry's most generous providers of maternity and associated benefits. The personnel director questioned whether equal opportunities for women was still a concern, arguing that their EO policy was 'very well established . . . and has been for some time . . . it's almost taken for granted'. A senior male manager commented: 'The company is heavily reliant on women with youngish children . . . at very senior levels it is dominated by a lot of women with children'.

Interviews within the company supported the view that women there did not have to make a choice between children and career. It was reported that increasing numbers of women were returning from maternity leave (this was reported in other companies too). But as well as generous maternity leave and financial assistance, reasons cited for this were concern for job security in a recessionary climate and changing expectations amongst women. In a period of little staff turnover the need for maternity leave cover had provided some opportunities for movement of employees; however the cost of cover caused some concern.

Union representatives felt there was scope for improving the financial support offered and that there was a need for crèche provision. However, the recessionary climate had made it difficult to negotiate on these issues. They reported that managerial attitudes towards women wanting to change their hours following return from maternity leave had not always been sympathetic. Arrangements such as job sharing were: 'not that well promoted or encouraged really – it comes about rather than being actively encouraged by personnel'.

Corporate cultures, occupational segregation and women's progression

Publishing attracts women in large numbers, particularly white middle-class graduates. The effects of recession, changing expectations and improved maternity provision mean that more women are choosing to stay in the industry. The 'feminisation' of publishing does not, however, operate in a uniform way; it is influenced by contrasting corporate cultures and managerial strategies (as reflected in Tables 2.2 and 2.3). Different companies can have a distinguishable 'masculine' or 'feminine' culture even though employing similar proportions of men and women. This orientation can be expressed in a number of ways.

Masculine/feminine cultures

A masculine culture is associated with the perception that a particularly aggressive approach is needed to get to the top, such that only 'atypical' women succeed. Successful men were often described as being more career-oriented and empire-building than women managers, who were often credited with superior negotiating and diplomatic skills. Yet many interviewees thought that for women to succeed they 'have to be considerably better than men', 'to have strong views on things' and 'women who have reached directorial levels or just below . . . tend to be forceful and have a reputation for getting their own way'. Women may have more difficulty in asserting their authority with male subordinates who may 'go running off telling . . . they'll blame it on a woman . . . but take it from a man'. They may also be the particular target of gossip: 'the derogatory remarks about women in senior positions . . . who they've been to bed with'.

A culture may be described as more 'masculine' where there is a sharper separation of functions along gender lines and where male areas are perceived to have higher status. In a company where all but two of the commissioning editors were young men these roles were particularly powerful and prestigious. The organisational style reflected theirs: 'the company likes to think it's young, aggressive, attractive' and was also described as a: 'macho culture, work till you drop'. One of the two women editors perceiving the social activities as: 'mainly male . . . football, cricket' felt it was difficult for her and her colleague to 'break into that . . . we don't go out with the lads'.

In contrast, mainly 'female' clerical areas and functions such as desk editing are felt by many male managers to be both attractive to women and appropriate to their skills. However female areas were sometimes described as 'unhealthy'; as a female manager of an administrative area commented: 'It's nice to have a man in the department, all women together does sometimes get a bit bitchy'. In another company, after she appointed a man in sales administration, the manager 'had all the men come up to me and say why did you employ a man, is he gay? . . . they found it strange for a man to be working for a woman . . . assumed he must be totally effeminate'. It is assumed that men will be put off working in a 'woman's area', and yet women may feel that without a significant male presence the area will be perceived as a 'female ghetto' and not taken seriously.

Within publishing distinctions are drawn between male and female markets and clients (i.e. authors). In an academic house we were told 'Male authors are more confident if their books are in male hands'. A woman publisher of academic books avoided publishing women's studies texts: 'we don't want to be known as a feminist house . . . I don't think that's good for our authors'. In these cases academic prestige was thought to be compromised when associated with women editors and women's issues.

In trade publishing, certain lists such as children's books, cookery and health are usually commissioned by women in departments with few men; male editors are more likely to commission 'upmarket' lists such as literary fiction. A male publisher described his search for an editor of popular fiction by women authors: 'I wanted to hire a woman because a lot of the books we do are not me'. Feminisation of publishing even led to a male director thinking 'the male market is being overlooked' because of the increased number of women editors.

The metaphor of a 'glass ceiling' has often been deployed in describing the organisational level which women, though well represented lower down, have difficulty in achieving. Organisations can be compared in terms of to what extent and at what level the glass ceiling operates against women.

In a large trade company the personnel manager expressed her puzzlement that: 'looking at the people I interview most of them are women, and then I look at [the company] and most of the senior managers are men and I want to know why?' The personnel director reported that: 'there is still the perception in some staff's mind that the glass ceiling exists' and that it was associated with 'male chauvinist attitudes', though he thought there were: 'enough people at board level who respect the worth of individuals irrespective of male and female'. He felt they addressed the problem through training women and developing their assertiveness, so they were less likely to have attitudes which would 'present barriers in any one's head'. The one woman on the board was 'disappointed' that after three years she was 'still the only woman there'.

'General:' shifts in corporate culture, occupational segregation and women's progression

As we have seen, 'General' was regarded as providing good equal opportunities provision. Its human resource management took place within a pluralistic framework with trade unions recognised and involved in negotiations, including EO matters. Relations between unions and personnel were regarded as generally good.

In 1993, 65 per cent of the workforce were women. Women were in the majority in all functions save computing (34 per cent female), sales representatives (33 per cent female), the warehouse (44 per cent female), management (48 per cent) and the board (33 per cent). Some interviewees felt the company was significantly 'feminised', particularly those coming from other industries such as the new woman personnel director: 'If anything it's a more female oriented company than a male oriented company' and 'the company is already predominantly female . . . [it would be] healthy to have some more men in'. A male director considered women had a powerful presence in significant business functions: 'not sales and finance particularly but elsewhere, particularly the entrepreneurial end of the business, commissioning, marketing, rights . . . things where you're dealing with outside organisations and have an immediate financial impact'. A sales manager reported his response to the marketing managers who complained that all the sales managers were men: 'Hang on a minute, all your marketing department bar one in the whole company are women!'

The personnel director put forward the view that women's progress was inexorable: 'A lot of male managers and directors are in the 50-plus age bracket, below 40 women outnumber men . . . it's just a question of feeding through over time'. However one interviewee described his perception of the political processes which may operate against women: 'in theory promotion prospects shouldn't be affected by being a woman. . .' but despite the numbers of women at departmental manager level there were relatively few at the very top: 'directors are responsible for hiring other directors, there's a laddish culture . . . the board has to present a united face . . . it would be disrupted by people who don't share that'. And senior women were not immune from having their 'competence called into question' and their 'forcefulness' perceived as being 'difficult' in a way not applied to men.

Increasing commercial pressures were seen to modify the 'liberal' traditions of the company; the liberal and informal editorial side was contrasted with the more 'business oriented' (and increasingly influential) sales and marketing area associated with the wearing of suits and a harder-nosed management approach. In this environment senior managers had to be 'forceful' and to be 'good at looking after the interests of their own department'.

Nevertheless, women seemed to have progressed in 'General' between 1988 and 1993. In order to establish the extent of women's progress in 'General', we present data in Table 2.5 (in addition to the data presented in Tables 2.2 and 2.3) which compares their relative positions in 1987–8 and 1992–3. Table 2.5 shows that the proportion of women in the company has increased and they now make up nearly half the managers. Similarly they had also improved their representation in the 'high earning' group in the company from 2 per cent in 1988 to 7 per cent in 1993 (Table 2.3).

Not all companies reflect this movement. The data on 'General' is shown alongside that of 'Academic', another large publishing house. Whilst the proportion of women employed in the company has also increased (women make up 68 per cent of the workforce), as has the proportion of employees in management roles, women are now more poorly represented in the management group. Their position in the 'high earning' group has only marginally increased from 1 per cent in 1988 to 3 per cent in 1993. Over the period in question 'General' had gained three more women directors and had two fewer male directors. In 'Academic' there are currently two women on the most senior company board, a similar representation to that of 1987–8.

TABLE 2.5   **Comparative data on women's representation in management in two publishing companies**

	% of all employees who are women	% of all employees who are managers	% of management roles held by women
'General'			
1987–8	61	13	41
1992–3	65	12	47
'Academic'			
1987–8	66	10	38
1992–3	68	14	31

Source: Surveys, 1988, 1993.

Both 'General' and 'Academic' have personnel departments and similar equal opportunity policies and provisions, both are regarded as industry leaders in this respect. These provisions in themselves therefore do not guarantee women's even progression. When interviewed in 1987 the 'Academic' personnel director also expressed the 'inexorable' view: 'I think that it will change [the low representation of women at top levels] . . . the barriers to getting to the very top are just the barriers of numbers'. The data presented by the company suggests that notwithstanding the equal opportunity provisions within the company, structural and attitudinal barriers seem to be preventing this happening at 'Academic'.

Accommodation, confrontation or transformation in a 'male' business world

In the previous section we explored gendering processes within publishing in terms of how occupations and roles have become gendered, and described the influence human resource policies and cultural variables may have in shaping and transforming these processes. The positions attained by individual men and women in publishing result from preferences and choices exercised by them as well as from the operation of organisational barriers which may impede the implementation of preferences. Preference patterns are influenced by gender and certain barriers operate specifically to affect the career paths and progression of women (Podmore and Spencer, 1986; Cockburn, 1991). In this section we explore women's career choices within the constraints imposed by the structural and attitudinal factors characterising the industry.

Trying to fit into 'masculine' organisations

As we have seen, entry into publishing for most women does not take place via a substantive publishing job or a trainee position but as a secretary or departmental assistant. To progress further it helps to have had 'a boss who had no preconceptions about what a secretary could do' and 'to work with people who give you a chance', for 'unless you have someone supportive you can get trapped and trampled on as a secretary'.

Working in 'female areas'

Having established themselves in a publishing role, women face the question of how to develop their careers, whether by moving upwards, sideways or following some other route. Some women may exercise a positive choice to work in so-called 'female' areas: 'I like being a desk editor because I like being involved with the book and authors, I wouldn't like to be on the commissioning side although that's seen as a progression'. In some cases commissioning reflected 'male and Oxbridge environments' and sales departments were perceived as 'aggressive' and potentially 'hostile' by woman employees.

Having stayed in such 'female' roles rather than moving on led one woman to describe her career trajectory as 'not amazingly upwards' but thought it was 'in a way my choice . . . I tend to be the sort of person who likes to stay in the same place for a long time'. But another felt trapped: 'My next job would have to be commissioning editor . . . only path open to me . . . apathy is making me stay and the fact that there aren't any good jobs around' (desk editor). Although often content with the work itself, many were dissatisfied with their promotion, status and earnings prospects reflecting the limited career ladders existing in predominantly 'female' areas.

Playing the 'men's game' to succeed

Some women agreed that women need to play the 'men's game' to succeed in publishing. One women director felt that if women wanted the top jobs in publishing they needed to 'start thinking like a man' although not necessarily 'acting like a man' in the way they approached their careers. She felt a significant problem was that 'women hadn't got time for the politics and to build up their power base, they're so fixed on their desk, they don't know what's going on around them until the man next door – who's not half so good – lands the top job.' Not all women do so uncritically: one woman manager admitted to using 'male tactics' but said 'it doesn't bother me when I'm using them [male tactics] because I quite enjoy using them but it bothers me in principle because I think it's immoral.'

Women also identified a difference between themselves and men in their style in dealing with organisational politics. Some felt that this had been of benefit to them: 'I am much more confrontational – I carry on the attack whereas the men don't want to make a fuss . . . I will fight where I think an injustice has been done or something has to be got to the bottom of'. However, another woman had been told: 'You're not a company woman and that is incredibly important in publishing . . . I've never been able to do that. I'm much better at being oppositional' and another: 'I have been hindered by the fact that I tend to say exactly what I think'.

A successful woman publishing director reported that in the early stages she: 'didn't want a big career . . . I was a slow starter'. She had found the transition from desk editing to commissioning the most difficult in her career: 'I had the role of managing editor which I could do standing on my head . . . I didn't know if I'd be a successful commissioning editor. . . . I had a lot of self-doubt, what happened was I did it very gradually'. She felt her slowness in moving resulted from not being 'aggressive enough'. In contrast another director had behaved ambitiously much earlier in her career, attributing her drive to the fact that 'I always felt that who was managing it wasn't doing it very well and I could do it a lot better'.

Small is beautiful?

The preference many women express for small companies reflects their perception that in larger companies political processes and the drive for power and status (generally perceived as 'male' preoccupations) are more important. Women are better represented on the boards of smaller companies where there are fewer hierarchical layers and where key women may individually negotiate flexible working arrangements. Women directors often pointed to the advantages in the early phases of their careers of having worked in small companies where 'everybody did a bit of everything . . . allows people to zig-zag'. A director who had built up a successful career in a large company felt it was more difficult now 'for people to get the range of experience and power base that I had, partly because it's so much bigger now..things were still relatively small so you could run publicity and design and sales and marketing . . . now it's huge'. However 'small companies can be a problem if there's no inbuilt career structure and a person can get stuck with nowhere to go'.

Children or career?

Working hard and working long hours were often identified by women as necessary for upwards progression: 'long hours and interest in it has helped', 'you have to throw yourself into it'. In this context women may perceive particular problems in combining their work responsibilities with children. Some may choose not to have children, though: 'It would not be impossible to combine my job with children . . . I would just pay someone to take care of them . . . I would work the same hours . . . [it's] one reason I don't have them', and 'I may not have a child because of the career/childcare dilemma'.

Women directors with children may have taken 'no maternity leave . . . I worked at home for six weeks' or gone 'on maternity leave but did work at home and hurried back'. Coping with children involved reliance on 'live-in nannies always' for one woman, another had 'never felt bad about leaving children with nannies . . . I can afford proper childcare which gives me peace of mind'; the costs of childcare for another woman had been offset by the fact she had been 'cushioned by my husband's income'.

Some women felt (and younger men) having children did limit the level of responsibility they wanted to take on; as one middle manager put it:

'I've got three children and I honestly feel I couldn't go on [to board level] . . . I couldn't have a full time with my family . . . I'm sure there are other women like me who want a certain amount of responsibility, but, because of other factors in my life I can't commit myself wholeheartedly to the organisation'.

A female director reflected on why there were not other women at her level in the company: 'there are a lot of women in the next layer down, most are married, most have children . . . being single may mean I have that extra push'.

Transforming 'masculine' organisations

Mentoring and networking

Women in senior management positions were able to provide important role models for women. Some were aware that they brought a different approach to management and actively sought to make their organisations more 'woman-friendly'. As one woman said, 'Being a managing director does make a difference . . . I do convey a different set of standards . . . Partly because I'm a woman, people don't make anti-woman jokes in this office.'

Another factor that was identified as important in career terms was having had mentors for guidance, support and inspiration (particularly in the early stages). Women most often mentioned having had women as mentors described variously as 'sympathetic', 'helpful', 'inspiring', 'brilliant at her own job'. Mentors did not only act as models: other roles included 'training me to take over from her' and 'advising me on jobs coming up'. Having a mentor was crucially important in helping women escape the many 'dead-end' jobs in publishing in order to climb on to one of the 'career ladders'.

Developing mentors and networking is important in career terms since at senior levels moves between companies are almost always initiated via informal approaches. In areas such as rights and publicity, the network is predominantly female; however, within the senior levels of publishing, it is predominantly male. Women wishing to go beyond the 'glass ceiling' need to be on one of the 'career ladders' and get themselves known in the industry. Cross-gender networking can be problematic because of the way in which women's social contacts with senior men can be interpreted. As one man commented on social functions 'the obvious ones that stand out are women making up to male bosses . . . I notice they seem to be successful at getting on . . . I suppose if you're ambitious you use everything available.'

Although women can network through the Society of Young Publishers, the Publishers Association and other professional publishing organisations, the difficulties encountered in gaining access to information ~~~~~~~~~~~~~~~~~~~~~~~~~~~ training and networking led a group of women working in publishing to establish Women in Publishing (WiP) in 1979. WiP was established to promote the status of women in the industry and its activities include running its own training programme, and monthly meetings and newsletters as well as publicity on issues of concern to women in the industry. Through WiP, women can network, learn about the industry and job opportunities in addition to campaigning for change. While many women welcome the opportunity to network with other women, and WIP's training courses are spoken of very highly, some women did not wish to become members on the grounds that they felt 'threatened', 'not feminist enough' or 'preferred to be with both men and women'. Its membership was described to us by a male trade unionist as: 'Girls who want to get on', principally serving the needs of young graduates aspiring to a publishing-specific career. In fact, Wip's membership during the time of study includes women active in their trade unions as well as those who were not.

Trade unions: organising for change

As women comprise the majority of publishing employees, it is not surprising to find that they are active at company level in the three unions (NUJ, MSF, GPMU) which represent employees in the book publishing industry. Our research indicated that positive developments in equal opportunities were most often found in companies where trade unions had pushed for equal opportunity policies, monitoring, equal opportunity committees and negotiated progressive terms and conditions including parental leave and childcare.

Where trade unions were active in companies, they had encouraged a more formal approach to equal opportunity policies and practices and negotiated employment benefits for women, offering what Collinson, Knights and Collinson (1990) have described as collective resistance to traditional 'masculine' structures and attitudes. This was particularly effective where there were enlightened personnel managers in post and a critical mass of women and men at senior and middle management levels who also supported equal opportunities. In the late 1980s, companies with such a pluralist industrial relations climate seemed to be moving towards developing a 'long equal opportunities agenda' (Cockburn, 1989) and a more 'woman-friendly' approach to HRM.

However, following the shifts in publishing between 1988 and 1993, trade unions have been marginalised or derecognised in the majority of publishing companies, membership has fallen and their influence has declined (NUJ, 1993; Gall and McKay, 1994). The trade unions are now struggling to 'maintain a voice at work in defence of members' interests' and are less able to take a proactive or confrontational role (NUJ, 1993).

Getting out of 'masculine' organisations

Research has shown that the number of women entering self-employment and small business ownership is increasing (Richardson and Hartshorn, 1993). In some cases, rising unemployment, unstable or unsatisfactory job conditions and prospects have 'pushed' women into creating their own jobs through setting up small businesses. A number of factors have also 'pulled' women into entrepreneurship, including ambition, self-realisation, economic returns and a desire for the flexibility which will allow women to combine family responsibilities with earning a living (Turner, 1993).

Three 'gender'-related motivations seemed particularly relevant to the women opting to 'escape' from 'male' publishing organisations. One group of women entrepreneurs were motivated by a need for autonomy and an income in a way that fitted in with domestic responsibilities. Another group were experiencing the frustrations of the 'glass ceiling effect' (Hymounts, 1986) and established businesses as a vehicle to escape these frustrations and realise their ambitions. A third group were motivated by their feminist principles and so sought to use their skills in order to work within 'woman-friendly' organisations, encourage women writers and recognise women as an important market for book publishing.

Going freelance

Many publishers suggest freelance work provides a potential route for women who wish to combine childcare responsibilities with a career. Indeed, the industry has rather taken for granted that, as long as women have this option, the industry need make no further provision for employees with family responsibilities. Although the majority of our freelancers had turned to this form of work because of redundancy/job loss (35 per cent), a number of women (and men) had chosen it as an option because of its flexibility, their desire to escape office politics and in order to facilitate childcare (21 per cent). A desk editor had 'often thought of going freelance' because of 'the sheer number of people and regimentation' in a large company. Another woman, particularly enjoyed working freelance because she felt she 'had no boss' and no longer 'had to fit into an office hierarchy with all the complex interaction that involves – bureaucracy, politics, sexism'.

Although women freelancers cited a number of advantages (flexible hours, independence, variety of work, time with children, work from home, etc.) they also identified disadvantages of this form of work (isolation, financial inse-curity, long hours, low rates, no benefits and stress).[9] A substantial number of those wishing to return to work in house (20 per cent) were women who had chosen to do so because of reasons related to childcare or job loss (Survey 1989 and 1993). However, a number of these women felt they would be unable to return to work in-house because of ageism and the low status awarded to freelance skills in the industry.

Going freelance was used by some women as an interim step towards moving out of publishing. Where women perceived limited career prospects in publishing, they opted to make a career change by commencing a pro-gramme of study, establishing a business, and so on, while working freelance to provide a source of income during the transition period.

Starting a publishing company

We interviewed several women who had chosen to establish their own pub-lishing houses; one woman did this right at the beginning, having declined the offer of a secretarial position and started her successful company from her front room. Another woman set up her company because 'I want things on my terms which would stop me getting to the top. You have to do things on other people's terms to get to the top . . . I want to continue to enjoy coming to work.' Yet another woman did so to encourage black and Asian authors and in order to serve what she as an Afro-Caribbean woman recognised was a growing demand for their books.

Women who had been involved in setting up their own companies identi-fied a different style of working: 'Compared to where I'd been before these were very real meetings . . . there is an agenda but informal . . . I prefer a small and intimate company to a large departmental based one'; 'We just get on with the job, we don't have lots of meetings . . . I would have to play those games [politics] if I became a satellite in a larger company'. A young woman director in a small company had 'no interest in going off and joining a big publishing company and working myself into the same position . . . my next step or ambition would be to start my own company'. In small companies, childcare leave was arranged on an informal and practical basis, as one woman MD with two children herself said, 'I am accommodating, they make the time up. It's no issue if someone's good, people have these things happening in their lives.'

Starting a feminist company

Feminism was an important driving force for some women encouraging them to get out of publishing organisations they had found 'personally destructive' in order to use their skills towards feminist goals. Thus women set up businesses run on feminist lines in order to publish books 'fuelled by a feminist perspective' and 'give women back their history' (Goodings, 1993). As one director of a feminist company has said, 'it was tremendously exciting to be caught up with a political movement and a job that was about me and my life. It is a great luxury in publishing to feel no split between yourself and the books you are working on' (Goodings, 1993). Other women established women's bookstores in order to 'provide a permanent outlet for women's writing' (Cholmely, 1991).

Although creating a feminist way of working was not without its tensions (Cholmely, 1991), we found that in a feminist house the women were generally very positive about the 'very supportive atmosphere'. 'It's both a very serious place and as casual as it can be.' In a women's bookshop, one lesbian cited 'autonomy and control' and the possibility of working in an organisation without fear of discrimination and homophobia as important factors for her in the establishment and running of the bookshop (Cholmely, 1991). Feminist publishing houses were an important force for change within the industry. They encouraged women writers, acted as training grounds for women who wished to work in the industry, and established that there was a market for women's writing across a broad spectrum of topics. They were also among the most pro-active companies in trying to improve black and Asian representation within publishing both as authors on their lists and as workers within the industry.

Conclusion

In summary, the women we interviewed attributed particular significance to informal processes in shaping their careers, such as mentors and networking. Similarly it was the informality of small companies that led many women to say they preferred them.

However, larger companies are more likely to offer 'formal' training programmes, career structures and official equal opportunity policies with associated benefits. The contrasts we have been able to draw between 'General' and 'Academic' suggest that within relatively large, formalised companies cultural and political processes impact differently upon women's career patterns. Similarly whilst in some small companies with liberal and relatively benevolent managers women may benefit from informally negotiated flexible arrangements, in others the atmosphere may not be so benign. The progress women make within a company does not just reflect their individual 'dynamism' and ambition but the operation of supportive structures, formal and informal. So for example in companies with equal opportunity policies, relatively generous maternity provision and a significant number of women in middle and senior positions we were more likely to be told that women in the company did not have to make a choice between a career and having children. Positive developments in equal opportunities were most likely to be found in companies where women members had pushed their trade unions to negotiate employment benefits for them.

This collective resistance to masculine attitudes and structures had begun to encourage the 'unpicking' of gendered patterns of job segregation in companies, particularly where there were enlightened personnel managers and a critical mass of women at senior and middle management level. However, the marginalisation/derecognition of trade unions in many publishing companies and the recession faced by the industry in the 1990s has led to restructuring, job-loss and a worsening of publishing employees' terms and conditions. The shift from a paternalist to a more 'woman-friendly' approach to human resource management in the industry as envisaged at the end of the 1980s has been replaced by a harder-nosed version which has at best stalled and at worst reversed formal equal opportunity developments for the majority of women within publishing.

Notes

1. Women account for 60 per cent of unit sales, whereas men account for 40 per cent according to Book Marketing (1995).
2. Publishing differs from other sectors such as manufacturing and transport where male managers and employees may consider much of the work physically or emotionally inappropriate for female workers (Cockburn, 1983; Robbins, 1986). Nevertheless, male publishing employees did perceive women as 'unreliable' in not conforming to 'male' standards and expectations.
3. The mergers, takeovers and closures which have occurred within the industry between 1988 and 1993 have created difficulties in comparing data for some companies for the two time periods.

4. The 'high earning' group for 1987–8 consists of employees earning above £19,000 p.a., and for 1992–93 consists of those earning above £26,000 p.a. Eight per cent of our total 1987–8 sample earned above £19,000; £26,000 is used as a basis of comparison for 1992–93 as the level above which 8 per cent of employees were now to be found.

5. 'Other' functions category must be treated with caution: companies have used it to categorise a mixture of computer services, maintenance, administrative and personnel staff. A few companies also placed managerial and secretarial staff in this category.

6. Interview with Nancy Duin of the National Union of Journalists freelance branch, 23 February 1994.

7. Trade publishing may be perceived within book publishing as more 'glamorous' than academic or educational publishing. Companies are mainly located in Central London; it deals with popular literature and high-profile literary authors, and must publicise its books and authors via launches, media campaigns, and so to an often unpredictable audience. Educational publishing concerns itself with textbooks for schools, colleges and universities utilising academic authors and relying on a more easily predictable educational market.

8. WiP has actively initiated research into issues of concern to women in the industry. In 1985 WiP established a Survey Committee which sought the assistance of business school researchers in order to provide a survey of the position of women in publishing and identify barriers to their progression (Colgan and Tomlinson, 1989). This was followed up in 1993 by a survey of maternity leave provision within publishing companies (WiP, 1993). In 1995 a group of senior women managers known as the Bentinck Group and the WiP Training Committee commissioned a study of the impact of corporate culture and exclusionary practices within publishing in order to highlight the continued existence of a 'glass-ceiling' affecting women's career prospects within the industry (Walsh and Cassell, 1995). WiP has, used these studies to campaign actively for improvements within the industry.

9. Long hours were common. Women worked an average of 35 hours a week, whereas male freelances worked an average of 45 hours a week. Howerver, this varied considerably through financial necessity or where deadlines had to be met. Women freelances' weekly earnings were on average 65% of those of their male colleagues (freelance surveys 1988 and 1993).

CHAPTER 3

Career aspirations – women managers in retailing

Anne Brockbank and Joanne Traves

This chapter outlines the structure and culture of the retail industry and describes the position of women within retail organisations. We report the experiences of some women managers, their attitudes and choices and their struggles to achieve seniority in a 'masculine' culture. The attitudes of retail employers to equal opportunities are assessed, while measures to improve the progress of women in the industry are explored and discussed.

Retailing

The industry

The activity of retailing is defined as 'the sale of goods and services to the ultimate consumer for personal, family or household use' (Cox and Brittain, 1991). Purchases for business or industrial use are not retail transactions and, by definition, retailing is a personal and family affair. Women are highly visible in the world of retailing, being the most likely shopper and, even more likely the shop assistant. Retailers, sometimes called middlemen, act as a bridge between the manufacturer and the consumer. Manufacturers employ mostly men, retail units are staffed primarily by women (Davidson and Cooper, 1992) and the majority of shoppers are women, who have 'traditionally acted as the family's main purchasing agent' (Kotler, 1991).

The retail industry is a major UK employer, providing employment for 2.2 million people, around 8 per cent of the nation's workforce (Department of

Employment, 1991). In December 1992, of the people employed in retailing, 62.3 per cent were female (Department of Employment, 1993). Published figures list retail data in conjunction with distribution, thereby masking the concentration of men in distribution and the concentration of women in shops and administration.

Across the UK there are 348,920 retail outlets, geographically spread, so that the industry is unique in that it maintains a substantial presence in every town and city. The everyday contact with consumers produces a total turnover of £132,704 million (Central Statistical Office, 1991a). Retail sales accounted for £134.96 billion in 1991, with Food Retailers taking £51.99 billion in sales (Central Statistical Office, 1991b). In addition to its high profile as supplier of basic essentials on a daily basis, the retail industry employs substantial numbers of workers, and is currently influential in the evolution of new concepts like shopping cities and out-of-town centres. Retailing has an enormous social impact through employment policies and business strategy (Sparks, 1987).

The range of retail outlets is varied and shops can be categorised roughly into independents, multiples, co-ops or department stores. Independent retailers (traders with less than ten branches) comprise four out of five retail outlets, but collectively account for only 40 per cent of sales (their share having decreased from 65 per cent in 1950 to 40 per cent in 1987). Typically such traders operate as small family businesses, often employing several generations and relatives of one family. Multiple retailers (organisations with more than ten branches), including variety chain stores, account for the major market share, particularly in food, having increased their share from 20 per cent in 1950 to 71 per cent in 1986, often at the expense of independents and department stores (Central Statistical Office, 1991a). Cooperative societies (retailing organisations trading on cooperative principles) collectively the UK's biggest retailer in terms of outlets, have declined in the period 1950 to 1982, halving their market share in the key grocery sector (Central Statistical Office, 1991a). Department stores (stores selling under one roof in separate departments, four or more classes of consumer goods, one being women's or girl's clothing) have declined since the Second World War, and presently account for 4.5 per cent of retail trade. Department store survivors of the competition from multiples offer particular benefits or unique factors to maintain a distinctive image.

Operational trends in modern retailing

In recent years the most successful multiple retailers have capitalised on the advantages of owning their manufacturing sources, giving economies of scale and considerable power. In addition, the biggest retailers have taken control from manufacturers over the distribution channel, either directly, or indirectly by sub-contracting. This advantage, together with the distribution strategy known as 'just in time', obviating costly over-stocking, has given the retail giants known as retail corporations the leading market position they now hold.

Furthermore, the role of information technology in getting the right products to the right place at the right time cannot be underestimated. The communication of sales information to head office almost instantaneously facilitates the actualisation of just in time distribution systems. However, in order to maximise the advantages offered by technology the three key players – retailer, manufacturer and distributor – must either act in concert or be one and the same. The EPOS, EDI and TRADANET[1] facilities enable such unified action to occur, and incidentally concentrate power and control centrally at the point of data capture. Such control has been identified as a contributor to the reduction and deskilling of retail staff, without consultation and reference to their needs and interests (USDAW, 1988). The evidence of the effects of EPOS in retail companies shows that information technology may also be used to enhance the autonomy of store managers, empowering unit managers and sales personnel to offer a courteous and well-informed service to customers. By contrast the centralisation of decisions such as buying and merchandising may lead to erosion of the entrepeneurial skills of experienced managers and staff (McLoughlin and Clark, 1988). New technology has affected workers in different ways and it has been suggested that women's work is particularly vulnerable to deskilling, with an increase in monitoring and control (McNeil, 1987).

The history of retailing suggests that control and centralisation is the key to survival in the market place, and therefore organisations based on bureaucracy and hierarchy are likely to feature as successful retailers. The development and evolution of retailing organisations has encouraged, indeed fostered, centralisation and the persistence of hierarchy to guarantee success or even business survival. Those retailers that eschewed the central power house, like the co-operative societies, are in decline, and they provide a warning to others. Consequently, today's leading multiples are highly centralised organisations with decision-making, information and power concentrated in head office at the pinnacle of a hierarchical structure. Those occupying the base of the organisational pyramid lose power, and in the case of retailing these are largely women.

Culture and power

The power of day-to-day meanings and models in an organisation can be understood in terms of *culture*. The culture of an organisation can be defined in sociological terms, that is, 'the pattern of development reflected in a society's system of knowledge, ideology, values, laws and ritual' (Morgan, 1986). Organisations are mini-societies and corporate culture is a product of history, powerful actors (sometimes called leaders), and what is known as the 'enactment of shared reality' (Morgan, 1986). The daily creation of such shared reality is achieved by maintaining the norms, images, symbols and rituals, by means of unconscious but highly skilled behaviour. For instance 'Many organisations are dominated by gender-related values that bias organisational life in favour of one sex over another' (Morgan, 1986). The culture of retail for example, has been described by Cynthia Cockburn as 'paternalistic, even patriarchal'[2] with 'the caring ethos, however, combined with an authoritarian management style' (1991). Authoritarian or power-type cultural styles (Handy, 1976) have been identified by Sherwood (1990) in a study of UK retail organisations.

In terms of history the retail corporations of today were not born ready-made. They grew from small beginnings as independent retailers, sometimes of the penny-bazaar variety. Such enterprises were typically run by one man, the owner, assisted by staff or family. The familial model with all that it implies is one which many retailers would recognise and indeed encourage as a means to achieve company loyalty. Staff in one leading company experience the comfort and security more often associated with a caring parent than an employer. The managerial control of dress for shop floor staff in multiple retail operations is a particularly visible example of the paternalistic nature of such organisations, and serves to emphasise the distribution of power and authority on gender lines. The controlling manager is likely to be male, the controlled staff female. Indeed the 'hierarchical division of gender is rarely random . . . men tending to occupy the higher and women the lower levels' (Hearn and Parkin, 1987). The tradition of male-as-owner has only recently been altered by the entrepreneurship of women like Anita Roddick and Sophie Mirman, but corporate boards are still almost all-male (Hansard, 1990). Clearly, the culture of today's retail organisations can be seen as product of their history, hierarchies run on paternalistic lines, benefiting staff to be sure, and taken-for granted by members of retail organisations, thus contributing to the models and symbols used to define day-to-day work.

The paternalistic nature of retail organisations gives retail managers legitimacy for demanding conformity from employees. The expectation that staff will rally around common objectives and suppress signs of conflict or questioning is essentially a *unitary* model of organisation. Retailing provides examples of unitary organisations where employees are required to respect the right of the manager to manage and the duty of employees to obey (Morgan, 1986). Senior managers in retail, predominantly male, tend to deny holding power and prefer to talk about leadership authority and control, concepts which coincidentally appear as criteria for selection and promotion.

Alternatives to the unitary frame of reference are those known as, firstly, *pluralistic*, where conflict and power are openly processed to the advantage of members, and, secondly, *radical*, where the organisation is the site of a wider social struggle in power relations like gender, class and race (Fox, 1974; Burrell and Morgan, 1979). Retail organisations may show signs of pluralism at senior levels where functional competition between male directors at head office leads to conflict and power struggles. Unfortunately the senior retail manager operates here at a disadvantage, having a unitary model as given, management of conflict may not be his strong suit. Management development at senior levels tends to have a heavy team-building ethos in order to enable resolution of such conflict. The cost of helping managers at this level to explore their managerial and interpersonal style will be discussed below. The retail industry does not have a history of social struggle, union membership is low, and there is little evidence of radicalism in retail culture.

A so-called masculine culture exists in retailing, a finding reported by Cynthia Cockburn (1989) in her work on equal opportunities. Judi Marshall (1984) noted that there was a widespread tradition of store management being the preserve of the male manager. She states that the desired characteristics of a commercial manager match closely the male stereotype and that women in store management may experience role conflict in consequence. The stereotype of 'manager = male', first identified by Virginia Schein (1973), continues to be held by *both* women and men (Schein, 1989).

The traditional sources of power in organisations are evident in retailing with resources, technology, procedures, decisions, networks, counter-organisations, meanings and models all identifiable as power bases for those who control them. Formal power in retail organisations lies with the network of male senior managers who are the decision-makers and resource controllers at head office. Informal power exists in the usual substructures of an organisation, the models used to inform work activity, the interpersonal networks and, where present, the counter-organisations like staff associations and trade unions. Work activity in retail reflects patriarchal models, and men dominate. Interpersonal networks are used by both men and women, but the old-boy network enables better access to power for men. Staff associations reflect the dominance of men in senior management whilst trade unions *have* provided some power for both men and women members. However retailing has traditionally attracted low trade-union membership. The Union of Shop, Distributive and Allied Workers (USDAW) represented approximately 14 per cent of the retail workforce in 1992 and women represented 60 per cent of this membership (USDAW, 1992a). USDAW, together with the General Municipal and Boilermakers Union and the Transport and General Workers Union, operate through collective agreements with the leading retail multiples.

Retailing and women

Women's employment in retail

Retailing in the UK is primarily a female occupation, particularly in the stores, where women are concentrated in the low-paid part-time positions. This gendering of retail work is reflected in the fact that one in seven, of all women who do work, work in retailing and that 'there is evidence of a continued *feminization of the workforce*' (Sparks, 1992).

The degree of feminization relates to product as follows: women employees dominate in the sectors of food, confectionery and tobacco, clothing and footwear and chemist, where they hold from 60 per cent to 85 per cent of jobs. On the other hand, in the sector selling motor vehicles/parts and household goods women hold from 30 per cent to 50 per cent of jobs (Department of Employment, 1993). Furthermore, employment patterns mirror consumer behaviour in that women dominate the buying of food and clothing, while men dominate the buying of motor cars and luxury household goods (Dibb *et al.*, 1991).

Alongside the relatively high number of women workers in retailing, the other most striking factor is the large number of part-time workers. NEDO (1988) records that 50 per cent of all employees in retailing are now working part-time, and published figures show that 81 per cent of these are women (Department of Employment, 1993). These two trends are connected so that the rising number of women participating in retailing comes from the increasing number of them taking part-time jobs. Estimates suggest that by the year 2000 there will be seven million part-time workers in the UK, a fifth of these working in retailing, and we can expect that at least 88 per cent of this part-time workforce will be women (USDAW, 1992b).

In contrast, however, to the high levels of participation by women in the retail sector, women are not evenly represented in all levels of jobs. L. Collins (1990) states of a national survey that 'although men were only 28 per cent of the workforce, they dominated all the top management positions except in personnel and that in the twenty largest retail companies only three board members were women'. This is further underlined by the NEDO report (1985) which asserts that 'for women who seek a career in retail management, the opportunities are generally fewer and qualitatively different from those available to men'. This view of horizontal segregation in the retailing industry is backed up by Cynthia Cockburn (1991), who, in a case study of a private high street retailer, noted that products and procedures have an influence on the gendering of jobs. In addition vertical segregation is apparent in the way the company is structured, a 'pyramid with its female base . . . topped by a pinnacle of men'.

Women and seniority in retail

According to Gillian Maxwell (1993) 'the preponderance and status of females in retailing is a major, if dormant, equal opportunities issue', particularly proportional representation in senior positions.

Opportunity 2000, an initiative funded by Business in the Community, was launched in 1991 to encourage women in business. The campaign was developed by the Women's Economic Target Team, chaired by Lady Howe, and directed by Liz Bargh. Some retailers have responded with enthusiasm and their activities were recorded in the First Year Report (Opportunity 2000, 1992). In a recessionary year many good intentions were not realised and members varied in approaches to the issue; for example, a strong male champion at board level made dramatic changes in one company, a history of ethical responsibility for employees stimulated a variety of solutions in another, and consumer/product gendering has led to significant redistribution of power at board level in a particular case.

Evidence from a study by Scarlett MccGwire (1992) reveals that 50 per cent of management positions in Littlewoods are held by women, with high participation at all levels. This has been brought about by a five-year action plan begun in 1986 which set target levels for women in management at all grades. Littlewoods has introduced job sharing, flexible working, career-breaks, and a nursery at its head office to facilitate this progressive stance. J. Sainsbury's introduced career-breaks to managerial staff from 1989. A report in 1991 stated that twenty people were on career breaks out of a total of 80,000 employees (G. Sheppard, 1991). Sainsbury's maintain that the steps taken have led to nearly 50 per cent of its management positions being held by women. However, out of 291 stores there are only 5 female store managers and 60 female deputy store managers (L. Collins, 1990). Marks & Spencer introduced job sharing for personnel managers and career breaks for managerial staff in 1991 (L. Collins, 1990). Tesco points to similar efforts to increase its number of women managers, but out of a total of 75,000 employees there are only 60 senior managers who are women. On reviewing W. H. Smith, 11 per cent of their retail managers are women. Out of their 461 stores, 26 have a women as a store manager and of the 162 deputy store managers in the company, 38 are women. At W. H. Smith Retail's head office there is a workplace nursery and an article in July 1993 stated that they were assessing the practicality of childcare vouchers (Jack, 1993). Boots claim that 25 per cent of their store managers are women, compared with 18 per cent in 1991 (*Milton Keynes Citizen*, 1993). Boots started in 1989 actively to encourage job sharing at supervisory and management level. Eighteen months later 30 partnerships had been created. The most typical working format was three days on/three days off, perfect for retailers who trade six days a week (Dawson, 1990). Thus job sharing has an important spin-off for employers in terms of management continuity. However, things are markedly different at one UK retailer, namely Mothercare. Mothercare's main board, previously all men, determining policy for the company's all-women store management team, has recently appointed women to the positions of chief executive, marketing director and merchandise director (McGarrigle, 1993). These changes in board structure have been noted as possibly leading a cultural change at Mothercare so as to refocus the business in order to maximise strategic advantage.

Dr Annette Lawson of the Fawcett Society, a pressure group which campaigns to break down the barriers blocking women's advancement, has reservations about the effectiveness of Opportunity 2000. She said in interview that 'some of the goals the companies set themselves are so vague as to be insignificant'. Yet she believes that Opportunity 2000 is correct in addressing the culture of an organisation and that as 'it will affect men, . . . it will have to be the men who change' (*Retail Week*, 1991). It seems likely that

> the character and composition of the retail labour force poses its own blend of problems and opportunities . . . As retailing is an industry dominated by women and managed by men, considerable scope exists to break down attitude barriers affecting career development and equal opportunities. (Howe *et al.*, 1992).

Those employed in retail on a part-time basis have little or no chance of promotion to management positions as these are specified as full-time. Opportunities for part-time managerial work in the retail sector are exceptional, reflecting the position for women managers generally which suggests that only 3 per cent are able to work part-time, whilst nearly half of the women holding non-managerial positions work part-time (*Labour Force Survey*, 1992). When such instances do occur they relate to particular functions, for example, personnel or training. Additionally such part-time managers have previously held the position full-time, and are often returning after maternity leave. Such arrangements are rarely encountered in line positions in stores. This confirms the traditional belief that in-store operational managers must be present all the time. The meaning of part-time and full-time, interestingly, varies depending on the type of work involved. Medical consultants, MPs and lawyers, primarily male, are rarely referred to as part-timers although many of them work on a sessional basis, in order to accommodate other commitments (Hansard, 1990).

The question of long and unsocial hours in retail management is often put forward as a reason for women's under-representation and the familial model again informs us. Traditionally the male shop-owner was omnipresent. He was there all the time to ensure that stock was replaced and proper service was given to customers, and at the same time exercise control of his staff. The influence of traditional ideas remains, with retail store managers being convinced that their presence is required for proper functioning of the store, especially at peak trading periods. Even if it were humanly possible, the prospect of one person covering a retail store with modern hours of opening, is unrealistic and European comparisons suggest that an ever-present manager is wasteful of a valuable resource. The hours issue may merit closer examination. The so-called reserve army of married women with dependent children are offered part time work to enable them to meet their domestic responsibilities. . .

> In response to the employer's needs, it may not be too surprising to note that women with domestic responsibilities and family commitments can often readily work a varied and flexible number of hours during the day or in the evenings and weekends. (Howe *et al.*, 1992).

However, when this is examined in detail, retail part-time employment is concentrated to cover peak trading times, that is, after 4 p.m. on Thursday and Friday, and all day Saturday and Sunday. These are the very times when domestic responsibilities are at their greatest, with children home from school and meals to be cooked. Evidence suggests that for women retail workers, employment protection and conditions deteriorate in direct proportion to the number of hours worked in a week. An increasing proportion of women in retail are working for less than 16 hours per week and many do not qualify for employment protection. The process of casualisation is likely to proceed further with recent legislation concerning Sunday trading, and 73 per cent of women shop workers surveyed were unhappy about working on Sundays (USDAW, 1992).

The research

The surveys and interviews

Surveys were carried out using two questionnaires, the first completed by 16 personnel directors/managers, who were mostly men, and the second by 36 women retail managers. Additionally, researchers undertook six semi-structured interviews with selected senior women retail managers.

The first questionnaire for personnel directors/managers included direct questions about the proportion of males and females employed in the company, their relative positions of responsibility, the company's equal opportunities policy, provision of flexible working methods and childcare facilities. Additionally, the first questionnaire sought to ascertain the company's attitude to women's opportunities in the firm, such as mobility requirements, training programmes and possible benefits to the business. All respondents were given an assurance that data provided by the questionnaires would be kept anonymous. Respondents gave their opinions as individuals and these may not necessarily be representative of the corporate view.

A second questionnaire for women retail managers was designed to test the proposition that women are under-represented in senior management because the cultures of retail organisations are biased against them, and that women are under-represented in senior management as a result of their own attitudes and choices. Questions covered issues such as: the extent to which different management styles were valued in the organisation, personal management style, career aspirations, career progression, promotion and support for career. The women retail managers were working in various functions in high street chain stores, department stores and out-of-town grocery stores. The women managers targeted were working at the level immediately below store manager because management positions at this level and below are filled predominantly by women, whereas positions at store manager and above are filled primarily by men. Responses from managers at this level would be likely therefore to provide an insight into the reasons why relatively few women progress beyond this level.

Information from both questionnaires was supported and validated by qualitative data obtained from interviews with six women managers in senior positions in retail. The interviews were designed to probe some of the issues highlighted by questionnaire data, such as: the women's opinions regarding their minority status as store managers, progression up the career ladder, particularly in relation to promotion and discrimination, the women's attitudes to the policies and practice of their employers in relation to equal opportunities.

Research findings

Representation of women in retail management

Personnel directors/managers generally agreed that they might be under-utilising the talents of the women in their workforce, and this was a matter of some regret. While most recruit equal numbers of men and women to their management trainee schemes, on equivalent criteria, they report that a majority of female entrants fail to climb the management ladder to the 'glass ceiling', let alone breach it. Findings confirm that employers (or their personnel managers) are genuinely mystified by the drop-out rate of female management trainees and would like to be able to do more about it. Such responses suggest that senior personnel, even in organisations espousing powerful equal opportunities policies, are unaware of their own part in implementing it, an example of the 'power of innocence' (Baddeley and James, 1991). Many male managers are embedded in a culture of innocence in relation to gender, where policy is separated from action which might alter the status quo.

The proportion of women employed in the responding companies confirmed published figures in the wider retail and wholesale sector. The proportion of women as a percentage of total retail employees ranged from 60 per cent to 93 per cent, the average being 77 per cent. Numbers of employees ranged from 1500 to 95 000 and retailers selling gendered products reported appropriately gendered workforces, confirming a degree of horizontal occupational segregation. This was particularly pronounced in one company which retails maternity and childcare products exclusively, where 93 per cent of employees were female.

Companies were asked for details of women in senior positions, and the results suggest that women retail managers do better than women in management generally, that is, retail women are reported to hold roughly 10 per cent of senior and boardroom positions. The most outstanding retailer for board room representation, a privately owned high-street chain, has received public recognition for the measures introduced to increase female participation at senior and board levels.

The women retail managers who completed the second questionnaire were middle managers, half in operations with the other half in support functions such as personnel or buying. This is encouraging, and contrasts with two management studies carried out in 1984 which suggested that at that time the largest proportion of women managers were in support functions (Alban-Metcalfe and Nicholson, 1984). Traditionally in retailing, store management has been primarily the preserve of men, and support functions primarily the preserve of women (Marshall, 1984). The 50:50 finding suggests that this tradition may well be changing.

Equal opportunities

Most companies have specific personnel, usually female, who are responsible for equal opportunities policy and implementation, often a lonely and thankless task. The reality of the struggle experienced by the lone female equal opportunities officer in high street retail was graphically described by Cynthia Cockburn (1991). In addition most companies undertake equal opportunities training for their staff, although only three have formal systems for monitoring equal opportunities, part of the EOC's model of good practice (Straw, 1989). Roughly half of the retail companies were making particular efforts to recruit and retain women as managers, and all respondents were revising their policies regarding matters which have been identified as indirectly discriminatory, for example, marital or parental criteria for selection as trainees, mobility criteria for promotion and access to training. Such revisions may have occurred in response to instances or threats of litigation (EOC, 1989).

The issue of positive discrimination/action was somewhat confused in the surveys, as personnel directors/managers were almost unanimous in their opinion that positive discrimination was not an appropriate method to achieve a gender balance in retail management. However, they all favoured a balanced intake at the recruitment stage. Regarding measures to improve women's opportunities, some organisations have reviewed their training programmes to be more accesible to women and a few would consider women-only training, although this was not a popular option. The statement 'women who leave to have a family should be given retraining on return' was agreed to by a majority of respondents. The powerful innocent, described above, has difficulty with any measures incorporating positive action to enhance women's opportunities, and findings confirm the resistance in retail to progressing women to responsible or demanding positions (Collinson, Knights and Collinson, 1990). Comments from personnel managers emphasised natural justice arguments such as:

- We discriminate on ability only for promotion;
- We are reviewing . . . selection criteria;
- We provide access to management development.

Seven of the companies were, or have since, become signatories of Opportunity 2000, and the initiative was perceived by senior women managers as encouraging companies to 'experiment' with promoting women. A variety of facilities were identified by our respondents as being designed to encourage women to remain or return to employment as retail managers. Table 3.1 shows the range of benefits/facilities and the retailers offering them.

The senior women interviewees did point out that they, as women, hold a tiny minority of senior positions in the company, and one respondent felt that such corporate efforts were 'tokenism' and that salary increases were held back on the grounds that 'she's only here for the pin money'. Five out of the six senior women had experienced the isolation of being the only woman, the issue identified as the greatest barrier to advancement for women managers (Coe, 1992).

Even when companies are 'supportive' and 'create strong policies', the problem lies with 'those in the middle who implement them' as 'they are scared by the idea of promoting women to store manager'. One of the women managers identified the presence of a female chief executive in her company as part of the reason for the increase in opportunities for women. When the women were asked to suggest reasons for the under-representation of women in senior management, lack of facilities A to F in Table 3.1 were again identified, and in addition:

- lack of understanding about women's career ambitions;
- lack of advice concerning career development;
- lack of support.

When asked about employer initiatives to improve women's opportunities, interviewees cited a variety of such initiatives, but found the pace of change very slow and traditional models of work rather persistent. For instance, the introduction of flexible work patterns, job sharing and part-time, were believed by respondents to be realistic options for senior management positions and could become 'the norm' in the future, replacing the belief that the store manager must be there 'all the time'.

TABLE 3.1   Facilities offered by responding retail companies to their employees

Retailers	A	B	C	D	E	F
1						
2	*					
3	*	*	*			
4	*	*	*	*		*
5		*	*			
6		*	*	*		
7	*	*	*	*		
8						
9	*	*	*			
10	*	*	*	*	*	*
11						
12		*	*	*		*
13	*	*	*			
14						
15						
16	*	*	*	*	*	

A = Child care/crèche facilities
B = Job sharing
C = Flexi-time
D = Career-breaks
E = Additional payment for childcare
F = Term-time contracts

The senior women were clear about the absence of any *overt* discrimination against them. However, all six women were aware of subtle negative attitudes which meant that they had had to work 'twice as hard' as their male colleagues to gain promotion. One of the women reported that she felt she had to 'prove' herself before being considered for promotion, and described putting in 'long hours', 'working at home' and being 'noticed because of ability to achieve commercial objectives'. One instance was reported of a senior woman being 'undermined' by male store managers, who were 'expecting me to blow it'. Sometimes the interview data is unexpected in what it reveals about the (possibly discriminatory) behaviour of the women's male colleagues. These findings illustrate the difficulty women themselves have in defining what is and is not discriminatory.

Progression

The women at middle management level reported that 83 per cent had experienced upward job progression in their last three reported positions. The same number of women also claimed not to have ever turned down a career move and 90 per cent of the women stated that their career decisions had not been affected by the degree of commitment required by their company. The women appear therefore to be highly motivated and highly committed to their careers, which supports other work which indicates that women managers are *as* committed and motivated as men or even more so (Davidson and Cooper, 1983; Nicholson and West, 1988). This contrasts with stereotypical attitudes which assume that women managers are less career-oriented and less ambitious than men managers.

Women at middle management level were predominantly childless (73 per cent), half were married, and only one of the six senior women had children. This senior woman admitted that she 'couldn't work without full time child care', and all confirmed that having a family had negative effects on women's career development. This supports other findings that reveal senior women as less likely to be married, have children, or have less children than men in equivalent positions (Davidson and Cooper, 1984). Successful women are confronted with a dilemma concerning children which presents them with a stereotypical male model of career which implies continuous employment, long hours and mobility, and they are forced to choose (White, Cox and Cooper, 1992). For those women who reject the male model the importance of other factors like personal relationships and lifestyle issues take precedence in their career plan (Marshall, 1984). Indeed one middle manager who had children, but who none the less wanted to progress her career, expressed her frustration with this attitude when she commented 'I work part-time and am seen therefore not to be as committed as a full time management team member.'

Overall, a healthy 73 per cent of the women middle managers aspired to move higher than their current level of management, with 80 per cent expecting to reach store manager and above at the peak of their career. When asked what level they realistically expected to reach at the peak of their career, three-quarters of the women still indicated store manager level or above. However, distinctly less indicated that they realistically expected to reach area manager or director level: although 40 per cent of the women wanted to reach this level, only 15 per cent believed they would. This illustrates that the women respondents believed very much in their ability as managers but perceived the existence of a glass ceiling at about area management level. Those who indicated a reason why they thought they would not reach their aspired level gave a variety of responses, though the highest response was the belief that job opportunities would not be given to them in their company.

Perhaps the high number of women *wishing* to progress their careers relates to the high percentage (70 per cent) who felt that to date their career had not been blocked. However, the desire to move higher in the company does not seem to be linked to the notion of a career plan, with only half the women managers having a career plan. This replicates the findings of Marilyn Davidson and Cary Cooper (1983), and gives some support to the idea that women, as found by Hennig and Jardim (1978), do not plan their careers formally, but instead are inclined to make the most of opportunities as they present themselves.

The majority of middle and senior women managers believed that their company did not have clearly defined criteria for promotion, a familiar symptom of possible discriminatory procedures (Collinson, Knights and Collinson, 1990). Of those women who stated that their company *did* have clearly defined promotion criteria, the majority said that these criteria were well communicated and consistently applied – an encouraging sign.

All the senior women had been with their companies for many years. This confirms other research which suggests that women at middle management level, who have established their credibility, find their best chances of promotion lie in staying where they are known and accepted rather than attempting to start again elsewhere (Marshall, 1984). Indeed, four out of our six senior women intended to remain with the company which had supported and challenged them, with five out of the six senior women reporting their experience of support from their employers and believing that any individual with ability could achieve promotion if they are 'determined , ambitious and perform well'. However, the senior manager with children complained that 'employers consider going off to have children resulted in a lack of continuous experience' and that 'people at the top are not understanding that some women want a family and a career'.

Management style and attitudes to work

In completing the second questionnaire the women middle managers were asked to assess themselves on the fourteen items, shown in Table 3.1, adapted from Morgan's lists of 'male' and 'female characteristics (Morgan, 1986).

TABLE 3.2   Morgan's list of 'male' and 'female' characteristics

Male	*Female*
Forceful	Intuitive
Independent	Spontaneous
Logical	Caring
Manipulative	Cooperative
Competitive	Flexible
Resilient	Emotional
Decisive	Thorough

The relationship between the male stereotypical items and the supposed nature of organisations has resulted in corporate values which reflect that stereotype. This may disadvantage women who are likely to display more of the female items. In addition managers were asked to rate the value placed on those items by the organisation. Women identified themselves more with the female list than the male, while the organisation was perceived as valuing a combination of both male and female items. This finding confirms the idea that successful modern organisations adopt a managerial combination of male/female, the so-called androgynous manager described by Alice Sargent (1983). The evidence is further supported by the work of Judy Rosener (1990) who found that the newly discovered 'interactive' leader, usually female, takes a valuable management approach, while the traditional male 'command-and-control' leadership style may not be the last word. A further survey of male managers' perceptions would strengthen the evidence for such an idea.

In examining personal management styles, and their perceived relevance, most women managers reported that they were comfortable or very comfortable with the mainly feminine management style they used at work. This suggests little or no conflict with their current management style nor any pressure to mute their preferred feminine style of management in order to achieve promotion. However, when asked if they would be comfortable working at the next level of management, the women were equally divided, with half confirming increasing lack of comfort with a rise in management level. This finding supports Deborah Sheppard's research which shows that women seeking promotion attempt to blend in with a male organisational reality and experience discomfort in consequence (D. Sheppard, 1989). Although this finding *might* point to the possibility that, at promotion, a different management style is required, an equally valid explanation would be a perceived increase in stress at the next level of management, which might be an inhibitory factor.

Senior women managers were asked about special qualities that they might bring to their work. They reported women managers as 'more caring' and 'understanding' but that they 'can also be hard and business-like'. Women also 'bring a different slant, focus on different concerns, but meet the same aim in terms of business objectives' and women 'have a greater understanding of the pressures of their staff', being perceived as 'more approachable'. Additional qualities mentioned by the senior women were 'strong interpersonal skills', an ability to 'appreciate the problems of those lower down', and women managers have 'more time for people'.

Attitudes of others

When personnel directors/managers were asked to comment on the underrepresentation of women in senior management positions they expressed serious concern (with one exception) perceiving the issue as potentially a matter of competitive advantage. When asked the reasons for women's under-representation at senior levels in the retail industry, respondents identified lack of the facilities shown in Table 3.1 and additionally cited the following barriers to women's advancement:

- Outdated attitudes to women's roles;
- Lack of female role models;
- Women's lack of confidence;
- Long anti-social hours;
- Physically demanding nature of retail work;
- Equal opportunities given low priority;
- Company culture and reluctance to change;
- Male dominance in the organisational hierarchy;
- Unequal access to training and development;
- Women reluctant to accept management positions;
- Women prefer to work part-time.

When asked to consider the possible effects of women's under-representation at senior levels on present or future performance most personnel directors/managers saw the issue as serious, affecting company image, recruitment and staff turnover. Some identified the people focus of women managers as a positive force for culture change, bringing a fresh management style to what has been a rather traditional industry. A minority could perceive no problem with their practice as competitors were operating in similar ways, and change would not be needed until it was legislated for, confirming a worrying lack of awareness of the business case for equality. This confirms interview data which suggests that 'the main thing is that males need to be educated to understand that some women want to have families and a career'.

One interviewee pointed out the crucial importance of 'how others see you' for women in senior positions and this was confirmed by comments about customer attitudes. These reported the degree of negative feeling displayed by *customers* (both men and women), who 'show surprise' when they meet a woman store manager, 'expect a store manager to be a man', and 'think the store manager should be male'. Senior women reported that some members of their staff, often older women *and* men, have remarked on a female as manager, confirming the research by Virginia Schein (1973), mentioned above, which established that managerial qualities were significantly associated with 'maleness' by both men and women. One instance of staff stating that they would 'rather work for a man', gives insight into the persistence of the Schein perception. One of the senior women believed that the presence of women in senior positions would, eventually, improve or alter negative attitudes to them. Some retailers were perceived by senior women managers as 'a bit behind and old-fashioned in their attitudes to women'.

Mentors

Most of the women managers did not have a company mentor to help them with their career planning and promote their interests, a factor known to influence successful careers of men managers (*Harvard Business Review*, 1978). Women managers as protegeés are high-risk for mentors, largely male, as their chances of success are low, and other factors may mitigate against them (Ragins, 1989). Therefore many women work in a careers vacuum, with little company-provided structure to help them progress their careers. Of those senior women who had a mentor, slightly less than half considered that having a mentor had helped them in developing the skills and personal qualities for promotion purposes. This is similar to research by Vivienne Arnold and Marilyn Davidson (1990) which reports that only 58.6 per cent of women managers interviewed found the career development role played by their mentor useful. Role confusion, between line management and mentoring, and cross-gender issues like stereotyping and gossip, were found to limit the effectiveness of some mentor relationships. This ambivalent attitude to the usefulness of mentoring shows that, for a number of reasons, it is not the simple solution to the problem of increasing the proportion of senior women managers that has been suggested in the literature (Ragins, 1989; Kram, 1988; Clutterbuck, 1991).

Conclusion

The under-representation of women in retail management is viewed with some concern, not simply because the implications for equal opportunities, but because many retailers are becoming aware of the business case for encouraging women to seek promotion. One of the most important outcomes of the research was the reported lack of clearly defined promotion criteria in many retail organisations. This indicates the need for retailing companies to look at reviewing their promotion policy and mechanisms for promotion. Further research will establish whether women are better represented at high levels in companies using clearly defined promotion criteria.

In addition the merits of mentoring were not perceived by all the women managers. This may well relate to a need for training and preparation for those involved in mentoring relationships so as to increase their value for women. Only half of the women had a career plan in the traditional sense, and together with the above observations it would appear that many women managers are operating without a career development framework that suits them.

The possibility that women are under-represented in senior management in retailing as a result of their own attitudes and choices is not supported by the evidence. It is clear that the women managers had very positive attitudes to their careers, and they showed high levels of motivation towards furthering their careers. Employment histories showed a clear pattern of upward movement, and their career progress appeared undaunted by the demands by their companies for job moves and the high levels of commitment required in the retail sector. Most significantly, three-quarters of the group wanted to move higher than their current level of management.

The assumption that women differ from men in their attitude towards their work is an enduring one, but research findings do not support it. Brief and Oliver (1976) studied male *and* female retail managers, and found no significant difference between men and women in motives for working. Our findings confirm this, as the women were overwhelmingly committed, ambitious and motivated to progress.

In addition, the large majority of the women did not feel that their career had been blocked, although they recognised other relevant factors such as children and the attitudes of others. Findings suggest that retail culture may not in itself mitigate against women, although management styles may play a part.

The managerial characteristics valued by the companies (as reported by the female managers) did not conform to a male model of management. On the contrary, a more androgynous set of characteristics was identified by respondents as valued by the companies. There was little support therefore for the notion that women are under-represented in senior management because the cultures of the organisations are biased against them.

Retail corporations, enjoying high performance with a largely male management force, may wonder why they should consider trying to change their gender structures by encouraging women to move into senior positions. Putting morality aside, are there good commercial reasons for enabling women to breach the glass ceiling? Demographic changes have led to a decline in high-calibre entrants to retail management and this particular labour shortage may become more visible as the recession ends. The high management turnover experienced by retailers in particular areas may become a liability for the business.

There is evidence that women, having adopted a company/employer as their own, and achieved some seniority, tend to stay loyal to that organisation, in an attempt to reduce some of the effects of gender stereotype (Marshall, 1984). This research supports that contention. Senior women managers may be less likely to move on, taking expensive training and valuable experience with them, as many men do. However women do report frustration with continued and unsuccessful attempts to shatter the glass ceiling and move on. Companies who are putting strategies in place to retain high calibre women can expect to hold a competitive advantage in the future. Retailers obviously have a valuable asset in their female managers and need to adopt strategies that harness their contribution at a senior management level.

Customer service or customer care is a key element for commercial success in retailing, and means more than accessible shops, credit facilities and refurbishment. The managerial style of an organisation cascades into interactions with customers and can affect the image of the organisation for good or ill (Desatnick, 1987). The best examples of customer care training result in assistants trained to walk the customer to the product location in store, or taking the customer to the relevant point of information. Store staff receive less successful training in conflict resolution, being required to passively absorb a customer's fury, discursive accounts and sometimes abuse. Outcomes are familiar: a senior member of staff, usually the manager, is summoned to deal with the problem, and company policy leads to managers increasingly giving away goods to appease irate customers. The style of interaction between manager/customer is often parental and the customer leaves clutching a replacement product, and recounts the event (to at least 9 others we are told) in terms of *the interaction* rather than the outcome (TARP, 1986; Day *et al.*, 1981). A new approach to customer care would identify the quality of the interaction as an opportunity, and women, with their acknowledged superior people skills may be a valuable asset here, particularly where the least desired outcome is a battle and the most desired outcome is consensus and compromise. Women, therefore, may offer potential for a more sensitive management approach in an industry where customer service is key.

Evidence is emerging which suggests that women managers may bring the qualities of 'visionary' and 'high regard for task' to their work as managers, rather more than men do (Vinnicombe, 1987; Rosener, 1990; Ferrario, 1990) so they may be a better bet all round than men! The nature of retailing is changing, as functions dealt with previously in-store are now controlled by central systems. This leaves the main role of a store manager and other senior managers to the leading and motivating of people to achieve performance levels. It is perhaps here that female managers, with their bias towards a feminine style of management, have a role to play in retail management.

Another consideration for retailers may be the cost of training and development for senior managers. Managers in increasingly pluralistic organisations are required to deal with political issues, and be able to manage colleague conflict as well as their own staff. The process of modification can be painful for managers and difficult, relying as it does on the manager reaching some degree of self-knowledge before even considering self-change. One well-established method for achieving the conditions for self-examination is the Outward Bound type of training where managers are exposed to physical challenges in the natural outdoors, a medium to which they are normally not attuned, and development is built on the breaking down of barriers between the men in the group. The benefits of this type of management development lies undoubtedly in its potential for bringing managers to the point of disclosure with their colleagues, and in spite of the expense involved, is considered worthwhile. Women managers who take part in such exercises will attest that it just is not necessary for them. Women do not need Outward Bound to reveal themselves to others: they are higher disclosers than men anyway, in fact the presence of women in a management training group is likely to increase disclosure by everyone, as research shows (Cozby, 1973). So, in terms of the cost of management development, women are cheaper, because they are less barrier-bound, they can change and adapt more easily, more quickly, and therefore more cost-effectively.

The retail industry is fast-moving and receptive to change in the multiplicity of its functions, and this includes management practice. The evolution of retail culture and management style may benefit from policies and practices that encourage women to contribute at senior levels. Successful retailers of the future are likely to take such matters seriously.

Acknowledgement

The authors wish to acknowledge the contribution of Ms Yvonne Airey, who was responsible for some of the data collection and analysis.

Notes

1. EPOS = Electronic Point of Sale (also EFTPOS=Electronic funds transfer at point of sale); EDI = Electronic Data Interchange; TRADANET = Electronic Interchange Network.
2. We are defining *patriarchy* here quite simply as 'a social system where men largely hold key positions of power and authority in business, economics and politics'.

CHAPTER 4

Women in personnel management – re-visioning of a handmaiden's role?

Larraine Gooch and Sue Ledwith

Introduction

This chapter is concerned with the role of women in personnel management and their future within both a changing occupation and a business environment newly focused on the management of human resources as a means of achieving competitive advantage. Given that women have been traditionally associated with the 'soft' (people and welfare) side of managing where they are able to use their caring skills and abilities, on the face of it, personnel as a function dedicated to the management of people would seem to be an 'ideal' job for a woman. Indeed it has been frequently noted that personnel management is a 'traditional stronghold of female (managerial) employment' (Marshall, 1984).

Nevertheless, the evidence is that women rarely make it to the top in personnel despite being the majority both working in the profession and in membership of the Institute of Personnel and Development (IPD). Thus rather than being a special case, Legge (1987) has pointed out, 'women's careers in personnel management provide an 'ideal type' model of the taken-for-granted subordination of women'. In this chapter we examine the patriarchal processes leading to this situation, and discuss the outlook for women in personnel in the future.

First, the development, location and perceptions of women's role in personnel are discussed and evaluated and compared with that of their male counterparts, revealing how roles and functions within personnel have become gendered. An examination of the emergence of human resource management (HRM) follows, and an evaluation of what has become known as 'hard' and 'soft' HRM helps to locate the position of women. This leads into an exploration of personnel's moves towards professionalisation, and the processes of gendered segregation involved in this. A survey of women personnel managers at the early stages of their careers is used to examine how their experiences and aspirations equip them for navigating their futures. Finally the prospects for women in personnel are debated.

Occupational segregation – women's jobs and men's jobs in personnel

Membership figures of the Institute of Personnel Development show that women made up 57 per cent of membership of the profession in 1995. Women also filled the majority of the junior membership positions in the Institute, with men dominating those at the top. Overwhelmingly women members of the IPD were also in the middle and lower levels of personnel management at work, dominating the lowest two rungs on the ladder, personnel/training officer and personnel/training assistant jobs. Women and men were almost equally represented at the middle level of personnel/training manager, but after that there was a runaway lead by men into the top jobs where they dominated senior executive, and director roles.

This evidence of gendered vertical segmentation within personnel has been revealed to be consistent over the years, across studies of the profession. In 1982 Long (1984) found that men moved faster through the lower grades and were over-represented at senior levels: 58 per cent of men were employed at personnel manager and above, compared with 30 per cent of of women.

MacKay and Torrington (1986), in comparing personnel management in the public and private sectors in Britain, found women more likely to be engaged in underdeveloped roles in medium and small establishments, and that they were absent from the senior roles in the largest establishments and organisations. Long (1984) found that women were more likely than men to occupy staff support roles with little or no supervisory responsibility. The continuation of hierarchical, vertical segregation has been accompanied by stereotypical horizontal differentiation of personnel work into 'feminine' welfare and 'masculine' industrial relations (Storey, 1994). Typically, such surveys also found that these differences were reflected in higher salary levels for men (Storey, 1994). Ten years after Long's survey for the IPM, Monks (1993) found that little had changed. In her survey of 103 personnel specialists in Ireland there were more men than women in the top and senior management personnel jobs and fewer men in the junior management posts. This was also the case among the few women in Diane Watson's (1988) study of industrial relations specialists.

Gendering the epistemology

The reality of women's presence in junior, administrative positions and men's in senior personnel and industrial relations (IR) posts has also been strongly reinforced in the mainstream academic literature. At the same time 'personnel' has been disparaged within both management and academic circles as being the 'soft' end of management (i.e. female), in contrast to the 'hard' business of industrial relations (i.e. male) (Townley, 1994). It is also notable that those writers examining the functions and roles of personnel practitioners and human resource management have been mainly men, in some cases using strongly gendered terminology to construct their epistemological models.[1]

One of the most widely used typologies has been Tyson and Fell's (1986; Tyson, 1995) metaphor of the construction industry, itself a singularly masculine preserve. Holders of senior personnel jobs were described as 'architects', involved in the design of organisational structures and having a background of wide experience in both line management and consultancy and, while probably graduates, not necessarily members of the IPD (Storey, 1995). At the middle level, and especially in the industrial relations function, were 'contracts managers', with 'clerks of works' being seen to carry out routine administrative and welfare matters. The clerk of works is also similar to Shipton and McAuley's (1994) 'welfare model' which was represented as a 'traditional, paternalistic view of the personnel function'. It had low power, was essentially reactive and had no role to play in the overall strategy of the organisation' being described as the 'sump of the organisational conscience rather than as a central core organisational activity'. 'Welfare' was identified as an activity to be 'visited on' individuals rather than as a 'corporate and contextual endeavour'. A second low-power, non-strategic role was illustrated by their 'administrative model' which existed to fulfill 'essentially bureaucratic commitments for the directorate'. High power roles were those of the eponymous 'business manager' and 'organisational development' models, both of which operated at strategic levels.

John Storey's (1989) research effectively reinforced these categories and their various designations of power and powerlessness. Storey (1989, 1992b) identified four main types of personnel practitioner. At the top were 'change-makers', those most 'in tune with the new human resource management initiatives'. Like 'architects', 'business managers' and 'OD' practioners, 'changemakers' were those making a highly pro-active, interventionary and strategic contribution.[2] 'Regulators' formulated, promulgated and monitored observance of employment rules, while 'advisers' acted as internal consultants, being in tune with recent developments, but left the running to line and general manager colleagues. At the bottom, and congruent with the 'clerk of works', were 'handmaidens' – a truly female categorisation! Handmaidens were identified as having a role as internal consultant, responding to their 'customers' in their offer of services; a reactive role (Blyton and Turnbull, 1994). Although Storey saw the 'handmaiden' role being to a certain extent a client/contractor relationship with line managers, he also located it within a 'subservient, attendant' framework.

Significantly for the gendered structure of personnel, Storey concludes that 'Personnel management in the UK is largely made up of 'clerks' and 'contracts managers' performing relatively routine administrative functions'. The number of 'architects' is relatively small; a ruling elite?

To add insult to this litany of women's injury, one of the 1990 Workplace Industrial Relations Study (WIRS-3) authors saw fit to comment that 'there did not seem to be much point in registering the gender of the respondents in the 1990 WIRS, since the great majority were men' (quoted in Storey, 1995). Storey (1995) concludes: 'Very few women occupy the senior positions in personnel . . . let alone fill the seats on the main boards.'

So, it is clear that top jobs in personnel remain located in the hands of men both in the rhetoric and the reality, while women are expected to carry out supporting roles in subordinate positions. What follows is an exploration of how this segmentation has developed, and its implications for gender relations in personnel.

Occupational closure and gendered segmentation in personnel

The manner in which horizontal and vertical segmentation has come about in personnel is a clear example of gendered takeover, exclusion and occupational closure in the interests of patriarchy and the male pursuit of professional status (Witz, 1992).

Historically, the function of personnel was owned by women. It was mainly women who in 1913 first set up the Welfare Workers' Association as a social and welfare institution. Women made up 29 of the 34 founder members, and were almost all of the estimated 60–70 welfare workers in factories at the outbreak of the First World War. These women saw their tasks mainly in terms of the 'selection and education of employees and the provision of health and safety, recreative and social institutions' (Niven, 1967) and by 1917 the organisation had expanded to become the Central Association of Welfare Workers. Its objectives were:

> To promote the well-being of the workers in securing, in co-operation with employers and employed, the best possible conditions of work . . . To help all efforts inside and outside the factory, to place industrial relations on a basis of good-will and understanding (Niven, 1967).

However, as early industrialist Edward Cadbury noted, that well-being, cooperation and goodwill comprised only half of the equation. For him, the 'supreme principle' (in industrial organisation) had been the belief that 'business efficiency and the welfare of employees are but different sides of the same problem' (Cadbury, 1912, quoted in Niven, 1967).

As Legge (1987) points out, this was to be the ultimate paradox for women. Initially the connection of welfare and efficiency served to promote women's position in personnel management. However, once it could be extended to connect personnel management – as a more general managerial (and masculine) activity – with efficiency, the days of women's dominance in the occupation became numbered (Legge, 1987). With a new title 'Industrial Welfare Workers', the emphasis shifted away from welfare towards labour management. In 1931 the word 'welfare' was removed altogether from the Institute's title, and it became the Institute of Labour Management (Niven, 1967).

The experiences of managing men in two world wars awakened further interest in the personnel aspects of management and in particular, good workforce relationships. Subsequently more men entered welfare/labour management and in 1946, for the first time, men exceeded women in the membership of the association, which was renamed the Institute of Personnel Management (Townley, 1994). These exclusionary processes continued as the personnel function expanded and developed, and women were increasingly channelled into activities involving the selection of women employees, training and welfare. This was evidenced by Niven (1967, cited in Legge, 1987); increasingly throughout the 1920s and 1930s it became the practice in large companies for the labour/welfare departments to be split into two separated functions: one for men and one for women. This was a division 'which some women found hard to accept especially as they could see themselves being relegated to specifically welfare aspects, leaving male colleagues to undertake the fuller functions of labour management' (Niven, 1967).

As the national concern with labour relations grew over the post-war years of reconstruction and full employment and then of inflation, recession and conflict, so the power of the personnel function increased proportionately to the extent to which it was able to define itself as an industrial relations function (Legge, 1987).

Watson (1977) found that this emphasis on the 'male' activities of negotiation, wage determination and the handling of industrial disputes, went hand in hand with distancing from and, at times, denial of the 'feminine' welfare function. Steadily, gendered occupational closure worked to segregate personnel work into 'feminine' welfare and 'masculine' industrial relations (Long, 1984).

Industrial relations was described by Diane Watson (1988) as a 'relatively distinct elite specialism or sub-specialism within the broader field of personnel management'. Major activities included negotiating with trade unionists, wage and salary planning, dismissing labour, joint consultation, and to a lesser extent manpower [sic] planning. It was a high-level role relating to 'seniority and experience', with functions such as recruitment and selection dealt with by subordinates. At senior level, a significant role for industrial relations was found to be the development of strategy and in some cases in policy-making at industry level through involvement with the employers' national bargaining machinery, especially in the manufacturing and engineering industries. Those involved at this level were all men.

It is likely that the 'cadre' of senior IR managers now holding top personnel posts came from the IR school described by Diane Watson (1988): industrial, shop floor and trade union backgrounds, where hands on experience counted for more than paper qualifications.

It was a career route which few women were able to access, as Monks (1993) also found; many of the women in her study had been promoted into personnel from clerical and secretarial backgrounds and did not have degrees. Their lack of general management experience was seen as crucial in preventing them moving into more senior positions. Among the small number of women IR managers in Diane Watson's study (1988), the lack of shop-floor experience was also seen to have narrowed their career options. It is also worth noting that the women in this study were working mainly in the public sector where, since their experience and background had been restricted, there was more emphasis on formal training.

However, the public sector IR managers who had believed that gaining IPM graduate qualifications would be a passport across the public–private sector divide had not found this to be the case. The trend towards professional qualifications was treated with wariness by existing IR managers, for whom hands-on experience counted for more in the 'theory and practice' debate, especially those in private sector jobs. There was, nevertheless, a recognition among public sector managers that, with the increase generally in higher education, professional qualifications were important for helping a career move and looking good on an application form. Diane Watson (1988) saw that such moves towards personnel as a 'graduate occupation' could bring benefits. Nevertheless, the WIRS-3 survey (Millward *et al.*, 1992) found that by 1990 still only 54 per cent of designated personnel managers (men) had professional educational qualifications.

The maintenance of the eminence of industrial relations specialists despite the reduced role of trade unions in the 1980s and 1990s (Beardwell and Holden, 1994; Millward 1994, Storey, 1995b) reflects interestingly on how such managers have been able to hold on to, and consolidate their positions. It is also notable that the industrial relations route, combined with management experience, has also provided the leadership élite in the professional Institute. The Director General of the IPD at the time of writing, like other senior officers, including general presidents and council members, had all followed such career pathways, several of them in the heartland of British industrial relations – the car industry. The implication here is that old attitudes such as a 'continuing preference for *men* [our emphasis] with line management experience' (Marsh, 1982 in D. Watson, 1988) continue to die hard.

Mechanisms to maintain closure and gender segmentation might include failure to provide supportive equality measures, such as childcare, career-breaks and training and development and further disadvantage women. In Long's study, wastage among women was attributed to family and childcare, while women had significantly less real chance to reach their potential than their male peers while employed in lower-level jobs, being less well counselled and developed, given less satisfying work and being less well paid than men (Long, 1984).

Women's concentration in 'velvet grottos' such as personnel, from which it is difficult to emerge into the mainstream heirarchy may also work to maintain segmentation. Kanter (1977) showed that channelling minority 'deviants' such as black people or women into dead-end jobs, or a 'women's slot', doing routine administrative tasks, ensured that they did not access the mainstream male-dominated heirarchy. She gave several examples of such women in personnel roles. In particular she put affirmative action and equal employment opportunity jobs into this category, saying that while many women would have welcomed the growth and challenge offered, they would not in practice touch such positions: 'the label makes it a dead end. It's a way of putting us out to pasture'. This is a particular irony, since the espoused objective of equal opportunities (EO) is to eliminate the discrimination of women's secondary status and position, not to reinforce it. However the very area of EO and its association with women practitioners is itself controversial and contradictory.

Personnel managers and equal opportunities

This is an area where there has been little research. However some of the findings of Collinson, Knights and Collinson's (1990) study of sex discrimination practices in 64 worksites of 45 companies in five industry sectors, in recruitment and selection, is revealing.

Overall, Collinson *et al.* concluded that both male and female personnel managers, junior and senior, failed to resist or challenge sex-discriminatory practices in their organisations. Instead they implicitly accepted the male 'breadwinner' ideology of line managers, and even sometimes contributed to the taken-for-granted reproduction of sexist customs. The personnel managers did so through explaining away sex discrimination by blaming the women themselves; blaming society generally; and by rationalising discriminatory practices as being the unintended consequences of management seeking to control the labour process at work. Similarly, Jewson and Mason (1986a) found managers justifying their 'circumvention by manipulation' of the formal recruitment process in the interests of efficiency among the racially mixed workforce in their study.

In Collinson *et al.*'s study, male managers in particular focused on the 'perceived incompatibility between economic production and biological reproduction' in justifying their selection preferences for women or men. Similarly, Liff and Dale (1994) also found that managers subtly distorted selection criteria or simply ignored the rules and justified their behaviour on the grounds of operational difficulties; managers generally have been seen to be adept at finding ways round such EO controls (Liff, 1995). The pressure on personnel managers for this 'normalising' and 'naturalising' of sex-discriminatory practices was, claimed Collinson *et al.*, particularly acute because of the public and professional commitment to establishing equality of opportunity required of personnel professionals. It was also especially significant because of the generally marginalised and subordinate role that personnel had in their own organisations, particularly at local level, and where such positions were often held by women. The function there was mainly advisory, administrative and welfarist, and lacked influence. In this situation, personnel's attempts to formalise and standardise selection procedures so as to render line managers more accountable and their practices more consistent, were often perceived as a direct challenge to line 'managers' prerogative and autonomy; described by one manager as 'impractical' and 'insulting'.

Given their insecure position within the managerial structures, personnel managers were seen to have an overriding concern for their own careers; in acquiring personal and professional credibility in the eyes of other senior managers (mainly male), even over their professional identity as personnel specialists.

Only one case was reported by Collinson *et al.* (1990) where a discriminatory recruitment decision was overturned. This was by a female corporate personnel manager with equal opportunities responsibilities in the banking sector who had been alerted by the woman concerned, who herself was able to draw on her trade union connections and skills to challenge the original decision.

The description of personnel in Collinson *et al.*'s study, although not adequately or systematically locating the gendering which goes on within the personnel function itself, does reflect the discussion so far in this chapter about the gendered and segmented nature of personnel. That Collinson *et al.*'s (1990) powerless personnel managers were mainly female illustrates well women's double subordination; as women in personnel, and as personnel managers in relation to line management within their organisational structures.

Customarily located within the personnel function, equal opportunities is often staffed by women. When Aitkenhead and Liff (1991) investigated the understanding within work organisations of equal opportunities they found their sample of those responsible for EO to be personnel specialists, of whom nearly half were women. They described the results of their survey as 'depressing' and, as others have found, there remains a lack of the commitment, resources and status (Hammond and Holton, 1991), or indeed a real understanding of the complex issues of discrimination and inequality, to do more than develop an EO policy mainly geared to the recruitment process (Aitkenhead and Liff, 1991). Although employers are increasingly carrying out monitoring, provide procedures and training to support equality recruitment practices, career-breaks, job shares and flexible hours (MccGwire, 1992; Opportunity 2000, 1994; Kandola and Fullerton, 1994) this is mainly within a relatively safe, EO 'liberal' framework (Jewson and Mason, 1986b). The more difficult and challenging aspects of discrimination such as issues of sexuality and sexual harassment are much less frequently dealt with. For example although studies show that a high proportion of women report experiences of sexual harassment – from 11 UK studies, between 16 per cent and 75 per cent of women at work, and 95 per cent of female students did so (reported by Wilson, 1995) – yet are rarely taken seriously. In one survey of 110 British companies, 61 per cent of women had experienced some form of sexual harassment at work. Yet over a third of personnel directors did not regard it as a serious management issue; 88 per cent had no policy statement and over half said that when a case was brought to their attention the harasser never faced dismissal (Wilson, 1995).

Dilemmas for personnel practitioners

The supremacy of the experienced IR-oriented senior male manager discussed earlier has itself recently been under threat from a new model of personnel: human resource management (HRM). This is now considered, prior to addressing the implications for women.

The concept of HRM developed in the 1980s as a response to industry restructuring fuelled by radical changes in the political and economic climate and the strong focus on business results. The route to competitive advantage was seen to be through improvements in the management of people and organisational structures; 'in other words, through better utilization of human resources' (Guest, 1987). Impatience with traditional personnel management for not delivering the business success led to line managers (predominantly male) increasingly taking on HR functions. The 1990 WIRS-3 survey (Millward *et al.*, 1992) found a continued absence of representation of a specialist personnel function at board level in something like two-thirds of even large organisations, and an increase in the role of line managers with personnel responsibilities (Storey, 1995b), while Purcell and Ahlstrand (1994) found managers increasingly questioning the role of the corporate personnel department. There is also a view that in an increasingly unitary climate, personnel's heavy involvement with IR and trade union issues may have led to its exclusion from strategic management decisions and segmentation into an isolated department (Marginson *et al.*, 1988, cited in Legge, 1995)

This shift from personnel specialism to mainstream management of human resources represents the latest phase in an ongoing contest (D. Watson, 1988) between two sets of managers – both predominantly male – for control of the personnel/HRM function in a time of restructuring, and a decrease in job opportunities, and one that line management seems to be 'winning'. Furthermore, the trends towards decentralisation of personnel's key activities have in part led to corporate personnel taking a more monitoring and controlling function and playing less of an operations role in the personnel sphere (Purcell and Ahlstrand, 1994).

The outcome of these tensions therefore is critical to personnel as a specialism which finds itself in a state of crisis and transition. The main elements of the crisis are now discussed.

First is the issue of credibility. As Legge (1995) cogently argues, personnel managers have always faced a problem of credibility stemming from the contradictions already identified, and from an ambiguity which is 'the hallmark of personnel' (Purcell and Ahlstrand, 1994). On the one hand it is personnel's special expertise which maintains the smooth flow of production and services through its relations with labour – both as individuals and collectively organised into trade unions. However, the very smoothness of these relations may render personnel invisible, with the risk of being starved of resources and excluded from decision-making (Watson, 1986, cited in Legge, 1995). Visibility on the other hand, arises through the resolution or attempted resolution of industrial conflict, both individual and unorganised such as labour turnover and absence, and collective disputes and industrial action. However the presence of industrial conflict is perceived by business as 'bad'; thus personnel and IR specialists become associated with negatives in the managing of human resources. Such negativity may be ameliorated in the short term through being identified positively as having resolved conflict, but overall the picture of personnel as problem-centred is not conducive to an image of a responsible profession. Legge (1987, 1995) refers to this as the 'vicious circle in personnel management'.

A second credibility gap arises through the feminisation of personnel. This is a question raised by Storey (1995) under the heading 'Still a Cinderella function?' when trying to account for the 'remarkable' significance' of the continuing absence of HRM specialists on company boards (30 per cent of companies). Moreover, Legge (1995) offers the observation that to 'background' the image of women in the profession (through subordination to junior roles and status) is to deny the origins and foundation of personnel as a specialist occupation. In this denial lies the danger of business raising questions about the validity and necessity for such a specialist occupation at all.

It seems clear to us that the dilemma that this woman question raises is at least partly dealt with within the profession by the gendering of 'women's' work into low-level roles such as those of handmaiden and clerk of works as discussed above. Nevertheless, if, as Etzioni (1969) has noted, an occupation which becomes dominated by women is assigned the status of a 'semi-profession', then ways of maintaining male domination become significant for personnel. It may have been thought that in addition to challenging personnel, HRM also offered a new route to credibility through its association with strategic management and business policy (Townley, 1994).

It was during the period of the rise of HRM that the Institute of Personnel Management (IPM) and the Institute of Training and Development (ITD), the two main professional associations, opened negotiations leading to their merger in 1994 as the Institute of Personnel and Development (IPD).[3] There is no evidence in the form and structure of the new Institute that gender issues, such as those raised here, were addressed in the merger talks, despite some evidence of female members' discontent. We return to this issue later in the chapter. Meanwhile, the next section discusses the impact on personnel of HRM, before moving on to examine personnel's situation as a profession.

Human resource management

The rise of HRM, as outlined in the previous section, has been extensively discussed and analysed (for example Guest, 1987, 1989a, 1990; Hendry and Pettigrew, 1990; Storey, 1989, 1992a,b, 1995b). Crossing the Atlantic from the USA (Fombrum, Tichy and Devanna, 1984) in the early 1980s, it has been identified variously as a 'vocabulary for managing the employment relationship', a revised set of titles for personnel jobs and education programmes; and the genesis of new academic journals (Legge, 1995). Much more managerialist in focus than personnel, HRM is an area of senior management responsibility and line management implementation (Townley, 1994). Its major themes are those identified in Guest's (1987) model: integration, commitment, quality and flexibility, all directed to supporting business strategically.

From all of this have emerged two main, overlapping, versions of HRM: 'hard' and 'soft'. The notion of 'hard' HRM emphasises the 'quantitative, calculative and business strategic aspects of managing the headcount resource in as 'rational' a way as for any other economic factor' (Storey, 1989, 1995b). Note the emphasis here on phrases related to the 'hard' business areas of finance and accounting such as 'quantitative' and 'calculative'. The implication is that 'hard', strategic HRM is about taking care of the bottom line of business – something that rhetoric had said personnel had failed to do.

'Soft' HRM, while still stressing the significance of integrating human resourcing with business strategy, is characterised by the emphasis on 'communication, motivation and leadership' (Storey, 1992b). There is an emphasis on gaining commitment using 'key levers' of 'nurturing', 'harmonisation' and 'teamwork' (Storey, 1992b). HRM sees employees as valued assets, worthy of 'trust' and 'collaboration' and capable of development through 'participation and informed choice' (Beer and Spector, 1985, in Legge, 1995).

The connotations here are of 'empowerment', of creativity, and enablement; employees are pro-active rather than passive inputs into productive processes; there is a mutuality involved in soft HRM (Legge, 1995). 'Soft' HRM could be described as the 'human' side of the enterprise.

However, even companies such as BP and IBM, Marks & Spencer, upheld in the literature as model employers of the 'soft' kind, have illustrated that when the bottom line shows up in the red, 'hard' 'quantitative' 'calculative' HRM strategies are adopted. A synthesing of hard and soft HRM in this way becomes 'tough love' (Legge, 1995), and by sugaring the pill of hard with the soft 'obscures the less than pleasant reality' (Guest, 1990 in Legge, 1995). Legge (1995) discusses this HRM 'mask' for the 'less acceptable face of enterprise culture' in some detail, exposing how the rhetoric involved seems both to preserve company images and to sanitize the reality of the workings of 'free' market forces. She concludes from a review of the research into practical HRM that there is little evidence of the 'soft' HRM approach, and that it is a 'mirage retreating into a receding' economic and political horizon.

This loss, if it is one, is also a loss for women in the profession, for whom the 'soft' HRM script might have been especially written. It was the women's movement which first launched the term 'empowerment' into the modern lexicon of personal release and self-fulfilment. The original values of the profession itself, of workforce cooperation, well-being and understanding were developed by the women Welfare Workers of 1913, and are echoed in the language of HRM such as its expression of the 'optimistic desire to improve the opportunities for people at work' and that the potential for human growth is central to the 'soft' HRM model (Guest, 1990, in Legge, 1995). The general management literature has recently also brought into the mainstream the creative, inclusive and 'transformational' side of management style, attributed particularly to women (Rosener 1990; Marshall, 1984; Morgan 1986).

By the late 1980s, however, 'the most perspicacious personnel managers' realised the need for a new rhetoric to assert credibility and enrol potential supporters; one that would 'perform the dual, if paradoxical, function of highlighting a new specialist contribution, while simultaneously locating themselves unequivocally within the management team' (Legge, 1995). The introduction of general management and finance as subjects into the IPM's stage 1 professional examination syllabus around this time represented a practical expression of such perspicacity. For the newly labelled personnel-turned-HRM professional, a 'skilful interweaving of the rhetorics of the hard and soft models' was intended to maintain both the paradox and the position (Legge, 1995). In updating his 'architect' model, Tyson (1995) provides a nice example. He offers two 'advanced versions': 'change agent' and 'business manager'. These are often 'new brooms' brought in to sweep away the old emotional baggage of personnel and 'envision' the future. The 'business manager' version offers 'credibility with senior colleagues', and 'orientation to relevance and value for money'. Meanwhile he suggests that the 'change agent' is likely to be on a short-term contract or a self-employed consultant. Thus, as Legge (1995) remarks, the new language offers personnel practitioners a mechanism for maintaining and enhancing their position, of having 'their cake and eating it'.

Moreover, as Monks' (1993) research confirms, this realignment between the notions of personnel – concerned with 'procedures', 'consistency', 'control' and 'monitoring' (Storey, 1992a) – and HRM, which is strategic, has been a gendered realignment. As Townley (1994) comments; 'Put bluntly, the focus of HRM – an agenda, in the main, prescribed by men – has been 'important' men in one field talking to, reflecting and reporting on 'important' men in another'. The 'skilful interweaving' described by Legge (1995) had performed the dual functions of attempting to regain the ground for personnel specialists in the new world of HR, while simultaneously achieving exclusion of women.

If this continues to be the case, then the partnership forged between the new rhetoric and new practices will have been effective in maintaining the gendered distinctions within the profession.

The Institute of Personnel and Development

We move on now to discuss the role of personnel and its project to become a profession. A profession may be characterised as an occupation which has successfully struggled for the right to control its own work and has thus been granted legitimate organised autonomy, usually by a dominant élite or the state (Freidson, 1970a, 1970b). The process by which this takes place is seen as a strategy of exclusionary occupational closure designed to limit and control the supply of entrants to an occupation in order to enhance its market value (Parkin, 1979). In 1975 the IPM first introduced its examinations which, together with three years' personnel experience, qualified members for 'corporate membership', thereby restricting voting on decisions in the Institute to this category of membership. Since men dominated the membership at this and higher membership levels, it is not suprising that there have only been three female presidents since 1933. Twenty years after the establishment of corporate membership, the new IPD's own figures still show, in Table 4.1, that the majority of corporate members are men – with women dominating the lower, non-voting categories, especially those at graduate education level and studying for IPD qualifications.

Black and Asian members are also mainly found at this level. analysis of IPM membership found that about 2.2 per cent were from ethnic minority groups, with a 'much higher proportion . . . concentrated at student-member level than are white members' (Paddison, 1991).

The authors of a 1992 survey of over 1100 IPM members observed that the 'qualification itself is thought to be hard work, but necessary for those entering a career in personnel'. In addition, the survey found that senior practitioners did not necessarily have the IPM qualification themselves, yet they did require it from younger staff – at whom they thought it was principally aimed and for whom they felt it had the most value (ICM, 1992).

As already seen, only half of personnel practitioners actually have professional educational qualifications (Millward *et al.*, 1992), suggesting that these are not a requirement for many personnel management jobs. The implication from this is that the IPD has not yet achieved full professionalisation.

TABLE 4.1   **IPD membership figures 1995**

Membership grade	Male	Female	% Female
Companion	197	44	18
Fellow	4 935	1 033	17
Corporate member	14 842	9 191	38
Graduate	3 391	12 124	78
Affiliate (studying)	2 208	10 486	83
Affiliate (non-studying)	2 156	2 340	52
Licentiate member	730	3 648	83
Associate member	4 662	5 582	54
Totals:	33 121	44 448	57

Source: IPD Membership Department, 1995.

The gendered nature of personnel is a central feature of its project of professionalisation. Simpson and Simpson (1969) argued that the dominance of women limited the ability of a profession to gain the full status of a profession, while Hearn (1982) redefined professionalisation as a patriarchal process where semi-professionalisation indicates a state of partial male dominance of an activity, and full professionalisation indicates complete male control. Witz (1992) has further fruitfully developed the analysis of the gendered nature of the process of professionalisation.

As explored in the previous section, these processes have been at work within personnel, systematically excluding women from senior, high status, high pay positions in both the personnel function and the Institute. Legge (1987) identifies the contradictions leading to this state as 'when an occupation is seen as peripheral to central management . . . concerns and far removed from strategic decision-making, then women may play a central role and reach the top.' Once the occupation becomes recognized as no longer peripheral and as a valid contributor to strategic decision-making, then women may be 'elbowed out' or 'politely pushed aside' – often with 'their own unconscious collusion'.

Such unconsciousness may also be a reflection of the gender-neutral language of the IPD's mission and objectives. These are centred on the dual aims of advancing the 'management and development of *people*' (our emphasis) and serving the 'professional interests of *members*' (our emphasis), implying tacitly that all members are equal. There is no explicit recognition of the gender (or race) differences among its membership. This has the effect of masking and thus effectively denying the actual situation of systematic subordination of its female membership.

There are some signs of a developing consciousness within the Institute; the membership is now monitored by gender, race, age and job category, but although available the figures are not routinely published. It is also possible for part-time work experience to be aggregated to enable membership upgrading into the senior, voting category of corporate member and above. Given women's careers, typically broken and containing part-time work periods to fit with children, this is an important facility. However, it is not widely known about and the main focus of the IPD's attention regarding equality issues is to produce a new best practice code[4] to highlight the importance of managing diversity in the workforce. A bursary award scheme is also planned to help people from disadvantaged groups to progress a career in personnel management. An annual prize has also been introduced for the best IPD management reports on equal opportunities (EOR, 1995).

A panel of equal opportunities experts within the IPD itself, and a titled officer exist, but the panel rarely meets, and the officer's job is focused mainly on preparing and offering guidance to the professionals, not on the membership itself. There is no formal association of women members and no provision for women to be proportionately represented on the ruling bodies. At the time of writing only one or two branches are known to have organised women's groupings, and although women in personnel do network, this tends to be done 'discreetly' to avoid the negative connotations which might be put on such practices by senior and influential members. And although the Institute was a 'supporter' of Opportunity 2000 (the voluntary campaign to improve the quality and quantity of women in the workforce by the millenium) at its start in 1991, by 1995 it was still not a member itself.

Although the message from the Institute is that there has been no pressure from grass roots to promote the role of women in personnel, there was some evidence of dissatisfaction from women in the 1992 ICM report for the IPM. Women's discontent centred on networking: in particular, access to region/branch activities, and opportunities to join special interest groups. Younger members were also much more dissatisfied about networking than older groups; many of the younger members are women. In addition, th

involvement of women members at branch/group and national level ran at almost 100 per cent (men's non-involvement was not much lower, at 82–87 per cent) with twice as many women as men finding the timing of meetings difficult, some of them because of their families.

In the light of the earlier discussion about the extent to which personnel is a profession, it also is interesting that this same study found extensive criticism by the membership of the IPM in its seeming inability to establish professional status.

Furthermore, the association of the 'élite' in personnel – the Society of Chief Personnel Officers (SOCPO) – is also male dominated. While SOCPO's two most recent presidents were women, there are only two women on its National Executive. In London and the south-east, membership is atypical, with up to a fifth being women. The Society, among whose members there is dual membership with the IPD, sees itself as providing a 'network' and route to government policy decision making for chief personnel officers of 450 local authorities within England and Wales. It has an equal opportunities working party whose purpose is to share good practice in their own local authorities. However, like the IPD, and which it meets every six months, there are no plans for addressing the gender issue within SOCPO itself, although their recent decision to open membership up to senior personnel officers may bring in more women.

Re-visioning of women in personnel?

Running alongside the rather depressing findings of women's continued subordination in gendered occupations and specialisms, is the case argued by Julie Storey (1994) for a 're-visioning' of women's careers in personnel from their own, female perspective. Such an approach gives voice and visibility to women's own perceptions of their careers, strengths and aspirations, which may be separate and different from those of their male colleagues. Storey describes this as a 'deliberate attempt to move away from socially-defined critera of success such as organisational status and salary towards individual perceptions of success and achievement of personal goals'. The concept of re-visioning also offers a wider space to include the whole of women's lives rather than compartmentalising them into rigid and unrelated spheres (Bell and Nkomo, 1992) especially work and family.

In Julie Storey's case studies of five women in personnel, she found that success was viewed in terms of the extent to which the women felt that their potential was being used. The women's primary career goal was self-fulfilment, and their main motivation derived from doing work which they enjoyed, made full use of their skills and abilities, and involved personal development. A number had discounted promotion opportunities where they had felt that taking them would not give them intrinsic satisfaction. They were also looking for recognition from others, including through status and salary – though it should be recognised that these will necessarily be shaped by the prevailing gender values in their organisation. Storey also found that concern for relationships was important; this included the balance between work and family roles and led to a view of themselves as one of 'connectedness' (Marshall, 1984, cited in Julie Storey, 1994).

Taking a re-visioning view of women's role and aspirations in personnel, it could be that the new HR packaging offers opportunities for women to reclaim 'soft' aspects of HRM and to seek openings into the changed world of HRM on their own ground. One area of personnel which at first glance does have significant potential, but which is neglected in the HRM debate, is training and development. In a post-modern era of rapid technological change accompanied by increased fluidity and flexibility of employment, has come the need for a workforce with a high level of skills and knowledge. WIRS-3 found that by 1990 increased emphasis was being put on training and competencies, leading to new demands for specialists in this area. Notwithstanding this 'felt need', the evidence seemed to be of a substantial fall in the number of designated training specialists, with 82 per cent of non-specialist managers regarding themselves as having the responsibility for training (Millward *et al.*, 1992). Also, training has not yet been a high status role on the personnel agenda, tending to be seen as representing a 'soft' area devolved to women (Townley, 1994); when it is high status it takes on a grander label such as Organisational Development (OD), and is managed by men. One feature of labour market changes and organisational down-sizing, decentralisation and restructuring is that training and OD specialists are moving out into consultancy roles (always an area boosted by redundancy). It may be that women's identified strengths as facilitators, and their preferences for self-development, could enable them to claim this as terrain for a re-visioning of their personnel careers both inside their organisations, and externally as consultants and entrepreneurs.

The approach of re-visioning is also helpful in considering the results of a larger study carried out by Larraine Gooch (1992) among 149 junior women studying on a part-time basis for examinations leading to graduate membership of the Institute of Personnel Management (IPM) in 1992.

The purpose of the study was to consider the motivations and career aspirations of women at the start of their personnel careers. It was felt that since women predominate at junior levels at work and as students within the Institute, they formed the very group from whom it might be expected that the more senior positions in personnel would be filled in the future. The women from colleges in each of the nine regions covered by the Institute completed a 12-page postal questionnaire.

Personal and family issues

Two-thirds of the women in the survey were under 35 years of age (see Table 4.2) and, with less than two years' experience in personnel, were just starting out on their careers in personnel. The majority worked full-time and, although they were employed by large organisations, the women themselves tended to work in small workplaces with less than 200 people. There was an equal spread of the women between public and private sectors.

As Table 4.2 shows, the majority of the women lived with a partner but had no children, although many indicated that they intended to have a family in the future. Among the 31 per cent who did have children, the strains of balancing family and work created conflict and mental stress, with two-thirds of the mothers having to restrict their career choice. For some it had led to loss of seniority at work. Less than half the employers of the women in the survey offered career-breaks, and only 22 worked for organisations where a crêche or nursery was provided, with seven women reporting holiday club provision. Long working hours and the tradition of personnel as a full-time occupation meant that few women (9 women) either worked part-time or expected to have that opportunity. Of the few who were able to work flexible hours, half said that these did not fit in with children's school times.

TABLE 4.2   Personal characteristics of women IPM students

			Single/ divorced	Married/ partner	Had children	
Under 35	35–44	45 +			Yes	No
103 (69%)	36 (24%)	10 (7%)	47 (32%)	100 (68%)	46 (31%)	103 (69%)

Work and career

It can be seen from the figures in Table 4.3. that 125 or 84 per cent of the women respondents in the survey were in junior positions.

By far the most common main activities of the women centred on recruitment (see Table 4.4), with only 13 per cent involved in employee relations and

TABLE 4.3 **Personnel jobs held by women IPM students**

Own job title	Number	%
Personnel director	2	1
Senior personnel manager	4	3
———————————————————————————————————		
Personnel manager	13	9
———————————————————————————————————		
Senior personnel officer	17	12
Personnel officer	52	36
Junior personnel officer	34	24
Other	22	15
Total responding	144	100

——— represents the divide between junior and middle jobs and then between middle level and top positions, i.e. the 'Glass Ceiling'.[5]

TABLE 4.4 **Main activities of current post compared with those of the most senior personnel person in their organisation**

Activity	Number of women	%	Most senior person's main activities	
			Number	%
Strategy	0	0	5	3
Policy	0	0	1	1
Employee relations	19	13	41	33
General personnel	18	13	44	35
Training/management development	17	12	4	3
Personnel administration	4	3	0	0
Recruitment	73	51	5	4
Other (equal opportunities, systems, manpower planning)	12	8	22	18
			(Other and not known)	
Total	143 responses		125 responses	

13 per cent in general personnel; the two main specialisms of the most senior personnel person in their organisation. These patterns reflect the gendered horizontal and vertical occupational segregation within personnel found in other studies and discussed earlier.

Many of the women seemed to be well aware of these patterns, and of what was needed to get on in their organisations. Although they themselves were all studying for the Institute's examinations, only a quarter of them saw the qualification as important for gaining credibility, or for promotion. A quarter of the women also recognised that for men the qualification was not considered important. As they said: 'Men tend to get the top jobs in any case.' and 'Men tend to obtain alternative acceptable qualifications', with one woman echoing the research findings outlined earlier: 'Few Personnel Directors are personnel professionals.' Such perceptions accurately reflect the career patterns of top men in personnel discussed in the section above on 'Occupational closure and gendered segmentation in personnel'.

For these women, 'personal development' was by far the most important reason that they gave for doing their IPM courses, with the material factor of pay, along with 'for job satisfaction' at the bottom of their lists of reasons.

Aspirations and expectations

From the way in which they reported their aspirations and expectations it would seem that the women in the survey had a good understanding of the effects of this gendering. Although two-thirds said that they had planned their career goals, only a quarter aspired to personnel director level, with a minute proportion, 11 per cent (16 women), expecting to reach it. A third aspired, and expected, to reach the middle level of personnel manager. It becomes clear that a 'glass ceiling' operates in personnel above this level. This was acknowledged by the women; for example: 'my experience suggests that in local government, tradition and traditional gender roles exist and are perpetuated. This bars women to some extent from reaching senior personnel posts.'

The reasons the women gave for their limited career hopes centred on the tensions between family and work and on their own lack of confidence in their abilities. From the comments of the 46 women who cited the effects of the home/work conflict it was clear that the main issues were that 'male dominated culture means working long hours', 'lack of flexible working hours', and career-breaks if taken, meant a loss of seniority and difficulties in re-entry into personnel. Indeed for a few of the women, their motivation for studying for the IPM qualifications was to get back into personnel work after having had children. On top of the reported stresses of parenting, 83 per cent of those with husbands or partners said that their partner's job meant a lack of mobility in pursuit of their own career, with 12 women identifying other dependants and children's schooling as other limiting factors. Nor is there always patience and understanding for such women among their female colleagues:

> I feel many women make a conscious choice to limit their career prospects by allowing family concerns to dominate, and it is therefore inevitable that some women will not reach senior levels. (Woman in personnel)

> Within my organisation, the most senior women in personnel are career women and are the worst enemy of those like myself whose career is important to them but not exclusive of having children and family life. In their opinion it is 'either or'. (Woman in personnel)

A feeling that they lacked ability in personnel, and the lack of opportunity to acquire this, also featured strongly in the reasons women gave for not expecting to reach the top. There were some who were looking for opportunities to use their skills and experience more fully, and to have them recognised: 'I would like to see a concerted effort by all to view males and females by their skills, knowledge and attributes and completely ignore gender.' and 'Women are an untapped resource who can be an invaluable asset if only given the opportunity.'

The women so far had had training mainly in presentation skills and team building. Only a third had been trained in assertion, leadership, communication and negotiation, with a mere handful having been on courses for confidence building and conflict handling. Some women suggested that the Institute could improve things for them by particularly considering the educational needs of women in personnel, and by providing refresher courses for women returners.

These views were coupled with their beliefs that the image of personnel as a female occupation was detrimental to women pursuing careers. Few of the women were able to identify female senior role models, and it was felt that this was an important factor in reinforcing the general view of personnel as a low status function in their organisations:

> Personnel is not respected. That is why few men wish to work within the function except at a more senior level. (Woman in personnel)

> My organisation is a highly dominated female workforce although it is rare for women to hold senior management positions – within both personnel and the organisation as a whole. (Woman in personnel)

Nearly a quarter of the women identified discrimination against women as a reason for the lack of career routes for women – this was despite the fact that over three-quarters of all the women reported that they worked for an 'equal opportunities' employer. However, we have already seen in the discussion around the family that few of the organisations where the women worked provided support systems such as childcare. Yet it was reported that in over half of their organisations it was the personnel department which was responsible for implementation of EO policy. It would appear that these employers were either not sufficiently committed to equal opportunities to ensure that it was effectively implemented, or their personnel departments had been insufficiently persuasive.

Other measures which are well known to help career progress – for both women and men – include mentoring (Arnold and Davidson, 1990; Clutterbuck, 1985) and networking (Beck and Steel, 1989; Coe 1992). These were both areas where the women in personnel reported gaps. Only a third had a mentor – and as can be seen in Table 4.5 – 60 per cent of those were men. Three-quarters of the women who had been mentored reported that their mentors had encouraged them to think about methods of achieving promotion. Over half of all the women surveyed said that they believed their career progress would have been helped by having a mentor.

As for networking, only nine of the women reported belonging to a women's networking group, with 94 per cent of the women not doing so. Nevertheless, the women did report informal support systems. Husbands provided two-thirds of the women with support, with female colleagues supporting 43 per cent and one in five getting backing from female friends outside work. Male colleagues also supported nearly a quarter of the women (see Table 4.5).

As students studying for the Institute's examinations, 84 per cent of the women thought that the IPM could do more to advance the career progression of women in personnel. The single most popular measure identified (by 62 per cent of the respondents) was to promote part-time working and career-breaks, with 'providing refresher courses for women returners' mentioned by just over half the women. A third thought that rendering women more visible through devoting a section of the Institute's journal to issues of women in personnel would also help. Increasing the proportion of women on the Institute's formal committees at national and branch level was seen by a quarter of the women as a way of improving things.

TABLE 4.5   Personnel women: mentoring, networks and support

Mentor		Belong to network		Other main support			Friends	
M	F	Yes	No	Husband	Colleagues		F	M
					Female	Male		
28	19	9	134	88	60	32	30	21
(60%)	(40%)	(6%)	(94%)	(63%)	(43%)	(23%)	(21%)	(15%)
47 responses		143 responses		Multi-response				

Women's strengths

On the benefit side, using Schein's (1976) work, the women were asked to identify and rank attributes which related to them. Top of the list were 'helpful' and 'aware of the feelings of others' and having human values, with 'competitive' and 'aggressive' at the bottom. These also reflected the women's perceptions of personnel as being about 'dealing with people' and which had led them to choose a career in personnel. While these attributes would not at first glance appear to equip the women well for fighting their way up the male career ladder, they may have relevance for a form of facilitative change agent, especially when coupled with the main motivators identified by the women. These were primarily having work which was challenging, where accomplishment was valued, and where there were opportunities to improve knowledge and gain advancement. These are similar findings to Julie Storey's, outlined above, and to other research (Marshall, 1994; Alban-Metcalfe and Nicholas, 1984), and do not in the main reflect the general negative mythology about women's motivation to work, especially since as found by White, Cox and Cooper (1992) they are also the motivators of male high-flyers.

With such evidence of women's strengths becoming increasingly available and being addressed by more mainstream management commentators, this does offer the opportunity for women's strengths and aspirations to gain increased visibility and currency. As one of the women in personnel put it: 'the work which many women in personnel pursue is being undervalued'.

In particular the concepts of re-visioning (Julie Storey, 1994) and 're-evaluating' used by Judi Marshall (1994) to describe the mid-life developments of women, may be helpful in changing attitudes to work and career more widely. Two of the women personnel respondents should have the last words on this:

> I feel strong and assertive in my role and do not view personnel as a weak function. (Woman in personnel)

> I feel that women ought to change their attitude, demand more and take a positive, pro-active approach to developing their career. (Woman in personnel)

Conclusions

It seems to be clear from the research evidence discussed in this chapter that gendered segregation in personnel exists to a high degree. This is both vertical and horizontal, with women being channelled into the lower level, supporting functions of recruitment, selection, welfare and administration, while men remain in senior positions involving industrial relations and the newer HRM. Vertical, hierarchical segregation also appears to give a low priority to equal opportunities and to issues of discrimination. This is maybe unsurprising, since top decision-makers in personnel are mainly men, who rarely have personal experience of discrimination and subordination. In addition, the promise that the new 'soft' HRM could offer women in personnel new opportunities has largely turned out to be false. There appears to be no HRM that is entirely soft, and the 'tough love' HRM discourse which has replaced it has effectively been constructed by and for men.

This has occurred largely as a response to the challenge of HRM to the traditional personnel-industrial relations focused male establishment, through a repositioning of personnel/HRM in both rhetoric and reality – although it is not clear how successful this has been in reclaiming for the profession the management of people, especially in the light of recent organisational restructuring, decentralisation, devolution and even contracting-out of personnel.

In this search for a role, some personnel managers seeking to embellish their self-image and organisational credibility in order to enhance their personal organisational careers have been found to reproduce and rationalise sex-discriminatory practices in their organisations (Collinson *et al.*, 1990). However, this rather harsh analysis does not adequately take into account the gendered structure of personnel itself, where women are consistently to be found in junior positions, largely in recruitment, and other low-power roles. Surely it cannot be purely chance that finds the role of professional gate-keeping – recruitment – to women's and men's organisational membership and careers, assigned to young, junior women personnel specialists? In Collinson *et al.*'s (1990) study, it was mainly these personnel managers whose role was downgraded by more senior, male, line managers who held the balance of power in recruitment decision-making, as 'an unproductive, welfare function best confined to administration'.

Nor should it be surprising that junior personnel managers (women), at the start of their professional careers, are keen to comply with the demands of their senior, male, managers who after all may well be key to their future prospects. It would be a brave young women who made an overtly feminist challenge, on her own, in a strongly patriarchal culture. Even in organisations with a seriously espoused commitment to equality, specialist equality officers have been found to experience opposition and difficulties: for example, one EO manager resigned her job after the three 'most painful' years of her career (Cockburn, 1991).

The junior women in personnel in the study reported here worked in organisations which, although they claimed to be equal opportunity employers, provided few practical support systems for women. This was in spite of the fact that over half of the women reported that personnel in their organisations had responsibility for implementing equal opportunities. It is difficult to avoid concluding that for EO, being associated with women, and being located in personnel, within the prevailing gendered structure and culture of personnel, is a recipe for impotence.

Meanwhile, evidence from research reported here echoes both recent (Julie Storey, 1994) and earlier findings (Long, 1984) that the values and aspirations of personnel women themselves are in a number of respects different from men's. Among these women there is a recognition of the difficulties and the personal sacrifices involved in climbing the traditional career ladder, together with a resignation about the lack of supporting measures for women from their own Institute, and to a lesser extent, in their workplaces. Reluctance to engage in a costly struggle to break through the glass ceiling of a personnel career seems to be coupled with a desire for a balanced life which includes family and self, and a more liberating and positive career on their own terms.

These findings broadly reflect those of other research about women in management generally. White, Cox and Cooper's (1992) study of high-flying women found that the women were motivated by the intrinsic desire to excel at their work and the demand for challenging and interesting work was stronger than the demand for promotion. These were also found to be motivations of high-flying men. However, a major difference between the sexes was that the theme of self-development was identified by a quarter of the women, but not among men. The women had experienced the common hurdles of occupational gendered segmentation and had overcome them using a dual approach. They had adapted and managed their material lives – family (fewer with children), ability to work long hours and be mobile, acquiring the necessary breadth of work experience including key 'hard' functions such as finance and business management – to the demands of largely male career routes. They had also been skilful in managing the gender and power structures in their organisations to achieve their goals. These included the use of mentors and sponsors, networking and alliances and a high level of accuracy and skill in reading and operating the political processes required.

The women in personnel in the study reported here in this chapter were mainly at the beginning of their careers. They were aiming for professional credentials which some hoped would benefit their progression. They were also aware of the lack of personnel qualifications among senior personnel practitioners (mainly male) and the tendency to favour the 'practice rather than theory' route to the top. While they were aware of the demands and barriers they would face in attempting to access mainstream career routes, these women had not yet developed the political strategies to deal with them, as illustrated by their reports of the lack of mentors, of using contacts through the Institute, and other networks and alliances.

We acknowledge that there is a gap here in our knowledge about the aspirations, consciousness and experiences of more senior women in personnel, and a research programme is planned to examine these. Meanwhile, we can conclude that for the women at the start of their careers in personnel there are a number of choices: to attempt to compete with men in 'their' career routes; to accept and continue in subordinate roles; to seek for fulfilment and personal development in other ways, perhaps via routes of training and development and external consultancy – as change agents (although these also have problems related to expectations of gender roles among clients, unsocial hours and travel, and instability and insecurity). There is also the prospect of working collectively with others in the profession to inform and change 'their' Institute of Personnel and Development and make it work for them. Whichever course, or courses of action women pursue, they will need to develop and use their political antennae if their challenges are to be effective.

Notes

1. Karen Legge is a major exception, especially her work on problematising the gendered aspects of personnel. Barbara Townley's recent text offers a Foucauldian approach to HRM which is also helpful in throwing light on the gendered nature of personnel.
2. Paradoxically Storey found when he tested the model in 15 case study organisations, that in only two instances were changemakers from personnel teams; most of the major change programmes had originated outside of personnel.
3. It is interesting to note that in the intense discussions preceding the merger in 1994 between the IPM and the ITD a proposal to use Human Resources in the title of new Institute was abandoned in favour of 'Personnel and Development'.
4. The current IPM (sic) Code of Conduct on Equal Opportunities is undated. It covers the legal requirements of sex and race and also covers disability and age. Sexuality is not explicitly addressed. While the code eschews quotas it 'sees no harm' in setting appropriate targets as a 'short term remedial measure' where there is serious under-representation of a particular sex or ethnic group (page 6).
5. 'For too many women there is a glass ceiling over their aspirations it allows them to see where they might go, but stops them getting there.' Women 'remain clustered in positions that fail to make full use of their qualifications and abilities' below this ceiling (Hansard Society, 1990).

CHAPTER 5

Something to declare: women in HM Customs and Excise

Amanda Martin Palmer

Introduction

HM Customs and Excise has been an award-winning government department in relation to equal opportunities. In 1992 the department was voted 'Public Sector Employer of the Year' by the Working Mothers Association (WMA) in a competition which had attracted a record number of entries that year. The competition was supported by the Opportunity 2000 initiative which the department had been quick to sign up to in 1991, being among the first organisations to do so.

Earlier, in 1990, the department won a joint advertising industry and Institute of Personnel Management award for its 'Tough Guy' recruitment advertisement, depicting a young woman as a successful Customs and Excise officer, counter to the stereotyped image of the department's work being for men. Indeed, it was the 'macho' image of the department and its efforts to overcome this which helped it win the WMA award.

Until 1972, HM Customs and Excise *was* primarily a uniformed male organisation apart from staff in headquarters. Customs officers *were* male except for staff required for the strip-searching of female passengers, and Excise officers were exclusively male. Women, where they existed, were engaged only at clerical and secretarial grades and could not rise to perform uniformed duties. Attitudes abounded that women were unsuited to 'rummaging' on board ship, that they could not do filthy checking work in engine rooms and were inappropriate for sea-going work on board the cutters, for shift work and surveillance duties.

The Sex Discrimination Act (1975) would have called these practices into question but prior to that, the abolition of purchase tax and introduction of value added tax (VAT) in 1973 gave the department a whole new range of responsibilities and the need for a much larger, office-based workforce. More women were recruited but, unsurprisingly, continued to feature primarily, although not exclusively, in the lower-graded occupations. (At this time, external recruitment was only at clerical assistant, clerical officer or executive officer grades.)

HM Customs and Excise was not alone among Civil Service Departments in displaying this pattern of employment. The Cabinet Office, in initiating its 'Programme of Action for Women in the Civil Service' in 1984, identified that women were over-represented in the clerical and administrative grades (now titled administrative assistant (AA), administrative officer (AO) and executive officer (EO)) and under-represented in the higher executive officer (HEO) grade and above. This pattern has persisted into the 1990s, albeit gradually improving (see Figure 5.1) and represents a 'glass ceiling' for women which divides supervisory posts from more managerial ones.

A common view is that the current absence of women at senior levels in the Civil Service in general, and in HM Customs and Excise in particular, is owing to earlier historical barriers which no longer exist; and that what is currently being manifested will be rectified automatically as women gain sufficient years of service to be promoted into the senior grades. However, after twenty years of espoused equality in Civil Service policies there has been plenty of time for women to meet the length of service requirements to be eligible for promotion, yet the inroads made by women into senior management grades have not yet put them on a par with men (see Figure 5.1). It is against this backdrop that the specific action taken by HM Customs and Excise should be viewed.

The department has sought to strengthen its commitment to equal opportunities through a wide range of structural appointments, policies and initiatives. Since 1984 it has had an equal opportunities unit attached to the personnel division at Headquarters and charged with the implementation of the 1984 Cabinet Office Programme of Action to achieve equality of opportunity for women. This unit has a broad responsibility for advising on policy and good practice in relation to all aspects of managing diversity, with the express aim of providing genuine equal opportunity to all employees and thereby ensuring that the highest calibre staff are identified and given the chance to work at their own highest level of competence, benefiting both the department and the individual. Departmental equal opportunity 'champions' have been both male and female, and the department has made top-level commitment to equal opportunity principles. Full trade union consultation has also been a feature of the equal opportunity initiatives introduced. Throughout the 1980s and into the 1990s a variety of policies have been introduced to enable women to take up or maintain careers in the department,

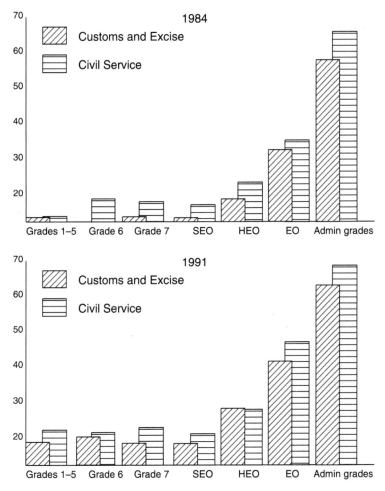

**FIGURE 5.1   Comparison of percentage of women by grade in Customs
and Excise and the Civil Service, 1984 and 1991**

and there has been a wide range of initiatives aimed at removing barriers to
women's career progression, most of which have been implemented since
1989 and some of which have been specifically introduced in response to data
gained from in-house research and surveys conducted during the 1990s. These
include:

- the introduction of a five-year maximum career-break scheme for all staff with
  the guarantee of returning to work in the same grade upon return;

- a departmental maternity leave scheme;
- the introduction of flexible working hours and part-time or job-share facilities wherever possible;
- the creation of departmental nurseries, six in total by 1994;
- the purchase of places in private nurseries;
- participation in holiday play schemes;
- the introduction of a *biodata* selection test for executive officer entry to encourage applications from women and others with non-standard academic qualifications or career histories;
- non-sexist advertisements openly challenging stereotyped images of 'masculine' and 'feminine' spheres of work;
- the production of a recruitment video 'Second Time Around' aimed at attracting women returners;
- revised promotion procedures (at some grades) aimed at providing opportunity for the diffident through which staff are automatically included for consideration if eligible on grounds of length of service in grade.
- the creation of local equal opportunity officers at assistant collector level in each 'collection'[1] in the UK, complete with external training by equal opportunity consultants;
- the creation of sexual harassment contact officers in most collections, trained to listen sensitively to claims of sexual harassment and advise or assist victims regarding options open to them;
- a formal complaints procedure for victims of sex discrimination or sexual harassment;
- the setting up of women-only management courses both in-house and via the Civil Service College, plus use of the Springboard training scheme;
- the production of updated manuals and booklets on equal opportunity policies and practice;
- an equal opportunity regular newsletter;
- both in-house and external training for staff on equal opportunity awareness;
- in-house research into the incidence of sexual harassment;
- research by external consultants into women's career barriers, both generally and in relation to specific areas of work in which women are substantially under-represented;
- monitoring of women's progress in the department;
- provision of a *forecast*, issued by the chairman in 1992, of the future representation of women at HEO grade and above for the years 1996 and 2000 for use as a yardstick against which to measure *actual* representation.

To what extent have these initiatives led to an equal distribution of women across the grade structure and work disciplines in HM Customs and Excise? Table 5.1 shows the 1992 national picture for women by grade, using personnel data from the Department's Chessington computer, indicating that there is still a barrier of some sort which causes fewer women than men to rise above the rank of EO. In addition, it is the case that there are far fewer women working in the Customs and Excise areas of work than in VAT, areas traditionally associated with the old, tough, aggressive 'macho' culture. The paucity of women in the London airports anti-smuggling teams reflects this, being an area of work which has failed to attract sufficient internal female applicants despite extensive drives to encourage women to come forward. In early 1994 a total of 369 men and just 69 women were engaged on anti-smuggling work across the range of grades, indicative of 'glass walls' as well as 'glass ceilings' (Davidson and Cooper, 1992). This horizontal and vertical segregation mirrors patterns of employment in many other sectors of the labour market (Dex, 1985).

Cockburn (1991) identifies some of the difficulties that a committed equal opportunities team can encounter in putting policies into practice, especially in relation to 'conservative' management attitudes and procedures adopted by middle and senior managers. In the light of a positive commitment to equal opportunities for women from the top in HM Customs and Excise, what are the barriers that remain? Do women 'vote with their feet' or are they squeezed out by structural contraints or prejudice? As previously stated, the department has undertaken research using internal staff and external consultants to

TABLE 5.1   **Women by grade level in Customs and Excise, 1992**

Grade	Total women	Staff in Post	Percentage		Comparison with 1 August 1991 Figures
			Dept Average	Civil Service Average	
Gr 1	0	1	0	0	–
Gr 2	1	3	33.3	7.0	–
Gr 3	1	9	11.1	7.0	–
Gr 4	0	1	0	5.0	–
Gr 5	5	74	6.7	14.0	–
Gr 6	14	133	10.5	11.0	+1
Gr 7	42	491	8.5	13.0	+4
SEO	143	1626	8.8	11.0	+21
HEO	1161	5270	22.0	19.0	+154
EO	3313	9125	36.3	42.0	−72
AO	3495	6082	57.4	67.0	−119
AA	2375	3364	70.6	73.0	−22
SUP GRD 1	100	184	54.3	N/A	−7
SUP GRD 2	296	662	44.7	N/A	−28
SUP MGR 2/3	8	13	61.5	N/A	+1
TOTAL	10954	27038	40.5	49.0	−67

investigate these phenomena. The subsequent sections of this chapter draw upon data gathered by such research in order to answer these questions.

Studies undertaken and their methodologies

The author was involved in three separate studies which served to inform the debate on barriers to women's careers within the department between 1989 and 1992. The evidence presented here relates to data gathered over these three studies and this period of time; a period of time in which equal opportunity issues were receiving systematic attention in the department, resulting in a number of initiatives such as the creation of (a) local equal opportunity officers at assistant collector level in each regional collection and, (b) sexual harassment support networks.

1. In 1989, the author interviewed 21 women at HEO level in the London area who were either in the field for promotion to Senior Executive Officer (SEO) or would soon be so. These respondents were selected at random from computerised personnel records of women who were eligible for consideration for promotion. The women were working primarily in head-quarters or in VAT offices, and as such the sample accurately reflected the areas of work in which women were usually found. Their ages ranged from late twenties to early sixties. All the women approached agreed to be interviewed and intensive, semi-structured, in-depth interviews lasting one to two hours were conducted with each woman, at a venue of her choosing, guaranteeing anonymity. Interview questions and discussion were wide-ranging but focused on:

   - the extent of their ambition and motivation;
   - the nature of any domestic constraints or difficulties;
   - personal experiences of the staff reporting and promotion system;
   - personal experiences of managers and colleagues.

   As a supplement to this study, 10 further female respondents on the SEO grade were added to the 21 HEOs to establish attitudes towards and willingness to work in both headquarters and the outfield (i.e. in the regional collections). This was of particular relevance as it was suspected in personnel that women were showing a distaste for some areas of work 'at the sharp end' (i.e. out in the collections) which might limit their all round experience and so reduce their promotion prospects. The additional women at the SEO grade were also interviewed on a one-to-one basis and guaranteed anonymity.

2. In 1990 the author acted as adviser to an in-house survey of sexual harassment of female staff in the Midlands area. This survey was conducted initially by questionnaires to all 382 women staff and then supplemented by in-depth interviews with a smaller sample of volunteer respondents. Again, anonymity was assured for all respondents. Fifty per cent of the women responded to the questionnaire and, of these, 10 per cent were subsequently interviewed in person.

3. Between 1991 and 1992 the author was granted access to interview all staff resigning over a nine-month period in two collections; one based in London, the other in the home counties. The purpose of these interviews was to establish the real and detailed reasons for leaving. There were 46 resignations during the research period and 31 people agreed to be interviewed. Here, also, respondents received a guarantee of anonymity and were free to choose where their in-depth and semi-structured interview took place. As a result, full and frank analysis of their situation was possible, and whilst it could be argued that people resigning might be expected to 'blame everyone else but themselves' it is the author's opinion that data collected accurately reflected lived experiences. Both men and women were involved for the original purposes of this research with broadly similar points being made by both sexes. However, findings relating specifically to issues of importance for women emerged from the dialogue with some of the 17 interviewed women who resigned, and their testimony has been incorporated here.

The studies listed above provided ample qualitative data to enable the identification of women's *own* perspectives on their careers, complete with motivators and demotivators. This data is presented and discussed in this chapter.

Motivators and demotivators in women's careers

Evidence from 21 women HEOs interviewed in 1989, all of whom were eligible for promotion to the SEO grade, indicated that approximately:

30 per cent were *seriously* interested in early promotion,
25 per cent *had been* interested in promotion in the past,
20 per cent were biding their time *before* applying, and
25 per cent were *not* seeking promotion at all.

From this it can be seen that career advancement was of interest to three-quarters of the sample interviewed with only one-quarter not interested in any progression. The factors informing these positions are of importance both to women in understanding how to unlock the door to success and to employers in understanding motivators and demotivators which affect women's career-related decisions.

HEO women seriously interested in early promotion

The most noticeable unifying feature about the six women intent on early promotion was their confidence in their own abilities and the additional contribution they could make if given the responsibility of the next grade up. Their commitment and positive thinking was striking, as indicated by their comments:

> I want to be a Principal [Grade 7] in Customs and Excise, that's what motivates me. . . There are no drawbacks for me in being promoted. I've got a lot to give and I can only give it if I'm promoted. I'm better at this grade than EO and I feel I'm more fitted to management. . . I go home each night with a feeling of elation, that I've really *done* something.

> I'm very interested in promotion. I want to be in a position to exert influence over what happens. . . I think that having sussed the situation out I am very innovative. I like things that are a mess so I can sort them out. . . Promotion means getting paid for what I do. . . I'd have more role power and credibility if I had the grade to go with it.

> I want to get as far as my ability will allow me to get. I tend to look two grades ahead. . . It's not just first and foremost the money, just the feeling of having achieved by my standards. . . also a feeling of recognition by the department. I feel loyalty to the department and it's like them rewarding me for my commitment.

A study of the individual circumstances of these six women did not reveal any evidence for a particular 'type' of woman interested in promotion. Three were single but two of these acknowledged that they would want to combine a career with having children at some point in the not too distant future. Two were married, one with a young child, the other with teenage children. All but the latter were in their late twenties and early thirties. The older woman had raised four children as a single parent during her career in the department. This career orientation strikes at the very heart of stereotyped attitudes which suggest that women's career motivation is less than men's. These women proved themselves to be as interested in promotion as men, in line with other studies (see Brief and Oliver, 1976; Davidson and Cooper, 1983; and Nicholson and West, 1988).

The women did come from particular 'backgrounds' in the department however. Half had obtained their major work experience in headquarters posts, while the other half had worked primarily in operational posts in local VAT offices (LVOs). None had achieved the majority of their work experience in the Customs or Excise field.

In consequence, their interest in promotion could not be traced to any particular set of domestic circumstances or particular 'history' in the department in terms of being headquarters or collection-based, but rather to to their own level of motivation and commitment to their work and their desire to retain and *develop* a part of their lives which they found challenging and interesting.

Three particular aspects of personal motivation were evident here: (1) confidence in own ability, (2) a desire to contribute (and be recognised for it), plus (3) a feeling of commitment and loyalty to the employer. None of these women doubted her ability and each was desirous of an opportunity to use it to the full. White *et al.* (1992) indicate the importance of women believing in themselves in developing successful careers. Bandura (1977) views self-efficacy as crucial and Waddel (1983) found that women who obtained higher-status positions believed in their own ability to affect the external environment. These women showed every sign of doing precisely those things, and in addition they wished to forge a career with their existing employer; loyalty was a major component of how women felt about their jobs. Marshall (1984) discusses women's preference for developing a career with one employer rather than with many, and these women were very departmentally orientated in their career aspirations.

Women who had once been interested in promotion

Four women had dearly wanted promotion in earlier years but their regular lack of success led to their eventual apathy or belief that it was 'now too late' for them on grounds of age or changed domestic circumstances. One woman had applied for promotion to SEO 'for some years' since 1982, a second had applied unsuccessfully between 1979 and 1981 before giving up, a third had applied regularly over the last ten years and a fourth had applied during the 1970s but gave up her ambitions (but not her post) upon having children. These women were now in their forties.

A *desire* for promotion combined with staff report gradings warranting *consideration* for promotion do not necessarily conjoin to make the individual the *best choice* for promotion in a competitive situation where only the top performers at interview and in reports will succeed. These women may well have failed to gain promotion based on valid and objective criteria. However, there are two important aspects of their failure to gain promotion. One is the demotivating effect of rejection and the other is whether the system *is* fair and *seen* to be so.

Overall, half the women interviewed (whether interested in promotion or not) had their doubts about the fairness of the staff reporting system and panel interview process. This was despite many efforts on the part of the central personnel directorate to develop an open staff reporting system, operate clearly publicised sift and interview criteria and train all interview panels for the task. Women were not alone in doubting the fairness of the system, but particular issues for women centred upon whether or not a certain type of 'macho' style and task orientation to work were viewed more favourably by their predominently male managers. Most criticisms were levied at the staff reporting system itself, which, until revisions to the system in 1993, involved the person's line manager acting as an annual reporting officer, grading each member of staff with a box marking (Box 1 = high, Box 5 = low) against a range of skills (e.g. oral and written communication, judgement) and in providing a similar box marking for 'overall performance' along with a 'promotability assessment' ranking from 'not fitted' to 'well fitted' for promotion. Individual reports were then countersigned by the reporting officer's line manager.

Criticisms of the system included (*a*) querying the ability of the reporting officer to judge the individual's merits against all the criteria, (*b*) querying the validity of the criteria themselves, (*c*) debating whether it is possible to identify 'potential' for promotion with any accuracy, and (*d*) favouritism.

> I had three 'well-fitteds' but then changed [job] and my promotability went down to 'fitted'. I didn't follow it up, perhaps I should have done. The time after that I got a 'well-fitted' from the Principal but was marked down by the Assistant Secretary [counter-signing officer]. . . He said I wasn't assertive enough, but he did have his favourites, there was one favourite who was well known.

> I think I have been regarded as a bit weak because I'm of a quiet nature.

> The impression they [management] were giving me was that I had the potential to be an SEO. . . I think perhaps the reports are not 'punchy' enough and that's why it gets rejected on sift. . . In last year's report, although it was a Box 2 on performance and management of staff, a clause was added 'but she expects too much of her staff'. I queried this and said it would have been a Box 4 or 5 if I hadn't chivvied staff, but the comment he parried to my statement was 'I feel she's over-reacting.'

Panel interview experiences were also referred to negatively, but in all cases repondents were alluding to interviews which had taken place before major, positive revisions to interview criteria and prior to the more objective interviewing techniques now employed within HM Customs and Excise.

It was a great worry to be honest. I felt I had to read everything in sight. I'd only been in a narrow area of work [VAT] . . . yet you're expected to answer questions on Customs, Excise – the whole area of the department's work.'

I didn't feel they were seriously intending to promote me. They asked if I would be a surveyor [SEO] in the outfield and I said, 'No, I prefer headquarters,' which I suppose did for me.

Demotivation ensued for these women. One threw herself more into her new family, another began to apply for Crown transfers to another department with this to say:

I'd played the game for ten out of fifteen years . . . I was now going to get out whilst I still had some self esteem left.'

Another reached a point where her obligations to an elderly parent made it subsequently impossible for her to contemplate managing the pressures of more reponsible work in combination with changed obligations at home. As this woman put it:

I look forward to retirement more than promotion quite honestly. . . My work is now more of a job than a career.

She was only in her early forties with up to twenty more years service ahead of her.

Interwoven in these and many other accounts were suspicions of:

- favouritism and stereotypical attitudes towards women;
- particular work 'profiles' helping or hindering career advancement;
- misjudgement of officers' strengths;
- assessments being made by countersigning senior officers too far removed from the individual to know their work and potential in any detail.

Davidson and Cooper (1992) emphasise the undermining effects of poor feedback or being undervalued by management, and certainly this lack of recognition for effort became demotivating for these women and the corollary of the motivating effects of the recognition anticipated by the hopeful promotees referred to in the preceding section. This points to an *optimum time* to reward women for their enthusiasm and commitment and the need to *develop* them promptly and appropriately if they are not quite 'making the grade'. This can avert the subsequent 'opt out' factor when domestic factors impinge upon the individual. It is unlikely that any of these women, if suitably developed and promoted prior to these life changes or changes of heart, would have requested demotion or still wanted to transfer out of the department.

Women biding their time prior to applying for promotion

One interesting group of women were those who wanted promotion at some point in the future but who did not consider themselves ready for it just yet. Four women fell into this category, three for job-related reasons and one for family reasons.

This last woman found herself on the horns of a dilemma. She wanted a second child, was already working part-time and was not certain how (*a*) part-time working would be viewed at the next grade up (SEO) and (*b*) whether she could cope with the new responsibilities and a new child simultaneously.

The other three women in this category were similarly keen to be promoted but felt that they were not yet in a position to meet with success if they applied. It was important to these women to get through the promotion board process if they applied. Failure to do so would have been interpreted as a rejection and as a blow to their self esteem. In this, the women felt that, unlike men, they did not simply 'throw their hat into the ring' to see what success they might achieve on a 'nothing ventured nothing gained' basis. Instead, they took the comments on their staff reports and the interpersonal feedback from their line managers very seriously and chose not to 'risk' putting themselves forward for promotion until they felt they could (*a*) fully prove themselves on paper and (*b*) acquit themselves favourably at interview. Women's lack of confidence in their abilities is indicated here, in line with the findings of Wallston and O'Leary (1991) that women attributed failure to lack of ability whilst men were more likely to attribute it to 'good' or 'bad' luck.

The ability to get strong marks on paper was closely linked, in the women's view, to length of time in current post. They expected their performance ratings to drop temporarily upon taking up new duties and were prepared to wait until these improved again. This backfired on one woman who, as a result, missed two promotion opportunities.

> When I was first eligible I'd just moved to . . . and it took time to settle in. I felt it was unrealistic to go for promotion because I was new in the post and not getting to grips with it as soon as I'd expected. . . This year I might have done. . . my boss was thinking of a Box 2 marking but was told not to, had to be harsher. My reporting officer came to put my mind at rest saying, 'I don't think this year but I see no problems next year.' There was then *great* embarrassment at sift because it was asked why I hadn't applied.

Such reliance, by women in particular, on staff reports and the opinions and advice of line managers could lead to disproportionate delays in their promotion, especially for those who move frequently (as capable officers often do) and in consequence are frequently 'new' in post, or for those who fall foul of negative attitudes from reporting officers. As previously stated, there was widespread dissatisfaction with standards of reporting and women felt that some reporting officers operated within a 'macho' culture and paradigm. An internal anaysis of staff report markings conducted in the early 1990s revealed that, at every grade, women received lower markings for overall performance and promotability than their male colleagues, so there is scope for women to be correct in their assessment. This important area will be returned to in a subsequent section on the culture of the department. Meanwhile, what is being emphasised here is that these women were being greatly influenced by what was thought *of them* rather than what they thought of *themselves*. Again, the importance of self-efficacy and of a belief in self and own ability to control the external world seems relevant to career progression, in this case working negatively and to the detriment of their career advancement.

Women not interested in promotion

Five women expressed no real interest in further promotion. Two women were already in their mid-fifties and had recently been promoted to HEO. One felt that she would no longer be considered for further promotion as she was too old and could not be of sufficient service in a higher grade before having to retire. In practice, the Department did consider people for promotion to within two years of their retirement and this respondent was in that category.

Just one woman cited primary commitment to her child as the reason for not wanting promotion. This woman was someone currently on maternity leave who had already decided to return for the obligatory one month to safeguard her pay before resigning. She had already lost intrinsic job satisfaction for separate reasons and doubted if she would ever return to the Department in later years. It could be argued that her loss of interest in her work rather than becoming a mother was the determining factor in her decision to leave.

Two other women *loved* their current work at their existing grade and put job satisfaction above promotion and the additional pay it would provide. Both were married women with working husbands who acknowledged they did not have to put financial considerations first. Neither ruled out accepting promotion altogether but other considerations were more important, for example:

> I'm interested in promotion but it's not my *raison d'être*. I'd rather be satisfied with my job and what I *do*. . . The first year I was in the field I'd only just moved and the second year my husband had been off for a major op. so this is the first year I've felt consolidated. . . As far as I can see, SEO is not as interesting as what I do now. There's a lot of paper work and clerical work as I've had it displayed to me. . . I would lose my technical work, lose work that's *yours*. . . I've got the best of both worlds here.

It could be argued that both these women could 'afford' not to consider promotion but, even so, they had not ruled it out completely. In addition, it should be noted that this was a minority view (less than 10 per cent) and many other women, with similar financial security, were very career-minded.

Overview for women HEOs in the field for promotion

One striking feature of the 21 women interviewed was that the vast majority (75 per cent) had once been, were, or would later be, interested in promotion. A further 10 per cent did not rule out a future interest in advancement altogether. This rather serves to refute claims that women are simply not as career-minded as men. What is apparent however, is that these women viewed their careers *differently* from men. Their priorities and their needs were related more to how they were treated at work than to what was happening in the home. This has major implications for the effective management of women, their career progression and hence optimum usage of their skills.

Aspects of departmental culture

Much play has been made of the 'macho' culture within HM Customs and Excise and how this disfavours women and officers displaying a 'feminine' style of management. As previously stated, historically the department was a male-dominated institution until 1972 and the need to recruit for office-based VAT posts. Since that time, it is largely considered that women have gained ground and seniority in the VAT field but made few inroads into senior-level appointments in both Customs and Excise work.

Much of both Customs work and Excise work is uniformed. Both men and women view this uniform with pride. Many recruits (especially males) are attracted to the department because of the uniform, yet the majority of posts lie within the non-uniformed field of VAT. In the late 1980s concern over staff losses within the first four years after recruitment and training for the EO grade led to a recognition that past advertising campaigns had been misleading, causing (mostly male) recruits to be disenchanted with the realities of life in a VAT office and female recruits to be conspicuous by their absence, having perceived the uniformed area's work as a male domain. The public image of the Department was still found to be very masculine. It is in this context that the award winning 'Tough Guy' non-sexist advertisement and 'biodata' questionnaires for non-standard applicants should be viewed.

The department has worked hard to alter its 'macho' image both internally and externally. (Witness the many initiatives listed earlier.) It would have been impossible for any officer of the department in the late 1980s and early 1990s to be unaware of the official shift in attitudes and practice. By 1994 there was the appointment of a woman chairman (a title she chose to maintain); a woman collector (i.e. Grade 5 head of a regional collection) and a woman deputy collector plus a range of women in other senior-level appointments. A general broadsheet, *Portcullis*, was frequently carrying articles about women's successes, sexual harassment awareness, new nursery facilities and new training initiatives. No officer could be left in any doubt that sexist attitudes, if acted upon or articulated, would be seriously frowned upon and could lead to disciplinary action.

What, then, did women over the three studies conducted say about the organisational culture and their experiences, as women, in the Department?

Departmental culture

Both men and women across all the grades in HM Customs and Excise confirm two things about the departmental culture. Firstly, that it is task-orientated rather than people-orientated, and secondly that it is a 'blame' culture. Neither feature sits very happily with the department's late-1980s 'People Initiative' (designed to value staff and their ideas more) or its 'Next Steps' programme (designed to pass decision-making down to executive units, giving them more budgetry responsibility and more freedom to take local 'risk' decisions in pursuance of centrally set goals and targets). The culture of operational units in particular appears to pull against the espoused aims and objectives set centrally by headquarters. More broadly in the Civil Service as a whole, the 1990s shift towards performance-related pay and the setting of individual rather than team targets has done much to reduce morale, create individual competition and reduce both risk-taking and team spirit as evidenced by an internal report within the Inland Revenue (*Independent*, 5 April 1994).

It is also apparent that this 'task' and blame' orientation does not mesh well with women's well-researched, preferred style of management (Rosener, 1990.) Although many successful women deny it, the *tendency* is for women to prefer to manage collaboratively, to prefer the 'carrot' to the 'stick' approach in managing staff and to aim for 'hearts and minds' rather than utilising an authoritarian approach. They prefer to persuade rather than tell, to encourage rather than impose.

Women in all three studies conducted between 1989 and 1992 felt that they had received negative treatment based upon some of the ideals supporting this culture. These ideals incorporated a belief that commitment is represented by working full-time (including coming in early and staying on late); that personal circumstances should not impinge upon work; and that a tough, aggressive officer is a good officer and will probably be male. Managers, in operating these ideals, were cited as being insensitive or unfair towards women.

> They don't come across as 'man managers' at all. You get the idea they spend their time collating figures and collecting stats rather than considering staff.

> I did an urgent job the day my son was very ill. I went in. . . and she said, 'I put this in your in-tray. You *must* do this.' I've spent I don't know how many years in management and I'd never use the word 'must'. She knew the details of my son's illness.

> It was the usual thing that if you were less than adequate people were less patient with you than with a man. They pin your inadequacies upon your sex. . . Women are perceived as unambitious, mobility is seen as a problem and women are seen as a short-term career prospect.

> Once I was put on a residential course and I couldn't go because of the possibility of my husband being away. [on departmental work]. I was told, 'If you've got children you should be at home, you should resign if you can't do courses.'

Two part-time women (an EO and and HEO) felt that their managers were driven by the pursuit of full-time targets irrespective of their part-time hours:

> I was marked down on stats when off sick and in half term. [She had taken annual leave for this.] A completely different emphasis to [my] training.

> He said. 'Unless your hit rate is as good as the HEOs [full-timers] you're out. . . You'll have a report in three months' time but I wouldn't expect you to improve because there isn't time.'

Some women returners coming into the department at HEO or EO level experienced resentment that they were utilising a non-standard route to senior-level posts. One woman's manager said –

> I've spent all these years getting to my position and you walk straight in.

Another found that working practices were not modified to allow for her part-time hours.

> It didn't work very well. People found it difficult to cope with me leaving at 3.30pm. I'd be called into a meeting at 3.25pm.

Women found that male colleagues as well as line managers could be insensitive or downright hostile, although sometimes it was difficult to isolate anything specific that was being said or done to their detriment.

The image of excellence is still that of a man, possibly an Oxbridge man.

It's very subtle, almost like a male club. We'll have to accept you but we don't really want to. It's even more subtle in Headquarters. It certainly comes through in the subtle wording of reports. . . There's your decisions, men above you don't trust your judgement. Quite frequently the reaction is that you're over-reacting because of your hormones or something. It's subtle but the feeling is there, your instincts are telling you, but that can be counteracted as paranoia on your part.'

The women speaking here were mostly SEOs and HEOs, a few were EOs. All were recounting experiences from the 1980s and 1990s, some ten years and longer since the passing of the Sex Discrimination Act of 1975. Some women had been thoroughly disenchanted by reactions to them and had handed in their resignations. Others reported being unaffected at a personal level but acknowledged that in general terms it was probably necessary to be better than a man to be considered equal to him. Women therefore knew that they had to try harder to prove themselves and would be more readily criticised for their performance than men. Not all women felt able to take up this challenge and it is difficult to assess the pool of talent lost to the department by virtue of such negative reactions to women officers.

Sexual harassment

Some negative attitudes towards women's presence in the workplace and to their style of working have been explored in the preceding section and could be described as discriminatory or bullying (see Adams, 1992). However, women can also be subjected to harassment of an overtly *sexual* nature which can be embarrassing, humiliating and undermine them in a professional context. A departmental guidance booklet on sexual harassment defines it as:

unreciprocated and unwelcome actions, attention or behaviour which are of a sexual nature and are deliberate or persistent.'

The department considers sexual harassment to be a serious offence and has introduced a series of contact officers in response to an internal study into sexual harassment conducted in 1990. These contact officers are trained to advise victims on courses of action open to them and to offer a variety of support. This was because, in the 1990 study conducted in the Midlands, many women stated that they would not wish to report an incident formally for fear of ridicule or not being believed, neither did they wish to cause trouble for the offender or for themselves.

Women nationally are the major victims of sexual harassment and men the major offenders. A recent police report (*Police Review*, 1993) based on a survey conducted with 1802 women in ten forces concluded:

> Nearly all policewomen experienced some form of sexual harassment from policemen.

Over 60 per cent of incidents involve a subordinate female and a male superior (Alfred Marks Bureau, 1991). A Mori survey revealed that men over 35 years of age are more likely to be offenders than their younger counterparts (*The Times*, 1 September 1992). Both a sexual and a seniority power game is being played out on most occasions.

Women report feelings of guilt if they fall victim to being harassed and often blame themselves for causing it in some way. They report mixed feelings of helplessness, anger, injustice, fear, humiliation and embarrassment. A good working relationship is frequently impossible once an incident has taken place, leaving management with the difficulty of moving one or other person to another location. Senior people can be hard to replace forthwith and there is a dislike of 'moving the victim'. Although the latter is often the easier option operationally, it would be a serious blow in terms of any expressed commitment to removing barriers to women's equal treatment at work.

Various surveys (e.g. Leeds, TUCRIC, 1983) indicate that over 50 per cent of women have experienced some form of sexual harassment at work. The 1990 survey within HM Customs and Excise indicated the following:

> 33 per cent of women had experienced unwanted touching;
> 35 per cent had experiences unwanted looks and gestures;
> 100 per cent had received sexist comments or remarks about their appearance.

Women in both the 1989 and 1990 studies were able to provide information about specific incidents from their own personal experience, either with line managers or peers. Many were quite senior women. Below are a few illustrations:

> I was in a meeting with my 38-year old boss. There's me trying to present a professional image and he mentions something about boobs, my boobs. I had to say to him it wasn't professional in front of people.

> An older but more junior man used to say things like – ask me if I'd had sex the night before and what positions I preferred. He only said it when the AA was in the room to undermine my authority, I was the EO at the time.

One officer calls women tarts. If I'm putting make-up on. . . he'll shout across the office, 'Now then, tart!''

You look knackered. Have you been on your back all weekend? You look like a missionary position to me.

Women were divided over whether such attentions affected their self-esteem. Many shrugged it off as an inevitable part of engagement with the opposite sex, but others saw the one-sided nature of such encounters and thought that as long as men responded to them in that way there was little hope of gaining their respect as colleagues and little hope of being treated seriously either in their present post or for promotion. In general, women saw their credibility at work as being undermined by such events, but did not report thinking less of *themselves* as a result. Indeed, some were determined to show that they were capable, in defiance of the stereotype of the woman as mere adornment. It is therefore difficult to assess the impact of harassment upon career prospects. For some it acted as an additional catalyst and spur to achievement, but it is difficult to estimate the extent to which underlying feelings of a lack of confidence and desire for managerial approval and positive feedback reported earlier are an expression of uncertainty fuelled in part by men's reactions to women as sex objects rather than colleagues in employment.

Women's strategies – overcoming the barriers

In the preceding sections of this chapter the confidence of some women within HM Customs and Excise has been celebrated, whilst the diffidence of others has been reported and analysed for its root causes. Much in terms of initiatives taken by the department has been mentioned representing good equal opportunity practice in the areas of flexible working patterns, nursery provision, revised promotion procedures and support for victims of sexual harassment designed to overcome some of the barriers and be *enabling* for women.

These initiatives have sent a clear signal to women that they are valued, and that child-rearing need not preclude a satisfying career in the department. Whilst these initiatives could be analysed in more detail to document their successes and failures in practical terms, this is not the purpose of this chapter. Instead, attention will now be focused on women's *own* strategies in getting on in their careers *within* the equal oportunity framework afforded them. This is because both promotion-seekers and non-promotion-seekers were doing things for themselves, enabling themselves in the present and preparing themselves for the future to assist their careers both in the short and longer term. Some women were not simply passive recipients of the organisational culture, of sexual harassment or of negative staff reports. They did not simply have children and trust to luck regarding how it would affect their career. Women took action. They made choices. In short, some women acted in a way which could be termed 'politically wise' (Arroba and James, 1987).

Strategies utilised in career progression

Three main areas were discernible in which women acted *strategically* to advance their careers. They can be categorised as follows:

(a) Getting the right profile;
(b) Planning for children and career;
(c) Dealing with the 'macho' culture and harassment.

(a)   Getting the right profile

One interesting and unexpected outcome of the 1989 study of 31 women HEOs and SEOs was the extent to which they had planned their career moves. Central Personnel had wondered if women's advancement to senior levels was being hindered by them eschewing certain aspects of the department's work, giving them restricted profiles and limited work experience. This did not prove to be the case for the women who had already progressed to the SEO grade, all of whom had a breadth of experience. Six out of these ten women SEOs had critically evaluated their experience to date, identified areas of work that would enhance their CVs and actively sought appropriate postings. For four of these women it meant deliberately gaining headquarters experience whilst for another it meant obtaining operational experience in the outfield. Either way, women were exercising a political judgement based on their knowledge of the organisational culture and what was *valued* in people and would enhance their propects of promotion.

> If you've tackled all the disciplines you're much more likely to be extended. There is a body of opinion that this is necessary. . . There are those who think that if you've not *done* the job you couldn't *manage* in that region.

> I'm far better off to be in headquarters now for promotion, but at principal level I would go out [to the outfield] as I've been advised it would be a career move.

Interwoven with the belief that breadth of experience was important to prove one's worth was the belief that 'getting noticed' was also beneficial.

Women spoke of utilising opportunities to undertake high profile work or be involved in key areas where they would be noticed.

> [Headquarters] helps if you want to get on. Policy work and 'flavour of the month'. You see the people who have the power as well. What you write is probably seen more often by people higher up.

> I moved to . . ., it was high profile and a good career move. It. . . involved management of staff. . . What I got from that was talking to high grade people and a high profile job.

Apart from deliberately obtaining experience in the outfield if it was absent from their CVs, the women successfully promoted to SEO mostly thought that headquarters work was the most beneficial for their careers. They saw it as providing:

- wider experience
- broader knowledge
- increased policy awareness
- greater kudos with promotion panels
- an opportunity to be noticed by influential others
- high-profile job opportunities.

Whether or not such 'games' should be necessary to demonstrate one's worth and potential is beside the point. What *is* salient is that these women could identify 'profile builders' and then took active steps to ensure that they fulfilled those, demonstrating their awareness of, and willingness to engage with, the organisational culture of success. In this they were demonstrating the myth exposed by Hennig and Jardim (1978) that women do not plan their careers.

(b)   Planning for children and career

Women SEOs, whilst not directly mentioning it in relation to themselves, also thought that headquarters work probably suited women with children more than outfield work as it could be relied upon to have regular hours, thus affording them a chance to plan childcare with some degree of certainty. It was also seen as offering more scope for flexible working hours and part-time working. Whether or not this was the case was not explored in this study but certainly there were more women interviewed from headquarters who were working part-time for childcare reasons than in the outfield. Just one woman working in the outfield visiting traders said that this suited her very well. She was working full-time and was able to manage this successfully because she had control over the timing of her visits and could stop work to coincide with school leaving hours and write up her case notes later at home.

One noticeable feature though of both the 1989 interviews with HEOs and SEOs and the 1992 interviews with resigners was the extent to which women had (*i*) planned their families to fit in with their careers, and (*ii*) chosen 'dead' time it which it would be least detrimental to either be away on maternity leave or be working part-time.

Women clearly felt that having time off work for childcare *did* affect their careers, and the majority of young mothers interviewed had taken the minimum amount of time off they felt able to before returning to their posts. They had also, in the main, waited until their thirties before having children, a pattern now common among career women as part of getting established prior to taking time off (White *et al.*, 1992). Rix and Stone (1984) suggest that

step off the career track for a short period, and certainly career-motivated women in the department who wished to have children simultaneously wanted to make it a 'damage limitation' exercise.

Ways in which they achieved this included planning maternity leave to coincide with 'dead time' in relation to promotion. In practical terms this meant timing pregnancy so that it came shortly *after* being promoted to one grade and *before* enough years in the new grade had accrued to provide eligibility for consideration for the next grade up. It has already been mentioned that women frequently saw the first year or two in a new post as a time in which they would not be able to 'shine' in their staff reports. Such time was capitalised upon so that otherwise ineffectual years could be used to serve family purposes with least impact upon career prospects. One woman, who wished to have a second child, was already working part-time in the HEO grade. She had researched promotion prospects to the SEO grade and judged them to be contracting. At the time of interview she was thinking very seriously about her best plan of action. Should she have another child as an HEO and risk the delay it would cause before she was back at work and in the field for promotion or go for SEO promotion now, deferring a posting after being accepted? This woman's decision was also being affected by how well she thought part-time working at the SEO grade would be received by management. She was concerned about a cool reception in this respect. All in all, she was determined to arrive at a family-planning decision which would do least harm to her long-term career prospects in the department. Whether or not she needed to be concerned about working part-time and when to apply for promoton is another question. In terms of departmental policy she did not need to. However, what is important here is her perception of what might be problematic and her desire to avoid any potential stumbling block to her own personal advancement.

These women also weighed up the pros and cons of returning to work full or part-time after return from maternity leave, and the benefits of using departmental nursery facilities. They naturally made decisions which best suited their financial and domestic circumstances, but two particular aspects of managing career and childcare featured in the women's decision-making. Firstly, the option to work part-time, whilst appearing initially attractive, often proved not to be cost or time effective. Buying childcare on a half salary, plus the commuting time each day made it a non-viable option for three women who therefore returned full-time instead. (The numbers of staff working part-time in the department is shown in Table 5.2). In addition, Departmental nursery facilities were not seen as a practical option by most of these women. Two women specifically mentioned that the journey into work carrying both child and baby equipment would be too tiring both for them and the child, and that childcare based closer to home favoured shared pick-up arrangements with either friends or a spouse/partner.

Overall, women who chose to have children showed strong signs of taking enormous care not to damage their careers by becoming mothers. Their work did not become secondary to the family, indeed it could be argued that job and career took pride of place, and women were determined that having a family was going to impinge as little as possible upon their career prospects.

One thing which *did* matter to some married women, however, was their career position in relation to that of their husbands. A number of woman expressed the desire not to 'overtake' their husbands in career or financial terms. For one woman this meant the future possibility of holding back from promotion until her partner, also in the department at the same grade, had risen one grade above her. For another it meant that she might have to relocate to allow his career to develop unimpeded. Only one married woman articulated the view that her career carried equal weight with that of her partner. As

TABLE 5.2   **Part-time staff in Customs and Excise as at 1 January 1991**

Grade	Male	Female	Total
Grade 6 (Legal)	–	3	3
Grade 7	–	1	1
SEO	–	5	5
HEO	4	44	48
EO	13	187	200
AO	4	188	192
AA	14	218	232
Other (including support and typist grades)	7	252	259
Total	42	898	940

Note: The total figure of 940 represents 3.4 per cent of the total staff. The figures include job-sharers.

a couple they had planned alternate career moves to date and had both a flat and a house which, between them, covered the main areas in which either of them might expect to be posted upon a promotion. It is therefore revealing that quite well-established middle managers should still have sensitivities towards the ideal of the male as major breadwinner. They were concerned for their husbands' feelings of self-esteem and self worth in a world which still largely views this as the male's primary function within the family. Richardson (1979) identifies no negative effects of women earning more than their men in middle-class households, yet still here we can see broader, societal pressures working counter to the culture of equal opportunities which the department wished to foster.

(c)   Dealing with the 'macho' culture and sexual harassment

Virtually all women interviewed agreed that a 'macho' culture still operated in the department: a culture which expected men to occupy senior positions of responsibility and women to work for them. In part, women's view of their own careers compared to those of their husbands referred to above is also a reflection of this culture which extends far beyond the doors of any organisation.

Examples of women's experiences as a result of this culture have already been documented in a previous section. How did the women respond to that culture and to harassment? In the above discussion of women's career strategies it has been suggested that women largely accepted the prevailing culture in all its forms, and attempted to gain profiles to suit what was expected of them. If they needed time off for child-rearing it was arranged so as to be 'away from the front line' at the least career-damaging periods of time. In relation to personal slights as women and to harassment the indications were similar, namely that the women did not overtly *challenge* men, nor did they demand to be valued on new and different terms. Instead, women chose to subtly *educate* men from within, seeking to demonstrate their worth as effective *colleagues* rather than as *women*, a strategy which, in view of the strength of the prevailing culture, was almost certainly a wise one.

Senior management (male) had a reputation for 'sticking together' especially in relation to handling complaints, and although the department would not wish a complaint of harassment to be treated anything other than seriously and fairly, it was widely thought likely that to pursue a case could be to the detriment of the complainant inasmuch as their career prospects could be damaged by virtue of 'having caused trouble' (see also Davidson and Earnshaw, 1990). It is against this backdrop that the individualised solutions to harassment selected by women should be viewed.

For example, one woman who tranferred to new Customs duties as an HEO found that she was the only female in the team: 'The attitude was, "There's a woman here now – make the tea!'" Her solution was not to openly challenge her colleagues but to indirectly demonstrate that this was not going to be her role: 'I drank water for days on a point of principle.'

Another woman HEO was subjected to having her bottom patted during her younger years as an AO. She responded thus: 'I solved it by slapping his, hard!.' This officer felt that she had always been aware of harassment from men in looks, gestures or comments. Over many years of frequent, unwanted attentions it had become wearing, running counter to the ethos of being an equal colleague to men. As an HEO she was still receiving comments on her appearance.

> Each day I get comments on my dress. If my hair is up it's 'Little Red Riding Hood' and a suit is an 'Air Hostess' or 'School Girl'. I've had to say, 'Please don't think of me as a *woman*, think of me as someone who *works* here.

Women therefore sought one-to-one and immediate solutions to harassment rather than make a bigger issue of it by formally complaining. They also operated a network to warn each other of men to avoid, although they did not tackle harassers directly in a collective fashion.

> One man was notorious. We all knew not to get in the lift with him.

Steps were also taken not to work for male managers known to have prejudiced attitudes towards women working in the department.

> I know I must avoid going into his district because I'll get blocked for promotion there.

These women were inclined to deal with harassment informally, operated a system of networking information about men to other women and thought carefully about career implications in any actions they took. That they chose 'low key' strategies indicated some fear of adverse consequences should they 'rock the boat' too vigorously in pursuit of a more gender-neutral working environment. Again, it would appear that the department was 'ahead of them' in wishing women to help management confront issues of sexism more openly, but that women themselves preferred to err on the side of caution, itself a pragmatic response and a strategy for long-term survival and success.

Evidence from some of the 17 women resigners also indicated that male paradigms still operated in the workplace in the early 1990s. No cases of *sexual* harassment were involved here, but four women resigned because of child-care or part-time difficulties culminating in experiences with line management that could be described as insensitive to the needs of women and as bullying or harassment in a broader sense. For example, one part-time woman trainee found that no allowance was made for her shorter working week:

As it came up to one year I was told my final probation report was coming up and I would have to be judged alongside any full-timers. No allowance for a part-timer's half experience.

Another part-time trainee felt that she was up against a brick wall of hostility from the outset:

I'm resigning because the feeling . . . was that I was a dead loss. . . but on my first day the [manager] called me in and, in no pleasant tones, I was asked what management experience and what accountancy experience I had. When I said, 'None,' he said, 'What good are you to me? . . . I've spent all these years getting to my position and you walk straight in.

For a few women then, there *was* no strategy for success other than to walk

of expertise and training effort for the department and a loss of dignity for themselves. Fortunately, theirs was a minority experience, but it indicates the difficulty in translating equal opportunity principles into practice through less-committed line managers.

Conclusion

This study would suggest that the majority of women in middle management in HM Customs and Excise were certainly career-minded. They listened carefully to management feedback on their performance and thought carefully about how to develop the right profile for career advancement. Those who wanted families organised the advent of children *around* their careers or selected 'down time' in which to temporarily work part-time by way of a 'damage limitation' exercise. Self-confidence was a striking feature among those who were forging ahead.

Stereotyped attitudes towards women as managers, sometimes spilling over into received sexist behaviour, were accepted as inevitable but subtly managed and challenged via informal and interpersonal channels in most cases.

Some of the departmental initiatives to promote equal opportunities for women were not always perceived as useful by the women in this study, for example part-time working (which was not always domestically practicable, financially viable or a working success) and formal sexual harassment complaints procedures (which were sometimes seen as too heavy-handed). Other departmental initiatives were well utilised. For example, working mothers *did* avail themselves of the maternity leave provisions. In addition, since these studies were completed, more women are reported to be coming forward *informally* in response to the sexual harassment support networks established following the Midlands study into harassment, and departmental nurseries are full and have waiting lists.

More important to most career-minded women in *this* study, however, was how they were individually managed and treated at work. Accurate feedback on, and recognition of, their strengths, plus relevant development of themselves by their line managers was of crucial importance. Much of this was articulated through the women's criticism of the staff reporting system. This system has undergone major changes during 1993–4 as it shifts its focus more towards identifying competencies in assessing the individual and performance related pay. In addition, job losses of 4000 over five years, 550 being customs officers (Elliott, 1995), will increase competition in the promotion systems. However, it is likely that issues for women will survive these changes for they centre on adequate *recognition* and *development* which will remain features of the new process.

Overall, the message was clear. Women loved their work and wanted to contribute more, finding ways and means to do this. Both work-related and family-related strategies were necessary in order to achieve their objectives, and women were prepared to put in this effort. The result was a body of committed managers whose loyalty was an invaluable resource to HM Customs and Excise.

Note

1. Great Britain is divided into geographic regions for the purpose of collecting both Customs and Excise duties, and also VAT. The regions are called 'collections'. Collections are further divided into districts for administrative purposes.

CHAPTER 6

Sisters organising – women and their trade unions

Fiona Colgan and Sue Ledwith[1]

Introduction

Women make up almost half of the British workforce. Yet only one-third of trade union[2] members are women, and within their unions women rarely reach the top; in 1994 there were four female general secretaries. Throughout the 1980s there were never more than five unions led by a woman, and in only a third were women represented on national executive bodies in proportion to their membership.

In a patriarchal society, where women's place is still seen as secondary to men's, this is perhaps unsurprising. Nevertheless, during the 25-year period of second-wave feminism, and since the introduction of government legislation rendering sex and race discrimination unlawful, a range of initiatives have been developed within the trade union movement to endeavour to ensure that a 'woman's place is in her union' (Hunt, 1982).

In this chapter we identify and evaluate these measures and explore some of the strategies and styles women themselves are developing in pursuit of more purposeful change. We do so first through an examination of studies of women and their trade unions, and then through some preliminary results of our study of women active in the newly amalgamated trade unions, the Graphical Paper and Media Union (GPMU – born of the merger of the Society of Graphical and Allied Trades (SOGAT '82) with the National Graphical Association (NGA)) and the new public sector super-union UNISON (constituted of the former National Union of Public Employees (NUPE), the National Association of Local Government Officers (NALGO) and the Confederation of Health Service Employees (COHSE)).

First however we set out the broad picture of female trade union membership in its political, economic and social context. This leads into a discussion of trade union structures and women's positions in these hierarchies. What we identify as 'liberal' trade union equality initiatives to 'let women in' (Briskin, 1993) are discussed and evaluated against an overlapping set of more 'radical' approaches. An emergent raft of alternative collaborative feminist projects are examined and identified, together with the strategies pursued by women in order to move them forward.

In mapping this potentially transformative terrain, we identify key influences and ideologies which have spurred women to become active trade unionists, and supported them in their endeavours.

Finally we weigh up the case for a long agenda as women's increasingly innovative 'struggle for equality' (SERTUC, 1994) within their unions offers the potential for creative change and union democratisation for all members, women and men.

The context

The context of British industrial relations altered radically after 1979 when the Conservative Government gained power (Millward *et al.*, 1992). Trade unions found themselves operating in an economically and politically hostile environment. Economic restructuring meant the expansion of service sector employment (often part-time) and the loss of jobs in the primary sector – the traditional base of British trade unionism (Jensen, Reddy and Hagen, 1988). As a result of the Conservative Government's campaign against what it saw as an abuse of trade union power and a lack of democracy, between 1979 and 1993 the legal framework governing trade unionism was transformed.

Since 1979 British trade unions have had to argue the case for their continued relevance to both employees (and their members or potential members) and to employers. This has been a difficult task, as can be seen in the overall decline of approximately 36% in membership of the Trades Union Congress (TUC) unions following the highwater mark of 1979. (Farnham and Giles, 1995). Although the extent of actual union de-recognition has probably been overemphasised, unions have found it much harder to gain recognition rights in new establishments in the newly expanding service industries (Gall and McKay 1994). Avoidance of existing trade unions by employers in more traditional workplaces has also been found to be extensive (Millward, 1994).

This changing landscape has led most unions to acknowledge the need to reconsider and reform their existing structures, policies and practices in attempts to make themselves more attractive to the workforce of the 1980s and 1990s (Bradley, 1993). The TUC's own investigations found the movement out of step with young people and women entering the labour market, and both the TUC and leading trade unions have remodelled themselves in the search for this new membership and a greater engagement with it, including increasing awareness of equality issues (TUC, 1994; Heery and Kelly, 1994).

Nevertheless, although the impact of labour market restructuring has been significant on male trade union membership, neither this, nor efforts by the TUC and its affiliates, have had much effect on union density among women in the union movement's traditional membership territory. At the end of 1992, 39 per cent of employed men in the UK were members of trade unions (down from 43 per cent in 1990). But the figure for women stayed the same at 32 per cent for the three years to 1992 (Labour Research, 1994).

However, trade union membership had increased, dramatically, among well-qualified, white-collar professional workers, a very high proportion of whom were female (Farnham and Giles, 1995). These women had joined non-TUC-affiliated unions, which Farnham and Giles (1995) have termed 'public-sector professional associations' and 'new model moderate unions', at a rate of increase between 1979 and 1991 of 130 per cent, bringing the female membership proportion in non TUC-affiliates from 48 per cent in 1980 to 62 per cent in 1991 (Farnham and Giles, 1995).

Clearly the differential trends of women's membership in the two types of trade unions need further study; however, this chapter is concerned with the position of women in traditional TUC unions, together with the more radical potential for change and renewal within the trade union movement offered by women's particular trade union activism. Over the past 15 years, trade union women have posed a creative challenge to the structures, strategies and ideologies of trade unions in Britain and elsewhere (Briskin and McDermott, 1993; Booth and Rubenstein, 1990; Coote and Campbell, 1987). Slowly but surely, as trade unions have realised that the labour movement needs women as new members, women (and some men) trade union activists have sought to shift the internal life within their unions in order to ensure that women's issues are taken up in negotiation, training courses are developed to suit their needs, and that unions are made more hospitable for women and men (Briskin and McDermott, 1993).

Nevertheless, as is evident from Table 6.1, there is still an enormous imbalance between the representation of women in positions of power and authority within the trade union movement relative to their representation as members (Colling and Dickens, 1989; Labour Research, 1994).

The list of putative causes for this under-representation is a long one: patriarchal attitudes, inequality at work, union rules on office-holding, inconvenient times and locations of union meetings, unequal sharing of domestic responsibilities and the lack of quality childcare provision have all played a part (Ledwith et al., 1990; Rees, 1990).

TABLE 6.1 Women in trade unions – the largest 10 TUC affiliates, 1994

	UNISON	T&GWU	AEEU	GMB	MSF	USDAW	GPMU	UCW	NUT	UCATT
Total membership	1,400,000	958,834	546,000	800,000	552,000	316,491	250,230	180,586	162,192	157,000
% as women	68	18	9	37	27	60	17	20	74	2
% on NEC	42#	5	0	36	24	61	5	20	27	0
% at Conf	46†	10	8	25	25	42	11	not known	48	1
% TUC del (1993 figs)	54	20	6	33	33	12	5	20	35	0
% National officers	20	9	11	13	18	19	5	17	16	0
% Regional officers	31	7	0	0	12*	21*	2†●	0*	11	0*

* 1993 figures.
# 1993 figures, the new Executive elections in 1995 achieved proportionality for women.
● 1995 Branches covering geographical areas are roughly the equivalent of Regions.
† 1995

Sources: SERTUC (1994); Labour Research; 'Women's Special – women in unions: still too few at the top,' March 1994; F. Colgan and S. Ledwith; Unison and GPMU research programme, 1995.

The relative absence of women in positions of power within the trade union movement is significant because it means that a lag is likely to remain between trade union policy and rhetoric on equal opportunities and much trade union practice. Although women represented by a union continue to enjoy better terms and conditions than those who are not (Martin and Roberts, 1984; Rees, 1992), the gap between male and female earnings has remained virtually unchanged for the last two decades, with women earning only 74 per cent of male gross hourly earnings and 63 per cent of gross weekly pay (Equal Opportunities Commission, 1993; EOR, 1994). Many issues of importance to women workers are still not addressed through collective bargaining, and there is evidence to show that women's disadvantage at work may be perpetuated by collective bargaining practices which do not question existing pay and employment structures (Colling and Dickens, 1989; Ledwith 1991b).

Trade unions have also been criticised for being slow to use legislative measures to improve women's position, such as the Equal Pay Act amendments and the transfer of undertakings legislation, both of which had the potential to improve and protect many women's terms and conditions since the early 1980s (Cunnison and Stageman, 1993; E. Lawrence, 1994.)

There is a growing body of evidence which suggests that many women trade union activists, although committed to improving conditions for both their men and women members, perceive the advancement of working women to be a central function of their union work. Women paid officials, for example, are likely to be 'more concerned' with, and thus make their priorities, organising women and addressing their issues (Heery and Kelly, 1988).

Gender differences appear to exist not only in bargaining priorities, but also in styles of collective bargaining, union organising, communication and representation (Dorgan and Grieco, 1993). Thus feminist critiques of existing trade union practices call for a trade union agenda which embraces such priorities and methods. A feminist trade union agenda requires that unions 'let women in' to current union positions and structures in order to represent and address the needs of women members. It also calls for a feminising and re-visioning of cultures and practices which often operate to exclude and marginalise women's interests and ways of operating (Briskin and McDermott, 1993; Cunnison and Stageman, 1993).

Women and trade union structures

In the traditional areas of trade unionism, despite the increase in women's labour force participation, conditions in women's employment which have always militated against female trade unionism persist. Women dominate part-time work, personal, health and welfare services in both private and public sectors. These are just the situations where the structural characteristics of small scattered workplaces, sporadic labour force participation due to family demands, low pay and low status jobs, plus antagonistic employers (including now swathes of the public sector) make trade union organisation of the traditional pattern costly and difficult. They also locate women's work as subordinate in the workplace hierarchy, with the result that women trade unionists representing mainly female members are sited low in the trade union organisational hierarchy. In other words, the union structure reflects the 'pecking order' at work (SERTUC, 1989). In turn this inequality is reproduced in workplace trade union relations, where management perceive and treat women representatives as being less important than the men. As a result, women activists typically are taken less seriously by managements than their male colleagues and have more difficulty getting time off work to represent their members (Fryer *et al.*, 1978; Heery and Kelly, 1988a; Colling and Dickens, 1989; Ledwith, 1991b).

Nevertheless, within the trade union movement itself women have been making incremental advances. Pushed by resolutions from feminist and socialist women at successive conferences, during the 1970s and 1980s the TUC's women's structures increased their profile and activities (Coote and Campbell, 1987). The duration of the TUC Women's Conference increased, delegates are now to be solely female, its committee was restructured to incorporate more democratic procedures such as rotating the chair. The term 'advisory' was dropped from its title, and an equal rights department was set up within the TUC. Charters for women within their trade unions and for women at work have both been adopted by the movement as a whole. Special measures, again stemming from Women's Conference resolutions on additional seats for women, now ensure a greater representation of women on the TUC General Council, including at least one black woman. The required proportional representation of women delegates has yet to be achieved. Women were only 27.8 per cent of the delegates to 1993 Congress, whereas the overall proportion of women members to TUC affiliates was 36.4 per cent. 'The General Council have noted the improvement this year over last year but are concerned that progress appears to have been confined to a limited number of unions, whereas in certain others there may have been little or no improvement' (Women's Committee Report, 1994). By 1994 women were not proportionately represented on the top decision-making bodies – national executives – in any of the largest 10 trade unions (Labour Research, 1994) and only four TUC unions had female general secretaries. (A peak was reached in 1990 when there were five women general secretaries.)

However, structural changes in trade unions over this period also complicate the picture. A substantial number of mergers and amalgamations took place, for example, reducing the total number of TUC unions from 84 in 1989 to 68 in 1994 (SERTUC, 1989, 1994). Since mergers ultimately mean streamlined organisational hierarchies, they also tend to reduce the opportunities for women and other minority groups to increase their representation up the union structures.

In particular the squeeze in the number of full-time, paid officer positions available seemed to come just when women were beginning to move on, up and through the barriers in their unions (TUC Women's Committee Report, 1994; SERTUC, 1994).

This is shown especially in the ranks of women's officers. In 1987 a survey of trade unions found 14 unions reporting the appointment of a full-time women's officer. Yet by 1992 the number was down to six, and only up to nine two years later (SERTUC, 1987, 1992, 1994). By 1994 nine of those 14 unions of 1987 had merged or amalgamated.

As the TUC Women's Committee commented in its 1994 Report to Conference: 'Further amalgamations are likely in the future, and as a result, large amalgamated unions may face difficulties in ensuring a fair representation' (TUC Women's Committee Report, 1994). Subsequently, an entitlement was agreed to additional women delegates to the conference.

Clearly size and structure are key variables in the attempts to encourage and support women's progression in their unions, and can partly help explain how 'unions remain such male institutions while taking so many exciting initiatives to involve women members' (SERTUC, 1989). However, it is the nature of the initiatives themselves and the equality strategies informing them that require closer study. Overwhelmingly, the equality initiatives taken by trade unions can be described as being within the *liberal* model as identified by Jewson and Mason (1986). The liberal approach emphasises the development of 'fair', and frequently bureaucratic, procedures in order to deliver equality. Although permitting positive action to redress past discrimination, it is criticised for failing to challenge or attempt to change the existing organisational power paradigm of gender and race (as discussed in Chapter 1).

In trade unions, liberal action typically includes the introduction of measures such as women's courses, childcare support, changing times of meetings so that they do not clash with women's family responsibilities, and the development of publicity materials. By 1994 the majority, up to three-quarters of trade unions, had such support systems in place. These sit comfortably with the current emphasis on a market-driven 'managerial servicing' relationship with members which Heery and Kelly (1994) have seen trade unions adopting in the 1990s. Market research carried out by both the TUC and some unions resulted in a felt need to attend to the needs of women. For example, the GMB prioritised equality bargaining on discovering that women members had different aspirations from those of men.

This approach, coupled as it was with the drive to recruit new members, has led unions to understand that their membership is not homogeneous, and that not only do different groups have different interests and goals but these need to be seen to be addressed fairly.

Nevertheless, managing traditional trade union values of unity among a newly discovered pluralist membership provides a significant challenge to traditional patriarchal trade unionism. And if Heery and Kelly (1994) are right about the core of this approach being one where union members are viewed as reactive consumers, then the development of a women's agenda raises the prospect of increasing contests across the power structures of trade unions – especially the existing male domain of national executives and national paid officials.

For women's demand for a more radical approach has been gathering momentum. This has emerged from coalitions of union women across a range of different women's perspectives. From one direction are women who, after years of working within the liberal tradition, have become increasingly disillusioned by the slow response of their trade unions to meeting women's needs:

> We have all heard the statements – 'Come on girls! We'll make sure you're looked after' – 'after' being the appropriate word. I think the women members of this union want and deserve more than that, don't you? (GPMU, 1993)

Increasingly, such women have been coming together to form alliances with those from more radical feminist and political strands (Coote and Campbell, 1987). After 25 years of second-wave feminism, women can draw increasingly on a wide and rich range of experiences and strategies of women's projects in their search for challenge, change and transformation; feminisation of their unions (Walby, 1988; Cockburn 1983).

Radical equality structures in trade unions

A *radical* approach to equality seeks to intervene directly in organisational practices in order to achieve fair representation and a fair distribution of rewards among groups. As such, it focuses on equity in outcomes, calling for positive discrimination and consciousness-raising in order to 'release a struggle for power and influence' (Jewson and Mason, 1986).

Only a small number of unions have gone down the radical route and developed separate women-only structures of 'positive discrimination' such as women's conferences, committees, officers and reserved seats on national executive – as they are empowered to do under Section 49 of the 1975 Sex Discrimination Act. See Table 6.2.

Women's conferences

These are important fora for women to meet, support, debate and learn from one another. For women in male-dominated unions, where women are very much a minority, are geographically widely spread and isolated, such conferences provide a vital lifeline and basis for networking with other women activists between meetings. Only a quarter of the unions in the SERTUC 1994 survey held a separate women's conference.

Even where they exist, the influence of women's conferences are often constrained by their remit to produce a report, or advice, to the supreme decision-making bodies – NEC and Conference – rather than make direct recommendations or resolutions.

For example, the TUC Women's Conference for years also debated that a certain number of the women's resolutions should go directly onto the agenda of the annual TUC Congress (often referred to by women as 'the men's conference') rather than, as at present, in a report to General Council.

Women's committees

SERTUC (1994) found that two-thirds of the TUC unions they surveyed had set up women's or equality committees by 1994, and a substantial number had committees at regional and industry level. This middle-ranking level is seen as important for women to gain experience and begin to consolidate their numbers and develop change strategies and skills, resourced by the more liberal support systems referred to earlier.

Women's officers

Only nine unions in the 1994 SERTUC survey had a separate women's officer, with a further nine having equality officers. And only 13 unions had an 'adequate' proportion of female paid national officers compared to their women's membership. As argued by Heery and Kelly (1989), although it may be a 'cracking job for a woman', women's officers and women officials also experience isolation and stress in their struggle for feminist-style agendas. As one woman described her experiences with male colleagues to us: 'when I'm negotiating on behalf of all the members, men and women, I'm one of the boys. When I'm raising women's issues, I'm that damn woman.'

TABLE 6.2 Radical equality structures in trade unions – the largest 10 TUC affiliates, 1994

	UNISON	T&GWU	AEEU	GMB	MSF	USDAW	GPMU	UCW	NUT	UCATT
Members	1,400,000	958,834	546,000	800,000	552,00	316,491	250,230	180,586	162,192	157,000
% as women	68	18	9	37	27	60	17	20	74	2
National Women's/Equality Officer	Y	Y	Y		Y	Y	N	Y	N	N
National Women's/Equality Committee	Y	Y	N	Y	Y	Y	Y	N	Y	N
Womens' seats on Executive	Y	N	N	Y	Y	N	N#	N	N	N
Women's Equality Conference	Y	N	Y	Y	Y	Y	Y	N	Y	N

Y = yes; N = no

\# Agreed at the 1995 Delegate Conference and on all elected structures within the union.

Source: SERTUC (1994); Labour Research; 'Women's Special – women in unions: still too few at the top,' March 1994; F. Colgan and S. Ledwith; UNISON and GPMU research programme, 1995.

National executives

National executives are one of the primary decision-making bodies within trade unions, and are jealously guarded in the espoused interests of delivering union democracy. Proposals for change are closely scrutinised and may produce resistance. Given the potential for feminisation and thus change in the gender power balance in unions, it is not surprising that reserved seats for women on such significant decision-making bodies 'raise strong feelings by supporters and opponents' (SERTUC, 1989). By 1994 there were still only six unions reporting reserved seats for women on their national executives. However, such measures do not necessarily guarantee proportionality.[3] Typically, reserved seats number one or two in an executive of 16 or upwards. In those unions with reserved seats, four had by 1994 come close to having women proportionately represented on their executives. In total, however, only a third of all the unions surveyed had executives which reflected the gender proportions of their membership (SERTUC, 1994).

Towards a long agenda

As the response within trade unions discussed above has shown, the radical approach to equal opportunity is viewed with suspicion by many male and female members. This is particularly the case where it is seen (or can be portrayed) as a vehicle for the pursuit of 'vested minority interests' by one group (women, for example) in order to gain power rather than to change it (Cockburn, 1989). Cynthia Cockburn argues that there is likely to be a greater potential constituency of support for a 'long' equal opportunities agenda which coherently argues the need to make changes to the organisation on grounds that the 'on-going chances of all groups are to be equalised and sustained, democratised and opened' (Cockburn 1989). This is especially relevant in trade unions, where membership and decision-making are based on values of unity and democracy. Traditionally these values have been unitary, and articulated in a gender-neutral manner – with the effect of them being gender (and race) blind. Increasingly trade unions are including in their objectives their commitment to non-discrimination and equal participation, notwithstanding the fact that in practice this is a long way from being delivered.

Thus it is recognised among some trade unionists that organising autonomously is an essential part of making the space to work for change and the delivery of real democracy for women (and other disadvantaged groups) (Cockburn 1984; Briskin and McDermott, 1993).

This raises dilemmas of contradictory and conflicting positions for trade union activists who are seeking to improve the position of women within the labour movement through a pluralist perspective involving separate women's structures.

In particular, where women's trade union activism aims to create transformational change rather than operating as just another vested interest group or faction, it is likely to pose the greatest challenge to traditional trade unionism, even if in the long run it is able to deliver real benefits both for women trade unionists and the union movement as a whole. (Colgan and Ledwith, 1994).

Women working on the long agenda tend to make alliances and coalitions with other activists: for example, those men and women on the 'Broad Left' who advocate a more participative approach to trade union democracy (Heery and Fosh, 1990) plus men and women in equality-seeking groups such as black, lesbian and gay members, and those with disabilities.

Opportunities to organise and push for a long agenda will differ between trade unions. It may be that the chance to do so can best be taken in a period of turbulent change when existing structures are fluid – as happened in UNISON, and as we describe later in the chapter.

Trade union women have found the pace of change 'snail-like' (SERTUC, 1994) and in a patriarchal, male-dominated union world the cycle of challenge and resistance continues. The SERTUC 1994 report illustrated both attack and resistance in the warrior-like description of women's 'battle':

> During the last two years NAPO has *spearheaded* the *attack* on the timing of Congress (clashing as it does with the first week of the school year for the majority of school children.) The *attack was successful* – the motion carried at the 1993 Congress *demanded* action in time for the 1995 TUC although at the time of writing there has been no sight of the promised consultation document. [Our italics] [The TUC has since acquiesced to this demand.]

In the words of SERTUC's Women's Rights Committee's report (1994), women are still 'struggling for equality' and are looking for mechanisms to develop and progress the long agenda in equal opportunities within their trade unions.

Separate organisation

As already indicated, a key mechanism in developing a long equal-opportunities (EO) agenda is a dual strategy of women's organising separately while at the same time continuing to work within mainstream trade union structures and systems.

As identified by Linda Briskin (1993), there are a variety of forms of separate organising within the union movement (e.g. women's networking, conferences, committees, women-only unions) and, despite significant differences among them, it is possible to imagine them along a continuum in their 'degrees of separateness'. She has argued that in a discussion of separate organising, it is critical to distinguish between separatism as a goal, and separate organising as a strategy. She provides the following useful definitions.

1. *Separate organisation* can be identified both as a goal, an end in itself, a means to an end. Such separate organisation 'often includes an explicit refusal to work with men and usually focuses on the building of alternative communities as a solution rather than the transformation of dominant social structures' (Briskin, 1993).

2. Separate organisation as a strategy — a means to an end, a way of building and empowering women in their struggle for equality.

The conflation of the two means that the latter is often criticised for being a divisive strategy in the union movement 'rather than as a means to strengthen not only the voices of women, but of the union movement as a whole' (Briskin, 1993).

In order to differentiate between the two, we refer here to *separatism* as a goal in itself, whereby women-only unions are seen as a means of ensuring women's control over their own union activities, over bargaining agendas, over modes of operating and of association, and of self-expression and self-development.

Contemporary evidence from Canada, Ireland and the UK, as well as the historical story of women's separate trade union organisation in nineteenth-century Britain (Drake, 1984; Davis, 1993) indicates however that women's separate organisation as an end in itself is too delicate an organism to survive where it is seen as competing with traditional patriarchal trade unionism (Briskin and McDermott, 1993; Ledwith, 1985). However Milkman (1985) provides some positive evidence of the success of independent women's organisations such as the '9 to 5', in organising women office workers in the USA.

Conversely, what we call *interim separatism*[4] can be seen as a strategy of separate organising by women (and other disadvantaged groups) in order to develop a collective feminist consciousness and empower women in their struggle to alter existing, mainstream political and organisational structures (Briskin, 1993). It is a strategy not unknown within trade unions, and like feminist strategies, the struggles of and resistance to a range of political and pressure group factions in trade unions are well documented. The stories of such conflicts also illustrate the complexity of the issues, the shifting terrain, and the long agendas for success and failure such as those experienced in the 'rebellion' in the National Union of Seamen between 1960 and 1974 (Hemingway, 1978).

Trade union activists of both sexes often assume that interim separatism as a strategy is only necessary until equality is achieved within the union movement. This view is based on that common commitment to the principle of trade union unity already discussed, and an antipathy to what is described in some union circles as 'trade union apartheid'.

Nevertheless, over the last 15 years, women and other marginalised groups (black workers, lesbians and gay men and disabled workers) have increasingly sought opportunities to organise separately in order to raise their concerns and work towards the transformation of their unions (Briskin, 1993).

So, in the light of the consistent failure of patriarchal trade unions to deliver equality through liberal – if any – measures, women have been pushing for a two-track approach. This involves women increasingly taking the initiative to propel their unions to move forwards from their preferred short agenda on EO into adopting a longer agenda through developing structures of interim separatism such as quotas, women's conferences, courses and committees (Briskin and McDermott, 1993; Cunnison and Stageman, 1993; Milkman, 1985).

How then are such changes achieved? It has been mainly women who have educated, persuaded and united in order to use existing trade union systems and structures to bring about change, as already illustrated by the work of the TUC Women's Conference and Committee. Over the years their proposals have been adopted formally as policy by both the TUC and constituent unions; a whole raft of initiatives flowing from their charters for women at work and women within trade unions were developed in the 1970s and 1980s (Coote and Campbell, 1987). Canadian sociologist Carl Cuneo (1993) takes the view that 'Feminism today is the most creative energy within the labour movement.' However, to what degree do women trade unionists themselves agree with this view? Are they organising around a feminist agenda, and how much support exists for a strategy of interim separatism and a long equal-opportunities agenda among British women trade union activists?

Trade union case studies: UNISON and the GPMU

Our research focuses on women's trade union activism within two British trade unions operating within different industry sectors and with differing structures and policies concerning the delivery of equal opportunities for male and female trade union members.

Research method

In the late 1980s we were engaged in research with the print and paper union SOGAT '82. Following its amalgamation with the National Graphical Association (NGA) to form the Graphical, Paper and Media Union (GPMU), we were interested in tracking equality initiatives within the new union. At the same time we approached another newly merged union, UNISON, with a view to carrying out some comparative work. This research is on-going, and in the following discussion we draw on the preliminary work carried out in 1994, in addition to our earlier research with SOGAT '82.

In 1994 we attended two trade union women's conferences where we administered self-completion questionnaires, and carried out interviews. A total of 77 women activists at all levels in both unions completed questionnaires (see Table 6.3), and group discussions and interviews involving 50 women have taken place.[5]

Early data from this study points to some patterns which are discussed later in this chapter. Figures in the tables here are derived from the self-completion questionnaires. Because the sample at this stage was quite small, and in order to ensure anonymity, responses from both unions were aggregated and the tables and discussion is based on this aggregation.

The two unions

The two unions have been selected to allow comparisons between an 'open' union with a large female membership which has embarked on an ambitious equal opportunities programme with a 'long agenda', with that of a 'closed', predominantly male craft/manual trade union following a more limited, and much contested, shorter agenda.

TABLE 6.3   Women trade unionists by levels of activism in their union (1994 study)

	Number	%
National	17	22.0
Local	26	33.8
Workplace	26	33.8
Member (not a representative)	8	10.4
Totals:	77	100.00

Structures of interim separatism are further developed within UNISON than the GPMU. Demands for self-organisation have been more slowly developed by GPMU women for a variety of reasons, including the strength of opposition to women's self-organisation which exists within the union. As we have already indicated, opposition comes from two overlapping groups, firstly those 'traditionalist' men and women within the union who see interim separatism as divisive to trade union unity, and secondly from an influential proportion of the union's predominantly male members who remain wedded to their union's patriarchal structures and culture.

The GPMU

The GPMU is a private sector, manufacturing union, organising in an industry which is male dominated, traditional, patriarchal, and highly occupationally segmented by gender with women dominating the low-paid, designated low-skill jobs. It was formed in 1991 following the merger of SOGAT '82 and the NGA. The print unions were traditionally strong, with a high level of membership density and pre-entry closed shops. Women made up a third of SOGAT's membership, whereas in the GPMU it is 17 per cent. The GPMU can be characterised as a closed union, whereby only members (with a minimum of five years) may stand for and be elected to office. The intention of such a constitutional requirement is to ensure that paid officers are representative of the union membership. However, it has been suggested by Heery and Kelly (1988a) that, ironically, such closure may work against attempts to improve the representation of women.

During the 1980s delegate conferences of both SOGAT and the NGA turned down separatist measures to improve women's chances and positions in their unions. The NGA Conference defeated a 1988 proposal for reserved women's seats on the national executive. Also in 1988 the SOGAT conference overturned an executive proposal for a union organiser with special responsibility for female members. The loudest applause in the debate was reserved for the woman speaker who declared: 'For years women have sought equality. If in that search we have to be treated separately, we will never be treated as equal' (Ledwith *et al.*, 1990).

In 1990, SOGAT '82's Delegate Conference finally voted that there should be an annual women's conference. Explaining this later, the female General Secretary, Brenda Dean, commented

At last year's BDC we had come through the glass ceiling. I saw woman after woman come up to the rostrum and speak, and hold their own with the best of the men in a male dominated union. It was like the culmination of a decade's work, of laying the ground, of encouraging and working with good women and creating a network. We knew when we went into the area of raising the profile of women in

SOGAT that it would create challenges. And after the slap in the face of the 1988 BDC [when a proposal from the NEC for a women's organiser was defeated by conference] I felt we were beginning to motor at last. (Ledwith, 1991a)

The Women's Conference was put into place in the run up to amalgamation with the NGA, which already had a Women's Committee elected from across the membership. Key women in both unions were determined that both structures should be embedded in the new amalgamated union's constitution. So were key men, who could also see that with the decline of the printing industry, male job and membership losses, and large numbers of unorganised women working in the industry, a woman-friendly union was vital for its long-term survival.

The GPMU therefore has a biennial Women's Conference and a national Women's Committee (first established in the NGA in 1980) which advises the National Executive.

In 1994 only 3 per cent of GPMU branch officials were women, and 5 per cent of the National Executive Council positions were held by women (SER-TUC, 1994). The disparity with the proportion of women in membership led the GPMU Delegate Conference in 1993 to accept the principle of proportional representation for women on its National Executive. The actual constitutional changes to deliver this were agreed at the union's 1995 rules revision conference.

However, there is no women's officer; the sole female industrial officer is responsible for 'protecting and administering' the interests of women members, but the Deputy General Secretary (male) has overall responsibility (SERTUC, 1994). Courses for women are organised and crèches or other childcare arrangements are provided for conferences and courses.

UNISON

UNISON was formed in 1993 from the merger of COHSE, NALGO and NUPE. It is a public sector union with 1 400 00 members (manual and non-manual) of which 68 per cent are women. UNISON can be characterised as an open union, whereby paid officials are normally appointed following public and open advertisement of positions and are seen as skilled experts hired for the specialist services they can offer to union members (Heery and Kelly, 1988a). Heery and Kelly (1988a) suggested that such open recruitment practices benefited women, as did the use of more formalised, bureaucratic selection procedures.

Structures of interim separatism were well established among its constituents NALGO, NUPE and COHSE prior to amalgamation in 1993, and were supported by a range of measures such as women only training and childcare support.

NALGO set up a national Equal Opportunities Committee in 1977 which in 1989 became a Women's Committee. Equal opportunities committees existed at district and branch level throughout the union. There was no formal women's officer – an assistant research officer had responsibility for encouraging women's participation.

NUPE was one of the first unions to introduce reserved seats for women on the Executive, in 1975, and on divisional councils. A Women's Advisory Committee was introduced in 1984, and there were divisional women's committees. A Women's Officer was appointed in 1983.

COHSE established an equality NEC sub-committee in 1979, and a Women's Committee in 1991. It had reserved women's (and men's) seats on regional councils, and a Women's Officer.

In the run up to amalgamation, women – in strategic alliances of both sexes and with other oppressed groups, and with key figures in the labour movement – worked to achieve these agendas, and to ensure that they were maintained and strengthened in the implementation. Women and their allies had worked on developing a long agenda by achieving constitutional legitimacy for separatist equality measures *within* the union's legitimate structures and boundaries.

So UNISON was born with a constitution based on proportionality and 'fair representation' for women, members of all grades, black members, disabled members and lesbians and gay men in order to establish a 'truly democratic union' (UNISON, 1994). Implementation is via a system of Self-Organised Groups (SOGs), and for women, a network of paid Womens' Officers at regional level. In putting all these into place, UNISON has 'taken the lead in the trade union movement in making the commitment to achieve proportionality throughout its structures' (UNISON, 1994). The aim is to accomplish the task, in the lay structures, by the year 2000. At the birth of the new union, when the executives of the three constituent unions came together as an interim body, women made up only 42 per cent compared with 68 per cent of the total membership. Among officers, only 20 per cent at senior national level were women, as were 31 per cent of regional officers (SERTUC, 1994).

Key mechanisms to achieve fair representation include a national Women's Committee, with a Women's Officer reporting to the Director of Equal Opportunities (as do officers for disabled members, black members and lesbian and gay members), and annual women's conferences at national and regional level. There are self-organised structures for these groups up and down the union; at national, regional and branch level. Women's proportionality was delivered at the first UNISON National Executive Council elections in 1995 whereby, under rule, the number of women elected to the new Executive was to be at least proportional to their membership at that time. In addition, 13 seats were reserved for low-paid women members.

Thus self-organisation (or interim separatism) has been legitimised within the constitution of the new union as a 'central plank in the union's goal of becoming a membership-centred union' (EOR, 1993b). The union also provides funding and other resources such as childcare and training to support the groups.

It is clear from union documentation, and reinforced by women we interviewed, that the ultimate goal of these measures of interim separatism is to increase unity, not to reduce it; to encourage active participation of women, disabled, black and lesbian and gay members in the union's mainstream structures, and to integrate equality issues in the core bargaining agenda.

As the Director of Equal Opportunities has put it, 'self organisation is not equated with separatism, it is about empowerment.' (EOR, 1993b)

Nevertheless, this innovative approach has led to some scepticism within the union as to how the ideal is to be achieved, according to UNISON's Women's Officer (Labour Research, 1994). However she is confident that 'just adopting the principle has caught women's imagination' and has created a 'momentum ' for women's expectations and activism within the new union (Labour Research, 1994).

Women trade unionists

As we have argued that women trade union activists provide a key element in the change and renewal of the trade union movement, the rest of the chapter will focus on women activists themselves, their activities, attitudes and their trade union experience. Specifically, it will discuss similarities and differences among feminist and non-feminist women activists, the women's perceptions of and support for a feminist trade union agenda, and their views on systems of interim separatism for women's organisation.

A typology of trade union women's consciousness

From our earlier work with SOGAT women, we developed a typology of trade union women activists (Ledwith *et al.*, 1990). Here we build on this, using the initial findings from the 1994 survey of UNISON and GPMU women; both studies are reported and discussed here.

The typology is derived from the concept of women's consciousness as a trajectory encompassing the range of attitudes from traditionalism to feminism, discussed in Chapter 1.

Being a traditional woman implies acceptance of women's gendered place in the family, the labour market and in the trade union. Traditionalism is closely aligned to a unitary perspective (Fox, 1966), whereby a trade union's values are centred on loyalty and unity, as enshrined in SOGAT's rule book:

> Unity is the most prized weapon of working people, and each and every member has a part to play in forging that unity. (Cited in Ledwith *et al.*, 1990)

From this perspective, challenges to existing gendered structures by feminists, or any factions, or 'entrists' seeking changes, may be seen as attacks on the union's ideology of unity, and its integrity in delivering to the members.

A trade union feminist is a woman whose values, knowledge and understanding, her consciousness, informs female strategies aimed at the transformation of patriarchal structures and obstructions in her union and the wider labour movement. A feminist is likely to have a pluralist (Fox, 1966) or more radical perspective (Hyman, 1975) on trade unionism.

Traditional women

Traditional trade union women typically pursue a liberal approach to equality for women in their union, within existing structures and traditions. They would not wish to call themselves feminist, seeing such radicalism (and separatism) as divisive and anti-pathetic to their own trade union experience and values.

These women were often uneasy about interim separatism as a strategy, arguing that they did not seek 'special treatment'. They wished to promote strict 'equality' as opposed to differential treatment based on sex. They had normally learned their trade unionism within the patriarchal structure and culture of the print industry where they worked in traditional female production jobs, and the print unions. Often their partners also worked in the industry and were involved in the union.

Feminist women

At the other end of the spectrum were two sub-groups of feminists:

Feminist socialists. These women had initially become politicised outside trade unions for example, during their post-school education experience, such as student union politics, community organising and the women's movement, and in black, lesbian and gay and disability campaigning groups. With this background these women quite quickly became active participants in their union at the workplace and were thus spotted and asked to formally stand for office. Their purpose was to introduce new styles of organising using feminist practice and styles of democracy so as to deliver equality and democracy to all sections of the labour movement.

Socialist feminists. These women's feminist perspective was born out of their trade unionism and political consciousness, developed initially through socialist politics. Their mode of working for democracy for women in their union was informed by their experience of trade union hierarchy and especially their commitment to trade union and working-class unity. Sometimes these fitted uneasily with their feminism, and often they would be uncomfortable with being labelled as 'feminists'.

A key difference between the feminists and the traditionalists were that the former were actively seeking ways of challenging and changing their trade unions, albeit using subtly different approaches. The feminists saw interim separatism not as a divisive strategy within the union movement, but rather as a necessary means to empower women, oppose divisive sexist practices and thus strengthen the union movement as a whole.

Women in transition

A number of traditional women were increasingly questioning why their union was not delivering for women despite espoused policies on women's equality. We identified these questioning women as being in transition. Their exposure to and debate with the views and analysis of feminist women, particularly at women-only formal and informal meetings, opened up opportunities for a re-evaluation and critique of the structures and strategies which could be developed to ensure equality for all trade union members. Only time would tell if these women's trade union activism was likely to remain limited.

Welfarist women

A fourth group was identified, which we called welfarist women. These were women without a labourist family background and thus without a predisposition for active trade unionism. Typically they had been galvanised into activism by an injustice or particular problem at work experienced either by themselves or female colleagues. Without the development of an ideological commitment to either trade unionism or feminism to sustain them, such women's trade union activism was likely to remain limited.

Self-identification as feminists

Since feminist endeavours embracing interim separatism were clearly so central to moving along the road to a feminisation of their unions, we asked the women in the 1994 GPMU/UNISON survey whether or not they would consider themselves a feminist.

Just over a quarter of the women (19) said yes, they did consider themselves to be feminist. Over half said they did not (41) and 18 per cent (13) didn't know. More UNISON women were feminist: 50 per cent, with only 13 per cent of the GPMU women as self-declared feminists. This difference could be considered a consistent outcome of the culture of the respective unions and their industries.

As indicated earlier, women learn their trade unionism and their feminism in a variety of ways. Here we discuss a few key influences, taken from the preliminary analysis of our GPMU and UNISON women in order to provide a profile of our women activists. Then we move onto a discussion of their priorities, styles and strategies as trade unionists.

Early socialisation in the family

Sixty five per cent of the feminists had mothers who were socialists or liberals, so did 56 per cent of the non-feminists and 44 per cent of those who didn't know. A smaller number of feminists had trade union mothers (41 per cent) and fathers (53 per cent). But two-thirds of feminists had a socialist or liberal father (67 per cent).

The figures for the non-feminist or don't know women with socialist or liberal and trade union parents, were consistently smaller. Although too early in our analysis to draw any clear conclusions, the consistency of the links between those who were feminists and their early general and trade union politicisation came over quite strongly, echoing the experience of a SOGAT woman activist in our earlier study: 'We got our father's politics rammed down our throats so I was always politically aware. I've done exactly the same and my family are all political people' (cited in Ledwith *et al.*, 1990).

Altogether, half of all our women activists had fathers who had been or were members of a trade union, and 36 per cent had fathers who were active in their unions. Not surprisingly, fewer had mothers who were trade unionists (30 per cent) and only 9 per cent had mothers who were activists.

Work experiences

When it came to the women's workplace experiences, gendered occupational segregation was still very much in evidence: 46 per cent of our sample worked mainly with women, a quarter with about equal numbers of men and women, and 27 per cent with mainly men. However about half of both feminists and non feminists worked in mainly female areas. On the one hand the sisterliness of working together with women can provide an important basis for developing support and networking systems in women's trade union and feminist strategies.

Yet gender segmentation may also mask from women's view the informal patriarchal politics, structures and systems, so reducing opportunities for women to develop their political awareness. In addition, for women, gendered occupational segregation usually involves lower status, pay and thus control over their working lives than male colleagues in superior positions. Taking on union activism in these conditions often entails constant struggle with employers and fellow trade unionists (Ledwith, 1991b).

In addition, some women activists felt that in a number of work situations management had been able to exploit the divisions which existed between male and female workers. Male trade unionists who prioritised the interests of skilled and semi-skilled male workers over the interests of women who were considered low in the ' pecking order' were particularly criticised. Thus in the printing industry, a SOGAT woman activist reported taking on a union role because she could 'see where things were going so wrong for the women'. The view was often expressed that when it came to differences with management 'the women support the men but the men never support the women' (Colgan, 1988).

Family responsibilities

Women's family responsibilities impinge on their union role, and women who are active in their unions are forced to make choices – like this SOGAT official who had to choose between her union career and her child:

> I thought long and hard about standing [for the senior full-time branch secretary's position – she was already deputy.] A lot of the . . . members asked me why I didn't. But you need to do the secretary's job with a total commitment, to be there whenever you are needed, especially in a dispute. I felt it was wrong to stand for office knowing that if my family, my child, needed me, she came first. A union expects its officials to put it first. It's like being married to the union. (Ledwith, 1987)

Over half of the women in our 1994 study had children, and as we found earlier among SOGAT women, the age of their children made a significant difference to women's activism. As can be seen from Table 6.4 below, nearly two-thirds of the women had children aged over 11, and the mothers of pre-school children were the smallest group of all the activists.

TABLE 6.4   **Women trade unionists' current family responsibilities**
(1994 study)

Age of children	Women with children	% of women
Under 3	3	4
3–5	4	6
6–10	5	7
11–17	14	19
over 18	31	43

Trade union role

If gendered job segregation is significant for the development of women's consciousness and political skills, then gendered trade union representation will also be important for women in development of their feminism and women's strategies within their trade union.

Two-thirds of the 1994 sample of active trade union women represented mainly women at their workplace and at other levels in their union (60 per cent or more of members represented), with only 22.2 per cent representing men and women equally, and 13 per cent representing mainly men.

Gender differences were also evident when it came to asking the women who encouraged them to take on their first elected union role.

Of the 73 per cent of women activists who reported being encouraged to take on the role, feminists had mainly felt encouraged by female members (44 per cent), whereas only a third of the other women activists had mainly felt encouraged by female members (33 per cent).

However, substantially more feminists had also been encouraged by their male workplace representatives (50 per cent), whereas other women activists cited male paid officials (19 per cent), female workplace representatives (17 per cent) and their partners (13 per cent).

When the women were asked why they first became active in their union, they revealed that paramount was their concern to improve women's position. As shown in Table 6.5, both feminists and non-feminists took on their first elected trade union role to make sure that women were represented.

In addition, one of the main trade union activities the women would like to spend more time on was 'advising and representing *women* members'. This finding was similar to Heery and Kelly's (1988a) findings that, among their women trade union officers, activities which appeared to be unambiguously popular were the promotion of women's issues.

Reinforcing this focus on women, two-thirds of all the women, and 82 per cent of feminists among the GPMU and UNISON women, agreed with the statement '*I would only vote for a union bargaining agenda which contained women's issues.*'

Feminist attitudes and strategies

The 1994 preliminary results identified that only a quarter of the active women trade unionists considered themselves to be feminist. Yet consistently, substantially more women than self-identified feminists showed beliefs and attitudes which we would describe as feminist. There appeared to be a remarkable consensus among feminists and non-feminists about what needed to be done for women in their unions. Regardless of self-perception, trade union women's primary attitudes seemed to be in agreement with what can be labelled feminist principles and strategies.

Our findings here are similar to Sugiman's (1993) work on women trade union activists in the Canadian United Auto Workers (UAW). She suggests that although many trade union women denied that they held 'feminist' ideas and loyalties, as did our traditional and welfarist women, they had drawn on the principles and strategies of the women's movement and often allied themselves with feminist positions. As one of the UAW women she quotes indicated: 'That word feminist doesn't sit with me the way it should. I believe

TABLE 6.5   Women trade unionists: reasons for taking on their first elected position in the union?

Rank order of importance by:	Feminists (%)	Non-feminists (%)
Problems at work	18.0	13.8
Make sure women are represented	16.0	15.5
Asked to take on the position	16.0	16.4
To do a better job than existing representative	16.0	6.9
Interested in being active	14.0	6.0
No one else would do it	12.0	18.1
Could do a good job for for members	6.0	18.1
Make sure black workers represented	2.0	0.0
Job dull/interest in Union work	0.0	3.5
Other	0.0	1.7
Non-responses (number)	1	5
Total sample	19	58

that every human being has a right to choices. But nothing to do with male or female' (cited in Sugiman, 1993).

Sugiman suggests that given the fact that feminism was associated with preferential rather than equal treatment, women auto workers 'moved carefully and somewhat ambivalently between conventional womanhood, patriarchal unionism, and a working-class feminism or feminist unionism' (Maroney, 1986; Sugiman, 1993).

Similar contradictions can be seen in the views of British trade union women. SOGAT's former female General Secretary had this to say: 'I was switched off by feminism in the early 1970s and I would not describe myself as a feminist in accordance with the public interpretation of the word' (Kinnock and Millar, 1993).

Yet Brenda Dean went on to describe her commitment to the improvement of women's lives at work and in the union. It was unlikely that the industry's national agreements would have contained women's issues such as cancer screening, sexual harassment, childcare, maternity and equal pay, up front and non-negotiable, had a woman not been leading the union negotiations.

Similarly, a highly active woman among the 1994 sample described her extensive socialist political and trade union experience and know-how, yet did not see herself as a 'full' feminist although she supported a 'feminist' agenda within her union. 'I can't be a feminist; I'm married. One day perhaps.'

Another woman with a similar background, including a male partner also a trade union activist, did classify herself a feminist – now. Fifteen years ago she took a traditional line, and saw feminism as divisive of trade union and socialist unity. She attributed her arrival at a feminist position to the accumulation of her own and her women members' experiences over the years.

Another woman described her route to feminism as: 'I'm a socialist and a feminist. Women make up 50 per cent of the population and yet remain second class citizens – a source of cheap labour either inside the house or out at work . . .'

Traditional trade unionism itself had also triggered feminist consciousness – not always in a positive way: 'The trade union movement has made me a feminist. Inequality in trade unions highlighted the need to tackle this issue.'

For those women who described the experiences and influences which had led them to a feminist perspective, it was negative personal encounters with discrimination and oppression at work, in the union, in the family and in society which dominated the responses.

For others the road to feminism had been more positive: 'It was my mother's influence, women's lot in general, education, family.' 'I learned my politics and feminism as a student activist while at university.'

Although we found in our research that differences did exist between the women who would consider themselves feminist and those who did not, we found considerable consensus around a number of issues, plus significant support for a strategy of interim separatism.

For example, three-quarters (75.3 per cent) of all the women and 76.5 per cent of the feminist women, agreed with the statement '*I believe that women's equality at work is the most important issue for my union today.*'

A massive 98.5 per cent of the women agreed that they would vote for *special measures to enable women to be better represented in their union*. One hundred per cent of feminists and 97.5 per cent of non feminists agreed.

When asked if women trade union representatives/officials were *more likely to encourage women's participation in the union than male representatives*, 72 per cent of feminists and 84 per cent of non-feminists agreed.

On voting in union elections, if faced with *a female and a male candidate of equal ability*, 70 per cent said they would vote for the woman (78 per cent of feminists and 65 per cent of non-feminists agreed with this statement).

Three-quarters of the women (88.9 per cent of feminists and 67.5 per cent of non-feminists) were in favour of women-only training and education in the union.

However, while considerable support could be found for a feminist agenda, and a number of measures which added together could comprise a strategy which we can recognise as interim separatism, it is worth noting that 56 per cent of feminists and 85 per cent of non-feminists agreed with the statement '*I would not vote for any measure which might divide my union.*'

This serves as a warning to those seeking to develop a long agenda for the delivery of equal opportunities for women through the development of an interim separatist strategy. Currently there *would* appear to be support among both feminist and non-feminist women activists for this approach – the inequalities faced by women within trade unions and the intransigence of patriarchal union structures and cultures seem to have reconciled a majority of feminist and non-feminist women to separatism as an interim measure in addition to other supporting measures.

However as Cockburn has cautioned (1991), considerable care needs to be taken in developing such a strategy if it is to be perceived positively as a means of delivering trade union democracy for all rather than a form of preferential treatment for 'women who want to get on'. Although socialist feminist and feminist socialist women have provided the engine to introduce and gain support for a feminist agenda and a strategy of interim separatism within trade unions, they have been able to do so only with the support and participation of allies of both sexes within the union movement. In particular, we would argue, such support has come from the growing number of traditional women trade unionists whose consciousness we have characterised as being 'in transition'.

In this light, Inez McCormack, UNISON District Secretary in North Ireland, provides an inspirational spokesperson for the transformation being aimed for by feminist trade unionists and their allies: 'I'm interested in women taking power, but I'm more interested in them defining it as a way of challenging inequality in relationships and in society' (cited in Kinnock and Millar, 1993).

She is specifically concerned with how women are using the power they gain, and asks are they 'redefining it by opening up new processes? Are we about change rather than exchange?' (Kinnock and Millar, 1993). Where the vision for equality within trade unions can be articulated clearly in this way, it is more likely to gain support from those committed to improving trade union democracy and participation – both women and men. It also makes it harder for opposing forces to criticise the demands made by women trade unionists as furthering their own sectional feminist agenda at the expense of trade union solidarity.

Feminist practice – a new style of trade unionism?

However, as trade union women move into positions of power, what evidence is there that they wish to use these differently and to bring about a changing style to trade unionism?

When asked what they as *women* bring to their union, the GPMU and UNISON women identified attributes such as common sense, tolerance, empathy, a sense of injustice, the ability to compromise, realism and fair play, and in particular a new less-aggressive approach. A majority also emphasised the insight and perspective that they could bring to their union based on their experience as women, mothers and workers – often from part-time and low-paid sectors. One woman, for example, hoped that she brought 'an awareness of women's current priorities as trade unionists and [I] could function as a representative and speaker that helps to demonstrate that women are trade unionists in the active sense and have validity.'

Many expressed their support for their unions' policies on equality and their active support to see these put into practice. A number were aware that they could operate as role models and wished to 'help get other women more active in the union'. One woman also felt that her presence helped to keep her male trade union colleagues 'on their toes'.

We also asked the women about their styles in representing their members.

A third of all the women thought that there were differences in the way they carried out their responsibilities as a trade union representative compared to male representatives. Forty-eight per cent did not think they did things differently, and 16 per cent said they didn't know. Women feeling that there was little difference between themselves and male colleagues stressed the need to be effective and 'to treat them [all members] as equal whatever their sex'.

The comments made by the women who did see themselves as having different styles revealed a preference for openness, sharing, tolerance, friendliness and availability – as one woman put it: 'A softer approach. More tolerance. Some women [me] are not naturally aggressive' and 'empowering to other women.'

Another felt that she could make a difference:

> Because of my personality, as well as being a woman. I can make meetings less sombre and formal. Because of my ignorance, I can ask questions that make everyone think about current practice. Because the branch is predominantly male and I speak out a lot, women are remembered. We may be small in number, but we can have a large impact.

Male aggressiveness, significantly, was frequently derided. Women saw themselves as less aggressive than men. Women appear to take it (TU representative responsibilities) more seriously than some of the men. Less power-tripping and games than the men.'

Once again women's own experiences frequently informed their styles: 'I understand sexual discrimination and take it more seriously.'

The styles which these women used are in fact similar to those identified by feminist management writers such as Judy Rosener (1990). Rosener's 'transformational' women's management style is about women's collaboration, an interactive approach. In her interviews Rosener found her women managers making frequent reference to their encouragement of participation, sharing power and information, enhancing other people's self-worth and getting others excited about their work.

Networking and caucussing with women

Women were also found to be consciously developing their political skills in furthering the women's agenda in their unions.

Just as the 'pint in the pub' and other forms of networking and caucussing are used by men, so women were doing the same. As one woman put it: 'networking involves supports, enjoyment and educates women to the women's movement so that we can find ways to be viable.' Only 31 per cent of the 1994 sample said that they networked or caucussed with other women trade unionists. However, among those, 63 per cent of those who considered themselves feminists did so, compared with only 21 per cent of non-feminists.

Nevertheless, women often found caucussing distasteful wherever they are on our feminist political spectrum. Such secretive activities conflicted with women's espoused preferences for open and inclusive styles.

Women are not so bureaucratic, are more supportive and open, sharing and caring. Women are more keen to explore different ways of working. I perceive men, especially macho trade union men, as needing to hide behind the union procedures. We [women] don't meet in the bar, we don't carve up positions and decisions before meetings, we are more up front.

Even well-seasoned political women declared unease about caucussing, especially when it concerned their own particular advancement: 'I would find it difficult to ask someone I didn't know very well to vote for me. I would expect them to want something in return. It's easy to do with a friend; I'd do the same for them.'

On the other hand, as indicated by the quote above, women seem to be more comfortable meeting with their own sex: 'Networking with women is better, easier. I have a strong sense of belonging, I don't mind asking questions or asking for further explanation. Women don't privatise knowledge the way chaps do!'

Yet women's triple burden (in the case of trade union activists) made networking more difficult . . . 'due to other commitments. Our network is not as good as the "old boys" network.'

Nevertheless, we did find evidence of women networking/caucussing around women's issues: 'At present there is a women's agenda and caucussing with other women who are aware of it is focused on that agenda and that awareness.'

Making alliances and working for change

We have seen how interim separatism has enabled women to develop a feminist agenda and build and develop support among women trade unionists. A second important feature of women's strategies in their unions is making alliances with political groupings in search of equality. Each of our two unions provided a different terrain on which women activists had to work in order to seek support for equality measures.

In the GPMU for example, with its predominantly white, male membership, its small proportion of women (17 per cent) and women activists widely spread geographically, it is men who hold the majority of positions of power: therefore alliances to build an equal opportunities agenda with sympathetic male trade union activists were especially important.

All the branch officials I have personally encountered are male. Very few (if any) women attend branch meetings regularly. This gives more opportunity to network with male union colleagues – not a very satisfactory situation.

> Some women in the union are right wing and pessimistic and do very little to encourage other women, whereas some men are highly supportive.

Women activists in both unions reported working with a range of broadly left political groupings.

Women in UNISON have the advantage in that women comprise the majority of the membership, and there was already an organised network of equity-seeking self-organised groups including women, black, lesbian and gay and disabled members. Women activists in the survey reported working both formally and informally within and across these groups, plus male trade union colleagues who were supportive of equality issues. One woman active in the black and women's self-organised groups was clear that: 'The union has been very complacent and . . . it has to change. One thing self-organised groups have realised, there's no way we can work in isolation to one another, we have to be working together.'

Women from both unions were also prepared to recognise the need for and support strategies of interim separatism for other equity-seeking groups within their union. Ninety-five per cent of feminists and 92 per cent of non-feminists believed that there should be *special measures to help ensure representation of minorities (black, lesbian and gay members with disabilities) in leadership positions within the union.* Eighty-three per cent of feminists and 84 per cent of non-feminists were *in favour of reserved seats to ensure the representation of minority ethnic groups within the union.*

As illustrated by these comments, using networking and caucussing to get women's issues onto the trade union agenda illustrates a high level of political awareness and skills among active women. So does understanding of the requirements for getting on in the union – both informally and formally. Table 6.6 shows that both feminists and non-feminists were aware of the significance of showing commitment to the principle of trade union unity. Feminists seemed to be more politically aware of the efficacy of being part of informal networks than the non-feminists. Thus they recognised the importance of having a proven track record, the support of key activists and 'being one of the boys', while also being seen to be committed to TU unity and the labour movement.

The feminists also seemed more likely to consider 'going further' in their union either as a lay representative or as a paid official. Only 52.9 per cent of our total sample of trade union women considered this as an option, 25 (48 per cent) of the non-feminists compared with 12 (67 per cent) of the group of feminists. The four reasons for not going further in the union most commonly identified by non-feminists were: a lack of sufficient trade union experience, a lack of self-confidence, the view that they could do more at the grassroots, and because they felt limited by family responsibilities. Feminists who did not consider this an option also felt that they could do more at the grassroots, or were restricted by family responsibilities.

TABLE 6.6   Women trade unionists' views of what is necessary to get into a more senior union position? (Cite up to 3 most important factors.)

Rank order of importance by:	Feminists (%)	Non-feminists (%)
Commitment to TU unity	16	14
To have a proven TU track record	12	10
To be 'one of the boys'	12	8
Commitment to TU principles	10	18
Speaking up at union meetings	10	7
Support of key lay activists	10	4
Experience of negotiating with management	6	12
Attending union meetings and conferences	6	10
Commitment to labour movement	6	2
Support of a faction/group	4	2
Proven record of negotiated deals	2	7
To be 'one of the girls'	2	4
Support of senior paid officials	2	4
Non-responses (number)	2	10
Total sample	19	58

Conclusions

From this discussion we can identify key themes in women's projects and endeavours for equality within their trade unions.

Proven failure of and impatience with the approach of liberal incrementalism has energised some women and both energised and politicised others. 'Letting women in' to unions by methods such as membership-organising drives, information for women, espousal of equality aims, increased inclusion of women on delegations, for example, has clearly been seen by women not to be sufficient to deliver equality and democracy for them.

We have sought to identify the support that exists among women trade union activists for a feminist trade union agenda, and the strategy we have labelled interim separatism. Evidence from our preliminary research among trade union women activists from the GPMU and UNISON shows that there is strong support for a number of the key elements on the feminist trade union agenda, and for feminist strategies of interim separatism.

However, despite these findings and the women's strong desire to establish equality for women within the trade union movement, the majority (75 per cent) still would not label themselves feminist. We accept that differences in aims, style and perspective still exist between welfarist, traditional and feminist women. Nonetheless we would foresee some reduction in these differences, particularly between feminists and the traditional women we have characterised as being *in transition* as women develop their consciousness and political skills.

Significantly, 56 per cent of feminists and 85 per cent of non-feminists stated that they would not vote for any measure which might divide their union. Traditional and welfarist women in particular wished to make it clear that it was equality they supported rather than preferential treatment for women. Thus as we have seen, considerable care needs to be taken by women and their allies, in devising and working towards the long agenda for equal opportunities within trade unions. Although the intransigence of patriarchal trade union structures and cultures seem to have reconciled the majority of feminist and non-feminist women to the need for the current approach, it seems likely that this support would be conditional on its being perceived as good both for women *and* the trade union movement as a whole.

A feminist trade union agenda is about ways to attract and keep women members, while offering a point of reference for re-visioning for the labour movement which goes beyond merely letting women in (Briskin, 1993). In other words, letting women in by ensuring they are on delegations, can attend courses and so on, is clearly not enough. As already indicated in this chapter, feminising, re-visioning the union is ultimately about transforming structures, hierarchies, and cultures, towards a truly democratic trade union and labour movement.

Notes

1. The authors would like to acknowledge the funding provided by the Economic and Social Research Council (ESRC) which assisted in some of the research reported in this chapter.
2. Here we are concerned with 'full' trade unionism as exemplified by unions which are members of the Trades Union Congress, and which in Blackburn and Prandy's (1965) terms are fully 'unionate'. That is, they broadly comply with the following seven characteristics: (1) Declaring itself a trade union; (2) Registered as a trade union; (3) Affiliated to the TUC; (4) Affiliated to the Labour Party; (5) Independent of employers for the purposes of negotiation; (6) Regards collective bargaining and the protection of the interests of members, as employees, as a major function; (7) Preparedness to be militant, using all forms of industrial action which may be effective. In 1994 there were 72 TUC unions. The number had reduced from 108 in 1980, mainly due to amalgamations and mergers. (Two of the previously non-militant professional groups voted in 1995 to change their constitutions to

legitimise industrial action. These were the Royal College of Midwives and the Royal College of Nursing. In addition the Royal Society of Physiotherapists already a TUC union, voted overwhelmingly to take industrial action in pursuit of a pay claim in the summer of 1995.)

3. Proportionality is used here to indicate that the decision-making bodies of a trade union should accurately reflect the make up of that union's membership. For example UNISON's concept of proportionality in relation to women is that since 68 per cent of the union membership is female, women should make up 68 per cent of the decision-making bodies and committees of the union.

4. 'Interim' may be interpreted as either a stage on the road to transformation of existing union structures and cultures, or as a route towards separate structures altogether. We use it here in the former sense.

5. Subsequent research will involve a much larger sample of women and men trade union activists from the two trade unions. This further work with both unions is funded by an ESRC award. (We are grateful to Ed Heery and John Kelly for sight of their study of trade union women questionnaire; we have adapted some of the questions for our questionnaire in order to be able to draw some comparisons.)

Different careers – equal professionals: women in teaching

Geraldine Healy and David Kraithman

Introduction: 'a good job for a woman'

Teaching is often perceived as the ideal job for women. The mythologies surrounding this perception in the conventional wisdom include short hours, long holidays, job security, career-breaks: in short it is a job compatible with family responsibilities. Further, teaching is considered to be professional work which is rewarded with relatively (in comparison with most work carried out by women) good pay. Teaching is a segmented profession which at the primary level is feminised, and has become increasingly feminised in the secondary sector during the 1980s and 1990s. Despite its feminisation, it is a highly stratified profession, a disproportionate number of the top jobs going to men.

In this chapter we consider the mythologies surrounding teaching. We examine women teachers' different career patterns in the context of employment structures, educational, managerial and employment change. We then consider the structures that facilitate or impede teachers and the strategies that teachers use to make their different careers equal careers. Throughout we argue that the notion of professionalism provides its own dynamic that helps shape teachers' different strategies.

We draw on macro and micro data (Department for Education labour market data, a small pilot study[1] and semi-structured interviews with teachers) to better understand the impact of change upon teachers and teacher managers and on the changes in the nature of the professionalism of teaching.

Professionalism

At the heart of many of the controversies emerging from recent educational changes has been the issue of professionalism. The term 'profession' in relation to teaching is potentially problematic. 'Profession' is itself a muddy concept, but its most frequently mentioned attributes are: skill based on theoretical knowledge, provision of training and education, testing the competence of members, organisation, adherence to a professional code of conduct and altruistic service (Witz, 1992). A further dimension to professionalism of relevance to teaching in the 1980s and 1990s comes from a structural focus: that is, the way in which actions are structurally and historically constrained (Johnson, 1982). A link is made with exclusionary strategies of closure (involving the downwards exercise of power in a process of subordination as a social group seeks to secure, maintain or enhance privileged access to rewards and opportunities (Parkin, 1979).

It is helpful to relate the above aspects of professionalism to the collective reaction in the strongly feminised segment of primary schools against the Government proposal to introduce non-graduates as teachers of early years children, the so-called 'Mums' Army'. It is interesting to note here the contradiction along gendered lines of one group of professional women frustrating raised expectations of other women who aspire to the profession, effectively illustrating the monopolisation of opportunities frequently employed by one segment of the subordinate class against another (Parkin, 1979). Opposition to the Mums' Army proposals led to their withdrawal. What has followed has been a further attempt to formalise the introduction of less-qualified teachers by the Government. Pilot schemes were planned for 1994 of Specialist Teacher Assistants. The National Union of Teachers (NUT) argued that the training for assistants amounted almost to a job description for a teacher, but would be covered in the equivalent of nine hours training a week for one year (*Guardian*, 2 May 1994). Teachers take four years to qualify through a BEd degree or a degree followed by a one-year postgraduate certificate. In theory, the introduction of the specialist teaching assistants could benefit teachers involved in the education of young children. It could reduce the intensification of teachers' work and relieve them of some of the repetitive less-skilled work; at the same time it could benefit other women wishing to gain entry to work they would find satisfying. There is a danger that the reality may be different: schools under financial strain may start substituting assistants for properly qualified teachers. The outcome would be further deprofessionalising of teaching; but paradoxically some women would benefit by gaining entry to work previously closed to them, but this gain would be at the expense of other women whose opportunities may be crushed.

The establishment of teaching as a profession seems to be a continuing battle. It is suggested that teaching is not a 'full' profession, but a 'quasi-profession' or semi-profession (Etzioni, 1969) alongside other feminised occupations such as nursing and social work. A semi-profession has two defining features: it is an occupation located within a bureaucratic organisation and one in which women predominate. Witz (1992) argues that the 'semi-profession' thesis is based on an androcentric model of profession; she quotes Parkin (1979) 'if the semi professions were staffed mainly by men they would be far more likely to attain professional autonomy and closure – what might be called the machismo theory of professionalisation'. This discussion on the professional status of teaching is important in the light of current Government change, the continuing feminisation of the profession and the crucial link between professionalism and the new managerialism. Managerialism has during the 1980s become a 'supra-non-profession': that is, an occupation which has emerged from the ranks of the professionals, to run the profession from a managerial rather than a professional perspective. The irony, as we shall see, is that enhanced status is dependent on managerial rather than professional expertise.

Different career patterns: 'lesser careers'?

In this section we show how women's careers as teachers may take a different form from those of men, and we address the complex patterns of career that women teachers may experience. We start from the premise that the notion of career itself is a male construct (Dex, 1985). Our analysis would be weakened if we only considered career to be work centred, to involve continuous work experience and orderly development and promotion up and through an occupational hierarchy (Evetts, 1988). We share Evetts' view that the large majority of married[2] women can seldom fit or approximate such a model, and to try to match their experiences with some model of career centred solely on paid work is to distort the meaning of career for many professional women. We use the term career in relation to a person's multidimensional employment profile.[3]

The basis of women's different career patterns was identified by Dex (1984). Her framework had three broad phases: an *initial work phase* starts the work cycle after women leave school or college; a *family formation phase* begins for most women with the first pregnancy and childbirth, and a *final work phase* is the last phase of women's work cycles. Dex (1984) pointed out that different

patterns of working and not working can be found during the family formation phase. We build on the Dex framework by attempting to identify some of
the complexities that the family formation phase conceals by capturing some
of the implications of particular working patterns for the final career phase.[4]

We identify a range of types that attempt to capture the different work
patterns that teachers experience; types that are not necessarily the outcome of
pre-planned career development, but may be the result of a range of inter-
locking factors which include choices, constraints, change and critical incidents in life.

1. *Initial teaching phase*: This is a common first phase characterised by new
   entrants and by mature entrants to teaching. The development of the
   career will be influenced by original aspirations, opportunities and constraints, and the experience of teaching itself.
2. *The continuous career phase*: This teacher fits more neatly into the traditional
   male pattern of career. She does not have child-rearing responsibilities,
   and either by design or default is more likely to become a managerial
   teacher; however, this teacher may also find that her professional aspirations are fulfilled though her class teacher role. She also moves seamlessly
   from the initial teaching phase through to being a continuous worker and
   on to the final work phase.
3. *The dual career teacher*: This teacher has taken maternity leave and returned
   to teaching. She is continuing to develop her career and, at the same time,
   to bring up her children. She sees herself as a career teacher, but finds that
   she must constantly negotiate different demands upon her time. The older
   her children, the more likely she is to become a managerial teacher, but,
   like the career teacher, she may be satisfied with the classroom role of her
   choice. This teacher may also have returned to teaching following a career-
   break and working in lower status teaching role, and has now regained the
   level and role to which she aspired. She can be a continuous worker
   throughout her life cycle, or she may have experienced interruptions to
   her working patterns.
4. *The inactive teacher*: This teacher has left the teaching labour market; she
   will have done this for one of two reasons:
   (a) Because she wants a career-break , most likely (but not exclusively)
       because she is in the family formation phase and has chosen at this
       stage in her work cycle a domestic career. This may be permanent or
       temporary. The female inactive teacher may be constrained by geo-
       graphical, educational factors and familial factors in deciding to
       return to teaching.
   (b) Because she has chosen to redirect her career away from teaching
       because she no longer wishes to teach.
5. *The interim phase teacher*: This teacher has taken a career-break to spend
   time with her children; she tends to come back initially on a part-time basis

and gradually increases her hours. At this stage the teacher may choose more of the resource of time over income and ultimately more control over the division of time (Scheibl, 1995). The ability to teach part-time and to be a supply teacher sustains the mythology that teaching is a good job for a women. During this phase, she may seek fewer responsibilities than previously. This teacher sees this as an interim phase through which she will move to return as a career teacher. If there is a rapid recovery of occupational status, it might be appropriate to regard any downward occupational movements as temporary (Elias, 1988).

6. *The compromise stage teacher*: This teacher has been an inactive teacher and moved through the interim stage, but has been unable to move back to being a career teacher. She has found herself trapped in a compromise role to which she is not fully contributing at the level of her ability. Of critical importance to the definition of this type of teacher is that she will feel under-utilised. She is a teacher experiencing frustration of aspirations and is often the victim of ageism. This teacher will be more likely to be on a fixed term contract, be a supply teacher, teaching subjects other than her preferred subjects, be applying for different jobs or resigned to her existing one. The more rapid the period of educational change during her career-break, the more likely it is that after the interim stage she will enter the compromise stage and recovery to her desired occupational status will be harder to achieve.

The typology does not presuppose any order of sequencing with the exception of the initial teaching phase. Women may move between categories according to opportunities and constraints that they face. The typology is not deterministic nor historically specific and aims to capture the fluidity of movement between different phases that can exist. Neither does it presuppose that all women at a particular stage will share the same aspirations. Aspirations will be shaped by the meaning negotiated in the culture of the workplace and . . . constrained by the patriarchal and other bargains available in the society at large (S. Acker, 1994). Thus structures create variable degrees of freedom and constraints for individual actors (Mouzelis, 1989).

Figure 7.1 uses this typology to demonstrate possible patterns of teaching profiles.

The framework employed captures a teacher's experience at a particular moment in time; it shows possible pathways from one phase to another. As applied to teachers, Figure 7.1 shows that women teachers might have continuous or discontinuous work patterns. A continuous work pattern can be followed by those not having children and those having children, in so far as they do not experience an inactive phase. The dual career can only be followed by a women who has gone through the family formation phase; but the profiles of such teachers could be continuous or discontinuous. However, as we have outlined above, the compromise phase (in the context of this typol-

FIGURE 7.1   The multi-dimensional career patterns of women teachers

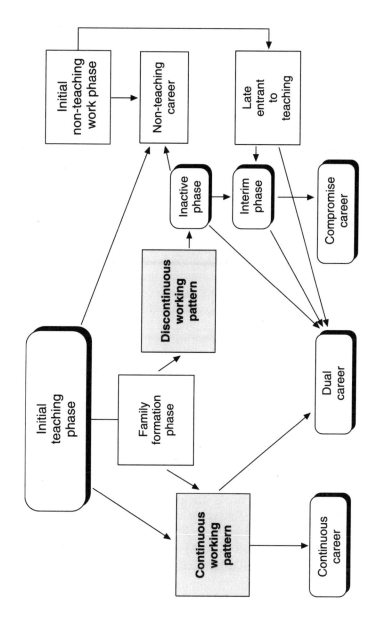

ogy) can only be reached by those whose hoped-for recovery of occupation status was unrealised during the interim phase.

Women's professionalism is often judged by their occupational phase: patriarchal values influence perceptions that different career patterns are lesser career patterns and lesser career patterns are adopted by lesser professionals. We argue that traditional notions of career are inappropriate, and further that women's professionalism and commitment in teaching is not affected by alternative career patterns. Women have different careers but are equal professionals.

The professional teacher's career will take one of three overlapping routes: *managerialist*, where the aim is to develop a career hierarchically; *collectivist*, where the aim is to develop a career via a union role; *or classroom teacher*, where the aim is to develop her potential within the classroom.[5] We use evidence from our study to show how collectivism facilitates specialist roles and also provides a instrument of resistance to what is perceived to be unacceptable and imposed changes to the work of the classroom teacher. An examination of teachers' employment patterns in the next section highlights some of the complexities and contradictions, and also points to the patriarchal assumptions on which employment decisions are made. It further demonstrates how teachers' own aspirations are limited or facilitated by particular structures and how these structures may force women into one or other phase of working pattern and severely constrain the impact of their own agency.

Teachers' employment patterns and sustaining myths

Women face an unequal struggle in reaching senior, and thus well paid, positions in schools. Teachers in the United Kingdom are employed in different sectors and are trained for those sectors. The primary sector educates children to eleven years of age, and the secondary sector educates children to eighteen years. These two sectors are complicated by some geographical variation where middle schools are preferred (from nine to thirteen) and where sixth form colleges (sixteen to eighteen years) dominate. In addition, a small percentage of children are educated in the independent sector. Teachers working with younger children tend to be generalist and are expected to teach across the curriculum, whereas those working with older children tend to be subject based.

Sixty-four per cent of teachers in all public sector schools in England and Wales in 1991 were female, a rise from the 60 per cent figure that obtained in 1981. During this decade the total number of teachers fell from 503 000 to 444 000 (a fall of 11.7 per cent) so that we observe a relative feminisation of the profession in this period; the total number of male teachers fell by 21.6 per cent and the total number of females by 5 per cent. Table 7.1 shows the uneven spread of women across the primary and secondary sectors and shows that the proportion of women in both sectors has increased.

In 1980–81 new young women entrants (under 30 years) to the profession outnumbered men by a factor of 1.64; by 1990–91 nearly three times as many women got first jobs as men. For the over 30-year-old the corresponding ratios are 1.45 (1980–81) and 2.12. (DFE, 1991).

Occupational choice

Dolton and Makepeace (1993) point to the simultaneous decision about occupational choice and potential future family commitments and claim that a recognition of probable family role specialisation leads women towards teaching as a career. One of the reasons they cite is the ease with which one can return to teaching after a career interruption, i.e. women who are keen to keep working will, ceteris paribus, be more likely to choose teaching and to work (Dolton and Makepeace, 1993). Thus they found women who are graduates and teachers are more likely to be in work than non-teachers with the same family commitments, and this effect is particularly pronounced for women with heavy commitments. This supports the view that women's labour supply decisions are made in a different framework from men's and highlights the potential significance of women *re-entrants* to teaching.

Re-entrants

Figure 7.2 indicates that in most recent years re-entrants outnumber new entrants and that re-entrants are almost exclusively drawn from women. Changes in the organisation of schools and schooling introduced by the Government in recent years have considerable ramifications for re-entrants to teaching.

TABLE 7.1   Proportion (%) of women teachers in UK public sector schools

	Primary	*Secondary*	*All public sector*
1980–1981	78	45	60
1990–1991	82	48	64

Source: Based on DFE, 1991.

FIGURE 7.2   Patterns of teacher supply: entrants, re-entrants and women re-entrants

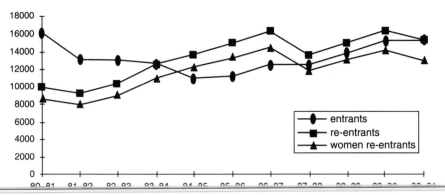

Source: Based on DFE (1991).

Vertical Segregation

The female professional teacher who wishes to follow the managerialist route will face deep-seated structural constraints. Whilst men comprise 18 per cent of primary school teachers, slightly more than half of those men will have posts as heads or deputies. The corresponding figures for women are 82 per cent of the workforce and about 16 per cent as heads or deputy heads.

Myths about women teachers' low status and pay

Explanations of women's low status and pay in teaching have included women's lower level of qualifications, years of service and their commitment to the labour force. An NUT study in 1980 addressed directly some of these 'truisms'. The study discounted from their comparisons part-time teachers (who are predominantly women) in order to offer a valid contrast with men. The NUT noted that whilst women supplied over three-quarters of the primary staffing only 43 per cent of headships of primary schools were held by women. They questioned the proposition that women were disadvantaged by lack of qualifications: they found that whilst 6 per cent of men graduates held headships, only 2 per cent of women graduates did so. They further found that, even after correcting for length of service, women teachers still earned less than men, thus dispelling any myth about the effect of any break for child-rearing on experience.

Commitment

A lack of commitment to the labour force is often put forward as a reason explaining gendered income differences, yet the NUT study (1980) found over 45 per cent of the women in their sample were the major breadwinners in the households and about one-third were unmarried. Most respondents expected to teach up to retirement age. Assumptions about women's lack of success in the promotion stakes is also the belief (unspoken and spoken) that women are just not as committed as men.

'Commitment' has achieved reified status in the managerialism of the eighties and nineties and is a term frequently reserved for full-time workers. Hakim (1991) argues that part-time workers demonstrate lower work commitment than males, but are disproportionately satisfied with their jobs. Our study suggests that women at the interim phase are committed to teaching but use this phase to enable an effective negotiation of competing demands. Scheibl (1995), in her critique of Hakim's grateful slave thesis, argues that women may adopt a compromise orientation to work during child-rearing, but challenges the view that part-time work implies a lack of commitment to paid work as a life goal activity. She holds that, rather than demonstrating an anti-work orientation, part-time work indicates a rational response and resolution to the constraints imposed by time poverty within the context of the sexual division of labour which is defined and filtered by the gender order. In our study we noted a particularly interesting coping strategy adopted by a female head of department. She had returned to work via the interim stage and at the time of the interview worked on a 0.9 contract, but was effectively doing a full-time job. 'She is in school all the time to get the job done; it is not manageable part-time'.

This woman had moved from the interim stage to dual career phase, but on her terms. She recognised that full-time was more than full-time and therefore adjusted her contract, and pay, to enable her to work an acceptable definition of full-time, while in fact being part-time. The 0.9 head of department was working full-time and being paid part-time; this demonstrated very strong commitment to work and provided an example of a committed teacher working less than full-time to minimise time poverty.

The above example raises the question of the length of the hours of a full-time job. In teaching the hours tend to increase as a teacher moves up the hierarchy.[6] It was suggested to us that: 'women with families find it difficult to commit the long hours – the expectation was a lot above and beyond normal'.

This is a far cry from the short hours associated with the mythologies of teaching. In the United Kingdom we have a long-hours culture that mitigates against women who want to develop their occupational potential but still leave space for caring responsibilities. Myths on women's lack of commitment are upheld by patriarchal notions of commitment associated with long working hours.

Promotion

The NUT (1980) study also showed that the success rate of women in internal promotions was about twice as high as at external boards, and a major effect the career-break had was that women 'ready' for a headship were often deemed to be too old. Discrimination based on a lack of understanding of the different career patterns of women teachers was thus underpinned by erroneous estimations of labour market and professional attachment by (largely male) selection boards.

AMMA (now the Association of Teachers and Lecturers (ATL) found that during the mid-1980s period of school closures and teacher redeployment all teachers had a pessimistic view of their promotion prospects, but married women were the most deleteriously affected (AMMA, 1985). Besides differing patterns of career-breaks between men and women, AMMA also noted that men's breaks were more likely to be for obtaining a higher qualification or to undertake research. Furthermore, when women did move they were more likely than men to make a horizontal move (because of changes in their husband's job) – thus women were less mobile. In contrast to the NUT study, AMMA found a relative lack of commitment to seeking promotion by women. The summary of the AMMA study concludes with the telling statement '. . . Heads, Governing bodies and LEAs decide who shall be promoted and, where there is an embarrassment of choice, the prudent course of action may seem to favour the young, ambitious male teacher at the expense of a women who might, in the view of those making the choice, leave to have a baby' (AMMA, 1985).

This last comment is interesting in that another study in the same vein conducted two years later by ILEA Research and Statistics Branch for the City of Birmingham Women's Committee (1987) reported that many women teachers had been asked about future family plans at promotion interviews, despite the fact that such practices might be indirect discrimination under the Sex Discrimination Act 1975. The reality or perception of an age-ceiling was also reported by returners in the Birmingham study. Given evidence in Birmingham that 'women are often on lower grades than men for work of equal responsibility, or with a similar length of experience', it seems that discriminatory practices did exist at that time. The Birmingham study investigated reasons for women teachers' disadvantageous position in addition to direct selection board discrimination. A major reason, they thought, might lie with difficulties women have on obtaining release for in-service training, particularly management training. Of course, this might be the outcome of discriminatory behaviour as well. One of the main findings of the report was the need for equal opportunities training of existing managers (ILEA, 1987).

Educational, management and employment changes

We have seen how discriminatory practices are built into teaching; we now consider the likely impact of educational reform on these practices. The changes can be categorised for simplicity's sake into three overlapping categories: educational, managerial and employment. Our focus is on those issues that particularly affect women, although we recognise that some of the issues we touch upon will also affect the male teacher; the impact of change on the careers of men and women and will be a subject of a later study.

Educational change

The two major changes in educational policy in the 1980s and 1990s were the introduction of the National Curriculum and the compulsory testing at the ages of 7, 11 and 14 as well as 16. The concept of the National Curriculum was generally welcomed. The reality was another matter, and curriculum overload became a major problem for the classroom teacher. Curriculum content was also a matter of concern with its UK-centric approach and its gender bias. Further, Shaw (1990) argues that if schools are viewed as 'curriculum delivery systems' subject to quality control, it might lead to a more instrumental rather than a moral commitment to work. The 'dedicatory ethic' would be reduced and professionalism threatened.

The introduction of compulsory, externally set testing led to deskilling, work intensification and constrained judgement; this was a critical example of the way change was deprofessionalising teaching. Testing became such an issue that the combined resistance of all teachers' unions led to a testing boycott. Again, testing *per se* was not seen as the problem, but the nature of the tests, the work involved in their implementation, their non-diagnostic nature and their publication were the major concerns. Tests for seven-year-olds were carried out, beginning in 1991; the time and workload involved in their implementation was immense and some of the rigidities in the marking scheme were deemed absurd. Because of the feminisation of the primary sector, women teachers were disproportionately affected by the introduction of these changes. Again, resistance led to some modification to the tests.

The general outcome of these changes has led to work intensification and a reduction in control by teachers of the curriculum and of the testing process.

The inability to use professional judgement in relation to marking the seven-year-olds' tests puts into sharp focus the issue of deskilling of the profession. Collective resistance included legal action.

Managerial and financial change

The issues of crucial importance to understanding the consequences of change for women's career progression were managerial and financial change. The introduction of local financial management of schools (LMS), the introduction of grant maintained schools and city technology colleges have forced schools to compete with each other for students. Under LMS, for the first time, schools have control over their budgets, which includes staffing. The funding formula delivers a sum for teachers' salaries to schools, based on the average salary across the local educational authority (LEA). The average funding formula provides a financial advantage to those schools who have a higher than average number of younger, and therefore cheaper, teachers (Sinclair *et al.*, 1993).

Schools are increasingly turning to young, inexperienced staff in order to make their budgets go further. Young women and men entering the profession will benefit from this. This has important consequences for the older (experienced and therefore more expensive) teacher who may be returning after a career-break (who as we have seen from Figure 7.2 is disproportionately female) or for the mature entrant to the teaching labour market. As we have shown, the number of mature entrants to teacher training now exceeds entrants under 26 years old, yet there are 'problems of finding teaching posts for these students on completion of their course' (Straker, 1991). If labour market conditions are not favourable, the opportunities for the interim stage teacher and the inactive teacher considering a return may be reduced. However, illustrative projections of teacher demand and supply are favourable to returners and indicate that returners will continue to provide around half of teacher recruitment to ensure an adequate supply of teachers in the years to come (STRB, 1994).

Potential opportunities for women seeking the managerialist route are also likely to emerge from future demands for senior teachers. Research into headteacher vacancies indicates that if the level of headteacher posts continue to be at around 3000 per year the choice available to governors is likely to be severely restricted (Howson, 1989). Howson argues that a solution to the shortage would be to ensure that suitably qualified returners were considered for accelerated promotion to their former grades and provided with suitable in-service courses, and that this should be linked with a campaign aimed at informing governors that such returners would be suitable for appointment. Shire counties generally have the least problem in recruiting headteachers, whereas the Inner London boroughs have the most difficulty (Howson, 1994). Labour supply factors seem critical in women's success in achieving these posts; Edwards and Lyon (1994) show how women were more likely to be successful in the south-east and in metropolitan areas (where turnover rates are highest) in becoming headteachers than in the non-metropolitan north and in Wales, where traditional values led to a preference for male heads. They argued that the cultural factors that formed the frames of reference of governors were important discriminators. These frames of reference may be sustained by governors' ability to recruit males to senior positions; thus patriarchal values coupled with favourable labour supply conditions collude against women with hierarchical aspirations. Or put another way, when the supply of senior teachers is limited, women's aspirations may be taken more seriously. This underlines the importance of equal opportunities awareness and policy compliance for decision-makers.

Equal opportunities developments in employment and education may be threatened by the decentralisation of financial management, and therefore the reduction in local authority influence. This gives schools freedom in the way they allocate their resources. In recent years some local authorities have demonstrated their commitment to equal opportunities by investing in training and by appointing specialist advisers; the use of advisers was found to be significant in helping equal opportunities move from policy to practice (Healy and Rainnie, 1991). It is possible that in the future only those schools which identify problems will invest in equal opportunity training or in the use of professional advisers. This may constrain schools' efforts to ensure that recruitment and selection systems operate in a non-discriminatory way, leading to more informal practices, which are prone to abuse. Essential aspects of good practice in equal opportunities may be frustrated without centralised guidelines and by lack of human resource management skills.

LMS brings the decision-making to the level of the school; organisational political skills will be essential in ensuring some share of a shrinking budget. The restructuring of schools shows how the contradictions in simultaneous centralisation and decentralisation force a growth of managerialism which can cope with a competitive market. Sinclair, Ironside and Seifert (1993) highlight the contradiction: 'Failure either to hold down their costs or to maximise their school's share of the market will have severe consequences for the school's future' and argue that 'the new system places immense pressures on school managers to embrace the ideology, assumptions and practices of private sector capital', which in recent years has included the techniques associated with human resource management. This creates a demand for a different kind of manager, although one who still has a shared occupational identity. A secondary deputy pointed to changing nature of the role of the deputy:

It is very complex; It is very different from what it was. Change to financial management is alien; some women find it off-putting, it is linked to confidence. The focus has shifted from pastoral and curriculum issues to health and safety and to the management of the premises.

The consequence of change suggests reskilling and possible upskilling in relation to managerial work, and a simultaneous deskilling in relation to the classroom teacher.

Employment relations change

Contractual change

For a woman who aspires to be an effective, professional classroom teacher and whose energies are concentrated on enhancing that professionalism, contractual changes may be perceived as a threat to her identity as a professional. The abolition by the Government in 1987 of collective bargaining for teachers and the subsequent state imposition of specified contractual conditions (directed time, non-teaching duties, training days) has further eroded the professional base of teaching. Clearly the *raison d'être* of teaching mediates against the extremes of low trust, but these changes highlight the contractual reduction of discretion and trust.

Job security

This was another part of the mythologies of teaching with which we began this chapter. Job-losses and redundancies are a major consequence of managerial and financial controls; because of women's different career patterns, some women may benefit and others may lose from this. Initially, recourse to compulsory redundancy was avoided by using natural wastage, premature retirement and restructuring to reduce the headcount (Bach and Winchester, 1994). The financial pressure resulting from the pay award in 1994 and 1995 has forced redundancies (in 1995 about 10 000 teaching jobs were shed) (MacLeod, 1995), since shortfalls in Government expenditure to meet the pay awards were to come from efficiency gains. Pay awards for some may mean early retirements or redundancies for others; in some cases women teachers at the interim stage in their career, working on a part-time or supply basis, may be substituted for the full-time teacher (who may of course be the older female teacher who has found herself at the compromise stage of her career). The impact of the increasing casualisation of teaching is felt most strongly by women; a recent NASUWT survey indicated that whilst 14.15 per cent of their respondents

(15 000) were on temporary contracts, 83 per cent were women (NASUWT, 1995). This is further compounded by the poor pay and conditions received by teachers employed by agencies (*Times Educational Supplement*, 30 June 1995). The increase of use of such agencies may force more teachers into the compromise phase. This is hardly a recipe for a contract based on trust.

Job losses are also accommodated by early retirement schemes. Teachers are given the opportunity to retire at 50. Whilst this is a voluntary decision, such teachers (older and therefore more expensive) feel that if they do not opt for early retirement, their staying on will negatively affect the well-being of the school. There are gendered consequences to the early retirement policy. Women demonstrate different patterns of career development and, using the model developed by White, Cox and Cooper (1992), we can show how potentially discriminatory this policy is. By the ages of 40–50 women are at a rebalancing stage: in other words they have resolved their career–family conflict and are in a period of stability and consolidation (White *et al.*, 1992). It is at 50 plus that they enter the *maintenance* stage which leads to continued growth and success. If at this stage they 'feel' they have to quit their contract of employment as a teacher, they will be unable to capitalise on the maintenance stage and so will experience occupational frustration. Further, schools will also be net losers in relation to the experience lost. We use the words 'contract of employment' advisedly, because many of these new retirees will return as casual supply teachers or on fixed-term contracts; they become embedded in the compromise stage and form part of the growing army of workers on alternative or atypical forms of contract.

The compromise phase seemed to have been reached by a 47-year-old woman in our study; she was on a part-time, fixed-term contract; a full-time post was not available. She argued 'it is impossible to develop owing to cash limitations – I'm only on a basic scale, therefore [only] the hierarchy are trained and receive promotion'. She also commented on the effect of age on job prospects, especially for women, and the problems faced by older women caring for aged relatives. This woman through a set of adverse circumstances found herself locked into a phase not of her choosing.

Collectivist responses: personal and professional

Teaching shares with other professional groups a central tenet of intrinsic levels of job satisfaction. This 'dedicatory ethic' (Lortie, 1969), or traditional public service ethic, elevates service motives and denigrates material rewards as the proper motive to work; such dedication can be seen as a form of subsidy to education which teachers give; but at a certain point the level of the subsidy becomes too much and collective action is taken to redress the balance. That is not to say action is taken to remove the subsidy but to get it back to what is perceived to be a more acceptable level. Part of the contract is the unwritten agreement that teachers trade salary for intrinsic rewards of the job. Nevertheless, there is an expectation that the contract should be perceived to be fair. Money was an important reason given by teachers in their decision to return to work; in the labour market generally money is a major reason why women with young children return to work (Martin and Roberts, 1984; Healy and Kraithman, 1989, 1991). Further, as a deputy of a secondary school pointed out 'It is not always recognised that a woman on her own needs financial independence'.

Notwithstanding the significance of money in the employment contract; pay has not been at the heart of recent collective teacher resistance. Instead the focus has been concern about the quality of education following educational reform. The gains from collective participation were professional. In teaching the evidence suggests that professionalism and trade unionism are inextricably linked (Healy, 1994). One of the interesting responses to collective resistance has been the direct involvement of its members by the NUT in its recent action against testing. The industrial action of the 1980s had an adverse affect on NUT membership; there was a severe haemorrhage of membership that benefited both the AMMA and to a lesser extent the Professional Association of Teachers (PAT) and the major part of this haemorrhage was women (De Lyon and Migniuolo, 1989). De Lyon and Migniuolo present the case not for unions to be less militant, but for unions to take action in different ways and give consideration to different approaches to action. The direct involvement of teachers by the NUT through frequent ballots would seem a response to this. Trade union action becomes more complex when the immediate cost may be children's education, albeit with a long-term view to gain. Direct involvement by ballot ensures that all union members influence policy.

Collectivism affects not only the professional world of teachers, but also their personal world. The standard use of the term 'collectivism' in the field of employment relates to the existence of independent, or quasi-independent organisations founded to represent and articulate the interest of groups of employees within the employment unit, the firm, the industry, sector or community (Kessler and Purcell, 1995). The women in our study show how collectivism has facilitated their career development and, interestingly, this also included their hierarchical development. Collectivist women, i.e., those women taking an active part in their union, will be at each of the career phases; the personal impact is felt by women who take a triple career role, i.e. women who have children, work and who are trade union representatives. A mature teacher (56 years) and mother of three, who had experienced career-breaks for childcare, but was now Head of a Sixth Form and a trade union representative pointed to the significance of her union participation: 'my involvement in the NUT has given me experience at high level meetings and opportunities to develop confidence and skills I lacked'.

This same teacher indicated the barriers she had faced in getting to her current position: 'Having three children fairly widely spread in age and geographical limitations of my husband's job. However, it did not appear to be so at the time – only in retrospect when considering 'if. . .'. This case is interesting; it is an example of an older woman carrying three jobs, but using one to benefit another and possibly both. She demonstrated a common pattern in return decisions: financial factors, proximity to home and the hours were all important to her.

Another deputy head, mother of two teenage children, who held a triple role also illustrated how her trade union involvement contributed to her career: 'My trade union involvement has made me a well informed member of the profession with an understanding of educational issues above and outside the school level. It has helped me to negotiate and to handle people'.

The above women demonstrated satisfaction with the intrinsic aspects of their work, but not with the pay and hours: in other words, they demonstrated a commitment to their work, but not to the employment conditions of the work. Whilst it is well documented that participating in their union activities may be difficult for women, the women in this study also show how their participation facilitated their personal and hierarchical development. The increasing feminisation of the teaching profession ensures that the promotion of women's issues has a mutual benefit for the unions and their survival, as well as the needs of their women members. The NUT, for example, is using its track record of protecting women members to enhance its recruitment of women – it is conducting a job-sharing and Women Returners campaign based on cases won under the Sex Discrimination and Equal Pay Acts (SERTUC, 1994).

Enabling career development: strategies and structures

In this final section we examine the factors of teaching that can facilitate or impede the woman teacher achieving her desired role. We consider structures such as the role of training, informal networks and of significant others alongside the strategies that women teachers use to accommodate their various and conflicting demands.

Training

Training is a central feature of professionalism (Witz, 1992); it has two, not necessarily related, functions: it is important as a means of enhancing the competence of the trainee and as an agent of career development. As Rees

(1992) argues, training opportunities could be transformative: that is, they have the potential to improve individuals' occupational life chances quite radically. It is also the case that the desire for training can be linked to high attachment to the labour market, indeed to commitment. Our pilot sample demonstrated the value of training, although teachers were alert also to the variable experiences of training. Further it was recognised that structural forces may impede the full utilisation of the training experience. A 47-year-old female deputy head noted that:

> general management and administrative skills acquired in previous posts and on courses not used because of full-time class commitment . . . . Training has improved my people management skills . . . . but existing training is inadequate, I want [training on] assessment, LMS and IT.

This case highlights the dilemma in many primary schools of deputies who are unable to get the training they need in essential aspects of management, e.g. LMS., and at the same time are unable to utilise the skills they have developed because of the high teaching load.

A part-time teacher highlighted the training problems faced by part-time staff. She was given access to training days, but not to training of her choice. Inequity of treatment between full- and part-time staff is common in all sectors of the economy, not least teaching. Part-time contracts are used by women at the 'interim stage' of their careers; given the current competitive climate teachers face, equality of treatment with full-timers would seem to be an essential aspect of women's development.

For many of the women in our pilot study, training enhanced job performance and development: '. . . can now use IT confidently with a new (younger) age range of pupils; could now take responsibility for IT. Existing training adequate although would like some more'.

These comments are particularly pertinent in light of the debate on women's commitment to work ; they are made by a 35-year-old supply teacher, a mother of one, whose primary school responsibilities include 'infant corridor, bus duty, pond upkeep and environmental care'. This teacher is clearly preparing for her move out of the interim stage. Other women commented that 'professional development was helpful and adequate, that it was helpful in maintaining some kind of job security'.

The transformative nature of training becomes clear in the case of a deputy who commented that 'management workshops helped me to think of what I would be moving in to'. From this interview the importance of *taking* the opportunities offered emerged; others emphasised personal development, so that a woman teacher commented 'training gave me confidence'. Access to training and professional development is clearly an important factor in shaping career decisions, and in providing a context of confidence and security for them to be developed.

Women-only training has been adopted by a number of local authorities as an attempt to redress vertical segregation. Al-Khalifa (1988) argued that whilst training women teachers is not a solution in itself to the disadvantage women experience, it has demonstrated how women seeking to change their situation can take the initiative and amply demonstrate their ability to work together for improvements in the education service which will benefit teachers and pupils. It also demonstrates how women teachers have strengths for action and organisation which are under-utilised and undervalued in schools. Notwithstanding the significance of women-only training, training is a key factor in enabling women to shape their careers according to their own choosing and potential; however 'training is [only] . . . one means among a variety of strategies for positive action aimed at effecting organisational change' (Al-Khalifa, 1988).

The informal network and the career-break

Much of the writing on women in organisations argues that women's opportunities are diminished by their exclusion from male networks. Networking for women is often seen as crucial as they do not naturally find themselves part of male networks. For black women, who face a different as well as a similar set of problems, it is seen as crucial:

> A network of support is crucial – it is absolutely essential . . . . from early on in my career I joined black women's groups – not just for friendship and support, but also for very positive advice in terms of careers and the sorts of courses we ought to be looking to and general career development. (Quoted in C. Walker, 1993).

In primary teaching, because of the feminisation of the labour force, any networks (apart from headteachers) tend to be female. Evetts (1988), in her study of career-breaks and returns of married women primary headteachers showed how important personal contacts and informal networks (i.e. previous colleagues some of whom were now in managerial roles) were in bringing women back into primary teaching. Evetts argues that a strategy whereby promotion achievements remain modest would constitute a successful resolution of the conflicting demands of family and work on the women's time and energy. She quoted Silverstone (1980)

> it could even be the case that the profession is secretly pleased to have a body of workers whose aspirations are not high and who thus ease the pressure on career posts within the profession. The danger lies in assuming all women will fulfil this role. They patently do not.

We would add that selectors should be sufficiently open in their thinking to accept that women's aspirations may differ from those of men's at particular moments in time; and, that when women want to move between phases this should be recognised as a normal, rather than deviant, part of their career progression.

Evetts' 1988 study is of particular interest to this chapter, as the women sampled were re-entering the labour market in the 1960s, 'a time of political optimism and economic expansion from which the education system bene-fited directly'. The impact of this climate is well expressed in this quote:

> One of the joys [of teaching] at that time was that you could happily leave in the knowledge that you could return when and how you wished. I mean I've often wondered what I would have done if things had been different. I've spoken to young [women] teachers who are terribly torn between pursuing their careers and taking time off to have their own families.

Thirty years ago, these women were in a strong bargaining position: they chose their school and could negotiate their childcare arrangements. Because women were persuaded to return to work through informal networks, frequently before they had planned to return, their breaks were short and partial, they did not therefore feel any anxiety about returns to teaching (Evetts, 1988). The break increased the self-confidence of the women; the interim phase facilitated the return to the desired job. This is very much in contrast to today. From the very brief outline of the changes in education, it is evident that the speed of change challenged even the most experienced of teachers, but for those taking a break for childcare, it acts as a deterrent to a return to teaching.

We have shown the significance of re-entrants to future teacher supply and it is recognised that more resources and effort should be put into the training needs of returners (STRB, 1994). Yet the transition from career-break back to teaching is not without problems. A study of 1813 NUT members (Healy and Kraithman, 1994) showed that 799 had taken a career-break; 665 women and 79 men (see Table 7.2). Only 10 per cent of this group had received updating training prior to returning to teaching. A higher proportion of men had received updating training than women.

When considering the duration of training, women's training tended to be shorter than that of men. The findings also suggested that a lack of updating training contributed to the difficulties experienced on returning to work. Updating training would have helped confidence, coping with competing demands, reduced the feeling of being out of date. It is also noteworthy that only a few of our sample did not experience problems on returning to work. The ease of the transition back to teaching will crucially influence the ability to negotiate conflicting demands and the final phase in which teachers find themselves.

TABLE 7.2   Teachers: difficulties experienced on returning to work

Reason	Total	Total (%)	Men (%)	Women (%)
Childcare	274	34	6	40
Coping with competing demands	347	43	23	49
Lack of training to up-date	165	21	10	24
Confidence	267	33	25	37
Feeling out of date	184	23	13	26
Teaching unfamiliar subjects	104	13	19	13
None	56	7	14	7
Other	66	8	11	9

n = 799 (79 men, 665 women)
Source: Healy and Kraithman (1994).

The career-break can put women very quickly into the compromise phase. Trevorrow's (1990) study of women who had taken a career-break well illustrates how they perceived their employment position: 'I now realise I was too old before I began [a course] . . . people like me are ten a penny.'

One teacher pointed to the no-win situation in which a career-break may appear to place a woman: 'too young before I had children and too old once I got myself established after returning'.

Whereas another negotiated her life to take account of home priorities: 'By 40, I had arranged my life so that my career took secondary importance to a variety of other interests'.

The contradictions in returners' positions and their adjustments of strategy are important, particularly in the light of the ageism they are experiencing. The following comment from a deputy head shows how a teacher can slip behind in the hierarchical race but at the same time how creative strategies during the interim stage are used to facilitate the move back to the career stage:

Obviously my career-break of seven years puts me seven years behind my male colleagues – my present head teacher is the same age as me, has fewer qualifications and has only ever taught junior classes – but has been a head for ten years and I've been a deputy for four years. However, I used my career-break to my advantage in interviews by explaining that during that time I taught everything from new born babies to 80 year old men and women!

Women develop strategies that include the use of different currency as evidence of career potential from many of their male colleagues.

In the mid-1990s women teachers face variable labour markets. Despite the changing economic environment and redundancies, it is still the case that in some geographical areas the informal networks put pressure on women to return: they 'came back not because they wanted to but because we wanted them to' (quote from a deputy head in the south-east, 1994). The likelihood that recent changes may force career choices at an earlier stage than women would like is real: a deputy head commented that: 'In the past few years more women are taking maternity leave and coming back, it is becoming more of a trend, the second income is important . . .If they have left for eight years now they would have real difficulty in returning.'

Thus educational change plus economic factors may force a polarisation of choice: the dual-role teacher may be reluctant to make this choice as she would really like longer at home; the teacher who opts to become inactive will be concerned that the changes will make her less employable in the future.

Influence of significant others

We were interested to know whom teachers perceived to be most helpful to them in their careers. The most commonly mentioned people were the heads of their current or previous schools. This is a similar finding to the Evetts study (1988). This is not surprising as heads have access to resources which can provide material support for the development of the teacher. What also seems to be emerging from our pilot study is the importance of colleagues of the same sex, although not exclusively. Given the feminisation of the profession, one cannot read too much into this at this stage; but it does merit further exploration. The identification of colleagues is important in the light of fears of 'increased competitive individualism of the market place' (quoted in Mac an Ghaill, 1992). The notion of team-work (an essential aspect of the new human resource management) is well rooted in teaching and, if anything, has been given a boost by the radical changes experienced (Healy and Kraithman, 1994); teamwork is an important counter to the imposition of unwanted and often undesirable changes.

Partners were also significant others in enabling women to progress; the role of partners is a recurring feature in the literature of women's achievement (for example see Ledwith *et al.*, 1990). Partners can enable or impede, or simply take up space. In our study we noted a secondary deputy head who indicated that her career developed when there were no significant others: 'the times I've got on was when I've not had men around'. She became a head of department following her divorce and a deputy headteacher when she was living alone. She argued that 'work becomes more important if you live alone, I might then want the challenge of being head. The idea of your own ship is very attractive.'

Critical life events, influenced by the lack of significant others, were key enablers in her teaching career. The role of significant others influences the variable degrees of freedom and constraint women have in shaping their careers to their liking.

Conclusion

Teachers face an employment context surrounded by two contradictory myths: teaching is a good job for a woman and the mythology that women teachers are less committed and less qualified than men. In refuting these myths we have argued that such myths sustain embedded discriminatory structures and warn that educational and managerial change may reinforce these structures.

Women teachers experience more varied career patterns than male teachers in order to cope with competing demands. This chapter has presented a typology to capture the complexity of women teachers' multidimensional career patterns, and it has argued that the ability to work continuously or to take a break and return to teaching will be partly dependent on the employment context teachers face. In the mid-1990s, teachers face a context of educational and managerial change leading to work intensification and reduction in professional autonomy; this may force greater compromise in the way women fulfil their domestic and occupational contracts. It is also the case that LMS forces increasing casualisation of work; women at the interim stage will benefit from this, but as they wish to move beyond this to more permanent employment they may meet frustration and find themselves not fulfilling their aspirations and spending their final work stage in a compromise phase. Thus change may force women to make more extreme decisions, i.e. to continue working without a break, or to leave for an indeterminate period of time, knowing that with the pace of change their options to return may be considerably reduced. The 'good job myth' is predicated on assumptions of women's low expectations and supported by pressures from the dual role of work and family to take low-level teaching work in the form of supply and temporary work; but, in the context of teaching as a flexible career for women, the good job myth is shattered.

The second myth influencing teachers' development is that women are not as committed nor as qualified as men. This myth cannot be sustained in the light of the evidence; however, as in other occupations, gendered structures (sustained by such myths) can lead to the marginalising of women who do not adopt the continuous career path. Women teachers have to operate within a highly political environment; therefore the importance of political skills will be critical; not least in respect of their ability to persuade selectors that different experiences are equal experiences. Women teachers will be operating within an increasingly feminised occupation whose professionalism is under assault. Resistance through collectivism may be an important means of survival; developing the benefits of collective skills outlined by some of the women in our study will be important.

Resources are important in career development; women in the study have identified the benefit of training as a development and as a confidence resource to them. Equally, the paucity of training when women return to work was an evident barrier to development. Informal networks provided important resources to re-enter teaching and to develop within teaching. The negotiation between women's caring and teaching roles have led women to develop a range of coping strategies that includes the 'interim phase' as the bridge between full-time childcare and a return to 'career teaching'. To move to the interim phase provides more of perhaps the most crucial resource: time. Change has led to an intensification of time in the teaching process and for those women with family responsibilities, their time scarcity may drive women into the compromise phase, albeit reluctantly.

The chapter has also shown that women (and men) teachers will be facing different labour markets depending on the type of school, the subjects they teach, their age and their geographical constraints. Some labour markets will provide greater opportunities than others, and we know that forecasted labour market demands may mediate against some of the negative consequences of change.

The complexity of women's career patterns demands serious reflection by decision-makers. To consider women's multidimensional career patterns as deviant is to condemn women teachers who have adopted discontinuous career patterns to feel obliged continually to justify their career decisions in the context of gendered structures. Equally, it is important that women teachers negotiate their share of limited resources, such as training and time, albeit in the context of constraint, to facilitate their development in teaching.

Acknowledgements

We are indebted to the teachers who took part in our pilot study either by completing questionnaires or being interviewed. We are also grateful to Judith Trevorrow and Fiona Scheibl for their insights on aspects of the study.

Notes

1. A pilot study was undertaken as part of the preparation for a major survey of teachers. The pilot consisted of 30 respondents, who completed detailed questionnaries which elicited considerable quantitative data, and five in-depth

semi-structured interviews and group discussions. A large quantitative study was undertaken in 1994 by the authors in collaboration with the National Union of Teachers to examine the impact of change on teachers' employment. Some preliminary findings were presented to the School Teachers Review Body (Healy and Kraithman, 1994).

2. It is hard to know why Evetts talks about 'married' women: the concern here is with teachers who have taken a break to look after children.

3. Evetts (1994) argued that there were at least three substantive issues that pose difficulties for women in achieving promotion in their careers, and that these issues need to be addressed if the concept of career is to be de-gendered and disassociated from the uni-dimensional model of a hierarchical linear career. The issues are (i) the combining of paid and unpaid work responsibilities; (ii) the unidimensional conception of management; (iii) the language of careers. She argues that the multi-dimensional career is more potentially satisfying for the individual and is in the best economic, as well as social, interests of work organisations.

4. Our previous research (Healy and Kraithman, 1989 and 1991) examined occupational aspirations of women with young children and found that women did not expect to achieve their desired occupation without additional enablers or retrieval forces (e.g. training, childcare). Further investigation suggested occupational frustration would arise if aspirations were not met. The typology of careers phases presented in this chapter have their origins in Healy and Kraithman (1995).

5. In secondary schools, head teachers tend to work 50 hours per week, deputies work 47.2 and other teachers 41.6. The average was 42.1 for all teachers (STRB, 1994).

6. We were influenced by the work of Mac an Ghaill (1992). He classified teachers as New Entrepreneurs, Old Collectivists and Professionals.

CHAPTER 8

Getting to the top in the National Health Service

Sylvia Wyatt with Caroline Langridge

The UK National Health Service (NHS) is the largest employer of women in Europe, but with few of them working in positions of power and influence.

In 1991 a programme to redress the gender imbalance in the NHS was put into place. A key part of this was the setting up a new Women's Unit. In this first introductory section to the chapter, Caroline Langridge, head of the Women's Unit, sets out the unit's agenda in the NHS. There then follows an analysis by Sylvia Wyatt of the organisational changes and the impact on women's career routes in the health service.

Women and new management in the NHS

Women have traditionally been seen as the gatekeepers in terms of their families' access to health care, and usually act as the carers in the family. They also tend to be more interested and knowledgeable about health. The World Health Organisation recognises the power of women in relation to health issues in developing countries, stating that the best way to improve health is to educate women and involve them in decision-making.

Over 78 per cent of NHS staff are women, although they are not so well represented in positions of power (Goss and Brown, 1991).

This gives the NHS Executive a particular interest in researching and meeting the needs of its largely female workforce.

This will become even more important in the future with the deconstruction of acute hospitals and their replacement by a network of interrelated largely community-based services. A primary-care-led NHS is unlikely to be susceptible to management by the old command and control or transactional management style. It is more likely to be using transformational leadership styles, working across boundaries, and adopting a collaborative, consultative, consensus-seeking style; using power based on influence and interpersonal skills (Rosener, 1990). This is what is also known as 'new management' (Brown and Parston, 1994).

As the largest group of NHS staff, women have a particular role to play in leading the way in implementing these changes, since evidence shows that they are more comfortable with transformational management styles. Also, as shown in an analysis of top women managers in the NHS (Proctor and Jackson, 1992), women are more likely to be given opportunities at a time of rapid change in organisational practice; they are often seen as ideal change agents, able to balance the dual roles of maintenance and facilitating change. Given the almost permanent revolution in the NHS, people able to manage change will be much in demand in the next decade.

However, in order to achieve power, women have first to get on and then climb the ladder. That so many have achieved power in the last three years is evidence of a major change in organisational culture in the NHS.

To reprise recent history, the 1991 Equal Opportunities Commission's highly critical report on *Women's Employment in the NHS* showed that, despite the widespread adoption by health authorities of equal opportunities policies, very little progress had occurred after a decade of such policies. Although women accounted for 79 per cent of NHS staff, they were heavily concentrated in the lowest managerial grades, with very few women in senior management. The position in medicine was even worse, with only 15 per cent of women achieving consultant status, although more and more women entered medical school following the outlawing by the Sex Discrimination Act of 1975 of restricting women to 30 per cent of medical school places. The Audit Commission (1991) had also drawn attention to the high percentage – 30 per cent – of women entering nurse training and leaving on or before qualification. Given the costs of training the NHS workforce, estimated at £2.3 billion in 1991, central policy-makers could no longer afford to ignore these issues. Ministers determined that as the largest employer of women in Europe, the NHS would be in the vanguard of change. The NHS became a founder member of Opportunity 2000 and launched a programme to utilise women in the NHS more effectively – thus also embarking on a major programme of changing organisational culture (NHSME, 1992).

The result has been a shift from a traditional equal opportunities policy framework with its concepts of social justice embedded in the language of rights, to a new business-focused approach based on competitive advantage, seeing women as a resource and not a problem.

An early priority was to identify and publicise the existence of credible role models, especially increasing the percentage of top women managers and of women medical consultants. To enhance visibility a profile of 27 top women managers was published, together with guidelines for aspiring women managers (Proctor and Jackson, 1992). In addition a national Career Development Register was established for women just below the 'glass ceiling', to enable them to compete more effectively for top jobs. In the first 30 months of the new initiative, to March 1994, women were appointed to 38 per cent of the chief executive posts advertised, and nearly 47.5 per cent of general senior management posts were filled by women at September 1994. By April 1995 women were 28 per cent of all general managers; see Table 8.1.

A key lesson in changing organisational culture is securing commitment at the top, not just to launch a programme, but for the sustained effort needed over a number of years to achieve results: the NHS had health ministers committed to the programme remaining in office for three years – a rarity in British government. Another key success factor is that the programme is

TABLE 8.1   Proportion of women as NHS general managers,* April 1995

	Women	*% of women*
All general managers	656	28
Acute units	71	25
Community units	70	42
Mental health	28	37
Conglomerate	16	18
Ambulance	2	5
Health authority	40	23
FHSA	22	34
Regional HA	1	12
All provider units	185	30
All purchaser units	62	26
Trusts		
First wave	14	19
Second wave	44	29
Third wave	63	29
Fourth wave	54	30
Fifth wave	5	28
DMU	6	46

* General managers defined as: regional directors, chief executives, district general managers, general managers of DMUs, director of operations, director of purchasing/commissioning if board-level post.
Source: NHS Women's Unit, Goal One Monitoring Exercise, April 1995.

clearly embedded within the overall business goals and strategic direction of the NHS and is not a bolt-on extra. In other words, it is part of the mainstream.

There has been a downside to women's gains, however. In the last three years there has been a steady rise of a male backlash. This is not surprising as the programme originated from ministers as a top-down initiative, moving forward on the basis of capturing enough key stakeholders to achieve change without waiting to get a majority of NHS staff on board. The NHS Executive's decision to focus initially on top women could be seen as élitist, but it was essential to achieve a critical mass of women in senior posts both to act as powerful role models for younger, more junior women in the NHS, but also to begin to change the dominant culture of the old macho model into one which empowers individuals to deliver better quality healthcare. However, men in the dominant group are unlikely to have felt comfortable with a frontal assault on their traditional power base, especially as the introduction of the Opportunity 2000 programme councided with significant downsizing in the NHS leading to a reduction of nearly 20 per cent in top manager or chief executive posts.

Nevertheless, if the future world of work is to be female, as many would have us believe, the NHS will need to make rapid steps towards becoming a family-friendly employer and aligning service delivery goals to fit the lifestyles and aspirations of its largely female workforce, and women, the main users of health care (Langridge, 1994).

Women managers in the NHS

The chapter now moves to a more specific analysis of the organisational changes and their impact on male and female career paths in the NHS.

Getting to the top in the National Health Service is defined in managerial terms and thus this section focuses on NHS managers, using the results of the Creative Career Paths Project (CCP) surveys, which reported on the responses of some 1714 NHS managers, both women and men. It describes who the managers are and some of the influences on their career paths, comparing different groups and identifying differences between genders. Aso described are some recent innovations which have brought the NHS to the forefront of good employer practice when trying to achieve more equality between women and men.

The NHS is one of the largest employers in Europe with a relatively young workforce comprising people with a very wide range of skills. In 1993 women made up nearly 80 per cent of this workforce but only 21 per cent of the NHS top managers in England. Women were over-represented at lower managerial levels.

For the first four decades of the NHS, getting into NHS management was restricted to people from managerial backgrounds. However, in 1985, when consensus management by 5–6 chief officers from different disciplines was superseded by general management with a single chief executive role, the top posts became accessible to people from any discipline and outsiders were actively encouraged to come into NHS management. This introduction of general management extended the length and variety of career paths to the top.

Evidence from the CCP surveys allowed the rate of career progress for NHS managers from different professional backgrounds to be compared, and some of the major influences on the progress up the managerial ladders for men and women to be analysed. The business case for making better use of women's skills in the NHS (Opportunity 2000, 1992) and other recent changes have resulted in the NHS leading the way in managing some gender issues. Ten years after the introduction of general management into the NHS and the first equal opportunities reviews, managers at the top are still predominantly 'homegrown' from within the NHS with managerial backgrounds, and women and nurses are still under-represented at the higher levels.

The structure and culture of the NHS

During the 1980s the NHS, like many other organisations in Western economies, underwent fundamental change characterised by:

- attempts to decentralise resources and decision-making within organisations;
- attempts to increase organisational efficiency;
- reduction of the number of levels in managerial hierarchies;
- an emphasis on horizontal integration of staff from different disciplines rather than vertical/functional divisions of labour;
- 'downsizing', as the euphemism has it, with a subsequent increase in 'outplacement' consultants;
- mergers of organisations, although the pendulum may be swinging back to the small-is-beautiful end of the spectrum;
- contracting-out technical and support services;
- establishing independent agencies to provide services previously contained within the organisation (training, information, estates management, for example) in the public sector.

In the NHS, as elsewhere, changes of these kinds were reactions to overwhelming economic forces from the continuing recession resulting in pressure on public expenditure and a political emphasis on market solutions. The result was significant changes in the employment culture of the NHS with the introduction of entrepreneurial ideas, competition, tendering for some services and the growth of managerialism, all of which had consequences for career paths.

The introduction of income-generation schemes into the NHS marked a symbolic shift away from public service values. The schemes themselves never produced much revenue, but they released health authorities from the existing restrictions on their freedoms to sell services for profit. This change increased the value of commercial skills and experience to the NHS, so that it was more willing to look outside to recruit non-NHS business skills (Robinson and Le Grand, 1994).

Competitive tendering for contracted-out services was politically attractive to the Conservative Government and had the added bonus of potentially increasing the efficiency of the NHS. Again the financial gain was less important than the principle that the core responsibility of health authorities was not to provide and manage but to ensure that services were available when and where required, at least cost to the authority and zero cost to the patients using them. The ancillary services with their predominance of women were most affected by this change.

In 1983 the Griffiths enquiry (Griffiths, 1983) recommended the introduction of general management principles in the NHS and as a result administrative and clerical staff became managers. The report placed more emphasis on appointing people with experience from outside the NHS to introduce more business skills into the NHS, and it opened doors to people with non-administrative backgrounds to become NHS managers. The implementation of the report in 1985 led to the appointment of unit general managers (UGMs), the predecessors to chief executives. A survey of newly appointed UGMs undertaken in 1986–7 (Disken *et al.*, 1987) identified that 62 per cent had administrative backgrounds, 6 per cent were from the armed forces and non-NHS management, 16 per cent were doctors or dentists and 11 per cent were from nursing backgrounds. Some 83 per cent were men and 17 per cent women.

The shift to an internal market in healthcare had its roots in extensive academic and professional discussion in the 1980s with growing realisation by managers that rational planning would not deliver the change necessary to meet the financial reductions. In 1985 Professor Alain Enthoven formally mapped out the potential form of such a market (Enthoven, 1985) in a paper for the Nuffield Provincial Hospitals Trust which later formed the basis of the White Paper, *Working for Patients*, and subsequently the NHS and Community Care Act in 1990. This resulted in major structural changes in the NHS with the separation of purchaser and provider functions.

Since 1990 there has been continuous change in NHS management with a general trend towards mergers between NHS organisations, for both purchasers and providers. The opportunity to get to the top in the NHS has halved since 1982 when there were some 1200 chief officer posts in England and when consensus management meant that there were 5 or 6 chief officers in every authority, compared to about 650 in 1994 when the 419 NHS trusts, 22 directly managed units, 8 regional health authorities, 112 district health authorities, 90 family health services authorities each had a single chief executive. The number will reduce further in 1996 when health authorities merge with family health services authorities.

In 1993, the NHS hospital and community services in England employed about 950 000 non-medical people; this equated to about 770 000 whole-time equivalents (WTEs). Figure 8.1 shows the overall proportions of the different types of non-medical staff.

Over 50 per cent (240 000 WTE) had a nursing qualification (excluding agency nurses) and about 90 000 were nurses in training. The second largest group was administrative and clerical workers, which included almost all the managers.

The workforce of the NHS is currently nearly 80 per cent women and they outnumber men in all staff groups except doctors, works and ambulance staff. The biggest group of women are nurses, where more than 85 per cent are female. Over 80 per cent of the administrative and clerical staff are women.

Figure 8.2 shows the relative proportions of women and men for non-medical staff.

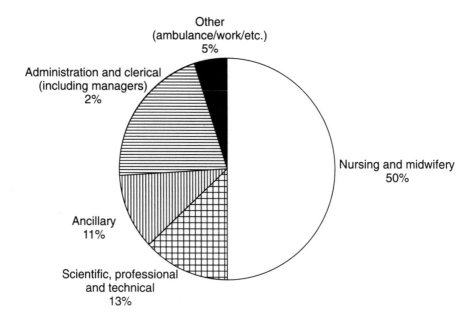

FIGURE 8.1   Non-medical staff by main group at September 1993

219

FIGURE 8.2 Non-medical staff by gender and WTE at September 1993

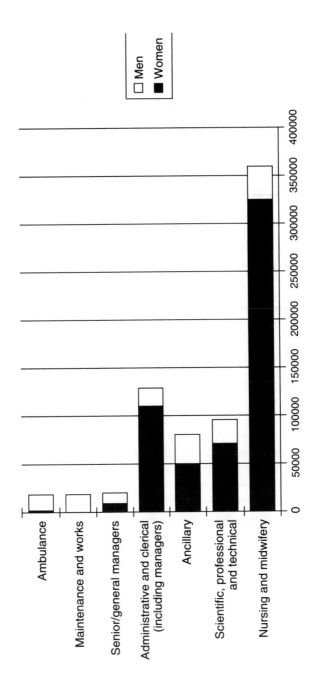

There has been a fall in the overall number of people employed by the NHS (a decrease of 8 per cent in non-medical staff between 1983 and 1993) and there are now larger organisations employing a smaller number of people. There has also been a reduction in the numbers of levels in the NHS hierarchies and more involvement of doctors and nurses, mainly consultants in (usually) managerial roles, often combined with clinical commitments. The overall effect has been to convert provider unit management structures from vertically organised professional hierarchies to structures based on multidisciplinary teams supporting the delivery of clinical services.

Career paths of the past

The current inequalities in status in the NHS between women and men managers actually represent a significant improvement over the position in the past. Until the mid-1980s, the NHS had hierarchical parallel career paths for doctors, nurses and administrators, and each of the many other professions involved. For those in clinical areas, the last rung of the career ladder was chief nurse (replacing the former matron), medical consultant or head of department. For administrators, the career ladders stretched from below hospital level to district to area and finally region. Movement between professional career ladders was almost unheard of.

These parallel career paths were most evident in the consensus management culture between 1974 and 1985 when doctors, nurses, finance officers and administrators (and works officers for RHAs,) formed district, area and regional teams of officers. The chief officers from different disciplines were technically of equal status (though did not enjoy equal pay) and were supposed to contribute equally to the decision-making process. Each considered themselves to have reached the top of their respective professions and worked in a complementary way with decisions made jointly. The career paths of nurses, doctors and administrators are described in more detail below.

Nursing career paths

Since Florence Nightingale first developed nursing into a profession, there have always been more women than men in nursing, but they have always been disproportionately represented in lower grades. The stereotype of a nursing career was a rigid hierarchy ending with a female matron figure at the top, running a hospital. The matron's status was always less than her medical consultant colleagues, implying that the nursing was a lesser profes-

FIGURE 8.3 NHS parallel career paths up to 1985

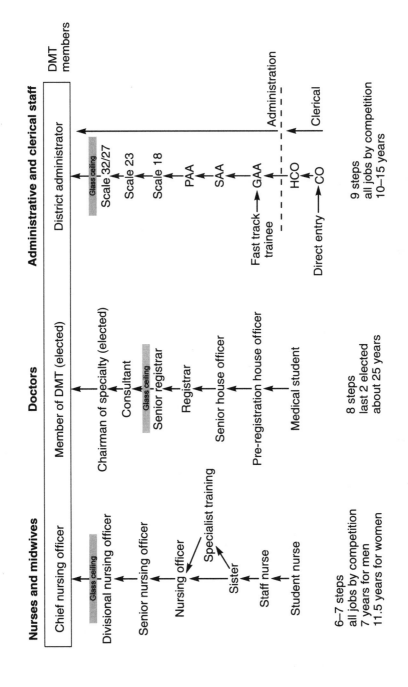

Nurses and midwives

Chief nursing officer — Glass ceiling

Divisional nursing officer

Senior nursing officer

Nursing officer ← Specialist training

Sister

Staff nurse

Student nurse

6–7 steps
all jobs by competition
7 years for men
11.5 years for women

Doctors

Member of DMT (elected)

Chairman of specialty (elected)

Consultant

Senior registrar — Glass ceiling

Registrar

Senior house officer

Pre-registration house officer

Medical student

8 steps
last 2 elected
about 25 years

Administrative and clerical staff

District administrator

Scale 32/27 — Glass ceiling

Scale 23

Scale 18

PAA

SAA

Fast track → GAA
trainee

HCO

Direct entry → CO

Administration

Clerical

9 steps
all jobs by competition
10–15 years

DMT members

sion. The Salmon Committee in 1966 led to the demise of the matron and was followed by the theoretical equality of consensus management. Progress from one nursing level to the next has always been reviewed by nurses themselves, largely against clinical standards set from within the nursing profession.

Men have been extraordinary successful in reaching the top in the nursing profession, despite being in the minority, This was investigated by Davies and Rosser (1986b) who showed that there was as considerable difference in the time taken by women and men to achieve their first nursing officer post: 17.9 years for women, 8.4 years for men and 14.5 years for women who took no career-breaks. This difference:

> was not explained by better qualifications, or earlier entry into the profession. The faster career progression rate was achieved despite the fact that 'the men appeared to break all the rules – they entered late, they went to the 'wrong' nursing schools, they did not chine particularly in terms of qualifications held and yet they progressed much faster than women.

This golden pathway was also identified by Davies and Rosser in the administrative field.

Medical career paths

Men have dominated the numbers in the medical profession and the stereotypical doctor is still a man. Progress up the medical hierarchy was and still is reviewed by doctors in an accreditation process organised by the Royal Colleges against standards set by the doctors. These formal rules, about the amount and type of clinical experience required to make progress, contrast with the actual barriers to career progress which were identified by Allen's (1988) study of 640 doctors. She identified the major barriers women faced as being:

- male attitudes and patronage;
- an inflexible career structure;
- the demands of having to be mobile;
- difficulties of combining career and domestic responsibilities (particularly if married to another doctor, of whom 50 per cent were);
- extremely long working hours;
- lack of time and opportunity available for studying for a higher professional qualification.

Although the proportion of women being trained as doctors has risen from 27 per cent to 50 per cent in the last 15 years, this equality in numbers still has to percolate to the top of the profession to redress the extant and recognisable horizontal and vertical segregation between women and men. In 1989, 15.5 per cent of all consultants were women and only 1 per cent of general surgeons were women. Only 5 per cent of the Fellows of the Royal College of Surgeons and 3 per cent of consultants in surgical specialties are women. There was (and is) horizontal segregation with women doctors concentrated in the less glamorous, less front-line specialties e.g. public health, anaesthetics, pathology, radiology and geriatrics. Most of the part-time female doctors are in general practice and few are principals.

Administrators, managers and clerical staff career paths

Administrators and clerical staff (later called managers) represented one of the largest predominantly female occupational groups in the NHS. Up to 1985, there was a single administrative hierarchy (and pay spine) starting with clerical officers and moving up through administrative posts to regional administrators (see Figure 8.3).

The career paths for administrators were far less formally defined than those for nurses and doctors, where the scope and amount of experience to progress upwards was subject to professional accreditation. There were two main entry points onto the old administrative/managerial career path: direct entrants and fast track trainees.

A significant number of people started out on the bottom rung of the managerial career ladder with secondary school qualifications and worked their way upwards, in most cases gaining professional (IHSM, MBAs or other administrative, business, personnel or financial) qualifications en route. These included people who started in clerical grades, as medical secretaries or medical records clerks with O level or equivalent qualifications.

The NHS has operated a training scheme for high calibre graduates or in-service candidates since 1956. This came to be recognised as the quickest route to the top of the administrative career ladder. Although the trainees in the first decade or so were primarily men, the numbers of women recruited gradually increased, and Dixon and Shaw (1986) reported that 52 per cent of the entrants were women between 1974 and 1981. In 1974 more women than men were recruited for the first time. Of those ex-trainees who were to be found working in the NHS in junior and lower middle management posts in December 1979, 57 per cent were female, which decreased to 14 per cent amongst those in senior management posts.

Progress up the administrative hierarchy was achieved by open competition for advertised jobs. Few standards were available to judge the levels of experience and competence and there was a high level of progress by patronage which tended to perpetuate the over-representation of men at the top of the hierarchy. Fast track trainees became linked with the 'golden pathway',

(Rosser and Davies, 1986b) requiring long working hours, geographical mobility, continuous employment with no career-breaks and remaining in the more glamorous acute sector. These constraints were more easily met by men than women and led to the golden pathway being described as male.

In 1991 Goss and Brown identified that: 'Men dominate in the glamorous hospital sector . . . whilst women move into lower-status family health and community services.'

The line between administrative and clerical staff was, and still is, difficult to draw accurately, and debates over the numbers of administrators have been frequent. However, whatever definition is used, women are concentrated in the lower levels of management.

In summary, until 1985 and the introduction of general management, separate career ladders for each profession were clearly defined, and the way to the top well-signposted. To get to the top you had to be on a ladder to climb and the best chance of getting to the top was to stay on the same ladder. There was, however, only one way to the top. With general management, the professionally defined career paths became linked to managerial ones, adding to the possible career path length and breadth of experience and others joined the ranks of managers. The top became defined in a single chief executive post. Thus to reach the top, doctors and nurses (and other professionals) had to become more than expert professionals and acquire general management skills to progress. For women professionals, this may mean that there are two glass ceilings. This is illustrated by Figure 8.4.

In the late 1980s and 1990s all employees, men and women alike, were affected by the fragmentation of the NHS into discrete management units and growth of local employment practices. In general, there was increasing concern (Wyatt et al., 1994) about the prevailing management culture in the NHS with its expectations of excessive workloads, unsocial working hours and a high level of geographical mobility. There were many voluntary or involuntary departures of experienced managers from the NHS, and traditional career paths within individual professions or functions closed down. If you had been climbing a ladder, by the time you got there the reasons for doing so might have disappeared.

Recent changes to increase the visibility of women in the NHS

The picture of women's employment in the NHS is fairly typical of the national situation. Women have shown a persistent pattern of lower rates of pay, under-representation in senior posts and over-representation in junior and semi-skilled jobs. There have however, been some innovations unique to the NHS, which have caused a wind of change. These initiatives are discussed

FIGURE 8.4   NHS: new career paths after the introduction of general management

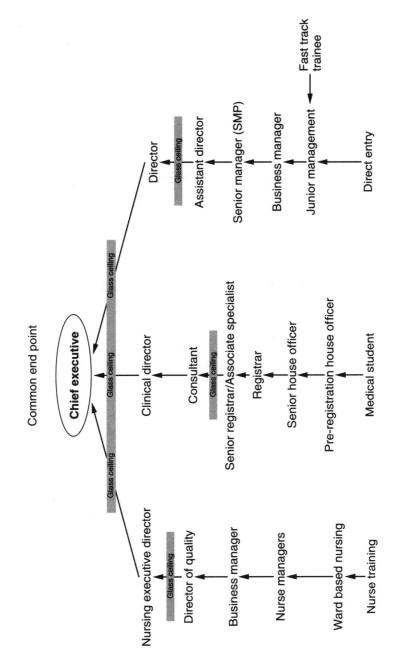

in below and the evidence to support the view that employer practices in the NHS are beginning to improve is reviewed in the next section.

Opportunity 2000 was set up by Business in the Community in 1991 in an attempt to address both the European Community's target for women's economic development and to improve employment opportunities for women. The Department of Health on behalf of the NHS was the first government department to become a campaign member of Opportunity 2000. This initiative aimed to increase the quality and quantity of participation of women at work and to see a demonstrable movement towards a more balanced workforce by the year 2000 and beyond. Opportunity 2000 focused on the problems and challenges faced by employers and the extent to which women provide the solutions. This business case emphasis represents a considerable shift from previous programmes for women's development, where employers had seen women and womens careers as the problem (Wyatt *et al*, 1994) to the point where employers are now being asked to respond to womens needs.

The NHS goal within Opportunity 2000 was to take full advantage of the potential of women in the NHS to provide the best healthcare for all members of the population. In 1991 the NHS Management Executive in England set a series of goals (DOH, 1992) for the NHS and established the NHS Womens Unit, tasked with the aim of reaching these goals by the end of 1994. These goals were:

Goal 1:   Increase the number of women in general management posts from 18 per cent in 1991 to 30 per cent in 1994. (28 per cent achieved by April 1995 and 5 of the 14 old RHAs had met or exceeded the 30 per cent target set.)

Goal 2:   Increase the number of qualified women accountants in the NHS.

Goal 3:   Increase the percentage of women medical consultants from 15.5 per cent in 1991 to 20 per cent by 1994, necessitating an annual increase of 10 per cent. Accelerate the rate of increase in the number of women consultants in surgical specialties from the current 9.7 per cent per annum to 15 per cent pa.

Goal 4:   Increase the representation of women as members of authorities and trusts from 29 per cent in 1991 to 35 per cent by 1994.

Goal 5:   Introduce a programme allowing women aspiring to management positions to go through a development centre with a view to establishing their own personal development needs.

Goal 6:   Introduce incentives for recruitment and retention to ensure that the number of qualified nurses and midwives leaving the profession does not rise.

Goal 7:   Ensure that, following a maternity leave or career break, all women (including those returning to nursing part-time or as a job share) are able to return at a grade commensurate with their leaving grade and to work of a similar status.

Goal 8:   Monitor the time taken for nurses to reach management positions to ensure that men and women have equal access to these positions.

The NHS Women's Unit has been actively pursuing these goals in England with considerable success. One of its early publications, was *Celebration of Success* (Proctor and Jackson, 1992) which contained case studies of the careers of 27 named top women managers from a variety of backgrounds, who received their education in the 1950s and 60s and whose career paths were established in the 1970s and 1980s. This study provided:

- visible role models of people enabling others to resolve choices and dilemmas in developing their own careers;
- examples of different routes to the top;
- a demonstration of the positive and distinct contribution women make in the management of the NHS whenever they are given or take the opportunity.

The Women's Unit set up the NHS Women's Career Development Register as part of Opportunity 2000 to help women with their own career development. Inclusion on the register was limited to women earning £30 000 or more and interested in senior jobs in the NHS. The register gave women access to career advice, personal development opportunities and counselling. The key objective was to raise the number of women at board level by helping them prepare and compete for more senior posts.

There was an almost overwhelming response from senior women managers to setting up the register, and membership has grown to over 700. It is not possible to identify how many more women might be eligible, nor how many men might be eligible for a similar register, but it is certain that this number only represents a small part of the whole. Some 39 per cent of the total membership have taken up a new post since joining the register, of these some 41 per cent moved to a higher salary band. Women who had used the register found 1:1 coaching the most useful, followed by advice about preparing their CV. One-third said that the biggest difference that the register had made was to increase their confidence (personal communication based on unpublished survey of managers on register). The ideas behind the register have been incorporated into the Human Resources Strategy for the NHS, and independent sources of career counselling and career development advice are being established at regional level, available to both women and men.

The NHS Women's Unit has been very effective in encouraging women to compete more effectively with men in a number of ways. It has helped women to overcome barriers which stand in their way, realising their full potential within the NHS, setting up local women's networks, acting as a focus for communicating information about best practice throughout the Service, identifying gaps in information and monitoring appointments procedures.

Creative Career Paths (CCP) Project

It was against a background of considerable organisational change in the NHS that the idea of carrying out a comprehensive study of career paths of NHS managers was conceived by the NHS Women's Unit in the summer of 1992. The aim of the study was defined as establishing the extent to which a flexible and imaginative career culture in the NHS could lead to a more cost-effective use and deployment of managers, greater satisfaction and motivation for individuals, and better recruitment and retention of talented managers in the NHS. The main part of the project comprised studying career paths of managers through four postal questionnaires of:

- a census survey of top managers in the NHS (population size 894);
- a sample survey of leavers from the fast-track training scheme and from top manager posts (sample size 213);
- a survey of a representative sample of managers from 15 NHS organisations (sample size 816);
- a census survey of senior nurses (sample size 695).

The survey populations were mutually exclusive, apart from the 52 top managers who were also nurses and who were resurveyed as part of the senior nurse survey. The findings of the Creative Career Paths (CCP) project for managers within the NHS are described through out the rest of this chapter and have been published as a series of four reports (CCP Survey Reports). Examples and data are drawn from all the surveys.

One of the most striking findings from CCP was the virtual absence of managers from ethnic minorities or who were disabled. However, the Secretary of State for Health recently launched a programme of action to improve this position in the NHS (DOH, 1993). This programme, which again has a series of goals, recognises that the majority of staff from black and ethnic minorities in the NHS are at lower levels of staff groups and professions, notably in lower nursing and ancillary grades, and that implementing equal opportunities policies has been patchy.

In relation to women, the CCP surveys show the continued under-representation of women in the managerial workforce and other inequalities between women and men relating to almost every aspect of their careers. The findings of the CCP surveys have partly refuted the 'men in grey suits' image of the managers in the NHS since women now form a significant proportion of the managerial workforce (see Table 8.2).

The figure above is supported by data from the NHS Womens Unit monitoring of progress towards the goals which found that 38 per cent (69 out of 198) vacant chief executive posts between April 1992 and September 1994 went to women (unpublished monitoring information from Women's Unit).

The CCP survey found that majority of the top managers still came from managerial backgrounds, but that the qualifications of senior middle and first line managers varied considerably. This is shown in Table 8.3 below.

The high proportion of top managers with administrative/managerial qualifications is almost certainly linked to the pre-1985 predominance of NHS management by administrators who had developed their skills within the NHS: few had clinical or professional backgrounds. The table shows the effect of introducing general management; the number of people with administrative qualifications is smaller further down the management hierarchy.

In contrast the position is reversed for nurses with a large number at first line manager level: this suggests that nurses are replacing 'traditional' managers, particularly in the business manager roles, and are entering management roles

TABLE 8.2   Proportion of women at different levels of NHS management in England

Type of managers in England	*sample size*	*% women*	*% women respondents*
Top managers:	894	16%	21%
Senior managers	110	41%	47%
Middle managers	210	52%	55%
First line	268	68%	69%
Senior nurses	695	na	71%

Source: CCP Surveys.

TABLE 8.3   Women at different levels of NHS management in England

Type of managers in England	*% of respondents with different types of primary professional qualifications (% women in brackets)*		
	Management/ administrative	*Nursing*	*Medical/dental*
Top managers:	54%(43%)	9%(26%)	7%(9%)
Senior managers	17%	16%	28%
Middle managers	16%	22%	9%
First line	9%	28%	1%

Source: CCP Surveys.

at a relatively early stage in their careers. This may, in future, help redress the imbalance still felt in nursing at higher levels where there are many more male nurses who have reached the top compared to women, despite the feminised workforce. In 1991 only 10 per cent of all nurses were men, but 45 per cent of the chief nursing posts were held by men, and again in 1993, 9 per cent of the top managers had nursing qualifications of which 47 per cent were men. This contrasts with the position for nurse executive director posts where 72 per cent were women.

The pattern for doctors is different again with a large number of doctors entering management at the senior level (as directors of clinical units) after a successful clinical career. This cohort of doctors have yet to move upward into chief executive positions and many return to clinical work, having had a taste ot management. The numbers of women top managers seem to suggest that they are competing successfully with men.

The age profile of NHS manager has changed dramatically in recent years with the average age of chief executives dropping sharply. Table 8.4 shows the average age and the proportion of managers who are over 50 at different levels in the NHS.

In 1981, the mean ages for men and women chief officers were 49 and 51 respectively (Dixon and de Metz, 1982) compared to 46 and 42 in 1993. It is interesting that the NHS top managers' average age has reduced and, more importantly, that the women managers are often younger than their male counterparts (in the cohort of young top managers aged 38 there were more women than men). No single factor has caused this change, but the Equal Opportunities Commission has contributed to the rise in numbers of women by focusing the spotlight on the situation in the NHS since 1988. Exceptionally senior nurses who were men were younger than their female counterparts which can be explained by the fact that fewer of the men have taken career-breaks.

TABLE 8.4   **Average age (male and female) and proportion of managers over 50 at different levels**

Group	Av. age (women)	Av. age (men)	Average all	% over 50
Top managers:	42	46	45	23%
Senior managers	41	44	43	17%
Middle managers	40	41	41	16%
First line managers	38	39	38	12%
Senior nurses	46	45	45	NA

Source: CCP Surveys.

Measuring progress to the top

In the CCP surveys, the time taken to reach a certain level were compared for different groups. The findings are given in Figures 8.5 and 8.6 below.

The average time for people who had spent the majority of their career within the NHS to reach top manager levels was 16.3 years. People with administrative qualifications or without children reached the level of top manager in the shortest time (16 years). People with financial qualifications have been at the top the longest. Surprisingly there was no difference in the time it took men and women to reach the top levels but men had been at the top for longer, reflecting perhaps the recent influx of a cohort young women top managers.

Yet the difference in the length of time for women and men to get to nursing officer posts identified by Davies and Rosser in 1986 was confirmed in the 1994 CCP survey of senior nurses. It was identified in goal 8 in the Opportunity 2000 initiative. Although the gap had narrowed by 1994, women had still taken on average 11.4 years compared to 6.9 years for men to reach nursing officer level.

In nursing there is a significant change in the representation of men in senior posts – 72 per cent of nurse executive directors were women of whom 46 per cent had taken career-breaks. This suggests that many of the women who are getting to the top now have family/domestic responsibilities. As part of the positive discrimination in training to help ensure that there is more equality of access to management positions, 270 nurses and 249 women and 21 men in professions allied to medicine (physiotherapy, occupational therapy, speech therapy, dietetics, etc.) are currently being sponsored to undertake management degrees as part of a £2.1 million scheme to get more professionals interested in management.

It is also interesting to compare changes in status for men and women managers during their careers. The proportion of upward and sideways moves made by the different groups were compared in Table 8.5 below.

TABLE 8.5 NHS managers' career moves

Group	% job moves sideways		% job moves upward	
	women	men	women	men
Top managers:	22%	14%	77%	85%
Senior, middle first-line managers	34%	30%	62%	66%
Senior nurse	23%	27%	67%	72%

Source: CCP Surveys.

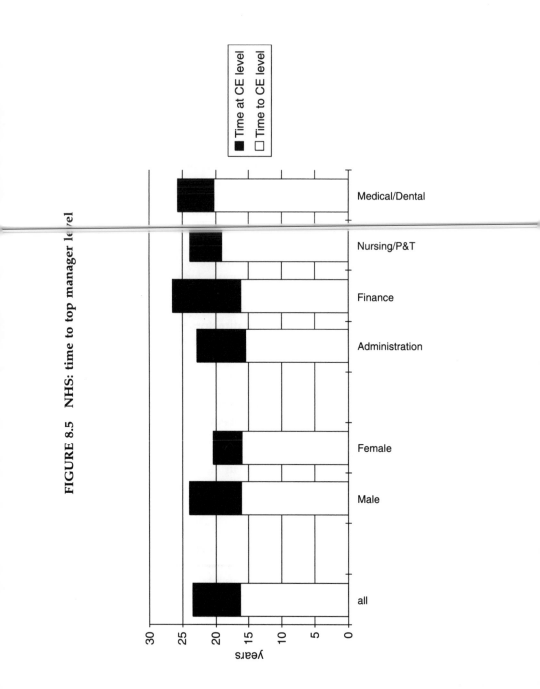

FIGURE 8.5 NHS: time to top manager level

233

FIGURE 8.6 NHS: time to nursing officer grade

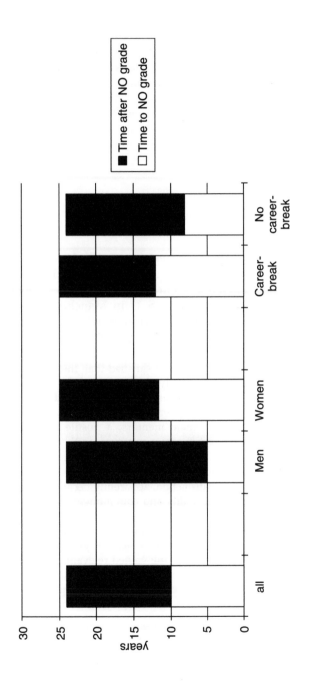

Men moved upwards more often and sideways less often than women. These findings are consistent with other research (Coe, 1992) which showed that women were more likely to have accumulated more qualifications and spent time in different functional areas than their male counterparts. This may also suggest that women managers in the NHS lack the confidence or opportunity to move straight up the career ladder or are expected to demonstrate broader previous experience than men. This female career pattern as been described as a lateral movement syndrome(Hardy, 1986). Hirsch and Jackson (1990) noted that men in the early years have achieved career progress while women have achieved career development.

Influences on career progress

The disparity between career progress for men and women is well described in a recent study of male and female ex-trainees (Carr, 1993) which focused on a sample who had attended a particular fast-track General Management Training Scheme programme (GMTS 1) in Manchester between the years 1983 and 1990. Following those individuals who had worked full-time as NHS managers since completing the programme, she found that:

> Most women earned less and were less satisfied than their male counterparts in the early years after GMTS1, seemingly due to a less forceful management style; sensitivity to the feelings of longer-serving but lower-paid colleagues; sex discrimination in promotion procedures; poor careers advice; lower availability; and lesser organisational influence of female mentors; a hostile managerial culture; poor feedback; and the low interest of senior managers in their development needs.

> In later years however, many of these women caught up with their male colleagues in terms both of salary and satisfaction, apparently because of increasing credibility in terms of both perceived flexibility and commitment.

> Many of these females ended up overtaking the men (again in both pay and satisfaction), perhaps owing to their first degrees generally being of higher class and more relevant subject; more having gained relevant qualifications since joining the NHS, and these being of a higher academic level; better managerial performance (suggested by higher Individual Performance Review bandings); having taken the time to build up basic experience; and employing a more effective management style.

The CCP surveys collected evidence about what managers felt had influenced their career moves. The reasons for managers leaving each of their jobs were analysed and categorised into:

- *career motivators:* promotion, increased financial rewards, career development, wider experience;
- *NHS circumstances:* Reorganisation, involuntary job loss, excess demands of the job, discrimination, networks, end of contract, to move in or out of the NHS;
- *personal circumstances:* family events or other personal changes

The proportions of each type of career move are summarised in Table 8.6. The reasons for top managers leaving their jobs were much more connected with their careers than for the other two groups, It would seem that NHS top managers systematically pursue an upward career path in spite of personal circumstances and recurring instability in NHS reorganisations. Men were more likely to describe their reasons for leaving a job as promotion than women who were more likely to attribute personal reasons. One in ten job moves made by women were for personal reasons compared to one in a hundred for men. These issues are explored in more detail below.

Career motivators (promotion, financial rewards, career development)

Although general management has opened doors to more people joining from outside, it is still difficult to move into a job in the NHS without previous healthcare experience, although evidence from the the CCP study of managers in 15 representative organisations suggests that there is some movement between the NHS and the independent sector. That the NHS does not value non-NHS experience very highly was demonstrated in the analysis of barriers to career progress in the CCP studies: men and women ranked prejudice about previous work experience as one of the most significant barriers to progress than they had encountered. As one male manager commented 'The NHS and particularly this organisation still too often behaves like an 'old-boys' network.' There is a definite 'in crowd' and it appears easier to 'get on' if you are in it.'

TABLE 8.6 **Reasons for NHS managers' career moves**

Group	Career motivators	NHS circumstances	Personal circumstances
Top managers:	84%	71%	4%
Senior, middle and first line managers	71%	12%	18%
Senior nurses	70%	11%	19%

Source: CCP Surveys.

There is still a long way to go to achieve Opportunity 2000 Goal 7, to ensure that following a career-break for maternity leave all women, including those returning to nursing part-time posts or as a job-share, return at a grade commensurate with their leaving grade and work of a similar status. As will be seen in Table 8.7 a significant proportion of NHS managers had taken career-breaks, but a large number of people had returned to a job of lower status after the break (though the break was not necessarily after 1991).

Some women returned to work part-time after a career-break, using the opportunity to consider and broaden their experiences, but this work was usually of a lower status with fewer promotion prospects than the full-time post they had held previously. This reinforced the loss of skills and confidence which career-breaks for child-rearing tend to result in. Dixon and Shaw (1986) observed that it was not the career break itself which affected the different achievements of women and men but that career breaks for child-rearing were assumed to reflect a lack of commitment to a career.

The rate of job change of NHS managers was shown to be high: on average managers moved jobs about every three years with a steady increase in rate of job change in the last ten years. Peaks in job moves coincided with NHS reorganisations in 1974, 1982, 1986 and 1991. Since 1992, 31 per cent of top managers and 38 per cent of senior nurses have changed their jobs – which is probably a consequence of the creation of NHS Trusts and changes in commissioning organisations and regions.

Top women managers in *Celebration of Success* believed it was important to move jobs partly to gain experience of different sectors of the NHS and partly the NHS culture encourages regular job moves among senior managers. The NHS is not unusual in this respect, as evidence from a national study of career development of British managers (Alban-Metcalfe and Nicholson, 1984) found that 'high fliers 'stayed in post only about 18 months. Anecdotal evidence from the *Celebration of Success* confirmed previous research findings, that women of equal status were expected to work harder than their male

TABLE 8.7   **Career-breaks by NHS men and women**

Group	% with career break (women)	% with career breaks (men)	% with lower status after break	% of breaks for child care and raising
Top managers:	53%	14%	11%	35%
Senior, middle and first line managers	57%	25%	22%	46%
Senior nurses	59%	16%	19%	56%

Source: CCP Surveys.

colleagues to be considered of equal competance. This is a double jeopardy – a woman has to work harder because she is considered less competent. Women moving between NHS regions found that their reputations were not as transferable as men's and often took a sideways or unconventional step to get into another region.

Financial rewards were not considered very important influences on career choices by top NHS managers. When asked about the importance of a number of factors on their career choices, both men and women rated financial rewards tenth out of a list of eighteen. Since the process of determining financial rewards is a decision-making process in which the balance between men and women is more transparent than usual it is a useful indicator of the current position.

There has been growth in the incidence of performance-related pay in the last decade. Several studies have identified negative outcomes of this shift for women. In 1991 a report from the Equal Opportunities Commission stated that:

> In the public sector, merit pay [performance-related pay] may be used primarily as a justification for paying large increases to [predominantly male] senior managers to bring their pay in line with their private sector counterparts . . . . The most objective and formal systems of merit pay and appraisal are likely to be applied to jobs performed by men than to those carried out by women. Performance of women's occupations often focus on the volume/quantity of work performed, attitudinal and or behavioural characteristics and casual judgements by line managers.

Up to 1991 pay and terms and conditions of service rates were determined centrally by the functionally defined Whitley Councils, some advised by independent pay review bodies being responsible for medical, nursing and Professions Allied to Medicine (PAMs). In 1991 a national survey of NHS managers' experiences of performance-related pay (Alimo-Metcalfe, 1994) found significant differences in the pay bandings reported by female and male general managers, with twice the proportion of male general managers reporting having received the highest rating, compared with the women general managers. The European Court of Justice ruled in the Danfoss case that 'it is inconceivable that work carried out by women workers would be generally of a lower quality than that carried out by men'.

Since April 1991 NHS Trusts have been able to opt out of national pay bargaining against the advice of the Equal Opportunities Commission who strongly advised against locally determined pay as it would probably be detrimental to women for a variety of reasons including: the lack of concern among local human resources officers for equality issues in the process of pay bargaining, less comparative information being available to employees and trade unions, and payment of larger pay rises to predominantly higher-paid occupational groups. Local benefit packages are being developed by Trusts aimed at reducing recruitment and retention difficulties, but, although most Trusts have so far continued to adhere to national pay rates, local pay determination is becoming increasingly important. The Institute of Health Service Managers having carried out a survey of managers' pay, may take on more of the trade union role in pay negotiations on behalf of its members, who represent the majority of NHS managers.

In 1993–94 the CCP surveys found no statistically significant difference between the pay levels of women and men managers. However, women managers reported receiving equal or slightly lower average salary bands in each UK country, each English region, and in every organisational type and level and for people with equivalent academic status. Only nurse executive directors of NHS Trusts who were women were paid more than their male counterparts, but this was linked to their older age.

Performance appraisal, if it is linked to personal development, should provide an opportunity for discussing openly achievements in the job, frustrations and barriers to improving performance. Studies in the UK (Corby, 1982) and US (P.J. Thomas, 1987) investigating gender differences in the appraisal interview have found that women are less likely to receive high quality feedback and are not valued in the same way and with the same conviction as are men.

In the national survey of NHS managers (Alimo-Metcalfe, 1994) investigated possible gender differences in the appraisal processes. Some significant differences emerged: that women found it more difficult to talk freely about what they wanted to discuss, to discuss their relationship with their appraiser, to give feedback to their appraiser and to identify their strengths. Women also felt more strongly than men that the appraisal process was linked to their relationship with their manager. This suggests that women are disempowered in the appraisal discussion and miss being able to make full use of the situation to discuss how their strengths could be maximised in the job and in their future career. Possible reasons why the gender differences in appraisal processes are found may be that women's successful or unsuccessful performance may be judged differently from that of men's. Studies have revealed that success in men is more likely to be attributed to ability and competence, whereas women's success is more likely to be attributed to effort or luck. Failure is, however, attributed to external causes in the case of men, such as bad luck, whereas for women, the more likely cause is presumed to be lack of ability (Wallston *et al.*, 1981).

In 1993, female top NHS managers identified the importance of gaining access to development programmes to support continuous self improvement, not least because it enabled them to compare their ability to that of men on the programmes and to be seen as 'capable of improvement' (Proctor and Jackson, 1992). Since it has been extensively and regularly established that think manager means think male', it is not surprising that female managers believe that their performance is being compared to that of the male dominant group.

NHS circumstances and managers' progress

Evidence from the CCP surveys showed that NHS management culture required very long working hours, considerable geographical mobility with few opportunities for flexible working – which generally suits men better than women. This poor working environment has further deteriorated in the turmoil of constant reorganisation, and managers have left the NHS voluntarily, involuntarily with associated perceived discrimination. It is arguable that the NHS has recently placed excess demands on its workforce.

The CCP surveys revealed that all NHS managers work extremely long hours compared to other managers in the UK. The average hours worked reported by the different groups of NHS managers are shown in Table 8.8, below alongside the hours spent on domestic duties. There was no variation in working hours between women and men, whatever their personal circumstances, though women spent considerably more time on domestic commitments than men.

CCP surveys also confirmed that NHS managers moved house frequently in their careers indicating a high level of geographical mobility. The findings from the surveys are given in Table 8.9.

TABLE 8.8   **Working hours and domestic commitments in the NHS**

Group	Av. work time per week	Domestic time per week (women)	Domestic time per week (men)
Top managers:	56 hrs	19 hrs	16 hrs
Senior, middle & first line managers	43 hrs	31 hrs	19 hrs
Senior nurses	52 hrs	26 hrs	20 hrs

Note: An Institute of Manpower Studies survey of non-manual working time in the UK in 1993 showed that managers worked an average of 35 hours per week.
Source: CCP Surveys.

TABLE 8.9   **NHS: house moves because of own and partner's jobs**

Group	Moved house because of own job (men)	Moved house because of own job (women)
Top managers:	87%	59%
Senior, middle & first line managers	96%	55%
Senior nurses	83%	47%

Source: CCP Surveys.

Even for senior jobs, men's job moves were more likely to determine the major upheaval of moving house than women's. The traditional picture of women following their partner's career location is still applicable. These findings confirm that the working culture in the NHS makes it more difficult for a women with family commitments to compete on equal terms with men because of the particular need for geographical mobility in the NHS.

There are also unequal opportunities for training. Allen found in 1986 that, not only was part-time training in medicine very difficult to find, it was only offered in limited specialities (e.g. community health and geriatrics) and in limited roles (e.g. clinical assistant). As a result she found that of the 40 per cent of women in her sample who were employed in part-time jobs, many of them regarded them as basically dead-end since they offered no training or career development opportunities.

In 1991 the Equal Opportunities Commission identified the lack of flexible working opportunities in the NHS :

Differences in promotion opportunities for women and men in the Health Service are apparent from research studies and surveys. There is an acute lack of part-time work or other flexible working arrangements in senior positions to enable women to combine career and family responsibilities.

In the NHS workforce overall 37 per cent of the women worked part-time particularly in nursing (41 per cent), ancillary posts (76 per cent) and administrative and clerical posts (42 per cent) usually at lower levels. At senior managerial levels flexible working opportunities are even rarer. Table 8.10 shows the proportion of managers in different groups who had ever worked part-time as part of their career.

The lack of flexible working opportunities affects nurses most, as almost half of the NHS nurses had either dependent adults or children at home, yet only 12 per cent reported that childcare support was available in their place of work. Nurses with family commitments (most of whom are women) seem to be disadvantaged in terms of career progression and entry into management,

TABLE 8.10   **Flexible working practice in the NHS**

Group	% part-time working (women)	% part-time working (men)
Top managers:	19%	1%
Senior, middle & first line managers	33%	5%
Senior nurses	39%	6%

Source: CCP Surveys.

although 46 per cent of nursing executive directors had taken career-breaks. A large proportion of female nurses work part-time, and evidence in 1993 indicates that the proportion continues to increase but there is difficulty in varying the work commitment from part-time to full-time, or to vary hours to meet changing personal circumstances.

For those who opt for a better balance between work and home, the outcome is often lack of career progression. General practice is a popular career choice for women in medicine as it offers an opportunity for part-time employment. Whilst almost half of all general practitioners (GPs) are female, 80 per cent of women GPs work full-time (General Medical Services Committee, 1992). Allen's (1988) study showed that women doctors were more successful in obtaining career posts in general practice as GP principals than as consultants in hospital medicine. She also found that women in career posts in general practice were much more likely to be working, or have worked, part-time than those in hospital medicine. Analysis of GPs, by grade by sex, showed that 92 per cent of the men in general practice were full-time principals, compared with 40 per cent of the women. Only 2 per cent of the men were part-time principals, compared with 19 per cent of the women. Most of those on the Doctor Retainer Scheme (a non-training scheme run by Regional Health Authorities for doctors under 55 years of age who currently do not work more than one day per week) are women. However, the career ladder is very short as in no other profession can one expect to reach one's peak so young – with only the prospect of becoming senior partner to anticipate. The main conclusion from Allen's study was: 'It is clear that the overwhelming requirement for women doctors is to alter the career structure in ways that allow interruptions and periods of part-time working without an inevitable cost to the final career.'

The NHS has to learn how to provide better flexible working opportunities so that it makes more use of people who want to work part-time and employs their skills to the full.

Personal circumstances and managers' progress

A person's upbringing may play a part in determining career choices. From the biographical details of top women managers in *Celebration of Success* interesting patterns about their background emerged. Most of them had had mothers who had been in paid employment and whom they regarded as powerful. The majority attended single sex schools (grammar or direct grant) having passed the 11-plus or gained a scholarship. They tended to be team-players and to join clubs and societies, sing in choirs, enjoy sports and some became the head girl. These extra-curricular activities provided them with what they later recognised as public speaking and leadership skills. Most went to universities, some to Oxbridge, some to polytechnics. Career guidance in higher education was poor and most joined the NHS by chance, though some used information provided by friends. Few had fathers who worked for the NHS but more had mothers who had.

The results of CCP surveys about level of academic qualification are given in Table 8.11 and are consistent with previous research (Dixon and Shaw, 1986, Alban-Metcalfe, 1984). All NHS managers were relatively well qualified but top women and middle managers had higher academic qualifications than men. Unusually, more male senior managers had a bachelors degree or higher than women: this distortion was due to the number of clinical directors included in this group. Nurses had relatively few degrees as they tend to obtain professional rather than academic qualifications. It is unexpected that male first line managers were better qualified than their female counterparts and there is no obvious explanation.

Career paths are often shaped by family circumstances and domestic commitments. A number of top managers married very early, before obtaining professional or degree qualifications, some to gain independence from home. Few of these marriages survived but early marriage and having children at a young age allowed some to take up the reins of their careers earlier than others. For those who succeeded in combining a family with achieving top manager's status, domestic responsibility took first place for them during early years of child-rearing. For some, in later years caring for an elderly relative has played an important role. Table 8.12 shows the proportions of managers by gender who were married and without children.

Women managers were more often childless and single than their male counterparts. Also there are many more male top managers with children than women. These findings confirm that men can usually have a career as well as a family whereas women still appear to choose between the two.

In summary, evidence from the CCP surveys and elsewhere showed that career motivators were still the most important factor in deciding career

TABLE 8.11   **Proportion of NHS managers with bachelors' degree or higher, by gender**

Group	% with bachelors or higher (women)	% with bachelors or higher (men)
Top managers:	73%	67%
Senior managers	55%	80%
Middle managers	57%	50%
First line managers	41%	57%
Senior nurses	59%	77%

Source: CCP Surveys.

TABLE 8.12 **Proportion of married NHS managers and those without children, by gender**

Group	% married (women)	% married (men)	% without children (women)	% without children (men)
Top managers:	66%	84%	50%	7%
Senior managers	57%	77%	43%	18%
Middle managers	57%	82%	47%	29%
First line managers	59%	77%	56%	34%
Senior nurses	59%	77%	49%	12%

Source: CCP Surveys.

choices. It seems that to compete effectively in the male working culture in the NHS, women managers' behaviour still has to closely match their male counterparts in many respects including:

- moving jobs frequently (every 3 years);
- working extremely hard and for long hours;
- having relatively few family commitments;
- gaining a reputation for achievement;
- establishing competence;
- recognising the need for self-improvement.

The comment from the Equal Opportunities Commission (1991) still holds true:

> It could be assumed that the NHS would offer conditions of employment commensurate with its dependence on female talent for delivery of care to patients. Such an assumption would unfortunately prove incorrect, as shown by comparison of their financial rewards, job and career prospects and working lifestyles with those of men working in the NHS. . . The NHS expects the majority of its workforce to conform to the working patterns of the minority.

The path to success for women

Although there has been a substantial improvement in the number of women in senior managerial NHS posts in recent years, the position of women overall, people from ethnic minorities and disabled people has changed little. The picture described in 1991 by the Equal Opportunities Commission has been confirmed by the findings of the CCP surveys:

- Women were under-represented in senior positions.
- Inflexible working patterns prevented many qualified and experienced women from returning to the NHS after having children.
- Part-time work was only available rarely and usually at the expense of down-grading.
- Part-time work was characterised by inferior terms and conditions of employment.
- Women are still paid less in every sector of the NHS management.
- Managers from black and ethnic minority groups or who are disabled are still virtually invisible in NHS management.

However, women in the NHS are becoming much more visible in management as the proportion of women working at senior levels increases. This change is being catalysed by the Opportunity 2000 initiatives including those promoted by the NHS Womens Unit which are enabling women to recognise their value and have the self-confidence to compete effectively with men. The evidence given above shows that these initiatives are beginning to have a significant effect.

General management and turmoil resulting from repeated reorganisations has meant that the career paths to the top have become less distinct. In some places narrow ladders have been replaced by climbing frames and it is now possible to change direction without having to go back to the bottom and start up a different ladder. The skill is identifying the next place that is best/safe to climb on and how the rules differ for women and men, and then challenge this state of affairs.

The balance between organisational requirements and personal requirements has, for years, been in favour of the organisation. Fewer people in the labour force and changes within the NHS are encouraging employers to take more account of their employees' personal requirements if they are to recruit and retain the skills they need. Women are poised to benefit from the fluidity of the NHS organisational structures and the current momentum to achieve more equality.

Acknowledgements

The CCP project would not have been possible without the generous support and funding from the NHS Women's Unit. I would like to thank Beverly Alimo-Metcalfe, my co-workers on the CCP project Sephie Disken, Jane Ball (researchers) and Maureen Dixon (Project Director, IHSM Consultants) for their contributions.

CHAPTER 9

On the move: women in the Toronto public transport sector

Fiona Colgan, Susan Johnstone and Steve Shaw[1]

Introduction

Throughout the world, women are in the clear majority as users of public transport. Far fewer women than men have regular use of a private car and they are therefore highly dependent on local bus and rail services (Hamilton and Jenkins, 1993). The quality of public transport has considerable significance for the quality of women's lives (Greater London Council Women's Committee, 1986; Rutherford and Wekerle, 1987; Corrigan, 1994). However, research has shown that the transport sector, has not sufficiently addressed the 'relevance of women, women's needs or women's issues to the plans and decisions which they make' (Hamilton and Jenkins, 1989). Many of the jobs with which the industry is identified, such as driving, planning and design, technical and maintenance positions are predominantly held by men. (Holland, 1988; EOR, 1992; Tradeswoman, 1993)

Although the women's movement has been slow to see transport as a feminist issue and 'one which has a vital role to play in the struggle for equality' (Hamilton and Jenkins, 1989), women's access to transport services and employment opportunities became one element in the feminist agenda during the 1980s. Women organised to support political parties with a commitment to equal opportunities, and sought to articulate women's concerns as consumers and employees through trade unions, user groups and political structures to those with the 'political will' and resources to implement policy which addresses the needs of women as well as men (Coote and Campbell,

1987; Barry, 1991; Adamson, Briskin and McPhail, 1988; Wine and Ristock, 1991; Backhouse and Flaherty, 1992)

In London, in May 1982, the newly elected Labour administration of the Greater London Council (GLC), under pressure from women's groups, set up a Women's Committee with the specific remit of promoting policies for the benefit of London women. One initiative launched by the Women's Committee was a survey of women's transport needs carried out between 1984 and 1986. The survey was 'a novel departure in the field of transport planning in Britain' (Focas, 1989). It found that London's public transport system was not geared to meet women's travel needs and that women often felt unsafe while using it (GLC Women's Committee, 1986). The GLC sought also to address equal opportunities in employment within London Transport (LT). Between 1982 and 1985, LT was under the control of the GLC. GLC-appointed board members placed pressure on LT to establish an equal opportunities policy and review employment practices. The outcome was the introduction of an equal opportunities policy and the creation of an Equal Opportunities Unit (Jewson, Mason, Waters and Harvey, 1990).

Unfortunately, a clash of ideologies between the Conservative UK Government and the GLC resulted in the loss of a unique opportunity to develop equal opportunities in employment and service delivery within London's public transport system. In 1984 the UK Government passed the London Regional Transport Act with the result that control of LT was transferred from the GLC to the Secretary of State for Transport. Under the terms of the Act, LT priorities shifted: the company was required to restructure and achieve the financial targets set by the Secretary of State. The Government's programme for transport based on free market principles set out to introduce decentralisation leading to deregulation and privatisation in the public transport sector (Labour Research, 1995).

This free market philosophy was also rigorously applied to employment rights. Arguing the need to free business from restrictive legislation and 'roll back the state' the British Government have progressively reduced employment rights for workers since 1979 (Ferner and Hyman, 1992). This means that UK workers have had to rely on European Directives and European Court judgments in order to maintain or extend many employment rights including those which concern equal opportunities (Labour Research Department, 1992; EOR, 1993).

Equal opportunity initiatives in public transport employment and service delivery similar to those developed by the GLC in London also developed in Toronto, Canada, during the 1980s. These developments provide support for the view that women's movements constitute a social movement accompanied by shifts in consciousness, demands for change and the international diffusion of ideas (Dahlerup, 1986; Barry, Honour, MacGregor and Palnitkar, 1994). Significantly, these initiatives had not been curtailed by the state in Ontario until 1995 (see postcript). Women's activism in community groups, trade unions and political parties in combination with the 'political will' of those elected at city and provincial level[2] had resulted in the development of a pro-active human rights and equal opportunities programme which provided a framework for employers including transport operators. Women's organisa-tions had both lobbied for and used the developing framework to try to ensure that women's travel and employment needs were met by public transport organisations.

This chapter will explore the following topics:[3]

- The role women have played as change agents in the development, formulation and implementation of human rights and equal opportunities legislation, programmes and practices in the Canadian Province of Ontario between 1980 and 1995.
- How the spirit and intent of statutes and regulations concerned with equal opportunities and human rights in employment and service delivery have been translated into action within two transport companies: the Toronto Transit Commission (TTC) and Government of Ontario Transit (GO Transit).
- The impact of the TTC and GO Transit's equal opportunities policies and practices on womens' access to employment opportunities and appropriate forms of service provision.

Creating a legislative framework for equal opportunities in Ontario

The legal framework within which anti-discrimination legislation developed in Canada is quite different from that of the UK. The UK system has been criticised as too complex and as creating a disincentive for women and the ethnic minorities to pursue claims (Leonard, 1987a, 1987b; Gregory, 1989). The Canadian approach is seen as a more positive way of dealing with the profound discrimination experienced by women and other disadvantaged groups in work and society generally (Jain, 1989; Skipton, 1991; Fudge and McDermott, 1991; McColgan 1994a; 1994b). There are a number of reasons which may explain why the law in Canada has developed in this way.

First, Canada had developed a human rights ethos. The Bill of Rights of 1960 recognised the need for equality. This was enshrined in the constitution in 1982[4] when the Canadian Charter for Fundamental Rights and Freedoms was given constitutional status.

Secondly, there is a strong network of campaign and lobbying groups of 'equity seekers' who have successfully made their voice heard and influenced political agendas. Pressure from disadvantaged groups (i.e. women, aborigi-nal people, 'visible minorities' and persons with disabilities) culminated in a

Canadian Royal Commission on Employment Equity in 1984 led by Judge Rosalie Abella which concluded that 'Equity in employment will not happen unless we make it happen' (Abella, 1984). Women have been active in organising for legislation at the national level through the National Action Committee on the Status of Women (NAC), and in Ontario through organisations such as the Ontario Equal Pay Coalition. Women who were active in the Equal Pay Coalition now hold senior posts in the Ontario Ministry of Labour and other government agencies.[5]

Thirdly, there was the political will to achieve equality. Political and public pressure by equity-seeking groups led to pro-active legislation at federal level in 1985, with all political parties pledging their commitment to employment equity. (Backhouse and Flaherty, 1992; Wine and Ristock, 1991). This set a precedent across Canada, and in Ontario in 1985 pay equity was one of the key issues of the accord on legislation signed by the minority Liberal Government

and the opposition New Democratic Party (NDP). Equity was firmly on the agenda of both parties. The NDP reconfirmed their commitment to employment equity when they came to power, with the new Premier stating 'We cannot afford to lose the skills and abilities of Ontario's population because of discrimination. My government is fully committed to both employment equity and pay equity.'[6]

The law in Canada operates at two levels – federal and provincial. To give effect to the Charter on Fundamental Rights and Freedoms, equality laws have been passed at federal and provincial level. However, Ontario has become widely known for its pro-active approach to equality laws (see postscript).

The law in Ontario

There are a number of statutes dealing with aspects of equality – the Human Rights Code 1981, the Pay Equity Act 1987 and the Employment Equity Act 1993.

Human rights legislation

The Ontario Human Rights Code prohibits discrimination on a wide range of grounds[7] and covers discrimination in employment and the provision of services.[8] However, it is largely complaints-driven, similar to the UK law, and this has led to dissatisfaction with the code as a means of redress, particularly from women's groups.[9] The Ontario Human Rights Commission recognised that it was criticised for being 'too slow, too inefficient and too out of touch with the needs of its clients' (Ontario Human Rights Commission, 1992).

In an attempt to deal with the problems, the Commission created a Systemic Investigation Unit in 1989. It was recognised that the individual complaint route was necessary but that those complaints were not eliminating discrimination. In one chief commissioner's view 'individual complaints usually do not target the worst cases of discrimination, because complaints about the worst places do not surface' (Ontario Human Rights Commission, 1992).

The aim of the unit was to enable the commission to initiate its own complaints where there appeared to be systemic discrimination, defined as 'deep-rooted, built-in patterns or 'systems' of discrimination' (Ontario Human Rights Commission, 1992). However, the vast majority of the Commission's work still entailed dealing with individual complaints.

Despite problems with the code, its mere existence and the threat of a case being brought under the code has been enough to encourage organisations such as the TTC and GO Transit to take the issue seriously. Both organisations have been very much aware of the code's requirements in relation to employment and service provision (for example, see the extract below from TTC's Annual Report).

The Pay Equity Act 1987

It is in the area of pay equity that Ontario first took a pro-active approach. The Pay Equity Act puts the onus on employers to 'redress systemic gender discrimination in compensation for work performed by employees in female job classes'.[10] It also established a Pay Equity Commission.

The Act requires employers to carry out a job evaluation, using a gender-neutral scheme, and to draw up a pay equity plan showing pay adjustments for women.[11] There is also a Pay Equity Tribunal, which can make orders to force employers to implement the law. Employers who fail to comply can be fined up to $50 000.[12]

The Employment Equity Act 1993

The employment equity legislation continued with the pro-active approach. It put the onus on employers to take positive steps to eliminate discrimination at the workplace. Employers[13] are required to carry out a workforce survey, institute an employment systems review to identify barriers to equity and to implement an employment equity plan to achieve equitable representation of designated groups[14] at all levels at the workplace. Each plan has to include qualitative measures and numerical goals set by the employer, who then has to make reasonable progress towards the achievement of their goals. The Employment Equity Commission oversees the implementation of the law and, again, there is a special tribunal to enforce compliance.[15]

Women campaigning for pro-active legislation

The impetus for the Pay Equity Act came from the Equal Pay Coalition – a labour-feminist alliance (Todres, 1990). They ensured that pay equity became part of every political party's agenda, and raised awareness amongst women generally. There had been the right to equal pay for equal work since 1951 (Female Employees Remuneration Act, 1951). What the Coalition wanted was an act which provided for equal pay for work of equal value and which required employers to implement pay equity.

The Equal Pay Coalition was established in the mid-1970s. It consisted of 23 different organisations including trade unions, community groups, ethnic minority, women's groups, as well as business and professional women. It was a 'grassroots, hands on lobbying organisation' and through 'a lot of persistence'[16] it brought pay equity to the statute books.

How did the women in this organisation achieve so much? A leading light, and founder member, was Mary Cornish, author of the Cornish Report (Ontario Human Rights Code Review Task Force, 1992). The women organised 'anything we could think of at the time to emphasise what women earned as a percentage of men . . . [for example] during elections the Coalition would do report cards on the various party's voting patterns'.[17] They gained the support of the NDP, (Canada's social democratic political party) which started to introduce opposition members' bills which were never passed but which opened up the issue for public discussion. Eventually all three parties (Conservative, Liberal and NDP) gave commitment in principle to pay equity. However, it was not until the election of a minority government in 1985 that there any prospect that commitment would be translated into reality.

The NDP's conditions for support for the minority Liberal Government (in a document known as the Accord), included mandatory pay equity within two years. Still the Coalition had a hard battle. They fought hard to prevent pay equity from dropping off the agenda in the negotiations over the Accord. However, the Liberals needed support from the NDP, and the NDP wanted to ensure continuing support from trade unions and community groups and from business and professionals. All those groups were represented in the Coalition. By their persistence, the women gained influence over Government policy.

However, it did not end there. Women in Ontario wanted legislation which was pro-active, which placed the onus for achieving pay equity on employers. The Liberals decided to hold public hearings across the province. So they appointed a panel of three business people to hear the views of the people. The Coalition objected, as the panel was not representative of the people affected. Again, an enormous organising effort was needed. The Ontario Federation of Labour (a federation of affiliated trade unions in Ontario, similar to the British TUC) worked with the Coalition to ensure that women's views were made known, and reported. They appointed their own panellist. Janis Sarra, now Vice-Chair of the Pay Equity Tribunal, recalled what happened:

> the Coalition announced that I was the alternative panelist. So I trailed around. They [the official panel] would show up in a city, and I would show up too. I'd pull up my chair beside them and they'd get the police and sort of knock me to the back of the room.

It was also organised so that there were supporters in the audience who would speak to 'members of the panel, and the peoples' member of the panel'.

Following the hearings, the Coalition published their own report before the official panel did. It set out the framework for the legislation they wanted. And, according to Janis Sarra 'probably the Coalition got 75 per cent of what it wanted, which is extraordinary'. How did they manage it? Janis Sarra sums it up:

> There was a lot of energy by an enormous number of people, women in particular. It was quite inspiring. I never met so many amazing people in all my life across the province. It was very much a collective effort . . . I think it's a classic example, and certainly in Ontario a very rare one, of just ordinary people pushing hard for something and being very organised.

The role of the trade unions was important. In the 1960s and 1970s women had developed strong women's committees within the unions. Carrol Anne Sceviour, Human Rights Director at the Ontario Federation of Labour, and another founder member of the Coalition, believes that the Women's Committee is one of the most powerful committees within the federation.[18]

Women involved in the Coalition are now in influential positions in the NDP Government and government agencies. Mary Cornish, for example, is a prominent labour lawyer and recently chaired a Government Commission on human rights. But the campaigning has not stopped. A Coalition for Employment Equity has been established and has been influential in the shaping of the Employment Equity Act. However, achieving change has become more difficult, not due to lack of commitment but to economic conditions linked to the recession affecting the Canadian economy.

For example, the Ontario government introduced amendments to the Pay Equity Act in 1993. For the Coalition, the fight for the amendments was tougher. It took six years to get the amendments and even then they were much weaker than hoped. The reason given by the NDP Government was the ailing economy. In introducing the amendments, the Labour Minister stated: 'Our resolve has not weakened, but the economy has. The long struggle to achieve pay equity will still be won but will take a few extra years to complete'.[19]

Impact of Ontario's equal opportunities legislation

Has the legislative framework led to, or in any way contributed to, an improvement in the position of women in organisations in Canada? In particular, has it helped improve the position of women in a male-dominated industry such as transport?

The pro-active approach has clearly been a positive step forward. Janice Killoran, solicitor for the Pay Equity Commission, believes the legislation is significant: 'the more important function of the legislation I think is as a tool to make people look at women's work differently, to attach value to what women do and to value it in ways that it has never been valued before'.[20]

Legislation can be used to persuade employers that some action must be taken, as this chapter will illustrate with respect to the TTC and GO Transit. The experience of Janice Killoran is that many large organisations are resigned to the legislation. 'They say, we might not like it but we don't have any choice – it's the law'.

Some employers believe that it will not be possible to achieve any change during a recession and have argued vehemently against the Employment Equity Act which they see as more 'red-tape'. Other employers see it as an opportunity to put systems in place to ensure a more balanced workforce when the economy improves. Much depends on the ethos of the organisation and these different views are reflected within the TTC and GO Transit.

Canadian public transport sector

In the UK, the organisations running local bus and underground services now operate as free-standing business units. The culture required is entrepreneurial, and survival necessitates single-minded attention to revenue and costs. Equal opportunity policies and practices, unless required by the law, must be demonstrably 'good for business.' Social costs and benefits for women (or other disadvantaged groups), whether as employees or as passengers, are no longer the operator's concern. The state does not seek to intervene in these transport businesses.

In Canada, public transport organisations are still required to operate as public services and to provide a wide range of social, economic and environmental benefits for the local population. Canadian cities such as Toronto, Ottawa, Montreal and Vancouver have developed a strong sense of civic pride in their public transport systems. Most undertakings are owned by municipalities and have a high profile in the agenda of local politics. They also have monopoly status in the geographical areas they serve.

Toronto Transit Commission

The Metropolitan Toronto Council (Metro) owns the TTC and has jurisdiction over public transport. Metro is a regional tier of local government encompassing the City of Toronto and twelve smaller municipalities.[21] The TTC's governing body is the Commission, a special purpose agency comprising five Metro councillors. In accordance with Canada's emphasis on open government, the TTC's meetings are held in public, and representations are quite frequently received from organisations representing women, disabled people, ethnic minorities and other campaigning groups.

The TTC's *Strategy for the 1990s* (1989) illustrates the key role it plays within Toronto's long-range development plan the *Livable Metropolis* (Metropolitan Toronto Planning Department, 1992). The TTC's broader goals include, providing mobility to the disadvantaged, preserving the environment, reducing dependence on cars and redistributing income (TTC, 1989a). Not surprisingly the TTC has a high public profile within Toronto, and developments are widely reported in the local news media.

The TTC operates the city's subway, bus and streetcars system. It employs over 10 500 employees, making it one of the city's major employers. However, only 12 per cent of the TTC's employees are women (see Table 9.1), even though the majority of the TTC's customers are women. In 1991, 59 per cent of the TTC's bus passengers and 57 per cent of the subway passengers were women (Joint Program in Transportation, 1986: 1991).

TABLE 9.1   Gender composition of the workforce: TTC and GO Transit relative to British public transport operators, 1992

	Total	*Men(%)*	*Women(%)*
Canada			
Total Workforce*	14 474 945	55	45
Transport*	550 580	81	19
TTC	10 181	88	12
GO Transit	1 125	79	21
Britain			
Total Workforce*	27 903 000	57	43
Transport*	1 777 100	79	21
LU Ltd	20 000	91	9
LB Ltd	18 171	93	7

Note: LU – London Underground Ltd.
        LB – London Buses Ltd.

Source: Company Employment Equity Reports 1992. Data marked * obtained from the Canadian and British Census, 1991.

GO Transit

GO Transit is a much smaller-scale organisation than the TTC, more recently established, and with the more specialised function of carrying longer-distance commuters into and out of Central Toronto. It was set up as a result of the 1965 *Metropolitan Toronto and Region Transportation Study*, which recommended public subsidy for a commuter rail service to 'reduce the need for costly construction or expansion of expressways' (GO Transit, 1992). Beginning as an experimental project in 1967, it was established as a separate Crown agency of the Province of Ontario in 1974 (GO Transit, 1992).

GO Transit's governing body is a board which reports to the cabinet through the Minister of Transportation. The board comprises a provincially-appointed chair, and representatives of Metropolitan Toronto and the five other regions served (GO Transit, 1992). GO Transit operates a network of seven rail and seven bus corridors, connecting with local transport in the suburbs, and with the TTC in the metropolitan area.

Overall it is a rather lean organisation, employing 1,125 employees of whom 21 per cent were women in 1992. The relatively high percentage of female staff at GO Transit is explained by the fact that many of the 'male' jobs are contracted out to Canadian National (CN) and Canadian Pacific (CP) Rail. Although GO Transit owns the trains and employs conductors on them, the track, rolling stock maintenance and train crew are contracted out to CN Rail and CP Rail (GO Transit, 1992). The bus services were originally contracted out, but GO Transit now employ the drivers and has acquired their own buses and maintain them in-house.

Since 1990 both the TTC and GO Transit have experienced revenue losses associated with rising provincial unemployment and a falling ridership. This has resulted in the shelving of some investment plans plus an employment freeze and a small number of lay-offs at each company during 1992–93. The TTC and GO Transit are mindful of the importance of retaining public support in a time of increased competition for provincial funding. Demographic changes and reduced urban densities are also increasing the number of, and dependence on, cars (GO Transit Business Plan, 1993a) which means that both companies are also aware that 'from a survival angle', they have to keep their 'customers, many of whom are women, happy and tap into other markets'.[22]

Structure and development of equal opportunities: TTC and GO Transit

The successful implementation of any substantial change programme, such as an equal opportunities programme, within an organisation is likely to depend on a number of elements (Hammond, 1992). These may include: powerful external influences such as legislation and political and social campaigns; internal factors such as strong leadership, resources to carry the project forward, the commitment of senior management, communication and acceptance of the need to change, focusing on the total culture not just organisational systems and making change the responsibility of all employees not just those in human resources (Cockburn, 1991; Hammond, 1992; D.C. Wilson, 1992; Ross and Schneider, 1992). A number of these factors help to explain the relative progress which has been made with regard to equal opportunities at the TTC and GO Transit.

Ownership, accountability and funding

The TTC's senior managers are accountable to local government via the Commission. GO Transit reports to the provincial government via the Board. Both organisations receive funding in the form of capital grants and revenue support from the public sector. Their policies and programmes require approval by elected politicians. Thus between 1980 and 1995 both have been encouraged to demonstrate good practice, as providers of a public service, to which designated groups should have equal access.

In 1980 the TTC introduced an equal opportunities programme which was focused mainly on women and operated from within the personnel department. This was in line with the affirmative action programme being practised at both municipal and provincial levels. Although there was a commitment to the principles of equal opportunities within the TTC, few resources were dedicated to the programme.[23] The development of an equal opportunities policy in 1991 at GO Transit seems to have followed a similar route as a result of strong pressure being placed on them by the NDP Government:

> Even though we are at arms length from the Ministry [of Transport], they are still there and if they question us and expect us to be doing something, we have to respond to them, we can't ignore them. It was external pressure, not internal pressure that led us to employment equity.[24]

Legal framework

Ontario's human rights and equal opportunities legislation has provided another major external stimulus to TTC and GO Transit to formulate equal opportunities policies and programmes.

As a GO Transit senior manager admitted, following an initial lack of enthusiasm for the intent of the Ontario Pay Equity Act 1987, senior management entered 'wholeheartedly into the job evaluation project', and they were 'committed to doing it within the time frame'. She felt that the need to meet the requirements of both the pay equity and freedom of information legislation had resulted in a fairer remuneration system for employees and that the company had benefited overall by 'improving corporate systems and policies'.

A senior manager at the TTC took the view that 'Legislation was needed', to spur companies to address equal opportunities. The external pressure placed on companies by equal opportunities legislation and the Ontario Human Rights Code acted as a useful lever for those opposing cuts in equal opportunities initiatives within the TTC. Impending legislation and the fact that one human rights complaint 'could cost us the cost of running HART for one whole year' had proved a useful line of argument when maintaining funding for a key equal opportunities management programme (HART). The same has been true with respect to services, where it has been recognised at the TTC and GO Transit that the Ontario Human Rights Code could be used as the basis for a complaint-driven litigation against a service provider.

Influence of user groups

Groups representing the users of public transport have used the legislative framework and political structures to make their presence felt in local politics. Voicing concern over the disadvantages experienced by the various designated groups, user groups have been established as catalysts for change. Their actions have eventually led to the establishment of permanent advisory bodies liaising with the TTC and other service providers such as GO Transit.

Women have been particularly active in campaigns to improve personal security and accessibility on public transport and in other public spaces. Well-organised local women's groups demanded action by local government, the police and the TTC in the early 1980s. A Metro Toronto task force resulted in the formation of METRAC (Metro Action Committee on Public Violence Against Women and Children), set up in 1984 as an advisory organisation funded by, but independent from, Metro Toronto. Urban transport systems and other public places were the subject of detailed investigation and appraisal. Collaboration between METRAC and other women's organisations such as 'Women Plan Toronto', the TTC and the Metropolitan Toronto Police Force resulted in a comprehensive audit of personal security with an explicit focus on sexual assault and harassment. The findings were published in a report *Making Transit Safer for Women* (1989), which has provided a springboard for demands by women for further improvements. Regular channels of communication have been established with the TTC's Equal Opportunities Department in order to ensure further improvements based on women's, ethnic minority and disabled user's concerns continue.

Senior management commitment and corporate culture

Partly as a result of these external pressures, the Chief General Manager and senior managers at the TTC have voiced enthusiastic support for employment and service equity since the mid-1980s. The TTC's policy statement makes it clear that equal opportunities should permeate the culture of the transit organisation, along with other key principles such as health and safety and service reliability.

> The Toronto Transit Commission is committed to Equal Opportunity. This commitment extends to every facet of our business involving the services we provide to our customers and the people we employ. A central theme of our corporate equality initiatives is a belief in the spirit and intent of the Ontario Human Rights Code and a recognition that Equal Opportunity at the TTC makes good business sense (TTC, 1992a).

The development of equal opportunities at GO Transit is more recent and the policy is more narrowly focused on employment. It states that

> GO Transit is committed to providing equal opportunities to employees and applicants without discrimination. GO Transit does not discriminate against anyone on the basis of race, sex, age, marital or family status, national or ethnic origin, citizenship, religion, disability, sexual orientation, record of offences, or any other ground as described in the Ontario Human Rights Code (GO Transit, 1993b).

As one senior female manager at GO Transit indicated with respect to the company's response to the Employment Equity legislation: 'the composition of GO Transit is basically white male . . . we have very few females in management . . . when you come to a group like that and say we have to institute an employment equity programme, they say, 'Why? What's the problem?

Certainly, support for Employment Equity Legislation at GO Transit was rather more muted than at the TTC. However, the view was expressed by a senior manager at GO Transit that once the Employment Equity legislation was in place they would comply with its requirements with the same commitment shown following the Pay Equity Legislation.[25]

Internal pressure for equal opportunities

A major reorganisation at TTC in 1985 led to the appointment of a Head of Employment Equity within the personnel department. Although the initial force pushing the TTC's equal opportunities programme along throughout the 1970s and 1980s was external political pressure, at least part of this development seems to have been spurred on by a very committed woman manager who helped to make the case for employment equity to senior management at the TTC.

> There was one particular individual who started the womens' programmes back in Personnel. She used to work in Personnel as a recruitment person and eventually she was given the responsibility for 'women's issues' and was seen as somebody who might drive that programme a bit further. She became the first Head of the [employ]ment equity] programme . . . She has been instrumental in a lot of the changes.[26]

Further change came in 1986, when the TTC's newly appointed Chief General Manager appointed consultants to undertake a culture survey of the organisation. Basically they concluded that the TTC was 'militaristic, paternalistic, very traditional with layers of hierarchy'. It was agreed that one of the vital components of culture change was a change in the way the organisation was recruiting and managing employees and that an employment equity programme could be a key lever within the organisational change strategy. Following the consultant's recommendations, the post of Director of Equal Opportunities was established with a department in the Executive Branch of the organisation. There seems to be little doubt at the TTC that the Director of Equal Opportunities effectively argued the business case for equal opportunities: she had 'made the programme go'.[27]

Significantly, the TTC Equal Opportunities Department, which in 1992 employed eight people, is responsible for 'advancing, supporting and ensuring the achievement' of both

- equal employment opportunity at the TTC, and
- equity of treatment in service delivered by the TTC.

This linking of employment and service equity initiatives illustrates the company's belief that it makes good business sense to do so (TTC, 1991). The TTC, in responding to legal and political pressure has recognised the diversity and changing demographics of the Toronto metropolitan area which provide it both with its workforce and its customers and has begun to address this as part of its corporate strategy.[28]

At GO Transit there has been no real internal pressure for this kind of equal opportunities development. A female recruitment manager in the Human Resources Department 'expressed interest in participating in the employment equity programme' and so when the company was pressured by the Government of Ontario the job landed on 'her doorstep.' She has three staff reporting to her in the Employment Equity and Recruitment section, but in 1992 employment equity remained a project rather than a concrete initiative with a budget.[29]

Trade union role

Three trade unions are recognised at the TTC and one at GO Transit. The union boards (all male) have been reactive rather than pro-active to company equal opportunity developments in both companies, on the grounds that there was no demand from their predominantly male membership for these initiatives. However, some changes in commitment have been evident over the last two years as the membership has become more diverse and the TTC Amalgamated Transit Union (ATU) local now has a female membership of 14 per cent. Women have established an ATU Women's Committee and are beginning to raise issues concerning their working environment, including sexual harassment.[30]

Equal opportunities and business strategy

By the late 1980s, equal opportunities had acquired a high profile in the corporate goals and programmes of the TTC. In the 1990 Annual Report, for example, the Chief General Manager's introduction emphasised that the year

> saw great advances in our long-standing commitment to equal opportunity. Employee rights were protected even further with the introduction of a new anti-harassment policy and training programme. We took special care too, in our approach to our changing community, with the introduction of a training programme to provide TTC managers and supervisors with the skills to work with employees and customers from diverse cultures (TTC, 1990).

In the body of the report, equal opportunities features as an integral function with regard to employee initiatives and customer service initiatives.

This is replicated in the TTC's Long Range Plan, approved in 1991. It charts the organisations's strategy for a course of action over a ten-year period. Of its sixteen key recommendations, four have direct implications for equal opportunities in employment and service delivery (TTC, 1989a). Following a review of corporate policy structure in 1992, 122 corporate policies were realigned into 12 broad policy areas. Equal opportunities was established as one of the twelve umbrella categories, establishing its importance within TTC's business strategy (TTC, 1992a).

GO Transit's operation is much smaller-scale than the TTC. In 1992 employment and service equity was not seen as a a core element in GO Transit's business strategy. The Human Resources Department had examined the position of women within the company in 1991–92 but had taken little action because they felt their procedures were fair and, in the words of one spokesperson they had been 'busy, like other organisations, with more pressing issues' partly created by the downturn in the provincial economy. Employment equity was designated as a project pending the introduction of Provincial Employment Equity legislation.

The organisation's position on service equity tends to be expressed in particular initiatives, rather than in comprehensive statements of policy. Nevertheless, the GO Transit Annual Report 1992 emphasises 'two . . . important areas: the safety and security of our riders, and accessible train services for passengers with disabilities' (GO Transit, 1993a)'. In 1991, GO Transit began a thorough review of security measures and features to improve safety, especially for women (GO Transit, 1992).

It is clear from this overview that both the TTC and GO Transit have primarily made equal opportunities changes in response to the external legislative and political pressures brought to bear on them in the last decade. The TTC provides evidence of a more substantial internally driven change programme and the remaining sections of the chapter will focus on the implications of the programme for women as employees and customers as well as the role they themselves play as change agents.

TTC: equal opportunities in action

This section will focus on the special programmes and practices overseen by the Equal Opportunities Department in both employment and service delivery.

Employment: women's representation in the workforce (1979–92)

The Equal Opportunity Department at the TTC has established an impressive statistical profile of its workforce which it monitors closely because it 'recognises the importance of measuring the success of its Equal Opportunity Program' (TTC, 1991). Since 1991 it has also been providing the statistical data necessary for the establishment of goals and timetables in line with the requirements of the impending employment equity legislation.[31]

The TTC has encouraged women to apply for jobs within the organisation. The company has been quite successful in increasing the representation of women within the TTC. Women comprised 12 per cent of the workforce in 1992, relative to 5 per cent in 1989. Between 1980 and 1990 the TTC experienced an average annual growth rate of 2.7 per cent which meant that the company was hiring, and it was primarily during this period that the gains in female employment in the company were made.

The TTC's original equal opportunity initiative also focused on improving the representation of women in the workforce, particularly in non-clerical (management and blue-collar) positions. As Figure 9.1 illustrates, the company has made some progress in reducing patterns of occupational segregation by gender within the workforce. In 1979, 92 per cent of the women

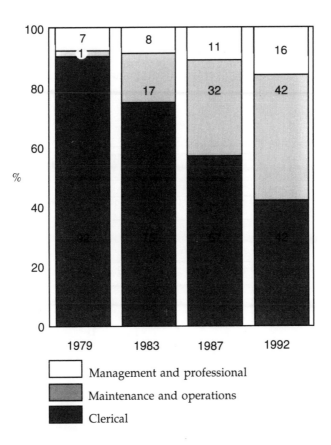

FIGURE 9.1   Women in the Toronto Transit Commission workforce, 1979–1992

Source: Toronto Transit Commission, *Equal Opportunity Report*, 1992.

employees working at the TTC held clerical jobs. By 1992, 42 per cent of the women employees worked in clerical positions, 42 per cent worked in the maintenance/operations branches and 16 per cent held management/professional positions. Thus women have gained access to a greater variety of jobs within the organisation.

Most of the absolute growth took place in the operations branch as women succeeded in gaining jobs as bus and streetcar drivers. However, women have also improved their representation in management positions, albeit in a limited range of positions as illustrated in Figure 9.2.

Figure 9.3 gives an overview of the TTC's progress with regard to a number of equal opportunity measures. It also provides an overview of women's representation in some key employment processes in 1991. In measuring equity for women in 1991, women's share of external recruitment (24 per cent) is very good in relation to their share of TTC applicants (17 per cent). The internal promotions rate (13 per cent) is also quite acceptable relative to TTC female workforce representation. However, women's share of turnover (22 per cent) is problematic when compared to their TTC workforce representation (12 per cent). The data concerns 'controllable terminations' (resignations and dismissals) and indicates that the TTC has a retention problem concerning

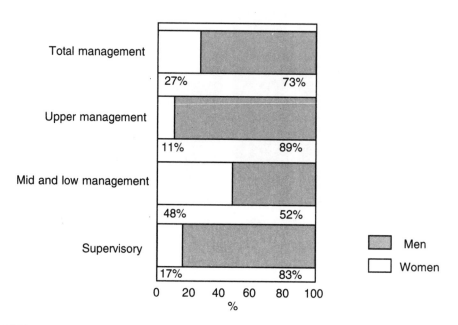

FIGURE 9.2   Growth of TTC management, 1987–1991: share of growth by gender

Source: Toronto Transit Commission, *Annual Statistics*, 1991.

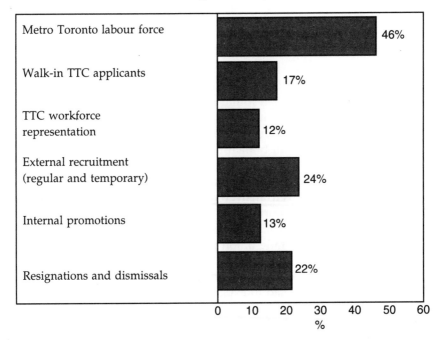

FIGURE 9.3   Representation of women in selected employment processes at the Toronto Transit Commission, 1991
Source: Toronto Transit Commission, *Annual Statistics*, 1991.

female employees. The fact that the TTC loses more women than it hires each year is recognised as a problem particularly in combination with an employment freeze or further downsizing which could lead to the erosion of the gains the company has made in female representation within its workforce.

Outreach and recruitment

The Outreach Programme is one of the initiatives which the Equal Opportunities Department credits for much of its success in hiring women and other designated groups.[32] It aimed to promote the TTC as an organization committed to hiring qualified designated group members. The TTC's recruitment staff participated in numerous job fairs, high school career days, workshops, agency visits, tours and so on in order to reach the designated groups. These activities included participation by employees of the TTC who are members of designated groups and act as role models.

Certainly a number of the female TTC employees interviewed for this research had learnt of job opportunities via TTC outreach sessions in the mid-1980s. For others, they applied as the 'word went around' and some were encouraged by seeing other women in transport jobs. 'I came to the TTC eight years ago – from a banking background. The decision to come to the TTC was because I was fascinated by streetcars. I never thought I could do it, but I saw a woman driving and I thought "if she can do it, I can" '.

Most women interviewed had found recruitment and selection procedures fair. Some, not all, did report finding male work colleagues hostile to them, particularly where they commenced work between 1980 and 1988. One wo-men working within the plant branch had found it upsetting to be told that, when she started work in 1985, 'my test was passed around to all the guys in my workgroup so that they could see that I had passed it legitimately'. When they found her test was well answered, rumours circulated that she 'had known someone in Equal Opportunities' so had been briefed as to the contents of the test. As the only woman, she was never really accepted by this work-group until she stood for a trade union position to represent them in 1990; at that point they began to accept that she 'wasn't just there to cause problems, [she] was there to try and make things better'.

Women agreed that they had to expend a great deal of effort on 'fitting in' with their male colleagues and the predominantly 'male' culture. One Afro-Caribbean woman who worked in the transportation branch had experienced both good and bad working environments. She realised that, as both black and female:

> It takes me longer to accomplish something than the average white person because I have this restriction: I'm black – so I have to go through this mode: – you will get to know me; you will know that I am sensitive to your culture; it is not my intention to do anything because you happen to be one colour and I happen to be one colour; I don't play favourites. Once we get past that, I get all the help.

Education and training

Another key equal opportunities initiative is the management training pro-gramme known as 'HART' – Hillcrest Area Rapid Transit which has been designed for all employees from senior management to supervisory levels. All TTC managers are scheduled to go on the HART programme which aims to provide the participants with the necessary skills and knowledge for mana-ging a diverse workforce. It has been developed as an important component in the company's culture change and, by spring 1993, 23 sessions had been run. Close to half the targeted management group have attended the programme which always includes at least two women and two ethnic minority partici-pants. HART focuses on four areas: employment equity, service equity, race relations and human rights. Graduates of HART participate in follow-up sessions and receive *HART-Beat* a newsletter to keep them informed of equal opportunity issues (TTC, 1991–93). Participation of ATU Executive Board members has also been encouraged by the company.

Other training priorities include workplace harassment, specific equal opportunities programmes for operative and supervisory staff plus modules within general training programmes, Women's Self Defence, and Sexual Assault Response Training – informing TTC employees how to respond effectively to occurrences of sexual assault, while remaining sensitive to the needs of assault victims (TTC, 1993b).

Although women staff members were positive about the TTC training initiatives in terms of aims and content, one problem that women described illustrates the dilemma faced by an organisation which undertakes equal opportunities training in a predominantly white, male workplace. It was recognised by some women that the Operator's Training Centre as currently constituted and described by some as 'little England' or an 'old boy's club' would have some problems finding appropriate trainers to deliver some of the equal opportunities programmes. This view seemed to be supported by the experience of one female equal opportunities course participant who suggested that she had found the experience 'very frustrating . . . because they were all white middle-aged guys; I was the only woman there . . . they knew what the right answers were, they were just going through the motions'.

Workplace harassment and discrimination

Since 1990, the Equal Opportunities Department has taken charge of the management of the policy. A human rights consultant now responds to human rights related enquiries and investigations of workplace harassment and discrimination. Awareness and utilisation of the internal complaints procedure and heightened awareness of workplace harassment following training sessions have meant that the number of complaints and enquiries increased in 1991 and 1992. Where particular departments seem to have recurrent problems, the two human rights managers will arrange training sessions with the agreement of line managers. A positive development in 1991 was a request from one of the ATU union representatives to run joint awareness sessions for trade union members.[33]

A large number of the sexual harassment complaints are being raised by women working in non-traditional areas. Women have experienced a variety of problems with rumours, sexual advances, gossip, graffiti and a case of sexual assault. One woman, who worked in an almost completely male area, suggested that at the TTC, some male colleagues perceive you as a 'hooker' if you're sociable 'but if you try and stay back then you're a lezzie'. She had experienced a number of problems with sexual harassment and felt that working at the TTC had toughened her up. She had begun to fight back following a harassment situation shortly after the harassment policy was put in place in 1987. A particularly large and offensive pornographic poster was placed at her work location.

> It was obvious, that they wanted to see what I would do so I just BLEW! I couldn't just leave that one aside, because it was a different feeling to know that they would try to antagonise me that much.

She had felt very alone in dealing with the situation. Her union president suggested she should go to management, and management had addressed the matter by holding a public meeting to publicise the sexual harassment policy because she insisted they do so. Following the incident her colleagues ostracised her. The harassment persisted and a second incident concerning obscene grafitti about her occurred so she complained again.

In 1988, a Human Rights Manager had been appointed to the Equal Opportunities Department and she investigated the woman's case. The woman said that she found the second incident was a lot easier to handle, partly because she found 'having a woman to talk to very helpful'. Following the investigation, a meeting was held with the woman, the Human Rights Manager, line management and male staff from the section 'to get the section working' and 'find out what's happened without placing blame on anybody'. This did not solve all the problems in the work area but the woman felt that it did enable male colleagues to see that she 'was just interested in doing [her] job and going home and not being a nervous wreck'. This woman became active in her union following this experience and now provides the kind of support for new women in the plant section which was unavailable to her early in her career.

Communication, networks and support

The Equal Opportunities Department has established a series of meetings for groups who may feel isolated in their work area: women workers, workers with disabilities and lesbian and gay workers.

One network is the Women in Management Network which was started informally by the Head of the Equal Opportunities Department and four other senior women managers, who would meet for lunch to 'maintain their sanity'. It broadened to include other women managers and Equal Opportunities agreed to arrange four formal meetings a year on a Friday afternoon which all TTC women managers were entitled to attend (on company time) in order to share common issues and concerns.[34]

Another series of meetings was held in 1989–90 for women working in 'non-traditional' areas within the maintenance and operations branches. These meetings allowed women to talk about issues, how they dealt with situations and just network. One woman reported finding these meetings very helpful, and had been surprised to find that she was not alone in finding her working circumstances difficult. 'It was really funny as nearly half of the women had their own little black books,' in which they would record problematic events at work so it would all be down there 'in black and white', should they need to provide evidence. She had contacted the Equal Opportunities Department in 1992 in order to ask them to restart the meetings for 'non-traditional' workers again, as she felt other women including a younger women in her department would benefit.

A number of male and female colleagues felt positively about two posters which the TTC had produced in co-operation with ATU Local 113. The posters showed photographs of a diverse workforce and some had been defaced. However, a woman inspector strongly supported the posters because she felt

that's something that people in the front-line can see and go 'Aha! – that is a reflection of who works for the TTC and there's a reflection of who our population is – it's not like it should be, yet, but it's moving.

Employment equity legislation

The TTC has taken a pro-active approach to implementing what it has perceived to be the requirements of the Ontario Employment Equity Act. Two integral components of the proposed legislation are: the requirement that organisations should establish employment equity goals and timetables, and the need for an employment systems review.

In 1991 and 1992 goals and timetables information sessions were conducted for senior management and within the HART management training pro-gramme. This has allowed misgivings held by some male managers about affirmative action programmes and 'quotas' to be dispelled by staff from the Equal Opportunities Department who reassure them that the TTC 'will have complete freedom in setting goals and timetables' and also to put positive arguments such as the following, 'we need to have a plan for anything we do, that's the way we do our budgeting, finance any of our capital projects so why not have a plan for human resources?'[35] In 1991 an employment systems review of the TTC's policies, practices and programmes was undertaken by an external consultant. The goal of the review was to identify and eliminate any artificial and systemic barriers existing in the TTC's employment systems. The findings of the study have informed the TTC's Human Resources Plan for the 1990s.

Both of these initiatives should address some of the concerns raised by women and ethnic minorities concerning their presence and progression in the company. Women felt that the biggest improvement that could be made to the quality of their working life was to 'get more women in'. They felt encouraged to find 'more and more women in positions other than janitor' and also to work with women as managers and professionals. A woman manager working in the Safety and Security Department for example spoke positively of working with a female station architect who 'had a good grasp of personal security'. Another woman manager felt liberated by the management style of her new female boss whom she described as having 'very much a team leader approach which is new to our department'. This more collaborative and interactive management approach is precisely the one that the TTC had sought to foster in embarking on its equal opportunities culture change programme in 1985.

However, TTC women employees recognised that in the prevailing economic climate where further staff reductions were likely, 'there'd have to be a magic formula to get them (more women) in so they'd be accepted . . . as having earned being there'.

In this context, the retention of women staff is recognised by Equal Opportunities as a significant issue. As a result of exit interviews, they know that women leave because of problems with shifts, inflexibility of work hours and the 'hostile' work environment. Although some of the more blatant hostility to women's presence has become less evident, as 'the older guys have got used to it or left' one of the Equal Opportunities managers acknowledged that

> Women don't feel they belong in this organisation. That has to do with being the only woman in a group or just simply by being ignored. I've seen it happen in meetings, jobs referred to as 'journeyman' and at the end of the meeting (the chair) will say 'gentlemen, I conclude', although there were women there.[36]

Employment: womens' views on the impact of equal opportunities at the TTC

In general, the women interviewed thought the Equal Opportunities Department was doing a good job, and that they were responding to their needs. They were concerned, however, that the organisation's policies still needed to be communicated more widely: 'The equal opportunities department is good. TTC's upper management policies are good. It's a matter of bringing them down to lower management and making sure lower management knows what's going on.'

A number were aware that the Equal Opportunities Department was perceived by male colleagues as the 'thought police'. A few felt this perceived surveillance made some male colleagues resentful of them. Thus they were not supportive of its attempts to change the use of permissible language (e.g. from 'ladies' to women) and they did not wish to see poor workers (regardless of gender) being able to 'hide behind equal opportunities'.

Most women felt, however, that there had been a definite improvement in the behaviour of their male colleagues as a result of the organisation's equal opportunities programmes and practices: 'The last few years there's been a real improvement . . . the guys themselves are a lot more . . . I hate to use the word sensitive! . . . well they're not as boorish as in the past.'

A few thought discriminatory attitudes and behaviour had just become less blatant. One women, however, felt that a recent wave of equal opportunity training had provoked a backlash from male colleagues similar to the one after the announcement of the harassment policy: 'I think because of that they are more hostile. Because they feel they are being told what they can and can't do, they feel there are quotas . . . and claim "we can't even make jokes anymore – because they're telling us what we can say'."

Others disagreed and were optimistic about the future: 'I don't think things have got worse: I think things have calmed down. The supervisory group went on the EO Human Rights course and now people are more sensitive as to what they say.'

Although most women acknowledged progress had been made, they still recognised that there was a long way to go before the TTC could be considered an equal opportunities employer, both in the eyes of new women employees – 'through my eyes . . . these women are being treated like gold compared to how I was treated but things are pretty backward as far as they can see' – and through the eyes of women who are now seeking promotion opportunities within the company. As one Afro-Caribbean woman said,

> I think that we have come a long way: I'm saying that as a double minority. . .. I will say though, if you remain an operator, or an inspector, you're OK. When you seek to go above those two levels that's where the problems begin . . . because you're becoming more and more their boss.

There are also a number of practical daily matters which need to be addressed by the TTC if women are to feel true parity of treatment with male colleagues. Increasingly, women are feeling confident to use established channels themselves, in order to make sure their needs are met within the organisation. One woman put in a grievance concerning the supply of uniforms to women,

> We still can't get clothing that fits us properly. The arrangement is that the local gets a clothing allowance and we get to pick the clothes we want. Up until a couple of years ago, you couldn't get any kind of women's clothing at all, now you can request it but I'm still waiting for pants.

The grievance went to management as a policy grievance for all the women's clothing, so the issue was being addressed in 1993 by Equal Opportunities and the trade unions representing women in 'non-traditional' areas. However, the female employee felt quite strongly that it was both an equal opportunities and a health and safety matter 'that should have been addressed a long time ago'.

The special employment programmes and practices developed by the TTC Equal Opportunities Department do appear to have encouraged women to work in a greater variety of occupations at the TTC. They have also been successful to a degree in changing the culture of the organisation from a predominantly white, male culture to one which values diversity and provides support for women and ethnic minority employees. The presence of women, their support of each other and use of company policies and union structures to pressure for change have also been important elements in making the TTC more 'woman friendly'. To what degree has this culture change permeated the TTC's provision of services to women?

Services: programmes and practices

Progress on service equity has developed through liaison with user organisations representing designated groups. It has resulted in action plans with wide implications for transit organisation, especially with regard to safety and security, personal development and training, marketing and outreach work. With regard to women as users of public transport, personal security has emerged as the central issue.

It is recognised that improvements to the passenger environment and operational practices will not stop sexual assaults and harassment (TTC, 1989b; 1992c). Nevertheless, such attacks are often crimes of opportunity and the safety audit's recommendations did identify a number of points which have been acted upon by the TTC. On surface transit, the 'Request Stop Programme' enables people travelling alone after dark and early morning to alight at places on the route other than regular stops. Following a pilot scheme in the Scarborough area of Toronto, where a serial rapist had followed his victims from transit stops, the scheme was extended system-wide. The design of bus shelters and their lighting has been improved and some stops relocated for security reasons. As from 1992 all surface vehicles have been equipped with two-way radio, and silent alarms, which allow assistance to be summoned from the police.

On the subway system, physical improvements have centred upon the 'Designated Waiting Area' (DWA) programme, also developed from the recommendations in 'Making Transit Safer for Women'. As from autumn 1992, all subway stations have clearly signed locations on each platform with a seat and:

- an emergency alarm button;
- two-way voice communication with station staff at the collector's booth;
- closed-circuit television surveillance, monitored by the station collector;
- a public telephone;
- improved lighting.

Design improvements to existing subway stations include mirrors to eliminate blind spots where assailants can hide in wait, better sightlines for surveillance, signage indicating exits as escape routes, and features such as extra benches, murals and public art to 'humanise' the subway. On the subway trains, the wording of the emergency alarm strips is being changed to explicitly include 'harassment' as a reason to summon assistance from the driver/guard.

METRAC and other women's organisations have emphasised the role of transit staff:

- to help prevent attacks by being alert to the hazards faced by women passengers;
- to respond quickly, sensitively and efficiently to incidents of assault and harassment.

It was recognised that transit staff might well be uncertain of how best to deal with personal safety issues, and might fear for their own safety in certain circumstances. The TTC's Safety and Security Department have worked closely with Equal Opportunities and the Human Resources Branch to provide guidance and training to 'front-line' staff and their supervisors. All employees have been instructed and issued with 'CARE' cards concerning the correct response to the emotional and physical reactions of a woman who has been assaulted or harassed:

- Communicate effectively.
- Advise Transit Control.
- Reassure survivor.
- Encourage the survivor to seek help.

A detachable section of the card provides information on how to seek help though a list of appropriate agencies.

Other initiatives which should benefit elderly women, disabled women and women travelling with children or an elderly relative include the Ontario 'Easier Access' programme, and the new generation of fully-accessible low-floor buses and streetcars which will replace existing vehicles.

Services: women's views on the impact of Equal Opportunities at the TTC

Meaningful dialogue between transit organisations and designated groups as users of public transport is an important pre-requisite for the development of service equity programmes. The TTC's 'Strategy for the 1990s' accepts that, in the past, the organisation received some criticism for' its perceived lack of openness to the community it serves' (TTC, 1989a). Today, however, community participation has become a key theme of Metro Toronto's planning for 'The Liveable Metropolis' in which public transport plays a leading role (Metropolitan Toronto Planning Department, 1992). The dialogue between TTC and its users has been assisted by public funding for METRAC. More recently, broad-based user groups have been set up with public funding to advise on disability, and on multi-racial access. How then, are the TTC's efforts perceived by women and other users?

A spokeswoman for METRAC commented that since the early 1980s considerable progress had been made towards mutual understanding and cooperation. Nevertheless, the continuing dialogue and pressure from women's organisations were still very necessary. For example, the initial take-up rate for the experimental 'Request Stop Programme' was disappointing, and there was

> quite a lot of resistance from the TTC to maintain that programme because the reports they were getting back from drivers was that very few people were requesting, but we urged them to hang in, perhaps do a little publicity to make sure people knew about it. And even with 150 people a month using it, it was still worth it.[37]

Further promotion of the scheme did indeed result in greater take-up, and the scheme was expanded to include the entire TTC surface network. METRAC also maintain the pressure for more sensitivity training, especially through the Canadian Urban Transit Association (CUTA) programme 'Yes, they have done training of staff, but we still get complaints. Women send us copies of their letters when complaining to the TTC about driver behaviour'.

Pressure from womens' organisations also helped to maintain the momentum to implement the Designated Waiting Area (DWA) programme on the subway. Furthermore, METRAC and 'focus groups' of women passengers were actively involved in the choice of design. Experiments with three prototype DWAs resulted in the rejection of the low-cost 'Basic' model, which lacked closed-circuit television surveillance. The principle of active participation by users is also fundamental to the safety audit developed by Gerde Werkerle and her colleagues at York University for subways and other public places.

> The basis of the audit process for us is that it must involve those who use, live or work in the place. If it doesn't it's not a safety audit. Indeed, the *process* is almost as important as the outcome, because of the way it raises awareness and how people are involved, including those who are in a position to do something.

Organisations representing disabled people in Toronto have also been a potent force for change. The Advisory Committee on Accessible Transportation, set up in 1993, should help to inform the development of policies and programmes. In its first six months, the committee was closely involved in some important initiatives including key station accessibility on the subway and the location of elevators, and the planning and design of new stations on line extensions and wheelchair positions in subway cars.[38] And again, staff training in awareness and sensitivity is a central issue. A partially-sighted woman passenger emphasised that increasing numbers of visually-impaired women are travelling on conventional transit, and that transit staff need to make it safe for them. She commented,

> operating staff generally seem very aware if you are unfamiliar with the geographical area. The operator of a street-car recently told me the traffic light was green when I got off. Another rang the bell when I was getting on to tell me where the vehicle was, and when the doors were open. They tend to do that now.[39]

Ethnic minority women may face the dangers of racially-motived attacks, as well as sexual assault. These concerns and fears were heightened in the Winter of 1992 when a serial rapist was preying specifically on Asian women, following them from transit stops. The TTC Equal Opportunity Department have emphasised the importance of communicating the recent safety initiatives using appropriate media and language to reach women in the various ethno-racial communities of the city. Multi-lingual and multi-cultural marketing are essential. Safety messages promoted through TTC leaflets are now translated into 15 languages, and the development of a manual and video for use by ethnic minority community organisations is also an important initiative. The TTC also recognises the need to obtain more information about the travel pattern, preferences and opinions of ethnic minorities.[40]

Conclusion

Public transport is an industry run by men and dominated by trades, crafts and professions in which women are grossly under-represented. In most transport organisations, 90 per cent or more of the workforce is male. Women tend to provide support functions as clerks, secretaries and administrators. The industry's patriarchal culture has implications for women, not only as employees, but also as customers. Typically, 60 per cent of the passengers are female. The 'traditional male values' of transport organisations are deep-rooted. Nevertheless, it would be wrong to assume that they are immutable.

In Canada, the principles of employment equity and service equity are enshrined in the law. It is recognised that discrimination can be systemic. Special policies and programmes of action may be required to redress the balance. Canadian public transport organisations are highly aware of the significance of human rights legislation, as they are major employers and provide a public service which has a particularly high profile. Unlike their UK counterparts, most urban transport undertakings remain in municipal ownership. Accountable to the local electorate, they must demonstrate even-handed treatment of all sections of the community.

This case study examining developments in public transport in Toronto suggests that where the political will is present, and where senior management is fully committed to equal opportunities, substantial progress can be achieved in a timescale of five to ten years. The case study also underlines the key role played by women, both as employees and as members of well-organised user groups. Without this internal and external pressure from women as 'change agents', it is hard to believe that the corporate culture of organisations can be transformed.

Postscript: January 1996

In June 1995, the election of a Progressive Conservative government in Ontario brought dramatic changes in policy concerning public sector funding and employment equity. Ontario's Progressive Conservative government immediately embarked on one of Canada's most extensive cost-cutting programmes, they aim to save the province $9.6 billion over three years and balance the provincial budget by 2000 (*Globe and Mail*, 1995c). Following government budget cuts, the funding to public transport systems has been cut substantially (*Globe and Mail*, 1995d).

One of our case study organisations, Go Transit, lost $3.8 million from its operating subsidy in 1995 (*Globe and Mail*, 1995e), and its capital subsidies are to be reduced by $20 million annually (*Globe and Mail*, 1995b). The TTC's operating and capital budgets have been cut for 1995 and 1996 (*Globe and Mail*, 1995a). As a result, fares have been increased, bus services cut and the Wheel-Trans service for the disabled has been drastically reduced. In addition, the Progressive Conservative government has cancelled the $740 million Eglington subway extension (*Globe and Mail*, 1995a). Despite these setbacks, the TTC's management have reaffirmed their commitment to equal opportunities in employment and service delivery.[41]

As part of the drastic overall change in political direction sought by the Progressive Conservatives, the Ontario Employment Equity Law (1993) has been repealed. This was one of the incoming government's top priorities after winning the June election in 1995. The Citizenship Minister, Marilyn Mushinski, claimed that the equity law was 'unnecessary, unfair and ineffective' and that the Tories were restoring the 'merit' principle (*Globe and Mail*, 1996).

Under the repeal law, passed in December 1995, employers are required to destroy any demographic information they have collected on the status of minorities in their organisations. However, this is being challenged by the Human Resources Professionals Association of Ontario (HRPA) and the Alliance for Employment Equity.

The HRPA of Ontario has asked the provincial government to change its employment equity reforms to ensure that Ontario companies can still press on with voluntary diversity programmes and strategies (*Globe and Mail*, 1995b). A number of companies stimulated by the requirements of the employment equity law have developed their own sets of standards and now see diversity strategies as crucial in developing a competitive edge in business. Under the Ontario Human Rights Code, employers are still allowed to put in place special programmes to help disadvantaged groups.

The Alliance for Employment Equity (made up of a number of equity-seeking groups) is trying to bring back employment equity via a constitutional challenge scheduled for February 1996. The Alliance contends that the bill repealing employment equity violates the Charter of Rights and Freedoms, which guarantees equal treatment under the law for everyone. The Alliance had also sought an injunction to overturn the Conservative's repeal bill and restore the Employment Equity Act in order to stop employers from destroying the demographic information on minorities they have collected in compliance with the law at least until after the constitutional challenge (*Globe and Mail*, 1996).

Sadly, our case-study chapter must recognise the uphill task now facing women and other equity-seeking groups in Ontario as they seek to counter the backlash to employment and service equity posed by the newly elected Progressive Conservative government. It is to be hoped that the substantial progress in employment and service equity made at the TTC (and within other public and private organisations in Ontario) will not be jeopardised or reversed, as we have seen was the case in London's public transport system.

Notes

1. The authors would like to acknowledge the funding provided by the Canadian Studies Institutional Research Programme of the Canadian High Commission which assisted in the completion of this research.
2. Canada has a federal system of government; the Canadian national government is based in Ottawa, the government of the province of Ontario is located in Toronto. Metropolitan Toronto is a regional tier of local government encompassing the city of Toronto and twelve smaller municipalities located in the metropolis.
3. This paper draws on research examining the implementation of equal opportunities in employment and service delivery within Canadian and British passenger

transport organisations. The research project focused on the ownership and regulation of passenger transport systems, corporate strategy and the legal and procedural basis for EO policies and practices. The Canadian research was conducted between May 1993 and August 1994. For this paper we draw on data collected from government and corporate publications, semi-structured interviews with public officials, campaigning organisations and trade unions, plus two in-depth company case studies. Within the two companies, semi-structured interviews (40 in total) were conducted with EO managers, managers, trade union officials and a sample of male and female employees.

4. Constitution Act 1982.
5. Personal interview with Brigid O'Reilly, Pay Equity Commissioner, Ontario Pay Equality Commission, Toronto 14 July 1993.
6. Speech from the Throne, 20 November 1990.
7. The Ontario Human Rights Code prohibits discrimination on grounds of race, ancestry, place of origin, colour, ethnic origin, citizenship, creed, sex, sexual orientation, age, marital status, family status or handicap.
8. Ontario Human Rights Code, Sections 1 and 4.
9. Personal interview with Janis Sarra, Vice-Chair, Pay Equity Tribunal, Toronto, 14 July 1993. Prior to the introduction of the Pay Equity Act, women had unsuccessfully sought redress through the Ontario Human Rights Commission.
10. Section 4, Pay Equity Act 1987.
11. Section 13, Pay Equity Act 1987.
12. Section 26, Pay Equity Act 1987.
13. Section 6, Employment Equity Act 1993.
14. Section 2, Employment Equity Act 1993. The designated groups are women, aboriginal people, people with disabilities and ethnic minorities.
15. Section 33, Employment Equity Act 1993.
16. Personal interview with Janis Sarra, Vice-Chair, Pay Equity Tribunal, Toronto, 14 July 1993.
17. Ibid.
18. Personal interview with Carol Anne Sceviour, Women's Officer, Ontario Federation of Labour, Toronto 16 July 1993.
19. Statement of the Ontario Legislature, 26 November 1992.
20. Personal interview with Janice Killoran, Solicitor for the Pay Equity Commission, Toronto, 21 July 1993.
21. This has been the case since reorganisation in 1988, before which the Commission comprised the Metro Toronto Chairman, another member of the Metro Council and three citizens appointed by the Council.
22. Personal interview with male TTC employee, 5 August 1993.
23. Personal interview with Estella Cohen, Equal. Opportunities Director, Toronto Transit Commission, Toronto, 19 July 1993.
24. Personal interview at GO Transit, Toronto, 15 July 1993.
25. Personal interview with Louise MacLean, Employment Equality Officer at GO Transit, Toronto, 15 July 1993.

26. Personal interview with Estella Cohen, Equal Opportunities Director, Toronto Transit Commission, Toronto, 19 July 1993.
27. Personal interview with two human resources managers at the Toronto Transit Commission, Toronto, 4 August 1993.
28. Personal interview with Cathy Dean, Equal Opportunities Director, Toronto Transit Commission, Toronto, May 1992.
29. Personal interview at GO Transit, Toronto, 15 July 1993.
30. Personal interview with John Brown, Amalgamated Transit Union, TTC Board Member, Toronto, 3 August 1993.
31. Personal interview with Estella Cohen, Equal. Opportunities Director, Toronto Transit Commission, Toronto, 4 August 1993.
32. Personal interview with female TTC employee, 4 August 1993.
33. Personal interview with Terri-Spinola Cambell, Equal Opportunities Director (Human Rights), TTC, Toronto, 4 August 1993.
34. Personal interview with Estella Cohen, Equal. Opportunities Director, Toronto Transit Commission, Toronto, 19 July 1993.
35. Ibid.
36. Ibid.
37. Personal interview with Susan McCrae Vandercoet, METRAC, Toronto, July 1993.
38. Personal interview with the Chair of the Advisory Committee on Accessible Transportation, Toronto, July 1993.
39. Personal interview with Kathryn Donnely, Toronto, 21 July 1993.
40. Personal interview with Ron Chong, Equal Opportunities Department, TTC, Toronto, 4 August 1993; TTC (1992c).
41. Personal interviews with TTC management, TTC, Toronto, July 1995.

CHAPTER 10

Movers and shakers: creating organisational change

Fiona Colgan and Sue Ledwith

Introduction

This book has focused on women and their work organisations during a period of extensive social and economic restructuring. In particular the case study chapters have explored some of the opportunities and threats to women's positions and progression within a range of different organisations. We have focused especially on the impact made by women themselves, through their increased presence in the workplace, by their individual actions in pursuit of their own careers, and by their collective strategies – in two main senses. Firstly whereby women use a collective or joint forum for the particular purpose of achieving their own individual career goals, and secondly where they do so as a strategic and explicit means of pursuing challenge and change to gender relations in patriarchal organisations.

To help our analysis, in the first chapter, we developed a trajectory of women's consciousness and activism and a model for evaluating the political skills and behaviour of women in organisations. Following the analysis of women's strategies presented in the case study chapters, we suggest that key ingredients in the liberation of women and of men in their organisations are women's and men's increasing awareness of gender politics, combined with a willingness to *actively* challenge inequalities and work towards organisational transformation.

Women in the case study chapters can be seen as change agents through their presence, and also through their own agency as women, as they assess their position and role in their work organisations, cope with gender politics, make alliances and work out and negotiate ways and means of progressing their own, and in some cases, a wider transformational equality agenda.

It is clear from the case study chapters that the breakdown of traditional career paths and organisational hierarchies, and the increasing fluidity of organisational structures and cultures has opened up opportunities for those – women and men – who are well informed, well placed and well organised. The main question for women is to what extent they have been able to develop strategies to take advantage of these opportunities. From the chapters within the book there seems to be grounds for both optimism and pessimism in responding to this question.

As we have argued that organisations are not gender neutral, it has been of importance within the book to recognise that organisations are shaped by a wide variety of historically contingent economic and social forces, gender notably amongst them. Nevertheless, it is possible to identify particular patterns of women's consciousness and activism within the case studies as women have negotiated their working lives and careers in the period since the mid-1980s. In this final chapter, we consider this activism and its impact on the case study organisations, and identify some possible directions for the future. In doing so we indicate the importance of links between women's activism within and across organisational boundaries taking into account the specific context faced by women in the UK and European Union. Thus we take the view that the influence of the women's movement as a key and influential social movement in most industrialised economies since the 1960s cannot be underestimated.

Changing organisations: women's activism

From the case study chapters, three elements emerge which we see as key in the progress of live and effective women's equality movements within organisations. First are the external conditions. These include the gendered political, legal, economic and social environment within which the organisation is operating. Crucial determinants in the formulation of corporate strategy could include, for example, the introduction of equal opportunities legislation, a shift in public policy such as the improved state provision of childcare or maternity/paternity leave and/or changes within current market conditions, particularly those affecting an organisation's labour markets and its stakeholders. Second is the organisation's internal patriarchal structure and culture and responsiveness to these gendered external changes. Third is women's activism, by which we mean the levels of consciousness, political skill and strategies women may use to bring about change both as employees and as users and customers of an organisation and as citizens within the society where it is located.

The strength of women's equality projects in organisations seems to depend on the dynamics of the relationship between these three elements. In organisations where women appear to be working most effectively in leading change, as change agents, challenging patriarchal organisational structures and cultures, it is in circumstances where women's activism is strong with 'supported women'[1] (Hoskyns, 1994) operating collectively within and across organisational boundaries. We see this as a strong dynamic of organisational activism by women: a 'women's vanguard',[2] whereby there is a real possibility of a longer or 'maximum' women's agenda being developed and progressed. This optimal position is illustrated in Figure 10.1.

We do not wish to discount here women pursuing their own career goals as individuals. As identified throughout the chapters, women have been and are successful in their organisations. The skills and strategies they must develop in order to negotiate their working lives in gendered and sometimes hostile working environments have been clearly identified in all of the case studies. However, the evidence does seem to point to the fact that individualist strategies on their own are unlikely to result in any significant changes in organisational gender relations.

FIGURE 10.1   Maximum dynamic of women's activism: the longer agenda

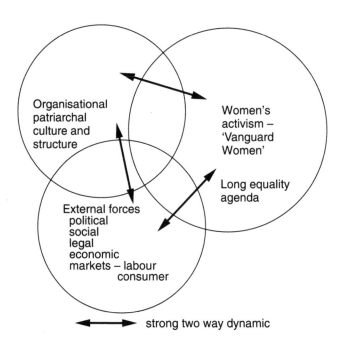

Where patriarchal external factors and strongly gendered organisational cultures and structures combine and dominate, women's consciousness and activism within organisations is likely to be weaker. Even where women may have a substantial presence as a proportion of employees (as, for example, in many retail organisations) challenges to the status quo seem to be individualistic, and any existing equality initiatives appear to be minimalised and marginalised, as illustrated in Figure 10.2. Women may operate as 'lone women' in such hostile organisational cultures until they experience 'burn out'. They may decide to try and 'play the system' instead of trying to change it thus becoming 'system women' (Hoskyns, 1994) internalising, operating within and sustaining the predominant oganisational patriarchal power paradigm. Or they may choose to leave the organisation altogether.

These different circumstances and the challenges facing women working as change agents within organisations are now discussed, drawing on evidence from the case studies.

FIGURE 10.2   Minimum dynamic of women's activism: the shorter agenda

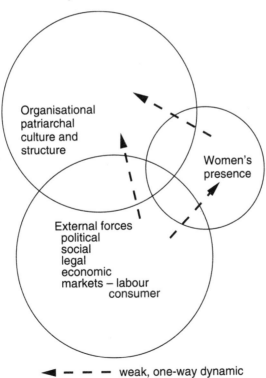

Strong women's activism – women as innovative change agents?

International comparisons suggest that gender equality is further advanced in public sector organisations which are publicly accountable, where collective bargaining is centralised and governments pursue active equal opportunity legislative and public policy programmes (Corcoran-Nantes and Roberts, 1995). Certainly this appears to be the case with respect to the case studies within the book: some of the most positive developments have taken place in the NHS, teaching and public transport case studies, particularly the public transport sector in Toronto, Canada.

Since 1979, in the UK, the external, political conditions which apply have contrasted strongly with those outlined in the Canadian transport case study. In the UK a private sector market orientation and the emergence of a 'new' managerialism have been widely adopted within the public sector (Clarke, Cochrane and McLaughlin, 1994). The UK Government's determination to introduce the discipline of the market to the public sector has led it to take an antagonistic stance to state-backed (including European Union) equality initiatives. One casualty of this ideological shift has been the retreat within the public sector from separatist equality structures such as women's and race equality units, on the grounds that they were an 'expensive luxury', especially in local government (Newman, 1994; Labour Research, 1995a). It has instigated public spending cuts and the abolition of collective bargaining within the public sector for groups such as teachers, while encouraging a shift to local pay bargaining in the National Health Service and other parts of the public sector. This has further weakened the collective push by trade unions for equal pay and conditions.

At the organisational level, the huge shifts driven by the free-market philosophy have led to women's and other equality initiatives being subsumed within an HRM (maximising human resources) and business efficiency management discourse which stresses competition and individualism (Newman, 1994; Maile, 1995). The danger is that within this context, as Newman (1994) suggests, attempts to provide 'a legitimating framework for the reworking of equality goals' means that 'the goals are stripped of their politics.' Nevertheless, as the various case study chapters illustrate this can be a means of women reclaiming the equality agenda as in the NHS or of losing it, as for example in personnel.

Tipping the balance, we propose, may depend on the state of women's readiness and preparedness to capture and adapt the new managerial discourse and use it for their own agenda. Their ability to do so will depend in part on how well women fare in the organisational restructuring and labour process changes affecting employment across the public and private sectors. However, as Newman (1994) outlines, it is likely that women's access to the power to shape this agenda will differ, given the parallel polarisations taking place around ethnicity, age and class linked to the growing split between 'core' and 'peripheral' female and male workers within restructuring organisations and flexible labour markets.

Where the conditions allow, we suggest that a key group of 'wise' women can usually be identified in the vanguard of change: change agents who can effectively read gendered organisational politics and work to innovate change within their organisation. These change agents are likely to be women-aware and/or feminist women. As innovative change agents they are less concerned with improving existing structures, instead they pursue change by reconstructing the problem and setting out to do things differently (Kirton, 1991). In UNISON, the NHS, the publishing company 'General' and the Canadian transport company, the TTC, the formal commitment for institutionalised women's equality programmes can be traced back directly to women actively working to make gender issues visible and central to the organisation, so re-visioning the existing patriarchal structures, cultures and practices which often operate to exclude women as employees and other stakeholders and limit both women and men to operate in gendered ways (Cockburn, 1985). Women sought to get the issues onto the organisational agenda, and then worked to ensure that the issues stayed there. It is these 'animating spirits' (Delmar, 1986) who form the vanguard from which a wider 'diaspora' of feminist and 'women-aware' actions may be developed over time, given the conjunction of a number of other conditions.

Accurate reading of gendered organisational politics: establishing the agenda and developing a strategy

The first of these conditions is a clear understanding or reading of the prevailing political, cultural and gendered organisational context by a critical mass of 'wise' women within the organisation and the development of alliances to push for change. This process can be seen most explicitly in the chapter on public transport in Toronto. Working collectively with other women, and men, across and among political, trade union, business and user groups, those arguing for equal opportunities were able to mount a well-organised, sustained and integrated campaign. In the larger transport company, the TTC, the result was a depth and strength, an *embeddedness* of equality. We suggest that the activism associated with a women's vanguard was present within the TTC with key women 'change agents' within the organisation being supported by a critical mass of women (and senior male) colleagues, in responding to changes in the external environment and specifically in identifying and responding to the demands of a key identified market – women public transport users. This momentum allowed an effective input to a corporate reassessment of organisational strategy and a challenge to be made to the prevailing patriarchal structure and culture. However, a heavily patriarchal organisational structure and culture at Go Transit and a lack of pressure from external women's user groups made it far more difficult for women change agents, who were mainly operating as lone women, in trying to move an equality agenda forward at Go Transit.

In the case of the NHS, the women-led Equal Opportunities Commission and the female researchers at Ashridge Management College (who produced the work on which Opportunity 2000 was based) were among the influential women using both existing formal institutional legitimacy, as well as political (both sexes) and 'women-aware' alliances to put the case for the women's NHS project. Within the publishing company 'General' a group of women active in their trade union (and in the pressure group Women in Publishing) negotiated with the company in order to establish a company equal opportunities group, which also involved women managers and supportive male colleagues in order to develop an equal opportunities policy and progress equal opportunities initiatives. In UNISON, labour movement women were among key movers working together across a range of socialist groups and academics (men and women) and both with and within the other equity-seeking groups: disabled, black and lesbian and gay trade union members. Women were able to ensure that their demands went into the agenda for the new union's constitution, and then were followed up to become practice within the union.

Thus feminist and women-aware women were able to develop their equal opportunities strategies both within and across organisational boundaries. Progress within these organisations involved specific equality strategies which made the case for equal opportunities not only on ethical or moral grounds but by linking equality with key strategic concerns such as quality, recruitment and retention and competition in the market place. Women within the TTC, the NHS, UNISON and 'General' sought for example to encourage their organisations that 'gender-blind' strategies were often wasteful and did not take into account the needs of women (and other marginalised groups) as employees, customers, suppliers or members. Thus, for example in the NHS, the annual cost (£2 billion) of training the predominantly female workforce was a forceful argument used by women change agents for a human resources strategy which put women at its centre. In UNISON, the argument for proportional representation was won not only on the grounds of democratic representation but also on the basis that women made up the largest group in the trade union 'market' from which UNISON needed to recruit in order to maintain and improve its strength and influence.

The longer agenda: changing the organisation

Feminist fingerprints can be traced not only on the equal opportunities (EO) strategies developed but also in the systems and structures women sought to put in place within their organisations. The development of a short agenda was frequently used as a springboard to develop a longer equal opportunities agenda. Women's collective and separatist (women only) strategies were key in this development, as can be seen within the TTC, the NHS and UNISON.

Major levers in the drive for equal opportunities, within the TTC for example, can be identified as firstly, establishing a commitment from senior management, which was clearly influenced by the powerful woman responsible for Employment Equity. From this developed a coherent integrated EO-HRM business strategy, which ensured that the role of EO was a key lever in the organisational culture change programme. The location of the equal opportunities department within the corporate executive, the careful provision of formal and interdependent EO provisions such as regular consultation with women's and community groups, staff training and development, monitoring, a communication programme plus women's networking, has proved successful in winning the argument for service and employment equity in the face of workforce cuts and the backlash from some of the male workforce.

A different, but similarly long, agenda has been built within the largest UK public sector workforce, the NHS. The women's project in the health service responded to the changing political context by using the 'new managerialism' as a springboard for a different kind of feminist project. Publicly supported at UK government level, centrally driven and well resourced, this has been a strategic programme utilising both a managerialist framework and a longer equal opportunities agenda, which includes the use of targets, innovative supporting initiatives and separate development opportunities for women. A particular feature of this was the formalised Women's Career Development Register, geared particularly towards the goal of 30% of general management posts being held by women by 1994.[3] As with the TTC, the Women's Unit was located within the most senior tier of corporate management and was headed by a feminist 'high-profile careerist' (Hammond, 1994). Even so, there is little sign so far of a change in the value system which sees the male career pattern as the norm: full-time, long hours, high mobility, and so on (Corby, 1995).

The seeds for UNISON's commitment to proportionality had been sown in 1975, when pre-merger partner NUPE first introduced the novel and radical practice of reserved seats for women on its national executive. A raft of additional positive action initiatives to support constitutional commitment had been put in place in all three partner unions over the ensuing years. In one of these in particular, NALGO, membership activism (including women) was bottom-up, grassroots and member-led (in contrast to the more officer-led system in the other partner unions), thus offering a different, complementary model of women's activism. As seen in Chapter 6, these different activist experiences plus the recognition of the need for gender democracy in a predominantly female union, have led UNISON to establish proportionality and the necessary organisational structures to deliver it (Cockburn, 1995b).

Following the years of campaigning by women (and other equity-seeking groups), UNISON now has a Director of Equal Opportunities, located at a senior level within the union, a Woman's Officer,[4] with dedicated regional women's officers and a range of formal structures at national, regional, industry sector and local workplace branch levels to ensure the proportional representation of women within UNISON. In particular, in UNISON, the formal legitimacy evident in the concept of proportionality for women, black members, lesbian and gay and disabled members, backed by rules and procedures and separatist self-organisation for these groups, ensured that within two years of its creation women were proportionally represented on the new NEC in 1995. They were also moving towards the target of complete proportionality in the remaining lay structures by the year 2000.

Most of the women we have discussed here have been working collectively as feminist or women-aware, 'supported women' within their organisations. We would agree with Ferguson (1984) that it is naïve to hope that once individual women have made their way to the top as individuals that they will inevitably work to make their own organisations more 'women-friendly' (cited in Billing, 1994). This will depend on their consciousness, their reading of the situation and their propensity to take action to address organisational inequalities. However, where feminist women (and in some cases women-aware women) take on senior roles and develop equality stategies which are supported both internally and externally by other women (and other equity-seeking groups), they may be able to take advantage of prevailing external and organisational conditions to move the equalities agenda forward, as illustrated in these organisations.

It is clear that the women working for equality within these organisations have also drawn on external networks of feminist and equalities consultants, trainers, researchers, networking and campaigning groups (e.g. METRAC, Women in Publishing) to work on programmes supporting equality initiatives, so making use of external links with women in order to progress their organisational agenda and the women's project more widely. It is also the case that all four of the organisations shared central altruistic values of service to their members, customers and users, which provide a strong underpinning ethos to the prevailing market and business case for equality initiatives.

Minimal women's activism – adaptive change agents, working in isolation?

In contrast, the case studies where equality initiatives stand out as being particularly marginalised are in the Customs and Excise Service, personnel and retail management and in some parts of the book publishing industry. In many organisations within these sectors, women are channelled into clearly labelled 'women's domains', and the majority of women appear to develop individualist strategies whereby they try to adapt to the gendered patterns of job segregation and the predominantly patriarchal structure and culture within which they work. Women actively opposing the gendered status quo thus find themselves working as a lone woman (Hoskyns, 1994), which can leave them exposed to hostility within their organisation and subject to burn-out (Cockburn, 1991).

Although women in the Customs and Excise Service make up 40% of the workforce, they dominate the 'softer' desk-orientated areas such as VAT and clerical and administrative work. Men are over 80% of those working in the 'tough' male jobs such as anti-smuggling (which seems to retain much of its pre-1972 exclusively male, uniformed culture) and make up 90% of the top management grades over all. In personnel, while women are slightly in the majority overall at 57%, they are invisible in top positions in management and in the profession, and are generally subordinated into the 'soft', 'handmaid' roles at work, with men dominating in the 'hard' domains of industrial relations and strategy, and more recently maintaining these positions in relation to women as personnel is recast into the new 'hard HRM'.

Even though retailing is a highly feminised industry, women make up the mass of the 'peripheral' labour force, doing routine tasks with little job security, whereas men compose the majority of the 'core' workforce, dominating career routes, especially at senior level, in most of the organisations. There are similarities here with 'routes to the top' in all our case study organisations, as for example with nursing and teaching management. Although nursing and teaching are 'feminised' professions, women take twice as long as men to climb career ladders and then are still disproportionately under-represented at the top.

This is not to discount changes resulting over time from the sum of individual women making choices and pursuing their own adaptive strategies independently. In teaching, Geraldine Healy and David Kraithman indicate, for example, that women in the 'interim' career phase who choose 'more of the resource of time over income and ultimately more control over the division of time', could in the long term be pioneering a more holistic approach to careers. This could, in the long term, be legitimised through its adoption by both women and men teachers who are seeking ways of managing the tension between work and family, and it also therefore challenges traditional concepts of patriarchy in the profession. However, we suggest that such incremental, adaptive action by individuals, unless organised in a coherent and conscious effort, is unlikely to effect significant change in the short term. In fact the means for a collective challenge are present, as can be seen in the teaching chapter in relation to NUT campaigns challenging women's low status and pay in the profession, but a specific strategy on gendered career paths has not yet been formally orchestrated by the professional organisations or trade unions within teaching.

The limits of the short agenda on equal opportunities

Where equal opportunities measures have developed within the Customs and Excise Service, retail sector and the personnel profession, they have mostly been externally driven initially by UK legislation, and by demographic changes in the labour-market, at the end of the 1980s. In most cases, where equal opportunity initiatives exist, they have been developed by employers as part of a short agenda on equal opportunities.[5] However, as illustrated in Figure 10.2, strongly gendered organisations and cultures appear to minimise and marginalise women's presence and influence within the organisation.

So, for example as suggested in the Customs and Excise case study, equal opportunity (EO) initiatives (some as much as 20 years old), although impressive on paper have clearly not been effective. When closely scrutinised, they almost entirely fall within the liberal tradition of equal opportunities measures, and are likely to remain largely tokenistic given the barriers to women posed by the overwhelmingly male organisational culture. Currently, no women's vanguard exists to drive them forward. Some EO measures can actually be seen as undermining career women's efforts since they run counter to this culture. For example, initiatives of the type intended to 'lighten women's domestic load' such as career-breaks and flexible hours, have caused resentment among male careerist colleagues for whom this sort of 'broken' career is not accepted as an option, and as a result these measures become marginalised.

In Customs and Excise, retail and personnel, the 'male' model of the career remains largely unchallenged. Thus women (and men) are expected to work long hours, deny life outside work and show total commitment to the organisation. This is in direct conflict with measures specified by the women in the cases, which in their view would enable flexible working and which recognises the appropriateness of a holistic and balanced family-work career structure. Women who want to proceed up the career ladder have so far seen no choice but to find their own individual ways of reconciling home and family. The women in Customs and Excise individually do provide some creative examples of accurate reading of this culture: for example, planning their family lives around these careers or choosing not to have children and networking informally with other women to warn them of male harassers. However, most of these initiatives remained largely privatised and individual.

As the personnel case study suggests, the individual women participating in the survey seemed to understand the limitations of their position well, tailoring their career ambitions to suit both their perceived subordination and their own wishes for a balanced family–work life. The junior women in personnel, in the study reported in Chapter 4, worked in organisations which, although claiming to be equal opportunity employers, provided few practical support systems for the women, despite the fact that in over half of those organisations, personnel had responsibility for the implementation of EO policy. Among the women themselves, none reported EO as their major activity. The ambivalent and contested relationship between personnel and line management generally and women's subordinate and compliant relation-ship both within personnel and *vis-à-vis* line management, combined with women's espoused individualism, makes them unlikely champions of equal opportunities in most organisations at the current time. This is a missed opportunity because research has shown that resistance to inequality is likely to be stronger in organisations where there is collective resistance to it on the part of women employees and managers, particularly where they enlist the support of personnel and the trade unions (Collinson, Knights and Collinson, 1990).

The women discussed in the retail management case study share some of the career characteristics and problems outlined for the Customs and Excise Service and personnel. Retail women remain a very small minority at the top with the interesting exception of Mothercare with three women directors promoted as part of the marketing strategy. Management roles in this industry also remain predicated on a 'male' model of long hours, full-time, full com-mitment, in sharp contrast as Anne Brockbank and Joanne Traves point out, to the use of flexible and part-time working by which retailers manage their businesses in response to their markets. This is also the dominant mode of working for the majority of women (almost two-thirds of the industry work-force). Nevertheless, the lead by Boots, of flexible working by job-sharing among senior managers, building on a well-established short equal opportu-nities agenda (integrated with the business strategy), could provide women with opportunities to progress such developments through their trade union USDAW or via their increased presence at management levels.

Currently, in retailing, most women reaching for senior management posi-tions find themselves required to comply with a male pattern of working as well as culture of working if they are to compete for the plum jobs. The highly segmented and gendered nature of their roles, plus an absence of female role models in top management and a lack of women's support groups, both shapes and masks their expectations of career progression. It is not surprising that the women in the study display anxiety and ambiguity about the different more 'masculine', styles they might be expected to adopt in order to progress in their careers. The women's strategies for progression appear to be indivi-dualistic, using the few EO measures available while experiencing role conflict as they adapt to the prevalent expectations of women as managers in the sector: 'working twice as hard' and 'being expected to blow it' by failing. As with the personnel women, faced with these hurdles, few women retail managers actually expected to reach senior levels.

Thus in these case studies, where individual women were seeking to operate as change agents, they were primarily constrained to do so as lone women, (Hoskyns, 1994), and as 'adaptors', trying to do better within the existing set of patriarchal rules and structures (Kirton, 1991). There was limited evidence of women with a women-aware or feminist consciousness. Such lone women were unlikely to take on the role of innovative change agents and equal opportunities champions within such overwhelmingly patriarchal structures and cultures. However, in order to initiate and progress change strategies appropriate to their particular needs and so try to make their organisations more 'women-friendly', women are likely to need to organise collectively within and across organisational boundaries. Otherwise, the majority of women within these organisations are likely to continue to have limited opportunities to develop and progress even where opportunities are opened up by change – such as the recent merger of the IPM and ITD into the IPD, or via changing consumer trends – as in the retail sector.

Building a women's movement within organisations: activism in transition

As indicated earlier, the key ingredient which may shift the organisational equality agenda from the minimum to the maximum model is the shape and direction of women's activism. We refer here to two stages. One is the developing consciousness of individual women, from a traditional or a questioning transitional consciousness to a more woman-aware or feminist perspective. As the diffusion of feminist ideas has influenced individual women so they may be increasingly aware of and more critical of the gender inequalities and other inequalities they perceive in their employment opportunities and the services they receive as customers. The second concerns the way in which existing women-aware and feminist change agents are able to link up with these women (and other equity-seeking groups) and over time and as innovators develop collective women's and equality strategies: in other words, the process by which 'lone women' in organisations begin to develop supports both within and outside their organisation, so becoming 'supported women' in order to challenge the patriarchal organisational barriers they perceive.

Such transitional situations can be seen particularly in parts of the book publishing sector, the teaching profession, GO Transit and in the trade union the GPMU. In book publishing, for example, feminist and women-aware women have collectively worked on establishing equality strategies within their organisations. Despite the adverse market and employee relations conditions described in Chapter 2, it is clear that women (with support from male colleagues) have also managed to hold on to some of the advances made prior to the recession in publishing. Women in publishing have made these gains largely through women's agency via a mix of individual women's ambition, collective action through the unions and also by developing support through the industry-wide network Women in Publishing. Women in Publishing has therefore played a key role in this transitional process, providing a supportive women-only feminist group for women, as well as having an educational and campaigning role within the industry.

Yet, while some organisational equality initiatives remain stalled in personnel departments, the Higher Education Equal Opportunities Network (HEEON), does offer a model for moving forwards for some women in personnel and education. The HEEON Network exists across and within higher education universities and colleges, and embraces a broad range of EO specialists, academics, and administrative and managerial women in the sector. An example of a separatist women's project, its members span a number of feminisms, and the network itself is supportive, developmental and transitional.

Within the GPMU, a small group of feminist change agents can also be seen to have been working on a transitional agenda to develop an integrated strategy, building on the existing short agenda of EO measures and working outwards to 'bring on' more women as activists. These initiatives have mainly been centrally located and officer-led, supported by a small but significant body of socialist feminists. In alliance with other key activists in the union, they have built into the strategy the market imperative of membership loss, particularly among women. This dual strategy reflects both the constraints and the opportunities of working within the union's existing patriarchal culture and structures. On the one hand, power is centralised at both the national and regional level and is in the hands of traditional male officials. However, opportunities do exist for women change agents to work together with women at the grassroots, many of whom currently seem to display a traditional or transitional level of consciousness concerning organisational gender politics.

Women moving forwards: challenges for feminism, feminists and the women's movement

Women's efforts to achieve equality and parity within organisations and society in general can be seen in a wider context than 'simply the story of feminism – or even feminisms'. Indeed women have always been involved in struggles which were about human rights and employment rights generally, not only about 'women's needs as women' (Rowbotham, 1992). Nevertheless, second-wave feminism of the late 1960s and 70s has been instrumental in shaping the values of many women. As a result of the combination of activism and economic change in the UK, for example, most women increasingly recognise the gender dimension in politics and support equality between the sexes, with less fixed gender roles with each new generation becomes more committed than the last (Siann and Wilkinson,1995)

The women's movement has developed over time and can be seen as not just one organisation, but 'the totality of a variety of organizations and individuals struggling to end the oppression of women' (Adamson, Briskin and McPhail, 1988). Analysis and debate has produced many feminisms – liberal feminism, radical feminism, cultural feminism, socialist feminism, post-modern feminism, black feminism, eco-feminism, to name a few. Feminist analyses diverge in a number of ways including the centrality accorded to the critique of patriarchy *vis-à-vis* other structures of domination (for example, capitalist and racist structures), their definitions of equality and the political programmes and strategies they advocate (Townley, 1994). As Rowbotham (1992) suggests,

> Real women are a complicated and argumentative lot. Instead of presenting 'women' as an abstract category, it is better to see 'women' as people who within particular historical situations are continually making choices about how they see and align themselves. (Rowbotham, 1992).

This complex reality is reflected within the organisational case studies presented in this book. From the evidence they present we would agree with Griffin (1995) that womens' activism is 'alive and well in the 1990s' in that many and different women are engaged in assessing their position at work and at home, discussing their concerns and ultimately becoming involved in 'organized activities designed to improve the conditions of women's varied existence'. We see the diversity of women as a positive force. Fluid and flexible, it becomes an *inclusive* body capable of embracing difference and so taking on a different shape in response to current challenges (Hoskyns, 1994). As Griffin (1995) points out:

> The condition of women's existence is *to be in movement*, to struggle towards transformations never fully realized, always superceded – even as they are attempted – by changes which in themselves demand adjustments of the goals set and of the tools, strategies and organizational structures used in the attempt to reach the desired ends. (Griffin, 1995)

This is not to underestimate the challenges facing the women's movement in the hostile climate of the 1990s. There are complex debates to be had, for example, about women's organising about 'single issue' or 'single identity organising' and the dangers and benefits in mobilising women (and men) of such localised politics (Griffin, 1995). Both the opportunities provided by and the difficulties of establishing coalitions and alliances in pursuit of equality initiatives have been fruitfully raised by feminist and other equity-seeking activists (Anthias and Yuval-Davis, 1992; Ben-Tovim, Gabriel, Law and Stredder; Cockburn, 1991; Tatchell, 1992).

Similarly, the advantages and difficulties of the institutionalisation and professionalisation of women's activism can work to both the benefit and detriment of women (Griffin, 1995). Clearly, women may benefit from having an organised voice either within decision-making organisations or formal channels through which they can address these, so they can intervene for the benefit of women (e.g. through the law, education, organisational policies). As Griffin (1995) suggests,

> The absorption into institutions and the establishment of specific organizations can mean that feminist activism is ingested into social and political structures to such an extent that its radical potential is masked or even eliminated. But it can also become the virus in the system which then acts as an agent for changing the whole.

The possibility of the latter appears to be the case certainly within the TTC and UNISON and to a lesser degree within the NHS, the publishing industry and the GPMU. Difficulties may also arise, however, from the possibility of compromise and the accusations of 'selling-out' frequently directed at those women who work from within institutions to effect change (Griffin, 1995). From the case study chapters it is clear that tensions and differences may arise between the 'women-aware' and feminist women in organisations in establishing equal opportunities priorities and deciding how to move the EO agenda forward. As Hoskyns (1994), drawing on Brenner (1993), suggests there has since the 1970s been a 'selective incorporation' of feminist demands in most Western countries. One danger of this, she argues, is that it prioritises equality over equality/difference and tends to cut middle class and professional (mainly white) women off from grassroots mobilisation. As Hoskyns (1994) suggests, this process may help to explain the apparent contradiction between the advances women seem to be making overall and the steady deterioration in the situation of those women with fewest privileges and least access to resources.

Thus in working to improve women's position within organisations, it is important that women's organising should recognise 'difference' within the social group 'women'(Cockburn, 1991; Cockburn, 1995a) and flexibly make provision where and when appropriate for the 'voices' of groups such as women of ethnic minorities, disabled women, lesbian women and older or younger women, to be heard. This is especially significant given the differential access to power, training and resources accorded different groups of women within organisations (dependent, for example, on their position in the labour market, ethnicity, etc.).

Recent research shows there is a younger generation of women entering the workforce, and particularly the professions, who have a different view of both their own position and of feminism. Such women are evident in retailing, book publishing and personnel in the research reported in this book. Their denial of feminist labels, proclaimed expectations of working together with men to develop an 'equality movement' rather than a feminist movement, looking towards androgyny and less fixed gender roles, all mean a shaping for such women, of perhaps one different kind of feminism (Siann and Wilkinson, 1995). Whether or not this will include the demands of the women in all our cases for a holistic, re-visioning of the careers of both men and women, to include a balance between work and family, remains to be seen.

Substantial challenges await women in the UK in the 1990s as they seek to address the organisational inequalities created and reproduced by the effects of the interrelationship between capital and patriarchy. Their activism is taking place within a context of considerable social change, severe organisational restructuring and public sector cutbacks. One of the results of this has been a lack of public and private funding for effective equality initiatives to empower women and promote equality and democracy within organisations (Griffin, 1995). The contours of feminism and women's activism are continually changing. The second-wave women's movement of the 1960s has laid strong foundations, and many of their values and strategies are now embedded. However, their successes have also generated backlash (Cockburn, 1991), not least from those espousing the new enterprise culture, including some younger women (Sian and Wilkinson, 1995).

Women and Europe: working towards equality?

In the UK, during the 1980s and 90s, European directives and the rulings of the European Court of Justice have frequently been looked to as a panacea for UK government actions and with some optimism by those looking to promote gender equality in work organisations and improve employment protections for both women and men (Gill, 1992; Labour Research, 1995b). Employee relations and HRM commentators have speculated about the negative and positive implications of a single European market for capital and labour. They have also debated the prospects for a changed employee relations climate within Europe, including the development of policies covering gender equality, working conditions, industrial democracy and so forth following the endorsement of the Social Chapter which was included as an annex to the

Maastricht Treaty on European Union in 1992 (Blyton and Turnbull, 1994; Hyman and Ferner, 1994; Legge, 1995; Teague, 1994).

The European Union[6] not only provides a framework within which equality and social justice may be sought, it also provides a contested terrain, whereby women – alongside other equity-seeking groups – are having to compete for representation and in order to get their needs for economic and social policy addressed. For women, as in most political and organisational arenas, there continues to be a gap between the rhetoric and reality of European policies geared addressing gender inequality. This is due in no small part to the different socio-economic, political and cultural traditions within member states. Further problems arise with respect to debates concerning the areas of EU competence and the question of subsidiarity.[7] Frequently it has been argued that subsidiarity has been used to block some of the more controversial aspects of policy that women have campaigned for, such as childcare, positive action, parental leave and maternity rights (Pillinger, 1992).

Thus women in the EU face a number of similar problems in their access to the proposed benefits of the Single European Market. In all EU countries women share experiences of inequality and marginalisation both as workers and consumers (Pillinger, 1992; Rubery and Fagan, 1994; Hegewisch and Mayne, 1994; Serdjenian, 1995). For a number of commentators, it is clear that without a substantial shift in organisational policies and practices and the public policy context at national and European level, women may well 'be the losers rather than the winners in the single market' (Pillinger, 1992; Cockburn, *forthcoming*). This is particularly true for women working in sectors sensitive to restructuring, unskilled women, women with poor access to training and education, and black and ethnic minority women (Pillinger, 1992; Hoskyns, 1996).

EU policy in favour of women since 1957 has shifted in focus over four stages of development[8] summarised by Pillinger (1992). During the fourth stage of development (1986–92), culminating in the passing of the Single European Act, Pillinger (1992) suggests the development of policy was geared to ensuring that a 'social dimension' became an integral part of the internal market, encouraging women to become more vocal in their demands for 'women-friendly' policies. While Hoskyns (1996) acknowledges that the women's policy is the most developed of the EU's social policy programmes and the only one where legislative measures have been activated by a mobilised political constituency over the last 20 years, she also recognises that the poor representation of women within European structures has substantially reduced its impact. This under-representation is clear within the higher echelons of the European Commission, the European Parliament, the Council of Ministers and the delegations of the social partners (employers and trade unions) (Hoskyns, 1994; Cockburn, 1995a). Thus the EU's formal institutions are seen by Hoskyns (1994) 'to reflect and reproduce the gender exclusions existing at the national level', with the result that it is hard to see how adequate representation for women can 'develop within the processes that spring from and are directly controlled by the governments of the member states'.

One result of this exclusion has been an on-going gender blindness on many European issues and debates, including the effects of the 1992 Programme and the Single European Act, the EU Poverty Programme, much EU employment policy and recent EU Directives on atypical work and works councils (Hoskyns, 1994). Hoskyns (1994) argues that despite the role played by lone women working within European structures in developing the European women's policy and raising gender issues more widely, two strategies of control and marginalisation have been used to develop and contain it. The first strategy is what she calls 'the imposition of hierarchy', such that policy discussion moves up the process of decision-making towards people who conform to the prevailing patriarchal norms and values who then take over and control the outcomes (usually men). Secondly, there is the ghettoisation of the European women's policy, so that where new developments take place, their effects are localised to specific units, poorly resourced and implemented and their permeation into other areas restricted (Hoskyns, 1994; Cockburn, 1995a).

Nevertheless, Hoskyns (1994) feels there may be grounds for optimism in that the EU Third Action programme for Women now gives emphasis to 'mainstreaming': the stated aim being to 'bring the objective of equal treatment into the formulation and application of all appropriate Community policies and programmes. She suggests that as the women's policy has developed it has achieved a degree of institutionalisation. It has a budget and a unit in the European Commission; advisory and consultative groups have been established; research and workshops are funded and organised. The European Parliament also has its own women's committee and a number of committed women members (MEPs) who collaborate with these developments. Indeed, Christine Crawley (MEP) has called for a Commissioner for Women to ensure that women's interests are represented at a senior level (Pillinger, 1992). The expectations of women have been raised and women's groups, pressure groups and trade unions have increasingly focused on the EU as a vehicle for change (Pillinger, 1992). This expanding transnational network of women's organisations in Europe according to Pillinger (1992) and Hoskyns (1994), has been key in helping to prevent the dropping or downgrading of existing policy gains, as cost-cutting and deregulation have taken hold. In turn, as Hoskyns (1994) suggests, these networks help to provide greater support and more connections for those 'lone women' actually involved in the EC policy-making process.

A further avenue of potential women's activism within Europe has been opened up by the enhanced role in policy-making given to the social partners in Europe under the Treaty of the European Union of 1992. Cockburn suggests that this may be supposed to place upon the social partner organisations a greater obligation than in the past, of internal democracy – including gender democracy (1995a). As she states,

> only if women are present among the delegates and staff of the social partner organizations in proportion to their presence in the constituencies they represent, and only if there is provision for women's particular concerns to be adequately voiced, can women play a full part in this new international forum and lend their efforts to make something meaningful of it. (Cockburn, 1995a).

However, she found that women are seriously under-represented on the various decision-making bodies in the social partner organisations and in social dialogue processes. This applies to both the employer and the trade union side. Women are half of the population of the member states of the EU and 40% of TU membership. Yet on the delegates of the social partners they are typically no more than 5–20%.[9] Cockburn (1995a, 1995b) reports that women are least well represented on higher-status bodies to which delegates are *ex officio* to leadership positions, and finds it particularly worrying that that they are under-represented in the newly developing fora of sectoral social dialogue and European works councils.

Cockburn (1995a) poses the question 'should women engage?' in what could be bureaucratic, time-consuming and undemocratic structures, and concludes that the answer has to be 'yes, if only for tactical reasons'. She argues that it is important that women consciously engage as the representatives of 'a large and diverse oppressed social group' in Europe, in unions and through the institutions and processes open to both social partners. She proposes a number of strategies for strengthening the representation of women in the social dialogue at workplace level, by employers and within trade unions and their confederations and at the level of European policy. Key among these is a system of sex-proportional democracy within mainstream structures and specially created women's structures within trade unions plus the necessary resources, information, education and guidance for women to help them gain access to 'Europe' (Cockburn, 1995a, forthcoming).

Thus the European Union as shown here is a contested terrain with diverse groups of women seeking to achieve resources, representation and a voice for their views, despite marginalisation and opposition within patriarchal structures and cultures. The opportunities available to women within EU sturctures are likely to depend on the configuration of social and political forces within its structures and the tensions between patriarchy and capitalism within both its member states and within Europe as a whole.

As Cockburn (1995a, 1996), building on the work of Jonasdottir (1988) and Young (1990), acknowledges it is currently 'in women's interest' as a disadvantaged social group to improve women's engagement in the structures and processes of the European social dialogue. However, she argues that it is incorrect to speak of women as an 'interest group', given that women's positions may differ (according to experience, culture, political perspective, age, sexuality, etc.). Rather she takes the view that it is likely that women's debate at the European level may focus on a number of 'women's concerns' (e.g. social provision of childcare, equal pay, harassment, etc.) and that it is only after women's experience and priorities have been publicly debated and consensus achieved that a 'woman's position' on any specific issue may be developed. This process will inevitably provide a challenge to the form and content of European debate taking place within national and Community level political structures and constituent organisations. These structures and re-sources can then 'be used by ordinary people [read 'women'] for political interaction, with the purpose of defining for themselves their own policy needs, or at least influencing meanings – instead of being passive recipients of policies defined by other people' (Meehan, 1993, quoted in Cockburn, 1995a).

Conclusion

From all the evidence weighed and examined throughout this book, it is clear that women's increasing presence in the labour market, their growing con-sumer power, plus their increased awareness of gender politics, combined with a willingness to challenge gendered organisational structures and cul-tures, is producing organisational change. An optimistic conclusion allows that feminist and women-aware women, particularly supported women work-ing with other equity-seeking groups, can make a difference in moving towards the vision of a transformational long agenda (Cockburn, 1991) 'to make large-scale organisations more democratic and more supportive of humane goals (Acker, 1990).

Equally however, the evidence shows us that the development of what we have termed 'maximum' and 'transitional' activism by women is uneven within and between organisations and is contingent on women's (and men's) agency within prevailing patriarchal environments and gendered organisa-tional cultures.

This leads us to be cautious of taking a 'falsely optimistic view of the future' (D. Sheppard, 1992), and to take account of the position of Juliet Mitchell (1986) who suggests that 'If women are the vanguard troops of change, it is not only because the whole society is becoming feminized or androgynized – though that is partly true. It is because, as women, we occupy a socially marginal and hence shiftable position.' In Mitchell's view, there is no straight-forward and inevitable progression to an ultimately androgynous society – assuming that this is what the ultimate goal might unreservedly be and with which we would not necessarily agree.

Instead, using a historical analysis, Mitchell (1986) claims that, within a period of critical change in capitalism, women are used within the economy as a temporary advance guard. They are the first, temporary inhabitants of the future, but once the transition of women moving into the labour market is effected, men take over and the landscape of employment is reshaped for both men and women. Men begin moving into these new occupations so perpetuating patriarchy and a sexual division of labour. Thus although 'Feminism may itself succeed in bringing about social change', it may find 'itself being used in the process of change to construct a confrontation out of which a particular future is made that feminism did not want' (Mitchell, 1986).

We conclude, however, that this is an overly deterministic and pessimistic view and suggest that women's activism can be a focus of resistance and a force for collective identity which empowers creativity and resourcefulness. As Billing (1994) observes: 'Too much is at stake in the world today to leave the important, powerful organisations to men.' So, we offer this book as a contribution to what we hope will be a growing area of study: namely, the ways in which women are developing their political and gender awareness and are becoming a significant force for change in organisations, moving in to open up and occupy the territory of organisational transformation.

Notes

1. Catherine Hoskyns (1994) in her discussion of the role women can play inside the EU bureacracy and in representative politics promoting women's issues has distinguished between three groups of women: 'supported women' who work for change and are members of women's networks both inside and outside the formal system, 'lone women' who are not supported in this way but who may still exert considerable influence within EU organisational structures as a result of their personal commitment and determination, and finally 'system women' who generally identify with prevailing organisational norms and so do not seek to challenge them. We have found this typology useful in our work examining the impact women's activism, both inside and outside the formal system, can have on organisations.

2. We use the word 'vanguard' here in a wide sense of leadership: e.g. 'those who lead the way or anticipate progress' (*Chambers Twentieth Century Dictionary*), and 'leaders of an intellectual etc. movement' (*Concise Oxford Dictionary*).

3. Significantly, the Women's Career Development Register was subsequently opened up to men – a move arising partly to ameliorate a male backlash and partly on the basis of its systems proving to be good HRM practice – this Women's Unit model has thus become the driver for a wider NHS HRM strategy of career development.

4. In addition to the Women's Officer, UNISON also has a Black Members' officer, a Lesbian and Gay Officer and an Officer for Disabled Members servicing each of the four self-organised groups and reporting to the Director of Equal Opportunities.

5. One notable exception to this in the retail sector is one of the case studies discussed by Cockburn (1989, 1991) 'High Street Retail' whereby a 'prime mover' and key internal corporate sponsor/champion for equal opportunities was the major shareholder, a male member of the founding family.

6. The Treaty on European Union in December 1991, adopted the name European Union (EU) and since November 1993, when the Treaty came into force, the term 'European Union' has been used instead of the term 'European Community' when describing European institutions and initiatives (Hoskyns, 1996).

7. The principle of subsidiarity allows that social arrangements must be implemented and provided for in as decentralised a manner within the European Union as possible, i.e. down to the national, regional or local level.

8. The three earlier stages of EC policy on women as outlined by Pillinger (1992) are as follows. Initially, between 1957 and 1969, she argues, its focus was primarily economic, and equal pay was included to prevent a competitive disadvantage for one member state. Between 1970 and 1979 the EC switched from its exclusively economic focus towards one that prioritised social policy, in particular action for women. However, by the third stage (1980–86), economic crisis halted the progressive development of policy in the Council of Ministers, with particular blockages to proposals coming from the UK. Still Pillinger (1992) argues that this period was broadly positive in that it was characterised by a wide-ranging set of measures being discussed by the European Parliament and the Commission including the rights of part-time workers, positive action and parental leave.

9. Cockburn (1995a) found that women were badly represented in the attenuated delegation process that leads from the workplace to positions on Works Councils and within Sectoral Social Dialogue. For example, in the case of Insurance Industry Sector Social Dialogue, she reports the union sent 14 men and 1 woman, whereas the employers organisations sent 14 men and 3 women. Thus the high (and growing) percentage of women working within insurance organisations is not being reflected by either trade union or employer delegations.

Bibliography

Abella, R. (1984) *Equality in Employment*, Ottawa: Royal Commission Report.

Abstracts, vol. 5, no. 1, pp. 10–18.

Acker, J. (1990) Hierarchies, jobs, bodies; a theory of gendered organizations', *Gender and Society*, vol. 4, no. 2, June.

Acker, J. (1992) 'Gendering organizational theory' in A.J. Mills and P. Tancred (eds) *Gendering Organizational Analysis*, London: Sage.

Acker, S. (1994) *Gendered Education*, Buckingham: Open University Press.

Acker, S. (ed.) (1989) *Teachers, Gender and Education*, London: Falmer.

Adam, B. (1987) *The Rise of a Lesbian and Gay Movement*, Boston: Twayne.

Adams, A. (1992) *Bullying at Work*, London: Virago.

Adamson, N., Briskin, L. and McPhail, M. (1988) *Feminist Organising for Change: The Contemporary Women's Movement in Canada*, Toronto: Oxford University Press.

Aitkenhead, M. and Liff, S. (1991), 'The effectiveness of equal opportunities policies', in J. Firth-Cozens and M. A. West (eds) *Women at Work*, Milton Keynes: Open University Press.

Al-Khalifa, E. (1988) 'Women in teaching' in A. Coyle and J. Skinner (eds) *Women and Work – Positive Action for Change*, London: Macmillan.

Alban-Metcalfe, B. and Nicholson N. (1984) *The Career Development of British Managers*, London: BIM Foundation

Alfred Marks Bureau, (1991) *Sexual Harassment in the Office*, London: Alfred Marks Bureau.

Alimo-Metcalfe, B. (1993) 'Women in management: organizational socialization and assessment practices that prevent career advancement', *International Journal of Selection and Assessment*, vol. 1, no. 2, pp. 68–83.

Alimo-Metcalfe, B. (1994) 'Gender and appraisal: findings from a national survey of managers in the NHS', in L. A. Heslop (ed.) *The Ties that Bind; Proceedings of the Global Research Conference on Women and Management in 1992*. Canadian Consortium of Management Schools.

Allen, I. (1988) *Doctors and their Careers*, London: Policy Studies Institute.

Allen, S. and Truman, C. (1993) *Women in Business: Perspectives on Women Entrepreneurs*, London: Routledge.

AMMA (1985) *Women Teachers' Career Prospects*, Assistant Masters and Mistresses Association.

Amos, V. and Parmar, P. (1984) 'Challenging imperial feminism', *Feminist Review*, no. 17.

Anthias, F. and Yuval-Davis, N. (1983) 'Contextualising feminism – gender, ethnic and class divisions', *Feminist Review*, pp. 62–75.

301

Anthias, F. and Yuval-Davis, N. (1993) *Racialized Boundaries*, London: Routledge.

Arnold, V. and Davidson, M. (1990) 'Adopt a mentor – the new way ahead for women managers?' *Women in Management Review and Abstracts*, vol. 5, no. 1, pp. 10–18.

Arroba, T. and James K. (1987) 'Are politics palatable to women managers: how women can make wise moves at work?', *Women in Management Review*, vol. 3, no. 3, pp. 123–30.

Atkinson, J. (1985) 'Manpower strategies for the flexible firm' *Personnel Management*, August.

Audit Commission (1991) 'Virtue of patients', NHS Report no. 4.

Bach, S. and Winchester, D. (1994) 'Opting out of pay devolution? The prospects for local pay bargaining', *British Journal of Industrial Relations*, vol. 32, June.

Backhouse, C. and Flaherty, D. H. (1992) *Challenging Times: The Women's Movement in Canada and the United States*, Montreal: McGill-Queen's University Press.

Baddeley, S. and James, K. (1987) 'Owl, fox, donkey or sheep: political skills for managers', *Management Education and Development*, vol. 18, pt 1, pp. 3–19.

Baddeley, S. and James, K. (1991) 'The power of innocence: from politeness to politics' in *Management Education and Development*, vol. 22, pt 2, pp. 106–18.

Bagguley, P., Mark-Lawson, J., Shapiro, D., Urry, J., Walby, S. and Warde, A. (1990) *Restructuring: Place, Class and Gender*, London: Sage.

Baker, P. (1993) 'Women's bank union activism' in L. Briskin and P. McDermott (eds) *Women Challenging Unions: Feminism, Democracy, and Militancy*, University of Toronto Press.

Ball, J., Disken, S., Dixon, and M., Wyatt, S. (1995) *CCP Survey of Senior Nurses in the NHS*, NHS Executive.

Bandura, A. (1977) *Social Learning Theory*, Englewood Cliffs: Prentice Hall.

Banks, O. (1981) *Faces of Feminism*, Oxford: Martin Robertson, cited in Delmar (1986) and in Mitchell and Oakley (eds) (1986).

Barrett, M. (1980) *Women's Oppression Today: Problems in Marxist Feminist Analysis*, London: Verso.

Barry, J. (1991) *The New Women's Movement in Britain: Critical Reflections*, University of East London Occasional Papers on Business, Economy and Society, no. 1.

Barry, J. Honour, H., MacGregor, S. and Palnitkar, S. (1994) 'The women's movement and city governance', paper presented at the Annual Conference of the Women's Studies Network, University of Portsmouth.

Beardwell, I. and Holden, L. (1994) *Human Resource Management – A Contemporary Perspective*, London: Pitman.

Beck, J. and Steel, M. (1989), *Beyond the Great Divide*, London: Pitman

Beechey, V. (1987) *Unequal Work*, London: Verso.

Beechey, V. (1988) 'Rethinking the definition of work: gender and work' in J. Jenson, E. Hagen, and C. Reddy (eds), *Feminization of the Labour Force; Paradoxes and Promises*, Cambridge: Polity.

Beechey, V. and Whitelegg, E. (eds) (1986) *Women in Britain Today*, Open University Press.

Beer, M. and Spector, B. (1985) 'Corporate wide transformations in human resource management', in R. E. Walton and P. R. Lawrence (eds) *Human Resource Management Trends and Challenge*, Boston: Harvard Business School Press.

Beer, M. and Spector, B. (eds) (1985) *Readings in Human Resource Management*, New York: Free Press.

Bell, E. L. and Nkomo, S. M. 'Re-visioning women managers' lives', in A. J. Mills and P. Tancred (eds), *Gendering Organizational Analysis*, London: Sage.

Ben-Tovim, G., Gabriel, J., Law, I. and Stredder, K. (1992) 'A political analysis of local struggles for racial equality', in P. Braham, A. Rattansi and R. Skellington (eds)

Racism and Antiracism: Inequalities, Opportunities and Policies, Milton Keynes: Open University Press.

Bennet, S. (1992) *Survey into the Training Needs of Editorial Freelancers in Publishing*, London: Book House Training Centre.

Bhachu, P. (1988) '*Apni Marzi Kardhi*, home and work: Sikh women in Britain' in S. Westwood and P. Bhachu (eds) *Enterprising Women*, London: Routledge.

Bhavnani, K. K. (1993) 'Talking racism and the editing of women's studies' in D. Richardson and V. Robinson (eds) (1993) *Introducing Women's Studies*, London: Macmillan.

Billing, Y. D. (1994) 'Gender and bureaucracies – a critique of Ferguson's "The feminist case against bureaucracy"', *Gender, Work and Organization*, vol. 1, no. 4, October, pp. 179–93.

Blackburn, R. and Prandy, K. (1965) 'White-collar unionism: a conceptual framework', *British Journal of Sociology*, vol. 16, no. 2.

Blyton, P. and Turnbull, P. (1994) *The Dynamics of Employee Relations*, London: Macmillan.

Book House Training Centre (1988) *Industry Training Survey*, London: Book House.

Book Marketing (1995) *Books and the Consumer*, London: Book Marketing, April.

Bookseller, The (1991a) 'Harper Collins – 60', London, 22 March.

Bookseller, The (1991b) 'Hundreds lose jobs as publishers retrench', London, 6 September.

Bookseller, The (1993) 'Adapting to misery', London, 9 April.

Bookseller, The (1993) 'Hodder Headline make 72 redundant – more to come', 6 August.

Bookseller, The (1993) 'Training – making gains out of change', London, 22 October.

Bookseller, The (1993) 'UK publishing growth continues', London, 26 March.

Bookseller, The (1994) 'Jobs go as Pearson dismembers Longman', London, 23 September.

Booth, A. and Rubenstein, L. (1990) 'Women in trade unions in Australia' in S. Watson (ed.) *Playing the State: Australian Feminist Interventions*, London: Verso.

Bouwman, R. (1994) 'Publishing's closely guarded secret', *Bookseller*, 22 July.

Bradley, H. (1989) *Men's Work: Women's Work*, Cambridge: Polity.

Bradley, H. (1993) 'Divided we fall: trade unions and their members in the 1990s' in *Unions on the Brink? The Future of the Movement, Management Research News*, vol. 16, no. 5/6.

Brant, C. and Too, Y. L. (eds) (1994) *Rethinking Sexual Harassment*, London: Pluto.

Braverman, H. (1974) *Labour and Monopoly Capital: The Degradation of Work in the Twentieth Century*, New York: Monthly Review Press.

Breugal, I. (1979) 'Women as a reserve army of labour: a note on recent British experience', *Feminist Review*, no. 3, pp. 12–23.

Brief, A. P. and Oliver, R. L. (1976) 'Male–female differences in work attitudes among retail sales managers', *Journal of Appllied Psychology*, vol. 61, no. 4, pp. 526–8.

Briskin, L. (1990) 'Women, unions and leadership', *Canadian Dimension*, Jan–Feb, pp. 38–41.

Briskin, L. (1993) 'Union women and separate organizing' in L. Briskin and P. McDermott (eds) *Women Challenging Unions*, University of Toronto Press.

Briskin, L. and McDermott, P. (eds) (1993) *Women Challenging Unions*, Toronto: University of Toronto Press.

Brown, H. (1991) *Women Organising*, London: Routledge.

Brown, H. and Parston, G. (1994) 'Managing beyond gender – an exploration of new management in the NHS', Office for Public Management, NHS Women's Unit.

Burrell, G. (1984) 'Sex and organizational analysis', *Organization Studies*, 5:97–118 cited in J. Acker (1990).

Burrell, G. and Morgan, G. (1979) *Sociological Paradigms and Organisational Analysis*, London: Heinemann.

Buswell, C. and Jenkins, S. (1994) 'Equal opportunities policies, employment and patriarchy', *Gender, Work and Organization*, vol. 1, no. 2, pp. 83–93.

Cabinet Office (1984) *Programme of Action for Women in the Civil Service*, London: HMSO.

Campbell, B. (1987). *The Iron Ladies: Why do Women vote Tory?* Virago Press.

Carr, S. (1993) *Women and GMTS1 A Study of the Promotional Prospects Available to Women who Complete GMTS1 Compared to their Male Counterparts*, Unversity of Manchester.

Carter, R. and Kirkup, G. (1990) 'Women in professional engineering: the interaction of gendered structures and values', *Feminist Review*, no. 35, Summer.

Carter, S. and Cannon, T. (1992) *Women as Entrepreneurs: A Study of Female Business Owners, their Motivations, Experiences and Strategies for success*, London: Academic Press.

Cassell and the Publisher's Association (1994) *Directory of Publishing*, London: Cassell.

Central Statistical Office (1991a) *Business Monitor SDA 25, Retail Businesses 1990*.

Central Statistical Office (1991b) *Business Monitor SDM 28, Retail Sales 1991*.

Central Statistical Office (1995) *Social Focus on Women*, HMSO.

Cholmeiy, J. (1991) 'A feminist business in a capitalist world: Silver Moon Women's Bookshop' in N. Redclift and M.T. Sinclair (eds) *Working Women: International Perspectives on Gender Ideology*, London: Routledge.

Clark, G. (1988) *Inside Book Publishing*, London, Blueprint.

Clarke, J., Cochrane, A. and McLaughlin, E. (1994) *Managing Social Policy*, London: Sage.

Clegg, S. (1989) *Frameworks of Power*, London: Sage.

Clutterbuck, D. (1991) *Everyone Needs a Mentor*, London: IPM.

Clutterbuck, D. and Devine, M. (1987) 'Having a mentor: a help or a hindrance?' in D. Clutterbuck and M. Devine (eds) *Businesswoman, Present and Future*, London: Macmillan Press.

Cockburn, C. (1983) *Brothers: Male Dominance and Technological Change*, London: Pluto.

Cockburn, C. (1984) 'Trade unions and the radicalizing of socialist feminism', *Feminist Review*, no. 16, April, pp. 43–74.

Cockburn, C. (1985) *Machinery of Dominance: Women, Men and Technical Know-How*, London: Pluto.

Cockburn, C. (1986) 'The relations of technology: what are the implications for theories of sex and class?', in R. Crompton and M. Mann (eds) *Gender and Stratification*, London: Polity Press.

Cockburn, C. (1988) 'The gendering of jobs: workplace relations and the reproduction of sex segregation' in S. Walby (ed.) *Gender Segregation at Work*, Milton Keynes: Open University Press.

Cockburn, C. (1989) 'Equal opportunities: the short and long agenda', *Industrial Relations Journal*, vol. 20, no. 4, Autumn, pp. 213–25.

Cockburn, C. (1991) *In the Way of Women: Men's Resistance to Sex Equality in Organizations*, London: Macmillan.

Cockburn, C. (1995a) *The European Social Dialogue: Strategies for Gender Democracy*, Equal Opportunities Unit, the European Commission.

Cockburn, C. (1995b) 'Women's access to European industrial relations', *European Journal of Industrial Relations*, vol. 1, no. 2, pp. 171—89.

Cockburn, C. (forthcoming) 'Strategies for gender democracy: strengthening the representation of trade union women in the European social dialogue', *European Journal of Women's Studies*.

Coe, T. (1992) The Key to the Men's Club, Corby: Institute of Management.

Colgan, F. (1986) 'Quebec's new policy on services for abused women: has anything changed?' in *Perception*, (Ottawa) vol. 9, no. 6.

Colgan, F. (1988) 'Women in SOGAT '82', Women in Organisations Seminar Discussion Paper, Business School, University of North London, June.

Colgan, F. and Ledwith, S. (1994) 'Women's trade union activism: a creative force for change and renewal within the trade union movement?', at the Work, Employment and Society Conference, University of Kent, 12–14 September.

Colgan, F. and Tomlinson, F. (1991) 'Women in publishing: jobs or careers?', *Personnel Review*, vol. 20, no. 5, pp. 16–26.

Colgan, F. and Tomlinson, F. (1994) 'Human resource management in a "feminized" publishing industry: formal policies and informal practices', at the 'Strategic Direction of HRM' conference, Nottingham Trent University, Nottingham, 14–15 December.

Colling, T. and Dickens, L. (1989) *Equality Bargaining – Why Not?* Warwick University/ EOC.

Collins, H. (1992) *The Equal Opportunities Handbook*, Oxford: Blackwell.

Collins, L. (1990) 'Managing in a man's world', *Retail Week*, 22 June.

Collinson, D. and Hearn, J. (1994) 'Naming men as men: implications for work, organization and management', *Gender, Work and Organization*, vol. 1, no. 1. January.

Collinson, D., Knights, D. and Collinson, M. (1990) *Managing to Discriminate*, London: Routledge.

Connell, R. (1987) *Gender and Power: Society, the Person and Sexual Politics*, London: Polity.

Cooper, C. L. and Davidson, M. (1982) *High Pressure. Working lives of women managers*, Glasgow: Fontana.

Cooper, D. (1994) *Sexing the City: Lesbian and Gay Politics Within the Activist State*, London: River Oram Press.

Coote, A. and Campbell, B. (1987) *Sweet Freedom*, Oxford: Blackwell.

Corby, S. (1982) *Equal Opportunities for Women in the Civil Service*, London: HMSO.

Corby, S. (1995) 'Opportunity 2000 in the National Health Service: a missed opportunity for women', *Employee Relations*, vol. 17, no. 2.

Corcoran-Nantes, Y. and Roberts, K. (1995) ' "We've got one of those:" the peripheral state of women in male-dominated industries', *Gender, Work and Organization*, vol. 2, no. 1, pp. pp. 21—33.

Corrigan, V. (1994) *Women and Transport – Moving Forward?*, University of North London: Centre for Research in Ethnicity and Gender.

Coward, R. (1992) *Our Treacherous Hearts*, London: Faber and Faber.

Cox, R. and Brittain, P. (1991) *Retail Management*, London: Longman.

Cox, T. and Blake, S. (1991) 'Managing cultural diversity: implications for organisational competitiveness', *Academy of Management Executive*, vol. 5, no. 3.

Cozby, P. C. (1973) 'Self-disclosure: a literature review', *Psychological Bulletin*, 79, pp. 73–91.

Craig, C., Rubery, J. and Garnsey, E., (1983) 'Women's pay in informal payment systems', *Employment Gazette*, April.

Crompton, R. and Le Feuvre, N. (1992) 'Gender and bureaucracy: women in finance in Britain and France' in M. Savage and A. Witz (eds) *Gender and Bureaucracy*, Oxford: Blackwell.

Crompton, R. and Sanderson, K. (1990) *Gendered Jobs and Social Change*, London: Unwin Hyman.

Cuneo, C. (1993) 'Trade union leadership: sexism and affirmative action' in L. Briskin and P. McDermott (eds), *Women Challenging Unions*, University of Toronto Press.

Cunnison, S. and Stageman, J. (1993) *Feminising the Unions*, Aldershot: Avebury.

Dahlerup, D. (ed.) (1986) *The New Women's Movement*, London: Sage.

Davidson, M. J. and Cooper, C. L. (1983) *Stress and the Woman Manager*, London: Martin Robertson.

Davidson, M. J. and Cooper, C. L. (1984) 'Occupational stress in female managers: a comparative study', *Journal of Management Studies*, vol. 21, no. 2, pp. 185–205.

Davidson, M. J. and Cooper, C. L. (1992) *Shattering the Glass Ceiling: The Woman Manager*, London: Paul Chapman.

Davidson, M. J. and Earnshaw, J. (1990) 'Policies, practices and attitudes towards sexual harassment in UK organisations', *Personnel Review*, vol. 19, no. 3, pp. 23–7.

Davies, C. and Rosser, J. (1986a) 'Gendered jobs in the health service: a problem for labour process analysis' in D. Knights and H. Willmott (eds) *Gender and the Labour Process*, (to follow).

Davies, C. and Rosser, J. (1986b) *Processes of Discrimination: A Study of Women in the NHS*, Department of Health.

Davis, M. (1993) *Comrade or Brother?*, London: Pluto.

Dawson, S. (1990) 'Filling jobs by halves', *Retail Week*, 11 May.

Day, R., Grabicke, K., Schaetzle, T. and Staubach, F. (1981) 'The hidden agenda of consumer complaining', *Journal of Retailing*, 57 Fall, pp. 86–106.

Delmar, R. (1986) 'What is feminism? in J. Mitchell and A. Oakley (eds) 1986) *What is Feminism?*, Oxford: Blackwell.

Delphy, C. (1984) *Close to Home: A Materialist Analysis of Women's Oppression*, London: Hutchinson.

DeLyon, H. and Migniulo, F. W. (eds) (1989) *Women Teachers – Issues and Experiences*, Milton Keynes: Open University Press.

Department for Education, (1991) *Statistics on Education*, London: HMSO.

Department of Employment (1991) *Employment Gazette*, November.

Department of Employment (1993) 'Employees in employment', *Employment Gazette*, May.

Desatnick, R. L. (1987) *Managing to Keep the Customer*, London: Jossey Bass.

Dex, S. (1984) *Womens Work Histories: An Analysis of the Women and Employment Survey*, Research Paper, Department of Employment.

Dex, S. (1985) *The Sexual Division of Work: Conceptual Revolutions in the Social Sciences*, Brighton: Wheatsheaf.

Dex, S. (1987) *Women's Occupational Mobility: A Lifetime Perspective*, London: Macmillan.

Dibb, S., Simkin, L., Pride, W. and Ferrell, O. C. (1991) *Marketing*, London: Houghton & Mifflin.

Dickens, D. (1989) 'Editorial: Women – a rediscovered resource?', *Industrial Relations Journal*, Autumn.

Disken, S., Dixon, M. and Halpern, S. (1987) 'The New UMGs – an analysis of management at unit level', *Health Service Journal*, 2 July.

Disken, S., Wyatt, S. and Dixon, M. (1995) *CCP Survey in 15 Representative Organisations in the NHS*, NHS Executive.

Dixon, M. and de Metz, A. (1982) *Management Development for Chief Officers in the NHS*, Kings Fund Project Paper no. 35.

Dixon, M. and Shaw, C. (1986) *Maximising the Management Investment in the NHS*, Kings Fund Project Paper no. 58.

Dixon, M., Wyatt, S. and Disken, S. (1995) *CCP Survey of Leavers from the NHS*, NHS Executive.

DOH (1993) *A Programme of Action: Ethnic Minority Staff in NHS*, DOH.

DOH (Department of Health) (1992) *Women in the NHS: An Implementation Guide to Opportunity 2000*, NHSME.

Dolton, P. J. and Makepeace, G. H. (1993) 'Female labour force participation and the choice of occupation – the supply of teachers', *European Economic Review*, vol. 37, pp. 1393–411.

Dorgan, T. and Grieco, M. (1993) 'Battling against the odds: the emergence of senior women trade unionists', *Industrial Relations Journal*, vol. 24, no. 2.

Drake, B. (1984) *Women in Trade Unions*, London: Virago (reprint from the 1920 edition published by Labour Research Department.)

Dunant, S. (1994) *The War of the Words: The Political Correctness Debate*, London: Virago.

Elias P. (1988) 'Family formation, occupational mobility and part-time work' in A. Hunt (ed.) *Women and Paid Work*, London: Macmillan.

Elliott, R. (1995) 'Will variety spice civil service life?', *People Management*, 19 October.

Enthoven, A. (1985) *Reflections on the Management of the NHS*, Occasional Paper no. 5, Nuffield Provincial Hospitals Trust, London.

EOR (1992b) 'Women in men's jobs: the transport industry', *Equal Opportunities Review*, no. 46, pp. 15–22.

EOR (1993b) 'Profile: Gloria Mills, Director of Equal Opportunities, UNISON', *Equal Opportunities Review*, no. 51, September–October.

EOR (1994) 'Slight reduction in gender pay gap', no. 58, November–December.

EOR (1995) 'Agenda 95', no. 59 January–February.

EOR (*Equal Opportunities Review*) (1992a) 'Equal opportunities in the legal profession', no. 45 September–October.

Equal Opportunities Commission (1989) *Towards Equality: A Casebook of Decisions on Sex Discrimination and Equal Pay, 1976–1988*, Manchester: EOC.

Equal Opportunities Commission (1991) *Equality Employment: Womens Employment in the NHS*, London: HMSO.

Equal Opportunities Commission (1992) cited in 'Equal opportunities in the legal profession', *Equal Opportunities Review*, no. 45, September–October.

Equal Opportunities Commission (1993) *Some Facts about Women*, Manchester.

Etzioni, A. (1969), *The Semi-Professions and their Organisation*, New York: Free Press.

Evetts, J. (1988) 'Return to teaching: the career-breaks and returns of married women primary headteachers', *British Journal of Sociology of Education*, vol. 9, no. 1.

Evetts, J. (1994) *Women and Careers: Themes and Issues in Advanced Industrial Society*, Harlow, England, Longman.

Faith, N. (1991) 'Giants collide in war of the words', *Independent*, 17 November.

Faludi, S. (1992) *Backlash*, London: Vintage.

Farnham, D. and Giles, L. (1995) 'Trade unions in the UK: trends and counter trends since 1979', *Employee Relations*, vol. 17, no. 2.

Female Employees Renumeration Act (1953).

Ferguson, K. E. (1984) *The Feminist Case Against Bureaucracy*, Philadephia: Temple University Press.

Ferner, A. and Hyman, D. (1992) 'Great Britain: still muddling through' in A. Ferner and D. Hyman (eds) *Industrial Relations in the New Europe*, Oxford: Blackwell.

Ferrario, M. (1990) 'Leadership style of British men and women managers', unpublished MSc Dissertation, University of Manchester, Faculty of Management Sciences.

Fine, B. (1992) *Women's Employment and the Capitalist Family*, London: Routledge.

Firestone, S. (1970) *The Dialectic of Sex: The Case for Feminist Revolution*, New York: Morrow.

Focas, C. (1989) 'A survey of women's travel needs in London' in M. Grieco, L. Pickup and R. Whipp (eds) *Gender, Transport and Employment*, Aldershot: Avebury.

Fombrun, C., Tichy, N. M. and Devanna, M. A. (1984) *Strategic Human Resource Management*, New York: John Wiley.

Fox, A. (1966) 'Industrial sociology and industrial relations', *Royal Commission Research Paper*, no. 3, London: HMSO.

Fox, A. (1974) *Beyond Contract: Work, Power and Trust Relations*, London: Faber & Faber.

Freedland, J. (1995) 'US: The Angry Vote', *The Guardian*, 20 June.

Freidson, E. (1970a) 'Professional Dominance', *The Social Structure of Medical Care*, New York: Atherton.

Friedson, E. (1970b) *Profession of Medicine: A Study of the Sociology of Applied Knowledge*, New York: Harper & Row.

Fryer, R. H., Fairclough, A. J. and Manson, T. B. (1978) 'Facilities for female shop stewards' *British Journal of Industrial Relations*, July.

Fudge, J. and McDermott, P. (1991) *Just Wages: A Feminist Assessment of Pay Equity*, Toronto: University of Toronto Press.

Gall, G. and McKay, S. (1994) 'Trade union derecognition in Britain, 1988–1994', *British Journal of Industrial Relations*, 32:3 September.

General Medical Services Committee (1992) London: General Medical Council.

Giddens, A. (1984) *The Constitution of Society*, Oxford: Polity.

Gill, C. (1992) 'British industrial relations and the European Community', in B. Towers (ed.) *A Handbook of Industrial Relations Practice*, London: Kogan Page.

Globe and Mail (1995a) 'Civic politicians need to know more before making cuts' (1 December, p. A7).

Globe and Mail (1995b) 'Employment equity concept is here to stay' (19 December, p. B24).

Globe and Mail (1995c) 'Operating expenses to be cut $3-billion' (30 November, p. A7).

Globe and Mail (1995d) 'Businesses will feel sting of Ontario's cuts' (30 November, p. B2).

Globe and Mail (1995e) 'Ontario economic statement' (30 November, p. A1).

Globe and Mail (1996) 'Judge refuses to reinstate employment equity law' (5 January, p. A3).

Glover, T. (1991) 'A house of many mansions', *Bookseller*, London, 16 August.

GO Transit (1992) *Twenty-Five Years on the Go*, Toronto.

GO Transit (1993a) *Business Plan 1993/94*, Toronto: March.

GO Transit (1993b) *Human Resource Policies and Procedure Manual*, Toronto.

GO Transit (1993c) *Employee Orientation Programme Manual*, Toronto: July.

Goffee, R. and Scase, R. (1985) *Women in Charge: The Experiences of Female Entrepreneurs*, London: Allen & Unwin, cited in Carter and Cannon (1992).

Gooch, L. (1992), 'The career experiences of women in personnel', unpublished MA thesis, Thames Valley University.

Goodings, L. (1993) 'Changing the office, changing the world', *Bookseller*, 4 June.

Goss, S. and Brown, H. (1991) *Equal Opportunities for Women in the NHS*, Report produced by the Office of Public Management, London.

GPMU (1993) *Biennial Delegate Conference Report*.

GPMU (1994) *Women's Committee Report to the 3rd GPMU Women's Conference*, March.

Grant, L. (1994) 'First among equals', *Guardian Weekend*, 22 October (previewing BBC 1 Panorama documentary 'The Future is Female', 24 October 1994).

Greater London Council Women's Committee (1986) *Women on the Move: Survey into Women's Transport Needs*, London: GLC.

Gregory, J. (1989) *Trial by Ordeal: Equal Opportunities Research Series*, London: HMSO.

Grieve, N. and Burns, A. (1990) *Australian Women: New Feminist Perspectives*, Melbourne: Oxford University Press.

Griffin, G. (1995) *Feminist Activism in the 1990s*, London: Taylor and Francis.

Griffiths R. (1983) *NHS Management Enquiry*, London: DHSS.

Guardian (1988), 26 January.

Guest, D. (1987) 'Human resource management and industrial relations', *Journal of Management Studies*, vol. 24, no. 5, pp. 503–21.

Guest, D. (1989a), 'Personnel and HRM: can you tell the difference?, *Personnel Management*, January.

Guest, D. (1989b) 'Human resource management: its implications for industrial relations and trade unions', in J. Storey (ed.) *New Perspectives on Human Resource Management*, London: Routledge.

Guest, D. (1990) 'Human resource management and the American dream', *Journal of Management Studies*, vol. 27, no. 4.

Gulati, A. and Ledwith, S. (1987) 'The silent trade union member' in D. Clutterbuck and M. Devine (eds) *Businesswoman, Present and Future*, London: Macmillan.

Gutek, B. A. and Cohen, A. G. (1992) 'Sex ratios, sex role spillover, and sex at work: a comparison of men's and women's experiences' in A. J. Mills and P. Tancred (eds) *Gendering Organizational Analysis*, London: Sage.

Hacker, S. (1979) 'Sex stratification, technology and organizational change: a longitudinal case study of AT&T', *Social Problems*, vol. 26, pp. 539–57, cited in J. Acker (1992).

Hakim, C. (1981) 'Job segregation: trends in the 1970s', *Employment Gazette*, December, pp. 521–9.

Hakim, C. (1991) 'Grateful slaves and self made women: fact and fantasy in womens work orientations', *European Sociological Review*, vol. 7, no. 2, September.

Halford, S. (1992) 'Feminist change in a patriarchal organization: the experience of women's initiatives in local government and implications for feminist perspectives on state institutions' in in Savage, M. and Witz, A. (eds) *Gender and Bureaucracy*, Oxford: Blackwell.

Hall, M. (1989) 'Private experiences in the public domain: lesbians in organizations' in J. Hearn, D. L. Sheppard, P. Tancred-Sheriff and G. Burrell (eds) *The Sexuality of Organization*, London: Sage.

Hamilton, K. and Jenkins, L. (1989) 'Why women and travel?' in M. Grieco, L. Pickup and R. Whipp (eds) *Gender, Transport and Employment*, Aldershot: Avebury.

Hamilton, K. and Jenkins, L. (1993) 'Women and transport' in J. Roberts *et al.* (eds) *Travel Sickness*, London: Lawrence & Wishart.

Hammond, V. (1992) 'Opportunity 2000: a culture change approach to equal opportunity', paper delivered at the Third Conference on International Personal and Human Resources Management at Ashridge Management College, 2–4 July 1992.

Hammond, V. and Holton, V. (1991) *A Balanced Workforce? Achieving Cultural Change for Women: A Comparative Study*, Ashridge Management Research Group for Opportunity 2000.

Hammond, V. (1994) 'Opportunity 2000: good practice in U.K. organisations', in M. J. Davidson and R. J. Burke (eds) *Women in Management: Current Research Issues*, London: Paul Chapman.

Handy, C. (1976) *Understanding Organisations*, Harmondsworth: Penguin.

Hannam, J. (1993) 'Women, history and protest' in D. Richardson and V. Robinson (eds) (1993) 'Introducing women's studies', *Feminist Theory and Practice*, London: Macmillan.

Hansard Society for Parliamentary Government (1990) *The Report of the Hansard Society Commission on Women at the Top*, London: Hansard Society.

Harding, S. (1986) *The Science Question in Feminism*, Milton Keynes: Open University Press, cited in Beechey (1988).

Hardy, L. K. (1986) 'Career politics: the case of career histories of selected leading female and male nurses in England and Scotland', in R. White (ed.), *Political Issues in Nursing*, New York: Wiley.

Hartmann, H. (1979) 'Capitalism, patriarchy and job segregation by sex', in Z. Eisenstein (ed.) *Capitalist Patriarchy and the Case for Socialist Feminism*, London: Monthly Review Press.

Harvard Business Review (1978) 'Everyone who makes it has a mentor', interviews with F. J. Lunding, G. L. Clements, D. S. Perkins, *Harvard Business Review*, July–August.

Haug, F. (1989) 'Lessons from the women's movement in Europe', *Feminist Review*, vol. 31, pp. 107–16.

Hayes J. (1984) 'The politically competent manager', *Journal of General Management*, vol. 10, no. 1, pp. 24–33, cited in B. White, C. Cox and C. Cooper (1992).

Healy, G. (1994) *Professionalism, Trade Unionism and Teaching: A Study of Members of the National Union of Teachers*, paper presented to Employment Research Unit conference, Cardiff Business School, September.

Healy, G. and Kraithman, D. (1989) *Women Returners in the North Hertfordshire Labour Market*, Report to Training Agency, Hatfield Polytechnic.

Healy, G. and Kraithman, D. (1991) 'The other side of the equation – the demands of women on re-entering the labour market', *Employee Relations*, vol. 13, no. 3.

Healy, G. and Kraithman, D. (1994) *Evidence to the Schoolteachers Review Body*, Business School, Hertford: University of Hertfordshire.

Healy, G. and Kraithman, D. (1995) 'Women's Aspirations, Choice, Compromise and the Interim Occupation', Business School Working Paper Series, Hertford: University of Hertfordshire.

Healy, G. and Rainnie, A. (1991) 'Evaluation and Monitoring Report 2: Best Practice in Equal Opportunities', Report for the Hertfordshire Training and Enterprise Council, Hertford: University of Hertfordshire.

Hearn, J. (1982), 'Notes on patriarchy, professionalisation and the semi-professions', *Sociology*, vol. 16.

Hearn, J. and Parkin, W. (1987) *'Sex', at 'Work': The Power and Paradox of Organisation Sexuality*, Brighton: Wheatsheaf.

Hearn, J. and Parkin, W. (1992) 'Gender and organizations: a selective review and a critique of a neglected area' in A. J. Mills and P. Tancred (eds) *Gendering Organizational Analysis*, London: Sage.

Hearn, J., Sheppard, D. L., Tancred-Sheriff, P., and Burrell, G. (1989) *The Sexuality of Organization*, London: Sage.

Heery, E. and Fosh, P. (1990) 'Whose union? power and bureaucracy in the labour movement' in P. Fosh and E. Heery (eds) *Trade Unions and Their Members*, London: Macmillan.

Heery, E. and Kelly, J. (1988a) *A Study of Women Trade Union Officers*, Department of Social and Economic Studies, Imperial College of Science and Technology and Department of Industrial Relations, London School of Economics.

Heery, E. and Kelly, J. (1988b) 'Do female representatives make a difference? – women full-time officials and trade union work', *Work, Employment and Society*, vol. 2. no. 4, December, pp. 487–505.

Heery, E. and Kelly, J. (1989) '"A cracking job for a woman" – a profile of women trade union officers', *Industrial Relations Journal*, vol. 20 no. 3, pp. 192–202.

Heery, E. and Kelly, J. (1994a) 'Professional, participative and managerial unionism: an interpretation of change in trade unions', *Work, Employment and Society*, vol. 8, no. 1.

Hegewisch, A. and Mayne, L. (1994) 'Equal opportunities policies in Europe' in C. Brewster and A. Hegewisch (eds) *Policy and Practice in European HRM*, London: Routledge.

Hellman, J. (1987) *Journeys Among Women*, New York: Oxford University Press.

Hely Hutchinson, T. (1991) 'Perceptions of change', *Bookseller*, London, 6 September.

Hemingway, J. (1978) *Conflict and Democracy*, Studies in Trade Union Government, Oxford: Clarendon.

Hendry, C. and Pettigrew, A. (1990) 'Human resource management: an agenda for the 1990s', *International Journal of Human Resource Management*, vol. 1, no. 1.

Hennig, M. and Jardim, A. (1978) *The Managerial Woman*, London: Marion Boyars.

Hewitt, P. (1993) *About Time: The Revolution in Work and Family Life*, London: IPPR/ Rivers Oram.

Hicks-Clarke, D. and Iles, P. (1994) 'HRM and the management of diversity: issues for theory, research and practice', paper presented at the 'Strategic Direction of HRM' conference, Nottingham Trent University, 14–15 December.

Hirsch, W. and Jackson, C. (1990) *Women into Management*, Institute for Manpower Studies.

Holland, L. (1988) 'Easy to say, hard to do: managing an equal opportunity programme', *Equal Opportunities Review*, no. 20, pp. 16–20.

Holland, L. and Spencer, L. (1992) *Without Prejudice? Sex Equality at the Bar and in the Judiciary*, Bournemouth: TMS Consultants.

hooks, b. (1984) *Feminist Theory: From Margin to Center*, Boston: South End.

Hoskyns, C. (1994) 'Gender issues in international relations: the case of the European Community', *Review of International Studies*, vol. 20, pp. 225—39.

Hoskyns, C. (1996) *Integrating Gender: Women, Law and Politics in the European Union*, London: Verso.

Howe, W. S., Couch, D., Ervine, W. C. H., Davidson, F. P., Kirby, D. A. and Sparks, L. (1992) *Retailing Management*, London: Macmillan.

Howson, J. (1989) 'Evidence to Department of Education and Science Select Committee', Oxford Brookes University.

Howson, J. (1994) 'Ninth annual survey of headteacher vacancies, School of Education', Oxford Brookes University.

Hunt, J. (1982) "A woman's place is in her Union" in J. West (ed.) (1982) *Work, Women and the Labour Market*, London: Routledge.

Hyman, R. (1975) *Industrial Relations: A Marxist Introduction*, London: Macmillan.

Hyman, R. and Ferner, A. (1994) *New Frontiers in European Industrial Relations*, Oxford: Blackwell.

Hymounts, C. (1986) 'The corporate women – the glass ceiling', *Wall Street Journal*, 24 March.

ICM Research (1992) *Report on IPM Membership Survey*, London: ICM.

IMS (1993) *Women Professionals in the European Community*, London: Law Society.

Independent, (1994) 'Tax Office pay system condemned by staff,' 5 April, 1994, p. 7.

Inner London Education Authority (ILEA) (1987) *The Birmingham Report*, London: ILEA.

Institute of Management (1994) *Management Development to the Millenium*, Corby: IM Books, cited in *Management Services*, September.

Jack, S. (1993) 'The fight to be friendly', *Retail Week*, 2 July.

Jain, H. (1989) 'Racial minorities and affirmative action/employment equity legislation in Canada', *Relations Industrielles*, vol. 44, no. 3, pp. 593–610.

Jenson, J., C. Reddy, and E. Hagen, (1988) *Feminization of the Labour Force*, Cambridge: Polity.

Jewson, N. and Mason, D. (1986a) 'Modes of discrimination in the recruitment process: formalisation, fairness and efficiency', *Sociology*, vol. 20, no. 1, pp. 43–63.

Jewson, N. and Mason, D. (1986b) 'The theory and practice of equal opportunity policies: liberal and radical approaches', *Sociological Review*, vol. 34, no. 2, pp. 307–29.

Jewson, N., Mason, D., Waters, S. and Harvey, J. (1990) *Ethnic Minorities and Employment Practice*, London: Department of Employment Research Paper no. 76.

Johnson Smith, N. and Leduc, S. (1992) *Women's Work: Choice, Chance or Socialization?* Calgary: Detselig.

Johnson, T. J. (1982) *The State and the Professions; Peculiarities of the British* in A. Giddens and G. Mackenzie (eds) *Social Class and the Division of Labour: Essays in Honour of Elia Neustadt*, Cambridge: Cambridge University Press.

Joint Progam in Transportation (1991) *Transportation Tomorrow: Survey for the Greater Toronto Area*, Toronto: University of Toronto.

Jones, N. (1994) 'British editing – the uncorrected proof', *Bookseller*, London, 10 June.

Jonnasdottir, A. (1988) 'On the concept of interest, women's interests, and the limitations of interest theory' in K. Jones and A. Jonasdottir (eds) *The Political Interests of Gender*, London: Sage.

Kakabadse, A.K. (1986) *The Politics of Management*, Aldershot: Gower.

Kalsi, K. (1995) 'The experience of Asian women in business and an insight into their management styles', paper presented at the 'Men in Management' conference, Thomas Danby College, Leeds, May.

Kandola, R. and Fullerton, J. (1994a) *Managing the Mosaic*, London: IPD.

Kandola, R. and Fullerton, J. (1994b) 'Diversity: more than just an empty slogan', *Personnel Management*, November, pp. 46–50.

Kanter, R.M. (1977) *Men and Women of the Corporation*, New York: Basic.

Kelly, C. and Breinlinger, S. (1994) 'Women's response to status inequality: a test of social identity theory', *Psychology of Women Quarterly*, Cambridge University Press, no. 18.

Kelly, C. and Breinlinger, S. (1994) *Involvement in Women's Groups and Campaigns: Why Women Do or Don't Get Involved*, Birkbeck College, University of London.

Kelly, C. and Breinlinger, S. (1995) 'Identity and injustice: exploring women's participation in collective action', *Journal of Community and Applied Social Psychology*, vol. 5.

Kelly, J. and Heery, E. (1994b) *Working for the Union: British Trade Union Officers*, Cambridge Studies in Management, no. 22, Cambridge University Press.

Kerfoot, D. and Knights, D. (1993) 'Management, masculinity and manipulation: from paternalism to corporate strategy in financial services in Britain', *Journal of Management Studies*, vol. 30, no. 4.

Kessler, I. and Purcell, J. (1995) 'Individualism and collectivism in theory and practice: management style and the design of pay systems' in P. Edwards (ed.) *Industrial Relations: Theory and Practice in Britain*, Oxford: Blackwell.

King, C. (ed.) (1993) *Through the Glass Ceiling*, Sevenoaks: Tudor Business Publishing.

Kinnock, G. and Millar, F. (1993) *By Faith and Daring Interviews with Remarkable Women –* Inez McCormack, UNISON, London: Virago.

Kirton, M. (1991) Adaptors and Innovators – Why new initiatives get blocked, reprinted 1984 in J. Henry (ed.) *Creative Management*, London, Sage, in association with the Open University.

Knights, D. and Willmott, H. (1986) *Gender and the Labour Process*, Aldershot: Gower.

Kotler P. (1991) *Marketing Management: Analysis, Planning, Implementation and Control*, London: Prentice-Hall.

Kram, K. (1988) *Mentoring at Work: Developmental Relationships in Organisational Life*, London: University Press of America.

Labour Force Survey (1992) Department of Employment.

Labour Research Department (1990) *Workers Rights and 1992*, London: LRD.

Labour Research Department (1992) 'The union derecognition bandwagon', *Labour Research*, London, November.

Labour Research Department (1992) *Union Law: The Latest Attack*, London: LRD.

Labour Research Department (1994) 'Still a long road to equality', vol. 83, no. 3, March.

Labour Research Department (1995a) 'Disappearing municipal equality', March, pp. 15–16.

Labour Research Department (1995b) *European Works Council*, London: LRD.

Labour Research Department (1995) 'Market madness on the BUSUS', *Labour Research*, February.

Langridge, C. (1994) 'UK health policy: the next 21 years', unpublished paper, November.

Lawrence, B. (1987) 'The fifth dimension – gender and general practice' in D. Podmore and A. Spencer (eds) *In a Man's World*, London: Tavistock.

Lawrence, E. (1994) *Gender and Trade Unions*, London: Taylor & Francis.

Ledwith, S. (1985) 'Why Irish women printers amalgamated' *Women at Work*, SOGAT Journal, October.

Ledwith, S. (1987) 'Mothers, workers and trade unionists', *SOGAT Women*, September.

Ledwith, S. (1991a) 'A woman's leadership style', *SOGAT Women*, SOGAT Journal, September.

Ledwith, S. (1991b) 'Sweet talk, soft deals? – gender and workplace industrial relations', Working Papers in Economics, Business and Management, no. 35, Business School, Polytechnic of North London.

Ledwith, S., Colgan, F., Joyce, P., and Hayes, M., (1990) 'The making of trade union leaders', *Industrial Relations Journal*, vol. 21, no. 2, pp. 112–25.

Leeds TUCRIC (1983) *Sexual Harassment at Work: A Study from West Yorkshire*.

Legge, K. (1984) *Power, Innovation and Problem Solving in Personnel Management*, Maidenhead: McGraw-Hill.

Legge, K. (1987) 'Women in personnel management: uphill climb or downhill slide?', in A. Spencer and D. Podmore (eds), *In a Man's World*, London: Tavistock.

Legge, K. (1995) *Human Resource Management: Rhetorics and Realities*, Basingstoke: Macmillan.

Leonard, A. (1987) *Pyrrhic Victories: Winning Sex Discrimination and Equal Pay Cases in the Industrial Tribunal*, London: HMSO, April.

Leonard, A. (1987b) *Judging Inequality*, the effectiveness of the tribunal system in sex. London: Cobden Trust.

Liff, S. (1995) 'Equal opportunities: continuing discrimination in a context of formal equality', in P. Edwards (ed.) *Industrial Relations: Theory and Practice in Britain*, Oxford: Blackwell.

Liff, S. and Dale, K. (1994) 'Formal opportunity, informal barriers: black women managers within a local authority', *Work Employment and Society*, vol. 8, no. 2, pp. 177–98.

Long, P. (1984) *The Personnel Specialist: A Comparative Study of Male and Female Careers*, London: IPM.

Lortie, D. C. (1969) 'The balance and control and autonomy in elementary school teaching' in Amitai Etzioni (ed.) *The Semi-Professions and their Organisation*, New York: Free Press.

Lovenduski, J. and Randall, V. (1993) *Contemporary Feminist Politics: Women and Power in Britain*, Oxford: Oxford University Press.

Mac an Ghaill, M. (1992) 'Teachers' work: curriculum restructuring, culture power and comprehensive schooling', *British Journal of Sociology of Education*, vol. 13, no. 2.

MacEwen Scott, A. (1994) *Gender Segregation and Social Change*, Oxford: Oxford University Press.

Mackay, L. and Torrington, D. (1986) *The Changing Nature of Personnel Management*, London: IPM.

MacKinnon, C. (1979) *Sexual Harassment of Working Women*, New Haven, CT: Yale University Press, quoted in J. Acker (1990).

MacLeod, D. (1995) 'Teachers' pay rise to drain budgets' *The Guardian*, 2 December.

Maile, S. (1995) 'The gendered nature of managerial discourse: the case of a local authority', *Gender, Work and Organization*, vol. 2. no. 2, pp. 76—87.

Marginson *et al.* (1988) *Beyond The Workplace: Managing Industrial Relations in Multi-Plant Enterprises*, Oxford: Blackwell.

Maroney, H. (1986) 'Feminism at work', in J. Mitchell and A. Oakley (eds) *What is Feminism?*, New York: Pantheon.

Marsh, A. (1982) *Employee Relations Policy and Decision-making*, Aldershot: Gower.

Marshall, J. (1984) *Women Managers: Travellers in a Male World*, Chichester: John Wiley.

Marshall, J. (1994) 'Why women leave senior management jobs' in M. Tanton (ed.) *Women in Management: A Developing Presence*, London: Routledge.

Marshall, J. (1995) *Women Managers Moving On*, London: Routledge.

Martin, J. and Roberts, C. (1984) *Women: A Lifetime Perspective*, London: HMSO.

Martin, R., Fosh, P., Morris, H., Smith, P. and Undy, R. (1993) 'The legislative reform of union government 1979–93', in *Unions on the Brink? The Future of the Movement, Management Research News*, vol. 16, no. 5–6.

Massey, D. (1984) *Spatial Divisions of Labour: Social Structures and the Geography of Production*, London: Macmillan.

Maxwell, G. (1993) 'The contribution of personnel management to UK high street retailing: reason and reality', paper presented to Seventh World Conference on Research in the Distributive Trades University of Stirling, September.

McGwire, S. (1992) *Best Companies for Women: Britain's Top Employers*, London: Pandora.

McColgan, A. (1994a) 'Legislating Equal Pay? Lessons from Canada', *Industrial Law Journal*, vol. 22, no. 4, December.

McColgan, A. (1994b) *Pay Equity: Just Wages for Women*, London: Institute of Employment Rights.

McGarrigle, I. (1993) 'Mothercare's childminder', *Retail Week*, 30 July.

McLoughlin, I. and Clark, J. (1988) *Technological Change at Work*, Buckingham: Open University Press.

McNaught, B. (1993) *Gay Issues in the Workplace*, New York: St. Martin's Press.

McNeil, M. (ed.) (1987) *Gender and Expertise*, London: Free Association.

Meehan, E. (1993) *Citizenship and the European Community*, London: Sage.

Metropolitan Toronto Planning Department (1992) *The Livable Metropolis*, Toronto, draft.

Milkman, R. (1985) 'Women workers, feminism and the labour movement since the 1960s' in R. Milkman (ed.) *Women, Work and Protest*, London: Routledge, pp. 300–22.

Millett, K. (1969) *Sexual Politics*, New York: Virago.

Mills, A. J. and Tancred, P. (eds) (1992) *Gendering Organizational Analysis*, London: Sage.

Millward, N. (1994) *The New Industrial Relations?* London: Policy Studies Institute.

Millward, N., Stevens, M., Smart, D. and Hawes, W. (1992) *Workplace Industrial Relations in Transition*, Aldershot: Dartmouth.

Milton Keynes Citizen (1993) 'Boots creates opportunities for women employees', 28 October.

Mitchell, J. (1986) 'Reflections on twenty years of feminism' in J. Mitchell and A. Oakley (eds) *What is Feminism?*, Oxford: Basil Blackwell.

Mitchell, J. and Oakley, A. (1986) *What Is Feminism?* Oxford: Basil Blackwell.

Monks, K. (1993) 'Careers in Personnel Management', *Personnel Review*, vol. 22, pp. 55–66.

Morgan, G. (1986) *Images of Organization*, London: Sage.

Morgan, G. and Knights, D. (1991) 'Gendering jobs: corporate strategy, managerial control and the dynamics of job segregation', *Work, Employment and Society*, vol. 5, no. 2, pp. 181–200.

Mountain, P. (1988) 'Is bigger better?', paper presented at the 'Women in Publishing' conference, London, 5 November, in Cassell and the Publisher's Association, *Directory of Publishing*, London: Cassell.

Mouzelis, N. (1989) 'Restructuring structuration theory', *Sociological Review*, vol. 37, no. 4.

NASUWT (1995) *The Career Prospects of men and Women in the Teaching Profession*, Report to Conference NASUWT, Birmingham 1995, Birmingham.

National Action Committee on the Status of Women (1993) *Review of the Situation of Women in Canada*, Toronto.

NEDO (1985) *Employment Perspectives and The Distributive Trades*, London: NEDO.

NEDO (1988) *Part-time Working in the Distributive Trades*, London: NEDO.

NEDO (1989) *Defusing the Demographic Time Bomb*, London: NEDO with the Training Agency.

NEDO/Training Commission (1988) *Young People and the Labour Market – A Challenge for the 1990s*, London: NEDO/Training Agency.

Nelson, G. (1991) 'Second among equals', *Bookseller*, London: 1 November.

Newman, J. (1994) 'The limits of management: gender and the politics of change' in J. Clarke, A. Cochrane and E. McLaughlin (eds) *Managing Social Policy*, London: Sage.

NHS National Steering Group on Equal Opportunities for Women, 1988. Equal Opportunities for Women in NHS.

NHSME (National Health Service Management Executive) (1992) *Women in the NHS: An Employee's Guide to Opportunity 2000*, London: NHSME.

Nicholson, N. and West, M. (1988) *Managerial Job Change: Men and Women in Transition*, Cambridge: Cambridge University Press.

Niven, M. (1967) *Personnel Management, 1913–63*, London: IPM.

Norton, J. (1993) 'Women, economic ideology and the struggle to build alternatives' in E. Schragge (ed.) *Community Economic Development: In Search of Empowerment*, Montreal: Black Rose.

NUJ (1993) *Magazine and Book Industrial Council Survey*, London: NUJ.

NUJ (National Union of Journalists) (1988) *Survey of January – May 1988 Agreements*, place of publication London.

NUT (National Union of Teachers) EOC (Equal Opportunities Commission) (1980) *Promotion and the Woman Teacher*, London: NUT/EOC.

O'Connor, M. (1994) 'Ambitious women should head for the City', *The Times Educational Supplement*, 20 May 1994:2.

Ontario Human Rights Code Review Task Force (1992) *Achieving Equality: A Report in Human Rights Reform*, Toronto: Government of Ontario, 26 June.

Ontario Human Rights Commission (1992) *Annual Report*, Toronto: Government of Ontario.

Opportunity 2000 (1992) *Opportunity 2000: Towards a balanced workforce, First Year Report*, London: Business in the Community.

Opportunity 2000 (1994) *Third Year Report, Executive Summary (and publicity notices)*, London: Business in the Community.

Ostergaard, L. (1992) *Gender and Development: A Practical Guide*, London: Routledge.

Ousley, H. (1995) 'Talent Spotting' in the *Guardian: Careers*, 25 February, pp. 2–3.

Paddison, L. (1991) 'Ethnic Minority Employees are Still the Losers', *Personnel Management* May.

Palmer, Amanda (1989) 'Report of research conducted into the careers of women officers in H.M. Customs & Excise', unpublished.

Palmer, Amanda (1992) 'Report of survey on reasons for leaving H.M. Customs and Excise, unpublished.

Palmer, A. (1993) *Less Equal Than Others: A Survey of Lesbians and Gay Men at Work*, London: Stonewall.

Parkin, F. (1979) *Marxism and Class Theory: A Bourgeois Masculine Critique*, London: Tavistock.

Peters, T. and Waterman, R. H. (1982) *In Search of Excellence*, London: Harper and Row.

Phillips, A. (1987) *Divided Loyalties: Dilemmas of Sex and Class*, London: Virago.

Phillips, A. and Taylor, B. (1980) 'Sex and skill: notes towards a feminist economics', *Feminist Review*, no. 6, pp. 79–88.

Phizacklea, A. (1983) *One Way Ticket*, London: Routledge & Kegan Paul.

Pillinger, J. (1992) *Feminising the Market: Women's Pay and Employment in the European Community*, London: Macmillan.

Podmore, D. and Spencer, A. (1986) 'Gender in the labour process – the case of men and women lawyers'in D. Knights and H. Willmott (eds) *Gender and the Labour Process*, Gower: London.

Powell, G. (1993) *Women and Men in Management*, London: Sage.

PQB (Publishing Qualifications Board) (1993) *The Future Viability of NVQs and the PQB in the UK Book and Journal Publishing Industry*, London: PQB.

Pratt, P. (1990) 'A review of sexuual harassment as it affects women', Customs and Excise, unpublished.

Pringle, R. (1989) *Secretaries Talk: Sexuality, Power and Work*, London and New York: Verso.

Proctor J. and Jackson, C. (1992) *Women Managers in the NHS: A Celebration of Success*, NHSME, Department of Health, London.

Purcell, J. (1995) 'Corporate strategy and its link with human resource management strategy' in J. Storey *Human Resource Management: A Critical Text*, London: Routledge.

Purcell, J. and Ahlstrand, B. (1994) *Human Resource Management in the Multi-Divisional Company*, Oxford: Oxford University Press.

Purcell, K. (1990) 'Research on gender: understanding the world in order to change it', *Work, Employment and Society*, vol. 4, no. 4.

Ragins, B.R. (1989) Barriers to mentoring: the female manager's dilemma, *Human Relations*, vol.42, no. 1, pp. 1–22.

Rai, S., Pilkington, H. and Phizacklea, A. (1992) *Women in the Face of Change*, London: Routledge.

Ramazanoglu, C. (1989) *Feminism and the Contradictions of Oppression*, London: Routledge, cited in Cockburn (1991), p. 7.

Redclift, N. and Sinclair, M.T. (1991) *Working Women: International Perspectives on Gender Ideology*, London: Routledge.

Rees, T. (1990) 'Gender, power and trade union democracy' in P. Fosh and E. Heery (eds) *Trade Unions and their Members*, London: Macmillan.

Rees, T. (1992a) 'The feminisation of trade unions' in *Women in the Labour Market*, London: Routledge.

Rees, T. (1992b) *Women and the Labour Market*, London: Routledge.

Retail Week (1991) 'Counter point: does Opportunity 2000 go far enough?', *Retail Week*, 22 November.

Richardson, M.S. (1979) 'Toward an expanded view of careers', *Counselling Psychologist*, vol. 8 no. 1, pp. 34–5.

Richardson, P. and Hartshorn, C. (1993) 'Business start up training: the gender dimension', in S. Allen and C. Truman (eds) *Women in Business: Perspectives on Women Entrepreneurs*, London: Routledge.

Rix, S.E. and Stone, A.J. (1984) 'Work' in S. Pritchard (ed.) *The Women's Annual*, no. 4, Boston: Hall.

Robbins, D. (1986) *Wanted: Railman*, Manchester: EOC.

Roberts, J. and Coutts, J.A. (1992) 'Feminization and professionalization: a review of an emerging literature on the development of accounting in the United Kingdom' in *Accounting, Organizations and Society*, vol. 17, no. 3–4, pp. 379–95.

Robinson, R. and Le Grand J. (eds) *Evaluating the NHS Reforms*. King's Fund Institute 1994.

Rosener, J. (1990) 'Ways women lead', *Harvard Business Review*, November–December, pp. 119–25.

Ross, R. and Schneider, R. (1992) *From Equality to Diversity: A Business Case for Equal Opportunities*, London: Pitman.

Rowbotham, S. (1981) 'The trouble with "patriarchy"' in R. Samuel (ed.) *People's History and Socialist Theory*, London: Routledge & Kegan Paul.

Rowbotham, S. (1992) *Women in Movement: Feminism and Social Action*, New York: Routledge.

Rubery, J. (1980) 'Structured labour markets, worker organization and low pay' in A. Amsden (ed.) *The Economics of Women and Work*, Harmondsworth: Penguin.

Rubery, J. and Fagan, C. (1994) 'Does feminization mean a flexible labour force?' in R. Hyman and A. Ferner (eds) *New Frontiers in European Industrial Relations*, Oxford: Blackwell.

Rubery, J. and Tarling, R. (1988) 'Women's employment in declining Britain' in J. Rubery (ed.) *Women and Recession*, London: Routledge & Kegan Paul.

Rutherford, B. M. and Wekerle, G. R. (1987) *Equity Issues in Women's Accessibility to Employment: Transportation, Location and Policy*, Toronto: City of Toronto Equal Opportunity Division.

Sandford L. T. and Donovan M. E. (1984) *Women and Self Esteem*, Harmondsworth: Penguin, originally USA Anchor Press/Doubleday 1984.

Sargent, A. (1983) *The Androgynous Manager: Blending Male and Female Styles for Today's Organizations*, New York: American Management Associates.

Savage, M. and Witz, A. (eds) (1992) *Gender and Bureaucracy*, Oxford: Blackwell.

Scheibl, F. (1995) 'Part-time workers: grateful slaves or rational, time maximising individuals? An examination of sociological fact and fiction in recent explanations of womens preferences for part-time work', Business School Working Paper, University of Hertfordshire, Hertford.

Schein V. E. (1976) 'Think manager – think male', *Atlanta Economic Review*, March–April.

Schein, V. E. (1973) 'The relationship between sex-role stereotypes and requisite management characteristics', *Journal of Applied Psychology*, vol. 57, no. 2, pp. 95–100.

Schein, V. E. (1989) 'Sex role stereotypes and requisite management characteristics:, past, present, future', paper presented at 'Current Research on Women in Management', conference, Queens University, Ontario 24–26 Sept.

Scott, J. (1986) 'Gender: a useful category of historical analysis', *American Historical Review*, vol. 91, pp. 1053–75, cited in J. Acker (1990) nd Beechey (1988).

Serdjenian, E. (1995) *Inventory of Positive Action in Europe*, Brussels: European Commission Women's Information, no. 42.

SERTUC Women's Rights Committee (1987) *Moving Towards Equality* SERTUC Women's Rights Committee Report on women's participation in trade unions, London: Greater London Trade Union Resource Unit.

SERTUC Women's Rights Committee (1989) *Still Moving Towards Equality – A Survey of Progress Towards Equality in Trade Unions*, London.

SERTUC Women's Rights Committee (1994) *Struggling for Equality: A Survey of Women and their Unions*, London: Southern and Eastern Region TUC.

Sharpe, S. (1984) *Double Identity: The Lives of Working Mothers*, Harmondsworth: Penguin.

Shaw, K. E. (1990) 'Ideology, control and the teaching profession', *Policy and Politics*, vol. 18, no. 4.

Sheppard, D. (1989) 'Organisations, power and sexuality: The image and self-image of women managers', in J. Hearn, D. L. Sheppard, P. Tancred-Sherrif and G. Burrell (eds) *The Sexuality of Organization*, London: Sage.

Sheppard, D. (1992) 'Women managers' perceptions of gender and organizational life', in A. Mills and P. Tancred (eds) *Gendering Organizational Analysis*, London: Sage.

Sheppard, G. (1991) 'A break with tradition', *Retail Week*, 8 March.

Sherriff, P. and Campbell, E. (1992) 'Room for women: a case study in the sociology of organizations', in A. J. Mills and P. Tancred (eds) *Gendering Organizational Analysis*, London: Sage.

Sherwood, D. (1990) 'How important is culture?', *International Journal of Retail and Distribution Management*, vol. 18, no 4.

Shipton, J. and McAuley, J. (1994) 'Issues of power and marginality in personnel', *Human Resource Management Journal*, vol. 4 no. 1.

Siann, G. and Wilkinson, H. (1995) 'Gender, feminism and the future', Working Paper no. 3 of *The Seven Million Project*, London: Demos.

Silverstone, R. and Ward, A. (1980) *Careers of Professional Women*, Beckenham: Croom Helm.

Simpson, R. (1995) 'The experiences of male and female MBA graduates at work and in the organisation', paper presented at The European Group of Organisation Studies (ECOS) Symposium, Istanbul, July.

Simpson, R. L. and Simpson, I. H. (1969) 'Women and bureaucracy in the semi-professions', in A. Etzioni (ed.) The Semi-Professions and their Organisation, New York: Free Press.

Sinclair, J., Ironside, M. and Seifert, R. (1993) *Classroom Struggle? Market Oriented Education reforms and their impact on teachers professional autonomy, labour intensification and resistance*, Labour Process Conference, 1993 (International Labour Process Conference, Aston University).

Sinclair, M. Thea. (1991) 'Women, work and skill: economic theories and feminist perspectives' in N. Redclift and M. T. Sinclair (eds) *Working Women: International Perspecives on Gender Ideology*, London: Routledge.

Skipton, S. (1991) 'Equal value: an alternative approach', *Employee Relations*, vol. 13, no. 1, pp. 17–23.

Sly, F. (1993) 'Women in the labour market', *Employment Gazette*, November.

Sly, F. (1994) 'Ethnic groups and the labour market', *Employment Gazette*, May.

Smith, D. (1988) *The Everyday World as Problematic: A Feminist Sociology* quoted in K. K. Bhavnani (1993) 'Talking racism and the editing of women's studies' in D. Richardson and V. Robinson (eds) (1993) *Introducing Women's Studies*, London: Macmillan.

Smith, P. and Morton, G. (1990) 'Notes and issues. A change of heart: union exclusion in the provincial newspaper sector', *Work, Employment and Society*, vol. 4, no. 1, pp. 105–24 (and amendments).

Sparks, L. (1987) 'Employment in retailing: trends and issues', in G. Johnson (ed.) *Business Strategy and Retailing*, Chichester: John Wiley, pp. 239–55.

Sparks, L. (1992) 'Restructuring retail employment', *International Journal of Retail and Distribution Management*, vol. 20, no. 3.

Stacey, J. (1993) 'Untangling feminist theory' in D. Richardson and V. Robinson (eds) *Introducing Women's Studies*, London: Macmillan.

Stageman, J. (1980) *Women in Trade Unions*, Hull: Industrial Studies Unit, University of Hull.

Stanworth, C. and Stanworth, J. (1994) 'Self-employment as a vehicle for workforce casualisation – the case of the book publishing industry', paper presented at British Union of Industrial Relations Association conference, Worcester College, Oxford.

Storey, John (1987) 'Developments in the management of human resources, an interim report', Warwick Papers in IR, no. 17, IRRU, School of Industrial & Business Studies, University of Warwick, November.

Storey, John (ed.) (1989) *New Perspectives on Human Resource Management*, London: Routledge.

Storey, John (l992a) 'HRM in action: The Truth is Out at Last', *Personnel Management*, April.

Storey, John (l992b) *Developments in the Management of Human Resources: an Analytical Review*, Oxford: Blackwell.

Storey, John (1995a) 'Human resource management: still marching on, or marching out?' in J. Storey *Human Resource Management: A Critical Text*, London: Routledge.

Storey, John (l995b) *Human Resource Management, A Critical Text*, London: Routledge.

Storey Julie (1994) 'Women's careers: a case study in personnel', Occasional Paper no. 21, Leicester Business School.

Strachey, R. (1928) *The Cause*, London: Bell, reprinted by Virago, 1978, cited in Mitchell and Oakley (1986).

Straker N. (1991) Teacher supply in the 1990s: an analysis of current developments' in G. Grace and M. Lawn (eds) *Teacher Supply and Teacher Quality – Issues for the 1990s*, Exeter: Multilingual Matters.

Straw, J. (1989) *Equal Opportunities: The Way Ahead*, London: IPM.

STRB (School Teachers Review Body) (1994) *Third Report 1994*, London: HMSO.

Sugiman, P. (1993) 'Unionism and feminism in the Canadian auto workers union, 1961–1992' in L. Briskin and P. McDermott (eds) *Women Challenging Unions*, Toronto: University of Toronto Press.

Tanton, M. (1994) (ed.) *Women in Management, A Developing Presence*, london: Routledge.

TARP (1986) *Consumer Complaint Handling in America: An Update Study*, Washington DC: White House Office of Consumer Affairs.

Tatchell, P. (1992) 'Equal rights for all: strategies for lesbian and gay equality in Britain' in K. Plummer (ed.) *Modern Homosexualities*, London: Routledge.

Teague, P. (1994) 'EC social policy and European HRM' in C. Brewster and A. Hegewisch (eds) *Policy and Practice in European HRM*, London: Routledge.

The Police Review, 12 February 1993.

The Times (1992) 'Old prejudice prevails as women strive for the top', 1 September, 1992, p. 5.

Thomas, P.J. (1987) 'Appraising the performance of women: gender and the naval officer', in B. A. Gutek and L. Larwood (eds) *Womens Career Development*, London: Sage.

Thomas, R. R. (1991) *Beyond Race and Gender: Unleashing the Power of your Total Workforce by Managing Diversity*, New York: AMACOM.

Thornton, P. and Lunt, N. (1995) *Employment for Disabled People: Social Obligation or Individual Responsibility?'*, University of York, Social Policy Report, no. 2.

Todres, E. (1990) 'Women's work in Ontario: pay equity and the wage gap', *Ottawa Law Review*, vol. 22, no. 3.

Tomlinson, F. (1987) 'What do women's groups offer?', *Women in Management Review*, Winter, pp. 238–47.

Tomlinson, F. and Colgan, F. (1989) *Women in Pubishing: Twice as Many, Half as Powerful?* London: Polytechnic of North London.

Tomlinson, F., Daniel, T. and Ledwith, S. (1992) 'The experience and progression of women business students', CERB Working Paper no. 1, Polytechnic of North London.

Townley, B. (1994) *Reframing Human Resource Management*, London: Sage.

Tradeswomen (1993) 'Women in mass transit', no. 16.

Trevorrow, J. (1990) 'A disincentive to teach? A Study of institutional constraints on the decision of women returning to teaching', unpublished MA Thesis, University of Kent.

TTC (Toronto Transit Commission) (1989a) *Back to Basic: A TC Strategy for the 1990s*, Toronto: TTC.

TTC (1989b) *Making Transit Safer for Women*, Toronto: TTC.

TTC (1990) *Annual Report*, Toronto: TTC.

TTC (1991) *Statistics*, Toronto: TTC.

TTC (1991–1993) *TTC HART BEAT*, September 1991–Spring 1993.

TTC (1992a) *Equal Opportunity Report 1991*, Toronto: TTC.

TTC (1992b) *Human Resources Plan*, Toronto: TTC.

TTC (1992c) 'TTC ethno-racial action plans', *Executive Summary*, Toronto: TTC.

TTC (1993a) *Equal Opportunity on the Move*, 1992 Annual Report', Toronto: TTC, p. 11.

TTC (1993b) *Corporate Training Plan*, Toronto: TTC, June.

TUC (Trades Union Congress) (1994) *Campaigning for Change: A New Era for the TUC*, London: TUC.

TUC Women's Committee (1988–1994) *Annual Reports*, London: TUC.

Turner, C. (1993) 'Women's businesses in Europe: EEC initiatives.', in S. Allen and C. Truman (eds) *Women in Business: Perspectives on Women Entrepreneurs*, London: Routledge.

Tyson, S. (1995) *Human Resource Strategy*, London: Pitman.

Tyson, S. and Fell, A. (1986) *Evaluating the Personnel Function*, London: Hutchinson.

UNISON (1994) *Getting the balance right – Guidelines on proportionality*, London: Unison.

USDAW (1988) *Retailing in the 1990's*, submitted by the Executive Council to the 1988 Annual Delegate Meeting.

USDAW (1992a) *46th Annual Report* Manchester: USDAW.

USDAW (1992b) *Women in USDAW – The Agenda for 1992*, 1992 Annual Delegate Meeting Executive Council Statement, Manchester: USDAW.

Vandevelde, M. and Forsaith, J. (1991) *Recruitment in Publishing*, London: BNIB Report no. 51.

Vickers, J., Rankin, P. and Appele, C. (1993) *Politics as if Women Mattered: A Political Analysis of NAC*, Toronto: University of Toronto Press.

Vinnicombe, S. (1987) 'What exactly are the differences in male and female working styles?', *Women in Management Review*, vol. 3, no. 1, pp. 13–21.

Vogler, C. (1994) 'Segregation, sexism and labour supply' in A. MacEwen Scott, (ed.) *Gender Segregation and Social Change*, Oxford: Oxford University Press.

Waddel, F. T. (1983) 'Factors affecting choice, satisfaction and success in the female self employed', *Journal of Vocational Behaviour*, vol. 23, pp. 294–304.

Wajcman, J. (1994) 'The gender relations of management', paper presented at the 'Work, Employment and Society' conference, University of Kent, 12–14 September.

Walby, S. (1986) *Patriarchy at Work*, Cambridge: Polity.

Walby, S. (1988) 'Gender politics and social theory,' *Sociology*, vol. 22, no. 2, pp. 215–32.

Walby, S. (1990) *Theorising Patriarchy*, Blackwell.

Walker, A. (1983) *In Search of Our Mother's Gardens*, London: Women's Press.

Walker, C. (1993) 'Black Women in Educational Management' in J. Ozga (ed.) *Women in Educational Management*, Buckingham: Open University Press.

Wallston, B. and O'Leary, V. (1981) 'Sex makes a difference: differential perceptions of women and men', *Review of Personality and Social Psychology*, vol. 2, p. 9–41.

Walsh, S. and Cassell, C. (1995) *A Case of Covert Discrimination*, London: Bentinck Group, Book House Training Centre.

Waterstone, T. (1991) 'Capitalism and culture in conflict', *Bookseller*, London: 20 September.

Watson, Diane (1988) *Managers of Discontent – Trade Union Officers and Industrial Relations Managers*, London: Routledge.

Watson, S. (1992) 'Femocratic feminisms' in M. Savage and A. Witz (eds) *Gender and Bureaucracy*, Oxford: Blackwell.

Watson, T. J. (1986) *Management, Organization and Employment Strategy: New Directions in Theory and Practice*, London: Routledge & Kegan Paul.

Watson, T. J. (1977) *The Personnel Managers: a Study in the Sociology of Work and Employment*, London: Routledge.

Webb, J. and Liff, S. (1988) 'Play the white man: the social construction of fairness and competition in equal opportunities', *Sociological Review*, vol. 36, no. 3.

Weber, M. (1947) *Economy and Society*, vol. 3, New York, cited in V. Beechey (1987).

Welsh, C., Knox, J. and Brett, M. (1994) *Acting Positively: Positive Action Under the Race Relations Act 1976*, Sheffield: Department of Employment Research Paper no. 36.

Westwood, S. (1984) *All Day Every Day – Factory and Family in the Making of Women's Lives*, London and Sydney: Pluto.

Whipp, R. (1992) 'Human Resource Management, Competition and Strategy: Some productive tensions.' Blyton, P. and Turnbull, P. (eds) *Reassessing Human Resource Management*, London: Sage.

White, B., Cox, C., and Cooper, C. (1992) *Women's Career Development: A Study of High Fliers*, Oxford: Blackwell.

Williams, A., Dobson, P. and Walters, M. (1989) *Changing Culture: New Organizational Approaches*, London: IPD.

Wilson, D. C. (1992) *A Strategy of Change*, London: Routledge.

Wilson, F. M. (1995) *Organizational Behaviour and Gender*, New York: McGraw-Hill.

Wine, J. and Ristock, J. (1991), *Women and Social Change: Feminist Activism in Canada*, Toronto: James Lorimer.

WiP (Women in Publishing) (1993) *Having it All?*, London: The Bentinck Group.

Witz, A. (1992) *Professions and Patriarchy*, London: Routledge.

Witz, A. and Savage, M. (1992) 'The gender of organizations' in M. Savage and A. Witz (eds) *Gender and Bureaucracy*, Oxford: Blackwell.

Wolf, N. (1994) *Fire with Fire*, London: Chatto and Windus.

Working Group on Employment Equity (1989) *Government of Canada Equity Programs*, Toronto: Ministry of Citizenship.

Wyatt, S. Disken, S. and Dixon, M. (1994) *CCP Top Managers Survey NHS Report no. 1*, London: NHS Executive June.

Yeandle, S. (1984) *Women's Working Lives*, London: Tavistock.

Young, I. (1990) *Justice and the Politics of Difference*, Princeton: Princeton University Press.

Zimmick, M. (1992) 'Marry in haste, repent at leisure: women, Bureacracy and the post office, 1870–1920' in M. Savage and A. Witz (eds) *Gender and Bureaucracy*, Oxford: Blackwell.

Author index

Subject index

329